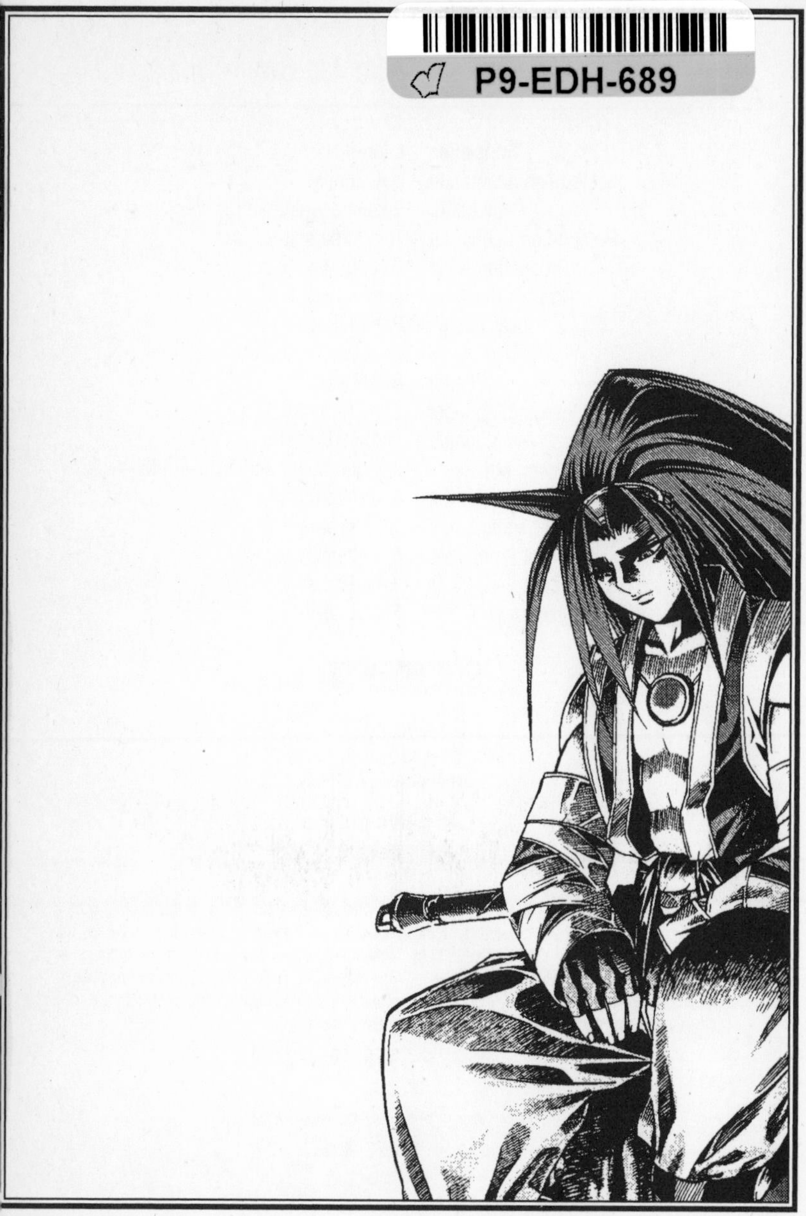

King of Hell Vol. 8
Written by Ra In-Soo
Illustrated by Kim Jae-Hwan

Translation - Lauren Na
English Adaptation - R.A. Jones
Copy Editor - Suzanne Waldman
Retouch and Lettering - Tom Misuraca
Production Artist - Vicente Rivera, Jr.
Graphic Designer - James Lee
Cover Design - Patrick Hook

Editor - Rob Tokar
Digital Imaging Manager - Chris Buford
Pre-Press Manager - Antonio DePietro
Production Managers - Jennifer Miller and Mutsumi Miyazaki
Art Director - Matt Alford
Managing Editor - Jill Freshney
VP of Production - Ron Klamert
President and C.O.O. - John Parker
Publisher and C.E.O. - Stuart Levy

A  Manga

TOKYOPOP Inc.
5900 Wilshire Blvd. Suite 2000
Los Angeles, CA 90036

E-mail: info@TOKYOPOP.com
Come visit us online at www.TOKYOPOP.com

ISBN: 1-59182-914-3

First TOKYOPOP printing: December 2004
10 9 8 7 6 5 4 3 2 1
Printed in the USA

VOLUME 8

BY
RA IN-SOO
&
KIM JAE-HWAN

HAMBURG // LONDON // LOS ANGELES // TOKYO

KING HELL

WHO THE HELL...?

MAJEH:

A feared warrior in life, now a collector of souls for the King of Hell. Majeh has recently been returned to his human form in order to carry out the mission of destroying escaped evil spirits upon the earth. There are two catches, however:
1. Majeh's full powers are restrained by a mystical seal.
2. His physical form is that of a teenage boy.

CHUNG POONG NAMGOONG:

A coward from a once-respected family, Chung Poong left home hoping to prove himself at the Martial Arts Tournament in Nakyang. Broke and desperate, Chung Poong tried to rob Majeh. In a very rare moment of pity, Majeh allowed Chung Poong to live...and to tag along with him to the tournament. Chung Poong's older brother-- Chung Hae--is also a student of the martial arts and is the "nephew" (martial arts inferior) of Poong Chun.

THE MARTIAL ARTS CHILD PRODIGIES

BABY/HYUR-AH/KWANG:

A 15-year-old from the infamous Blood Sect, Baby is several warriors in one...thanks to his multiple personality disorder. Baby is shy, gentle, and blushing, Hyur-ah is intense, unforgiving, and murderous, and Kwang is even scarier than Hyur-ah. The question remains: who--or what--else is also inside this young man?

CRAZY DOG:

A 6-year-old club-wielding hellion from a remote village, Crazy Dog definitely earned his name right up to the moment of his death at the hands of a demon-possessed martial arts master.

SAMHUK:
Originally sent by the King of Hell to spy on the unpredictable Majeh, Samhuk was quickly discovered and now--much to his dismay--acts as the warrior's ghostly manservant.

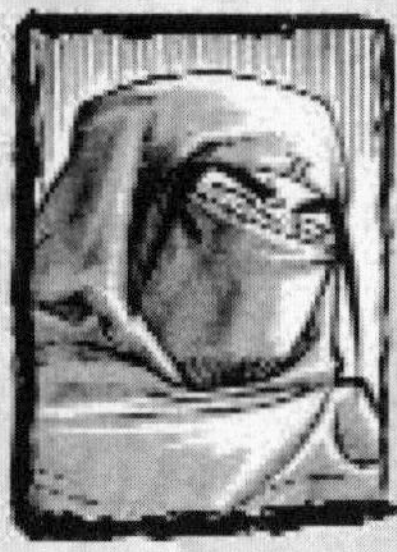

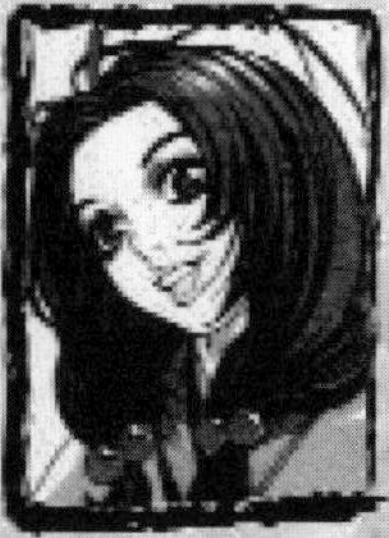

DOHWA BAIK:
A vivacious vixen whose weapons of choice are poisoned needles. She joined Majeh and Chung Poong on the way to the tournament.

KING OF HELL:
You were expecting horns and a pitchfork? This benevolent, otherworldly ruler reigns over the souls of the dead like a shepherd tending his flock.

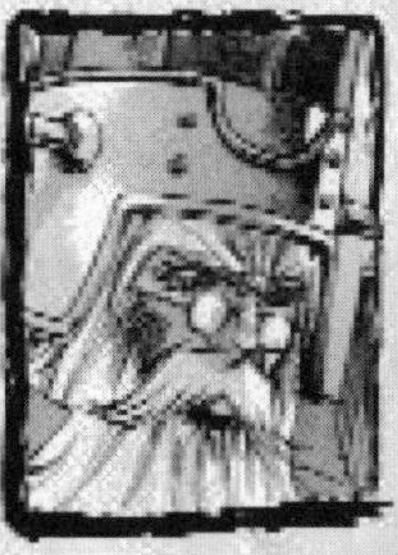

DOHAK:
A 15-year-old monk and a master at fighting with a rod, he is affiliated with the Sorim Temple in the Soong mountains.

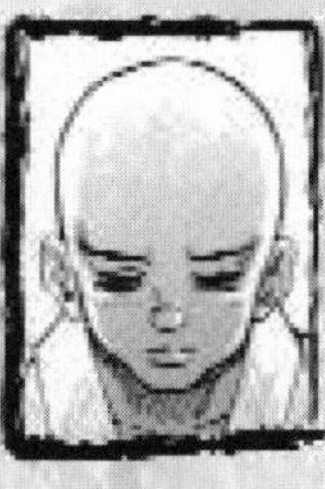

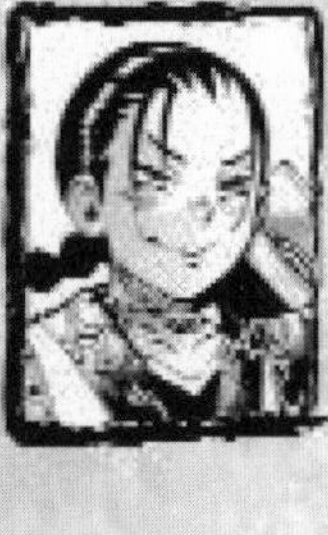

POONG CHUN:
A 12-year-old expert with the broadsword, he is affiliated with the Shaman Sect. Poong Chun is the "uncle" (martial arts superior) of Chung Hae--Chung Poong's older brother.

YOUNG:
A 15-year-old sword-master, possessing incredible speed, he is affiliated with Mooyoung Moon-- a clan of assassins, 500 strong.

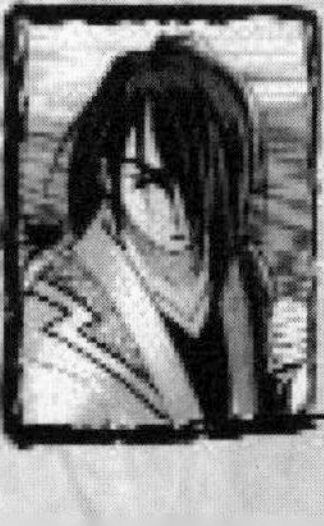

Hell's worst inmates have escaped and fled to Earth. Seeking recently-deceased bodies to host their bitter souls, these malevolent master fighters are part of an evil scheme that could have dire consequences for both This World and the Next World. It is believed that the escaped fiends are hunting for bodies of martial arts experts, as only bodies trained in martial arts would be capable of properly employing their incredible skills.

To make matters even more difficult, the otherworldly energy emitted by the fugitives will dissipate within one month's time...after which, they will be indistinguishable from normal humans and undetectable to those from the Next World. The King of Hell has assigned Majeh to hunt down Hell's Most Wanted and return them to the Next World...but Majeh doesn't always do exactly what he's told.

Majeh was a master swordsman in life and, in death, he serves as an envoy for the King of Hell, escorting souls of the dead to the Next World. Majeh caught Samhuk--a servant for the King of Hell--spying on him and, after making the appropriate threats, now uses Samhuk as his own servant as well.

The King of Hell has reunited Majeh's spirit with his physical body, which was perfectly preserved for 300 years. Due to the influence of a Superhuman Strength Sealing Symbol (designed to keep the rebellious and powerful Majeh in check), Majeh's physical form has reverted to a teenaged state. Even with the seal in place, however, Majeh is still an extremely formidable warrior.

Along with the young, wannabe-warrior called Chung Poong Namgoong and a femme fatale named Dohwa Baik, Majeh has made his way to the much-heralded Martial Arts Tournament at Nakyang--the most likely place for the warrior demons to make their appearance.

Shortly after arriving in Nakyang, Majeh and company met Chung Hae--Chung Poong's older brother--though it was far from a happy reunion. Chung Hae berated his younger sibling and ordered Chung Poong to return home. With Majeh backing him up, Chung Poong was able to stand his ground and stay for the tournament.

Though Majeh seemed to have forgotten his mission to capture Hell's Most Wanted, the escaped evil souls certainly had not forgotten him! While Majeh faced off against Crazy Dog, the tournament was suddenly interrupted. An elderly, one-armed, martial arts master--whose body was inhabited by one of the fugitive demons--forced his way into the arena and effortlessly killed Crazy Dog and another young martial arts prodigy. Despite his best efforts, Majeh also seemed on the verge of total defeat...though, as his life-force dissipated, the Superhuman Strength Sealing spell that limits his abilities was broken!

Freed from restraint, Majeh rose and quickly obliterated his opponent. Though Majeh recovered very quickly from his battle injuries, he was still surprised to learn that, while he was out, his fellow contestants--including Chung Poong's older brother--were kidnapped! After the attack, Mo Young Baik, the organizer of the Nakyang Martial Arts Tournament, cancelled the rest of the games and sent the martial arts prodigies home. However, of all of the contestants, only Baby reached his destination...and that was only with the help of his mysterious third personality known as Kwang.

The disappearance of the young martial artists quickly created suspicion among the sects which threatens to erupt into all-out war. At Mo Young's behest, Majeh set out to discover the fates of the missing young fighters along with Young, a member of the Mooyoung Moon assassin clan.

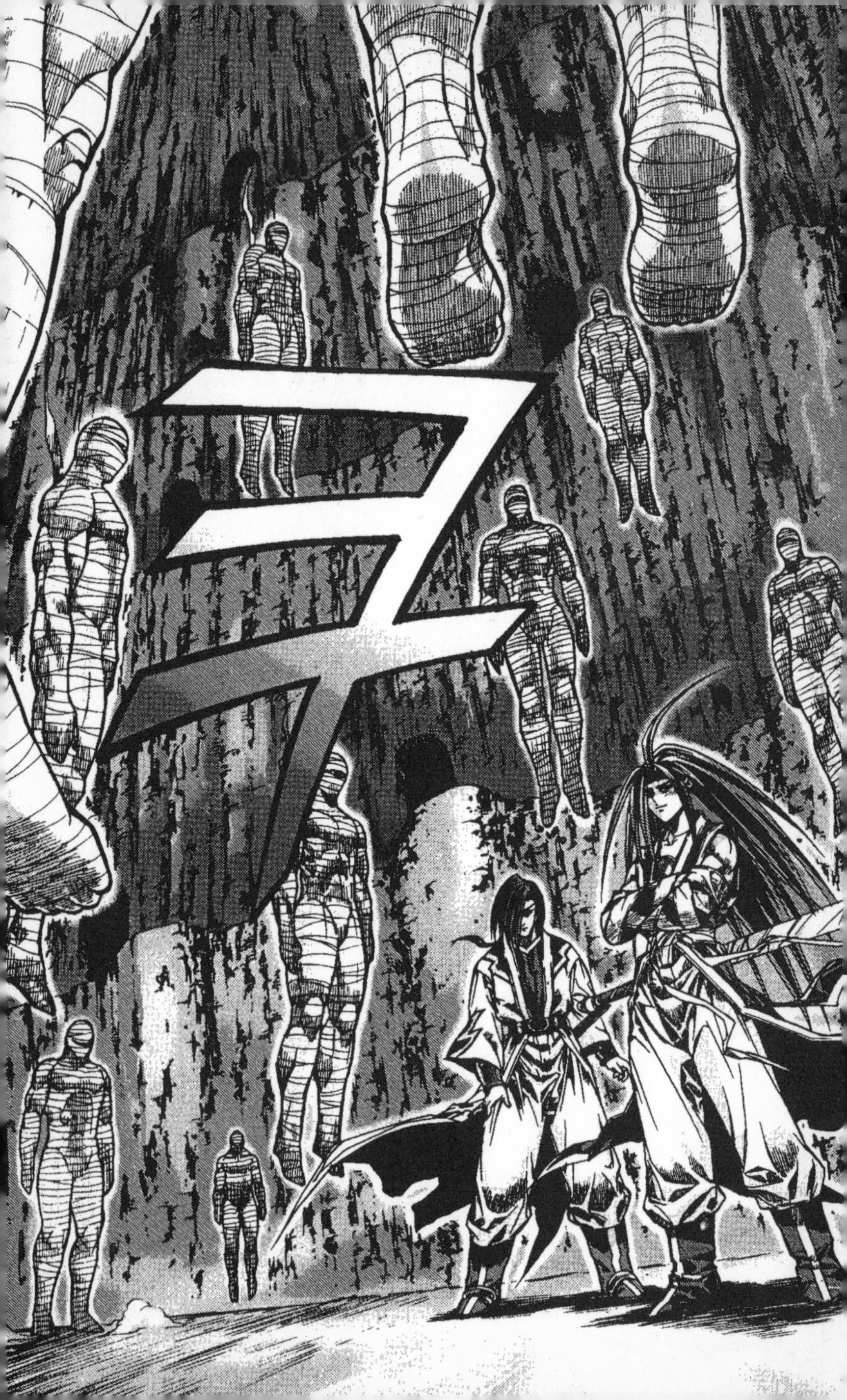
7

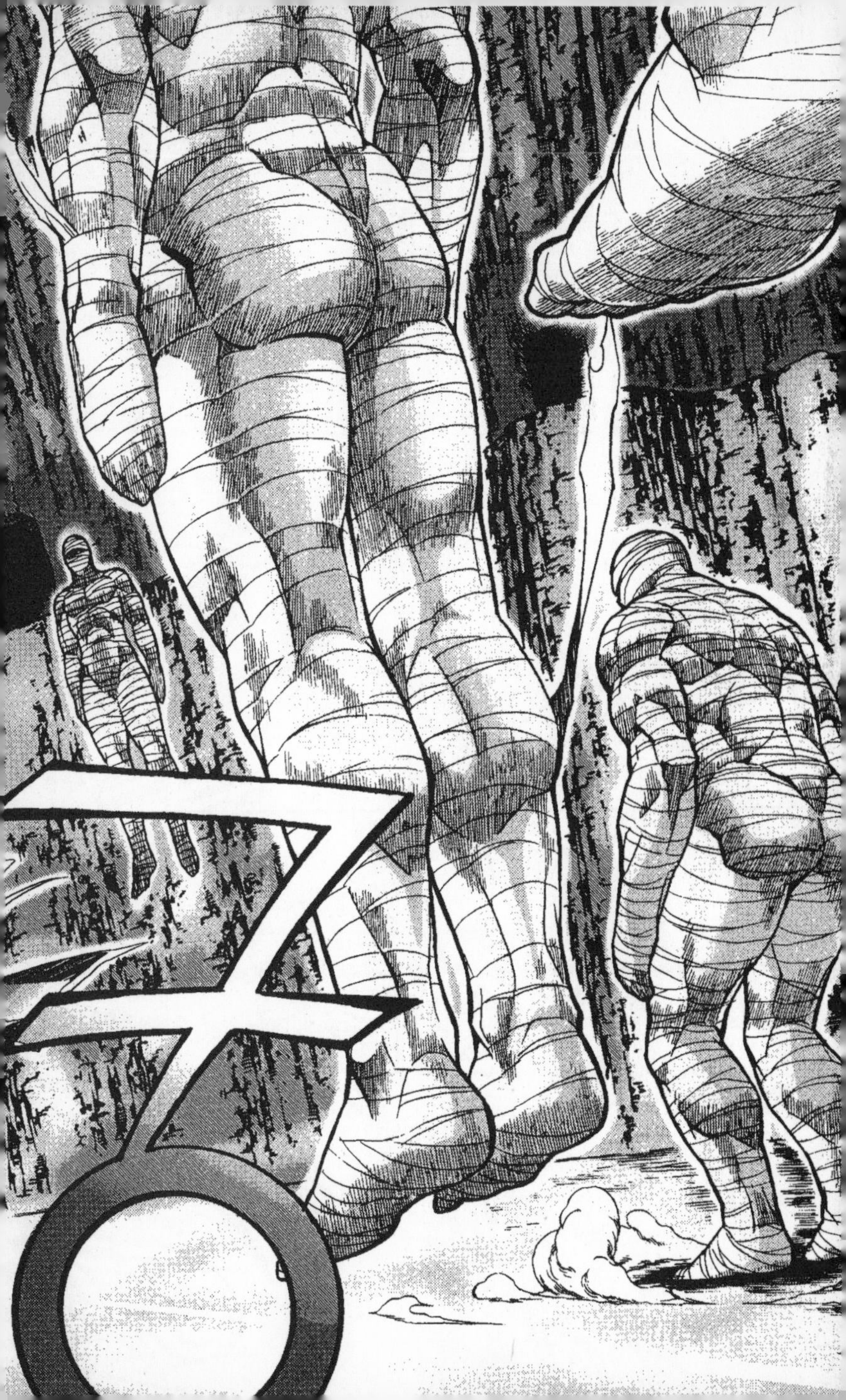
ZO

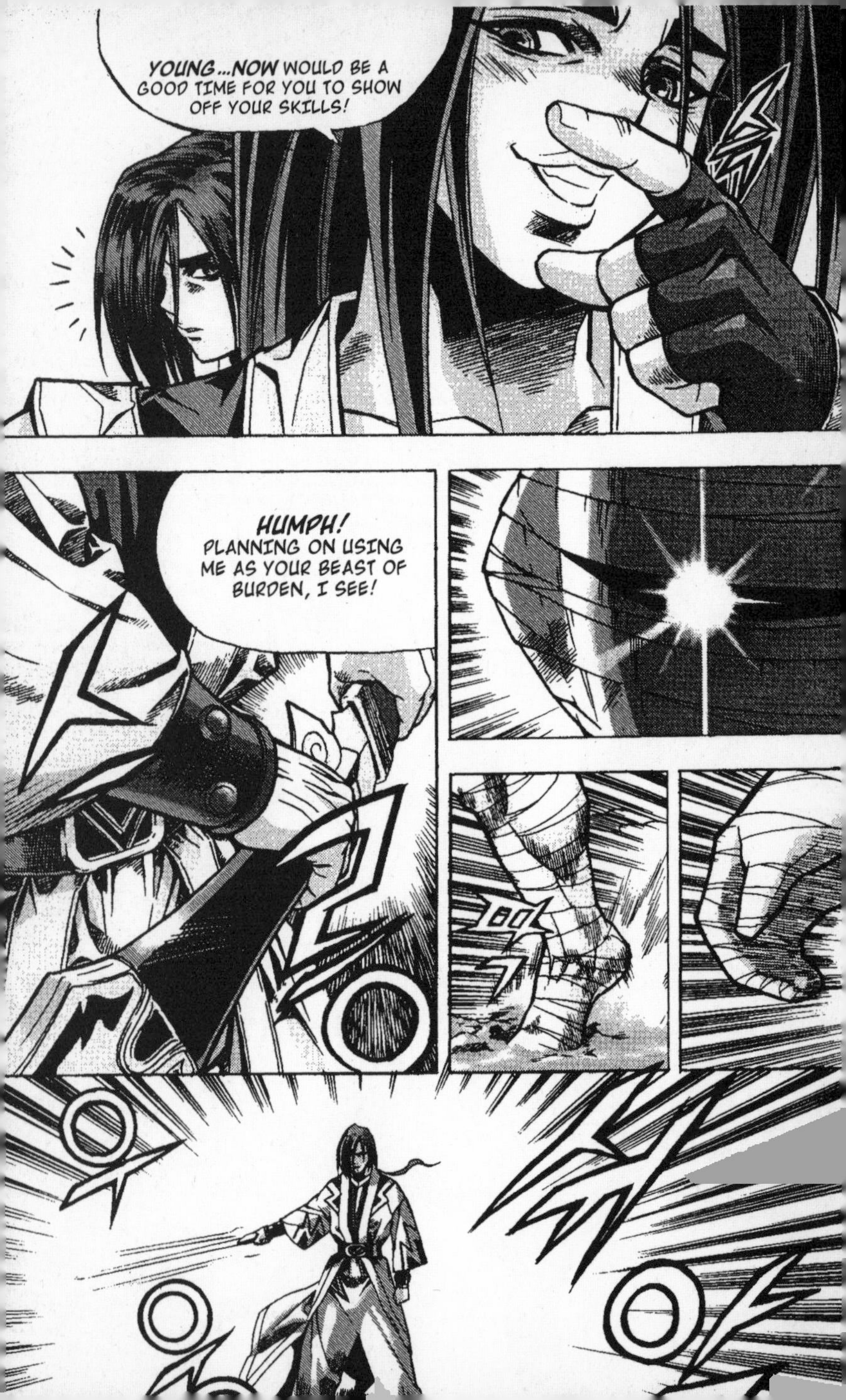
YOUNG...NOW WOULD BE A GOOD TIME FOR YOU TO SHOW OFF YOUR SKILLS!
HUMPH! PLANNING ON USING ME AS YOUR BEAST OF BURDEN, I SEE!

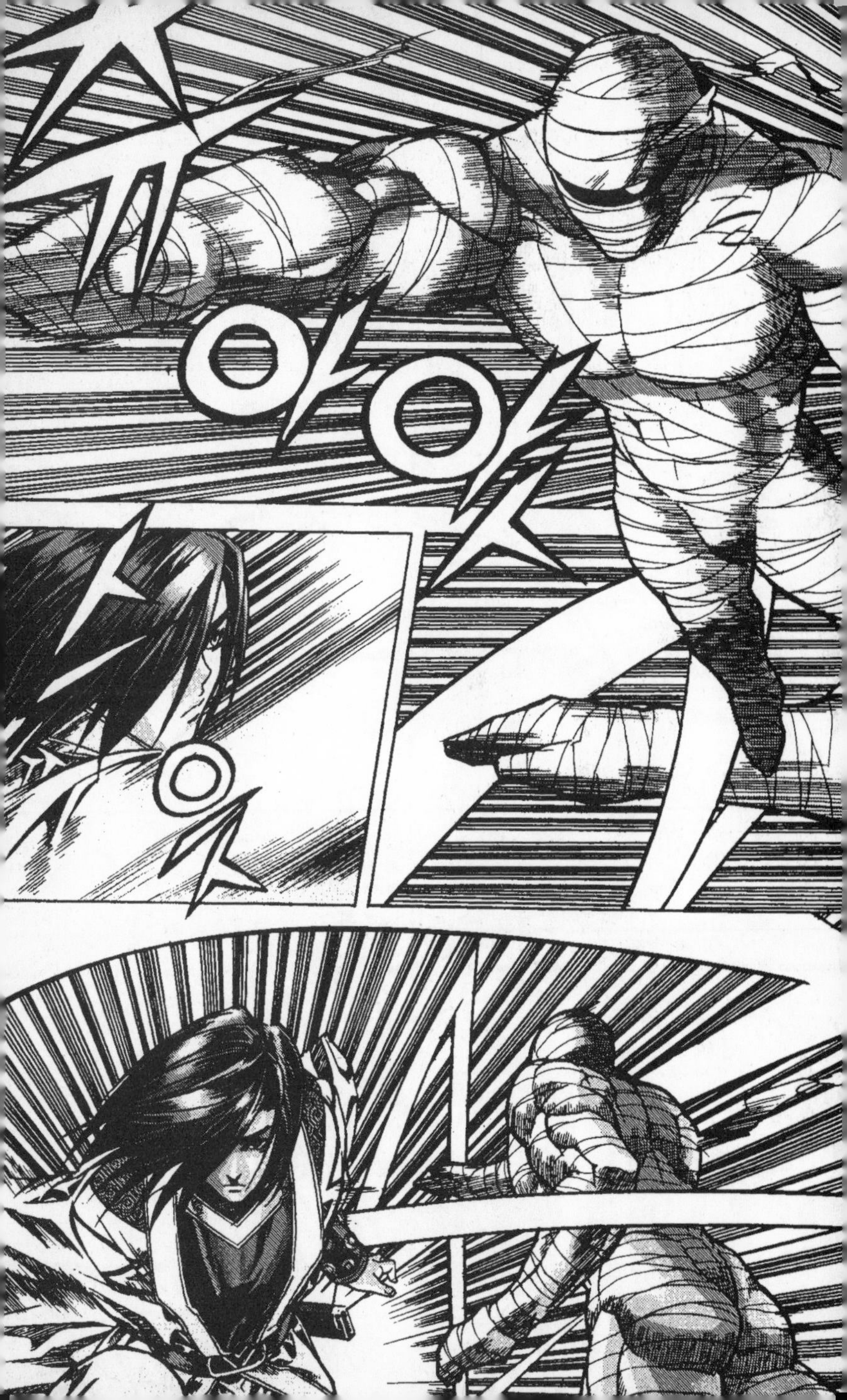

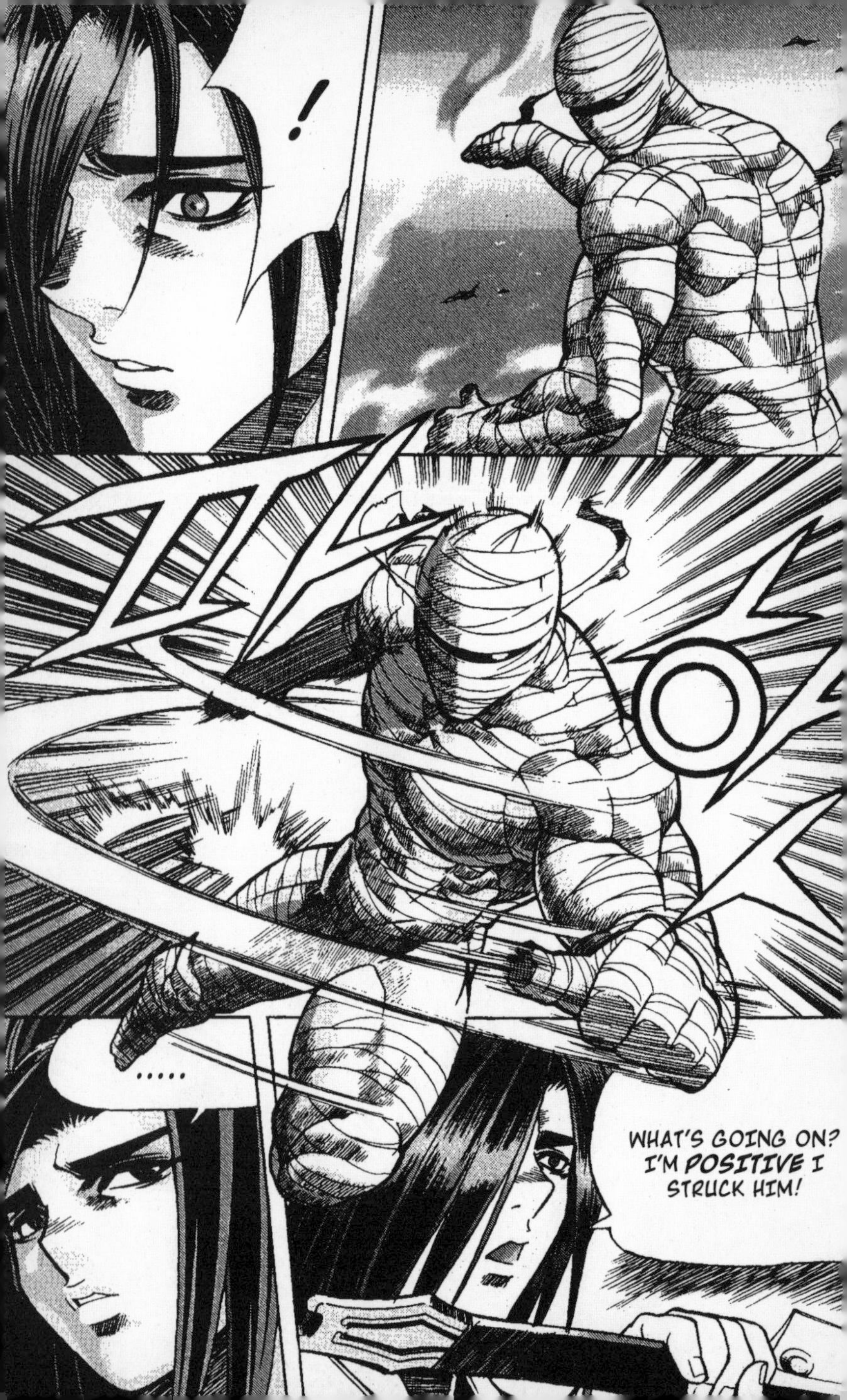
!
.....
WHAT'S GOING ON? I'M *POSITIVE* I STRUCK HIM!

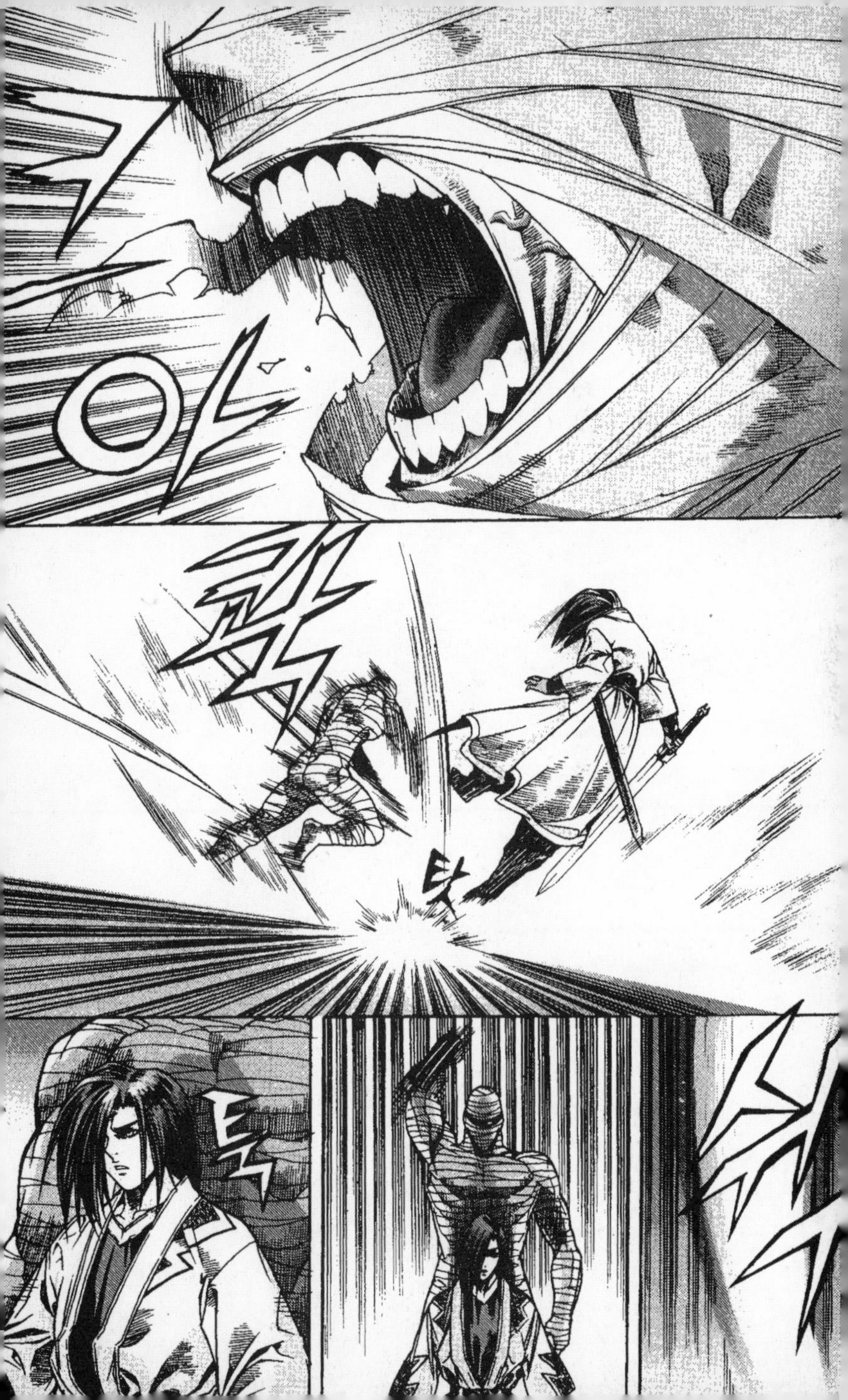
크아
탓

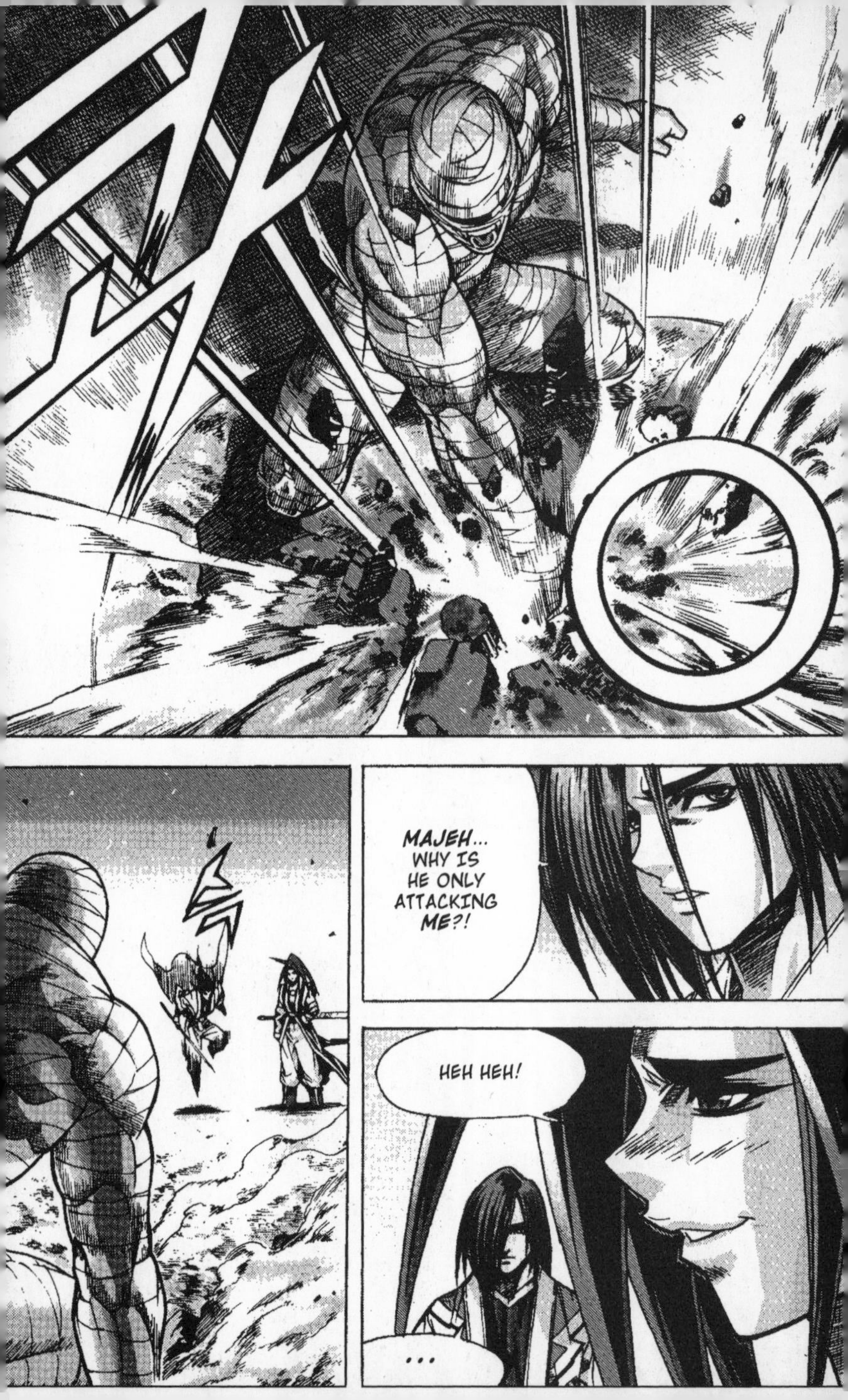
MAJEH... WHY IS HE ONLY ATTACKING ME?!
HEH HEH!
...

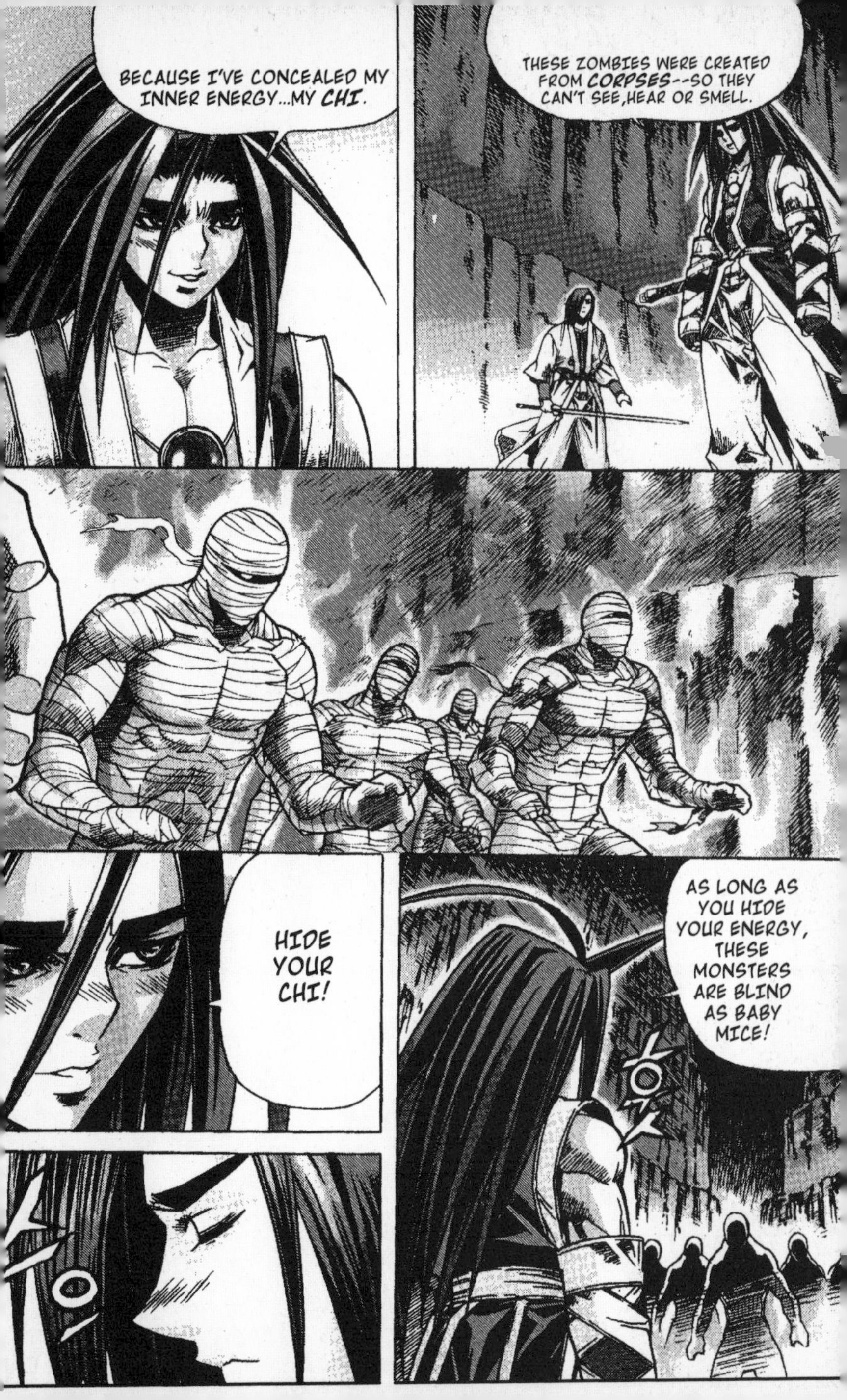
BECAUSE I'VE CONCEALED MY INNER ENERGY...MY CHI.
THESE ZOMBIES WERE CREATED FROM CORPSES--SO THEY CAN'T SEE, HEAR OR SMELL.
HIDE YOUR CHI!
AS LONG AS YOU HIDE YOUR ENERGY, THESE MONSTERS ARE BLIND AS BABY MICE!

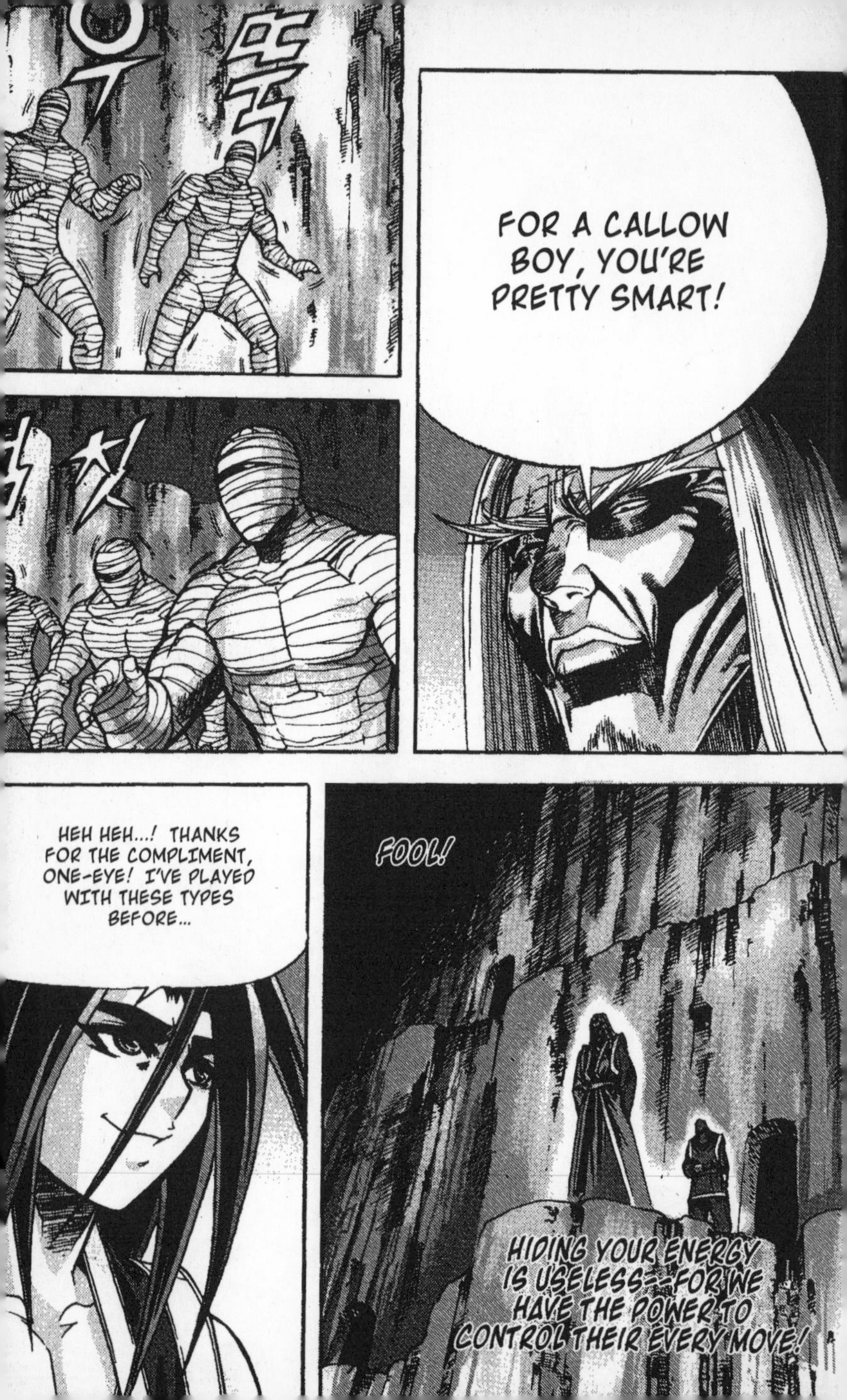
FOR A CALLOW BOY, YOU'RE PRETTY SMART!
HEH HEH...! THANKS FOR THE COMPLIMENT, ONE-EYE! I'VE PLAYED WITH THESE TYPES BEFORE...
FOOL!
HIDING YOUR ENERGY IS USELESS--FOR WE HAVE THE POWER TO CONTROL THEIR EVERY MOVE!

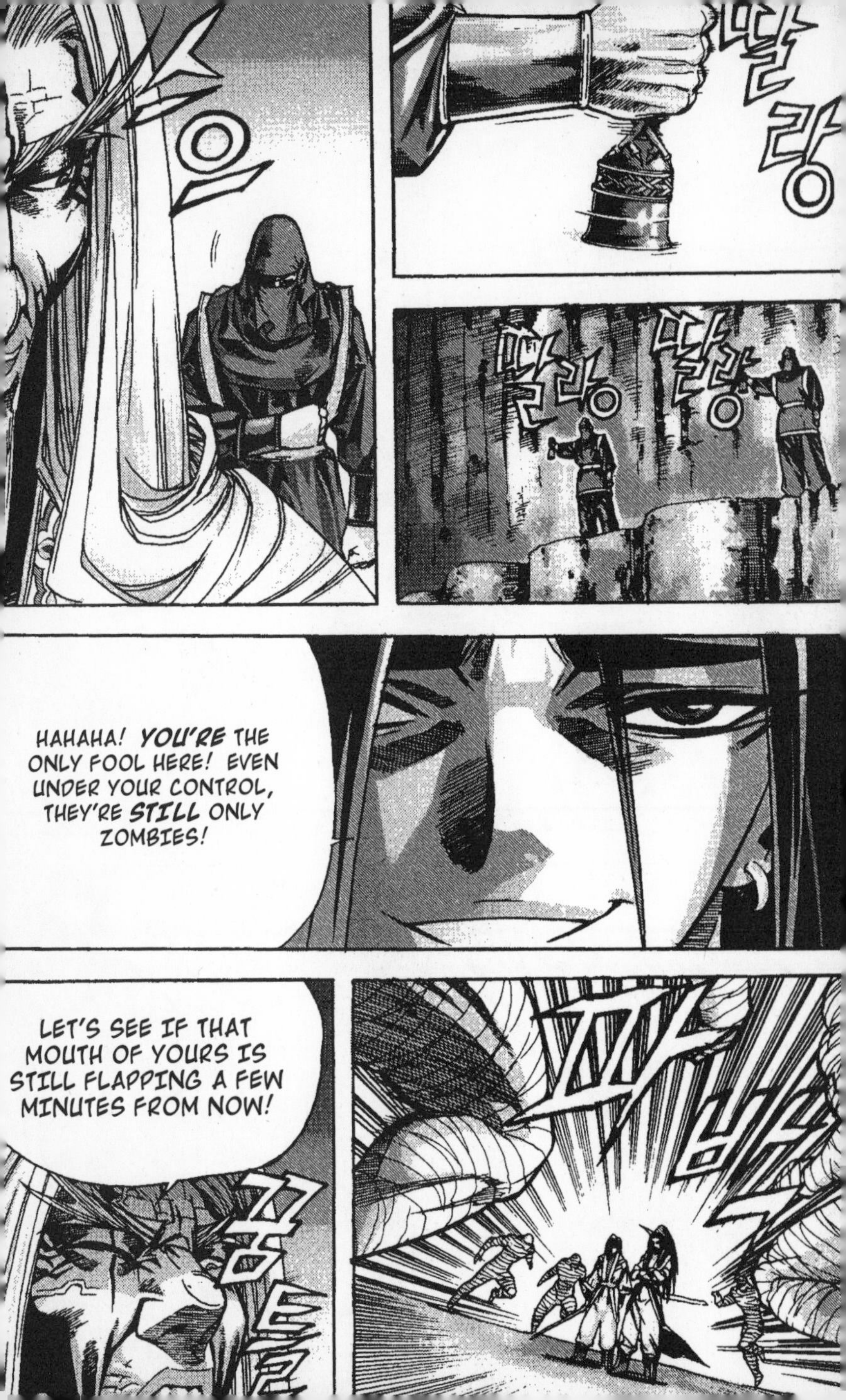
HAHAHA! YOU'RE THE ONLY FOOL HERE! EVEN UNDER YOUR CONTROL, THEY'RE STILL ONLY ZOMBIES!
LET'S SEE IF THAT MOUTH OF YOURS IS STILL FLAPPING A FEW MINUTES FROM NOW!

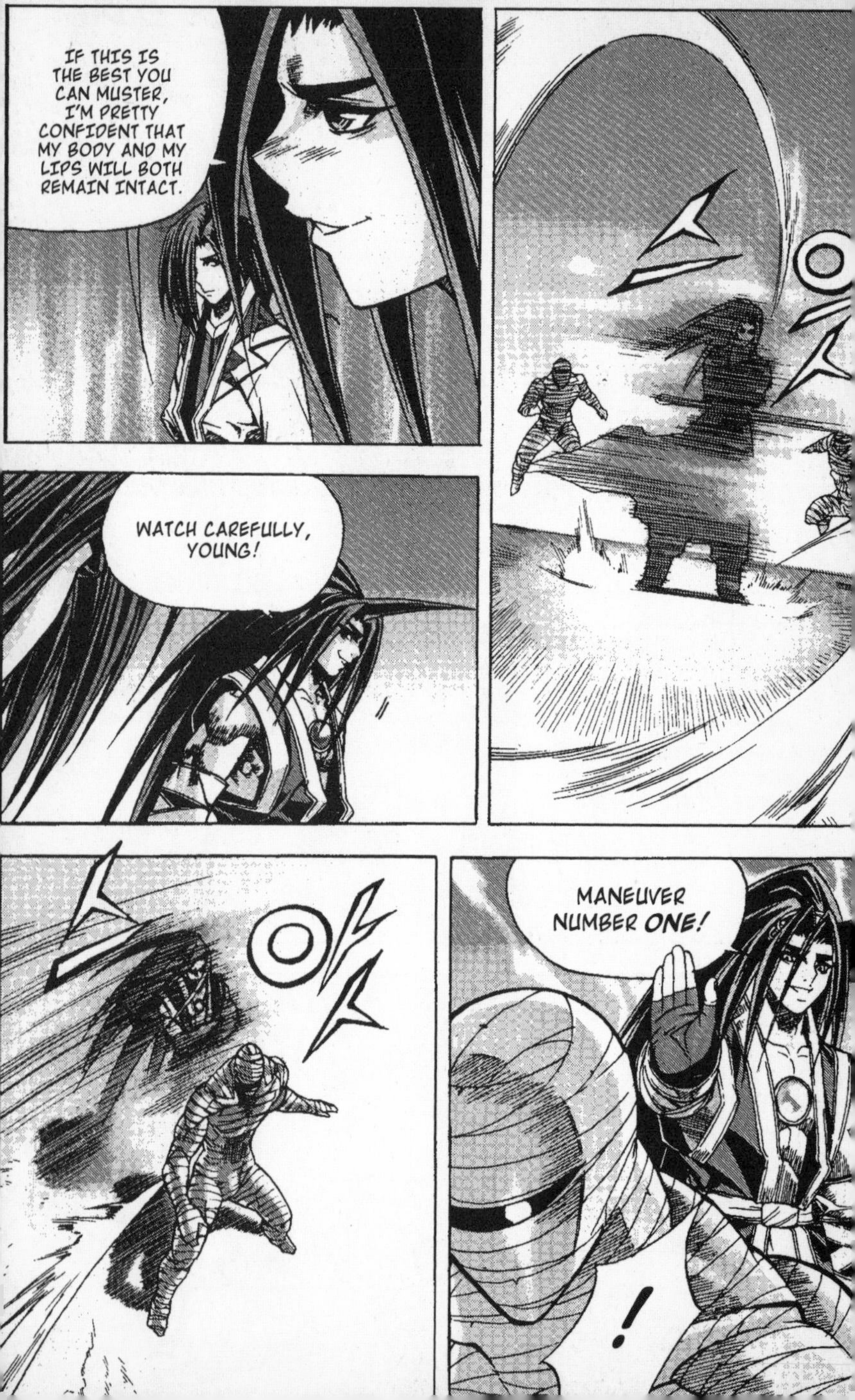
IF THIS IS THE BEST YOU CAN MUSTER, I'M PRETTY CONFIDENT THAT MY BODY AND MY LIPS WILL BOTH REMAIN INTACT.
WATCH CAREFULLY, YOUNG!
MANEUVER NUMBER ONE!
!

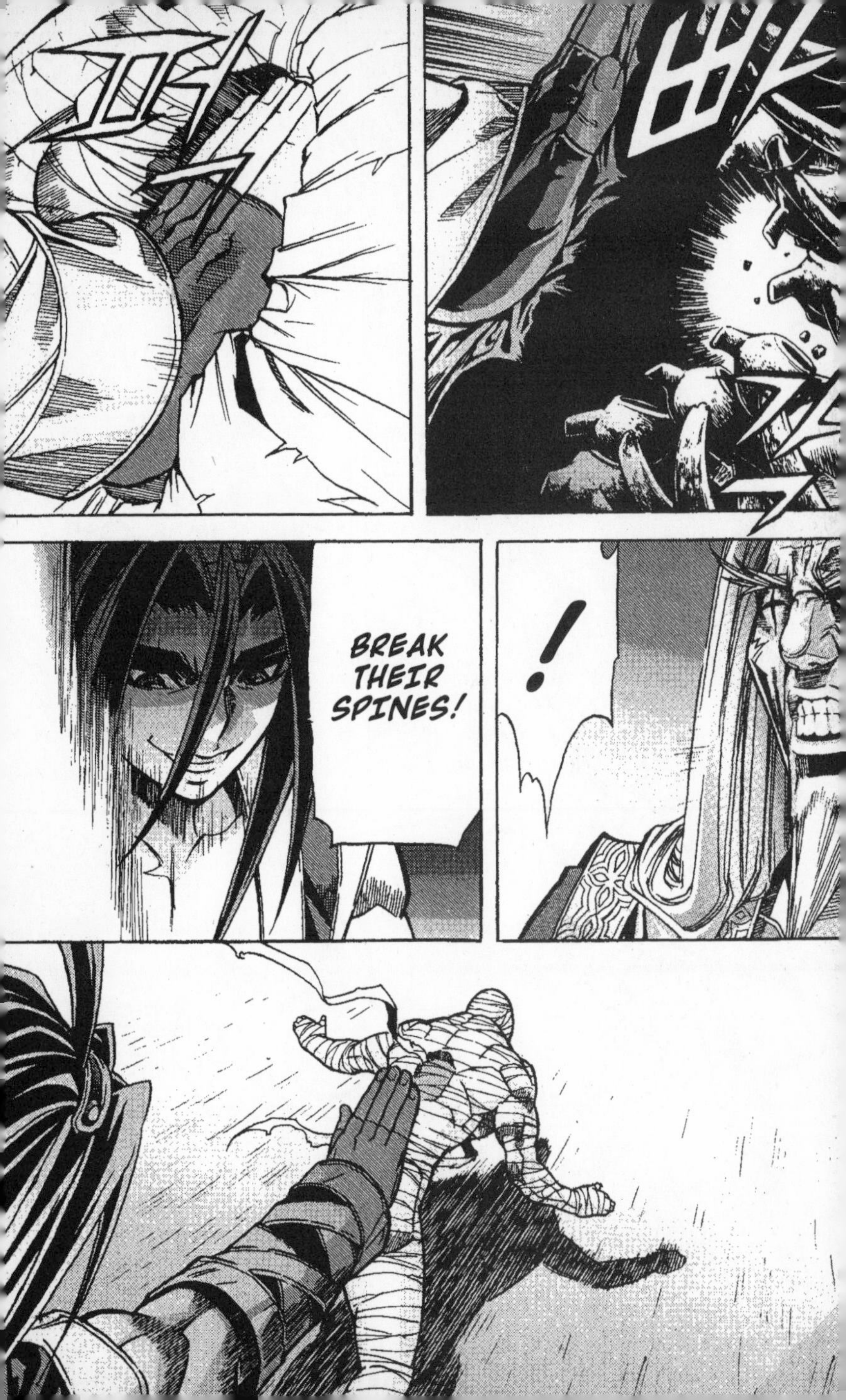
BREAK THEIR SPINES!
!

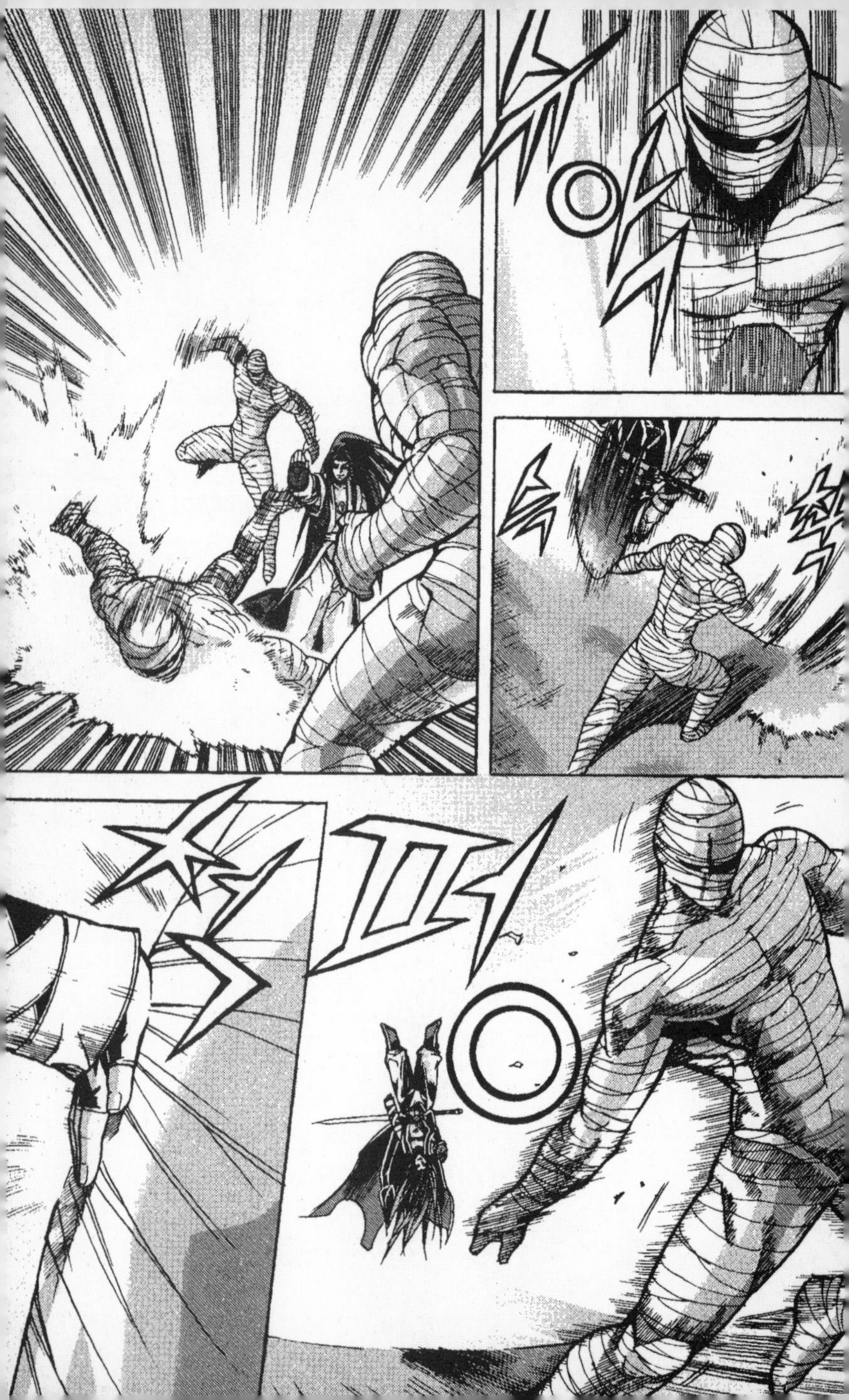

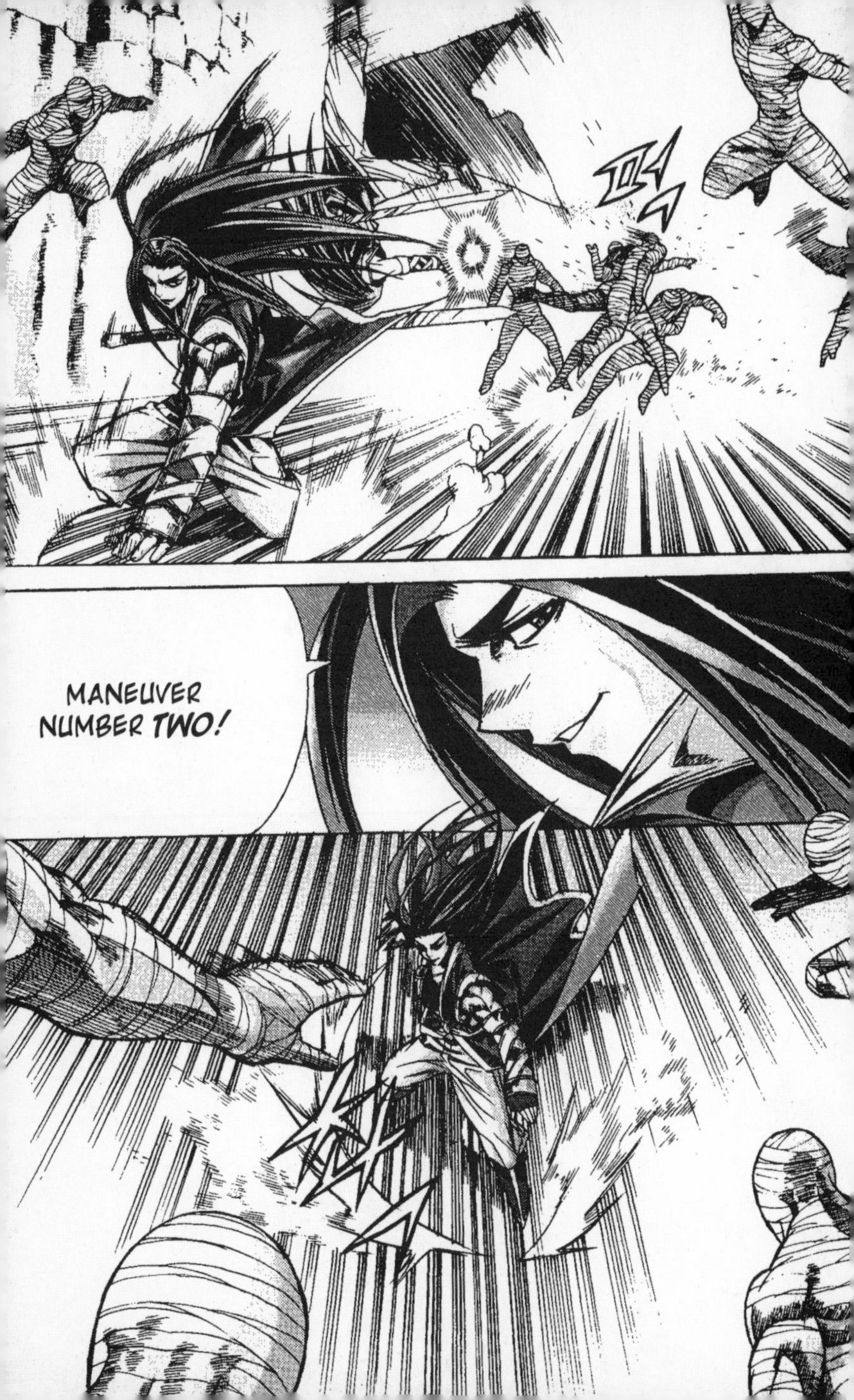
MANEUVER NUMBER TWO!

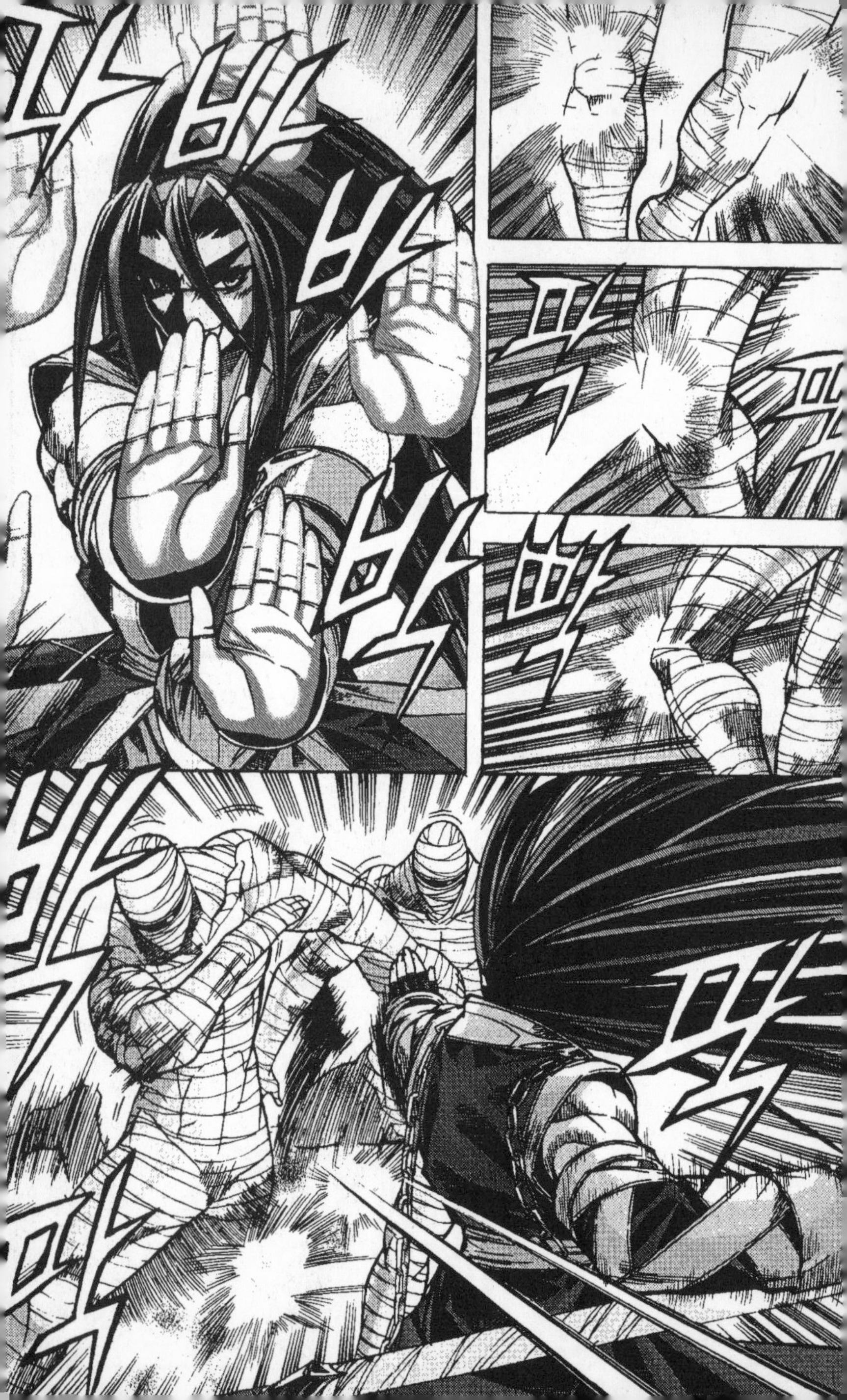

바
바
바
팍
빡
팍

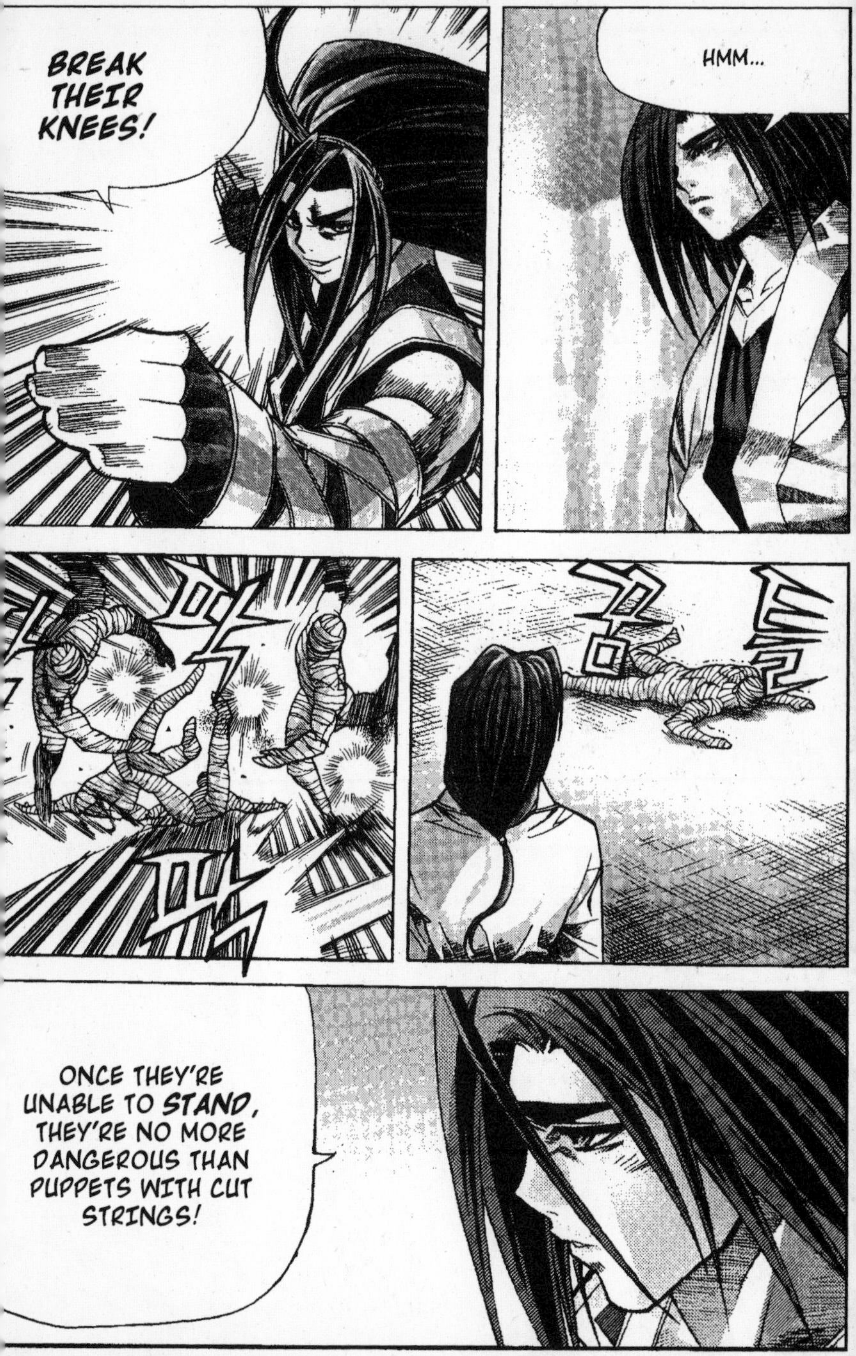
BREAK THEIR KNEES!
HMM...
ONCE THEY'RE UNABLE TO STAND, THEY'RE NO MORE DANGEROUS THAN PUPPETS WITH CUT STRINGS!

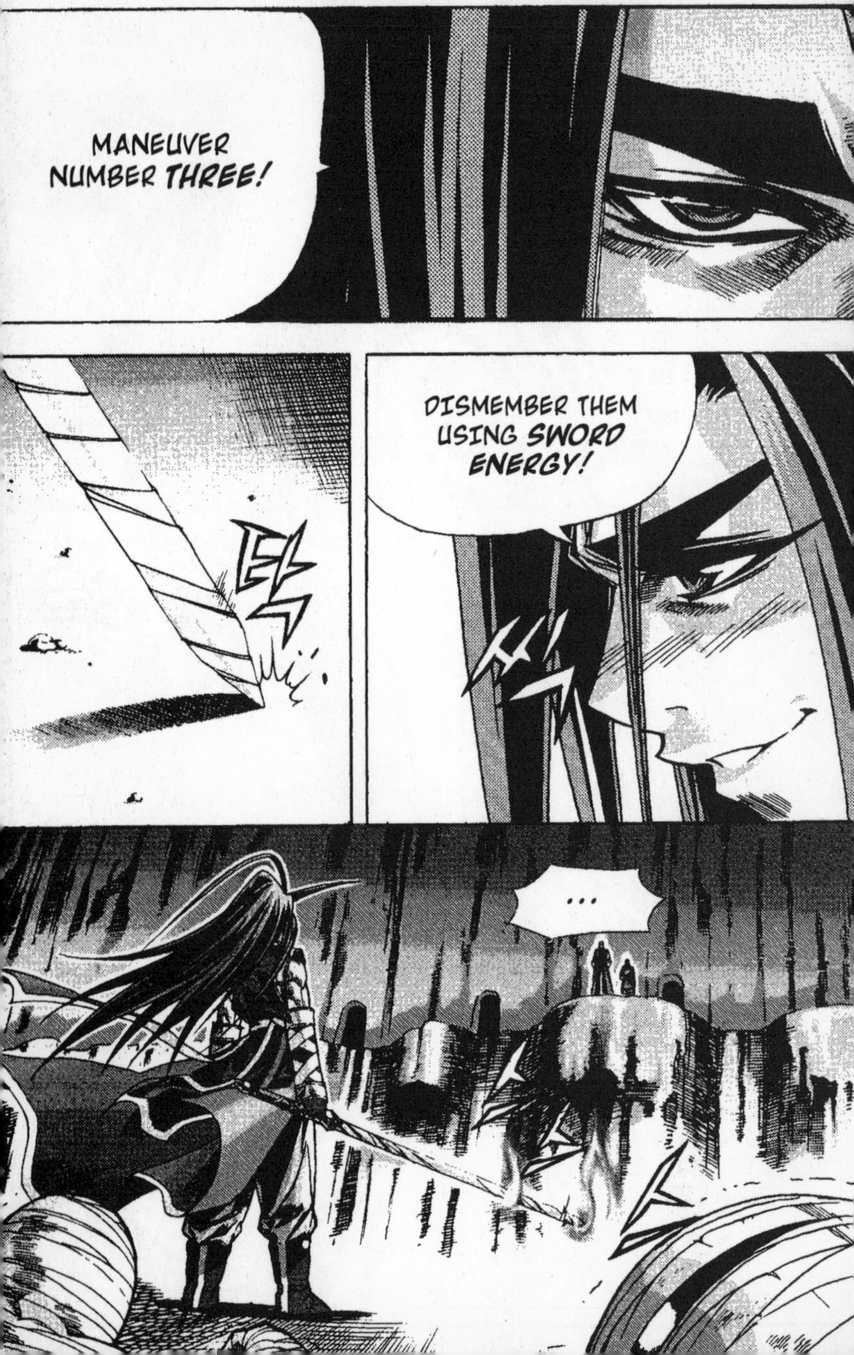
MANEUVER NUMBER THREE!
DISMEMBER THEM USING SWORD ENERGY!
...

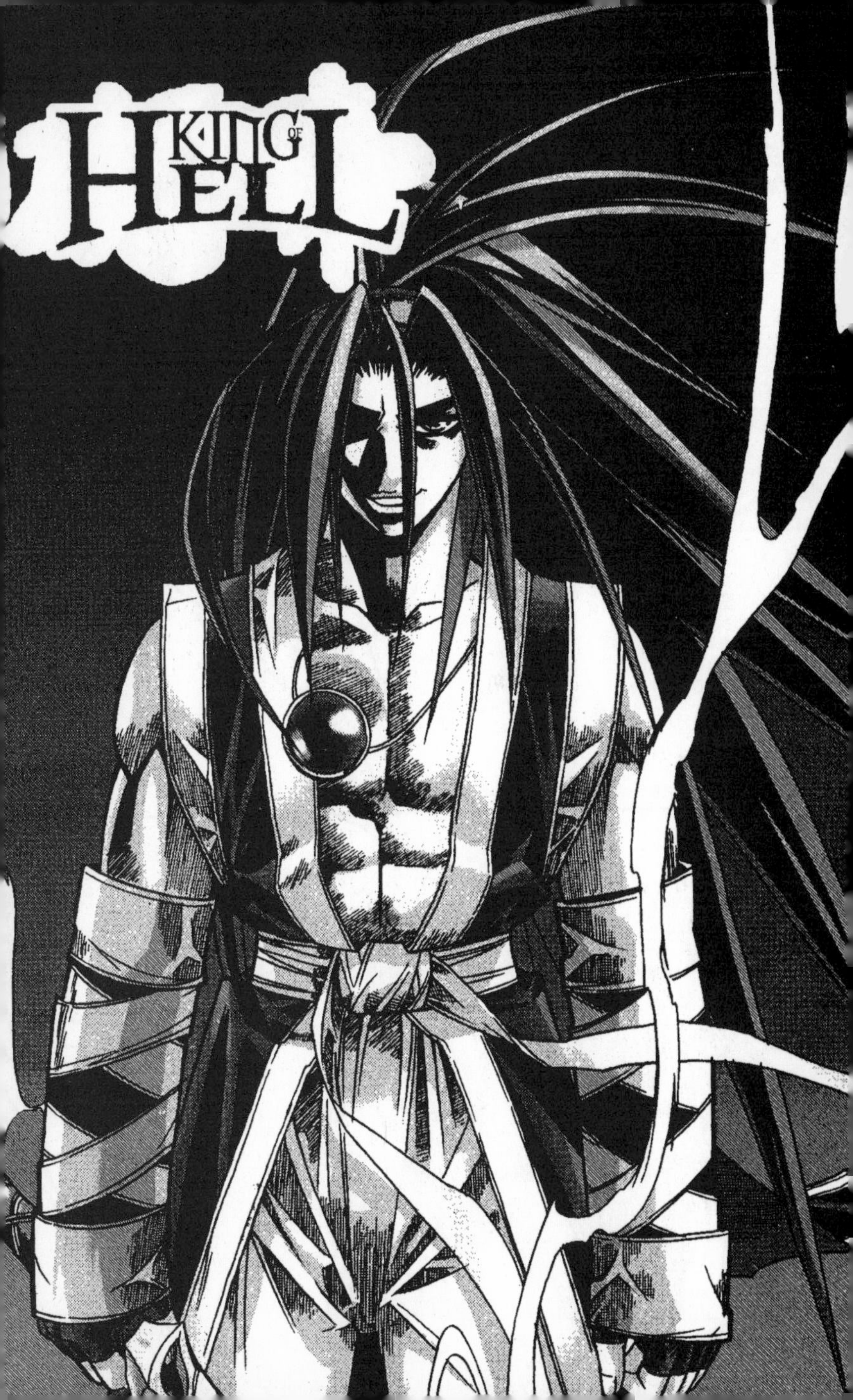
KING OF HELL

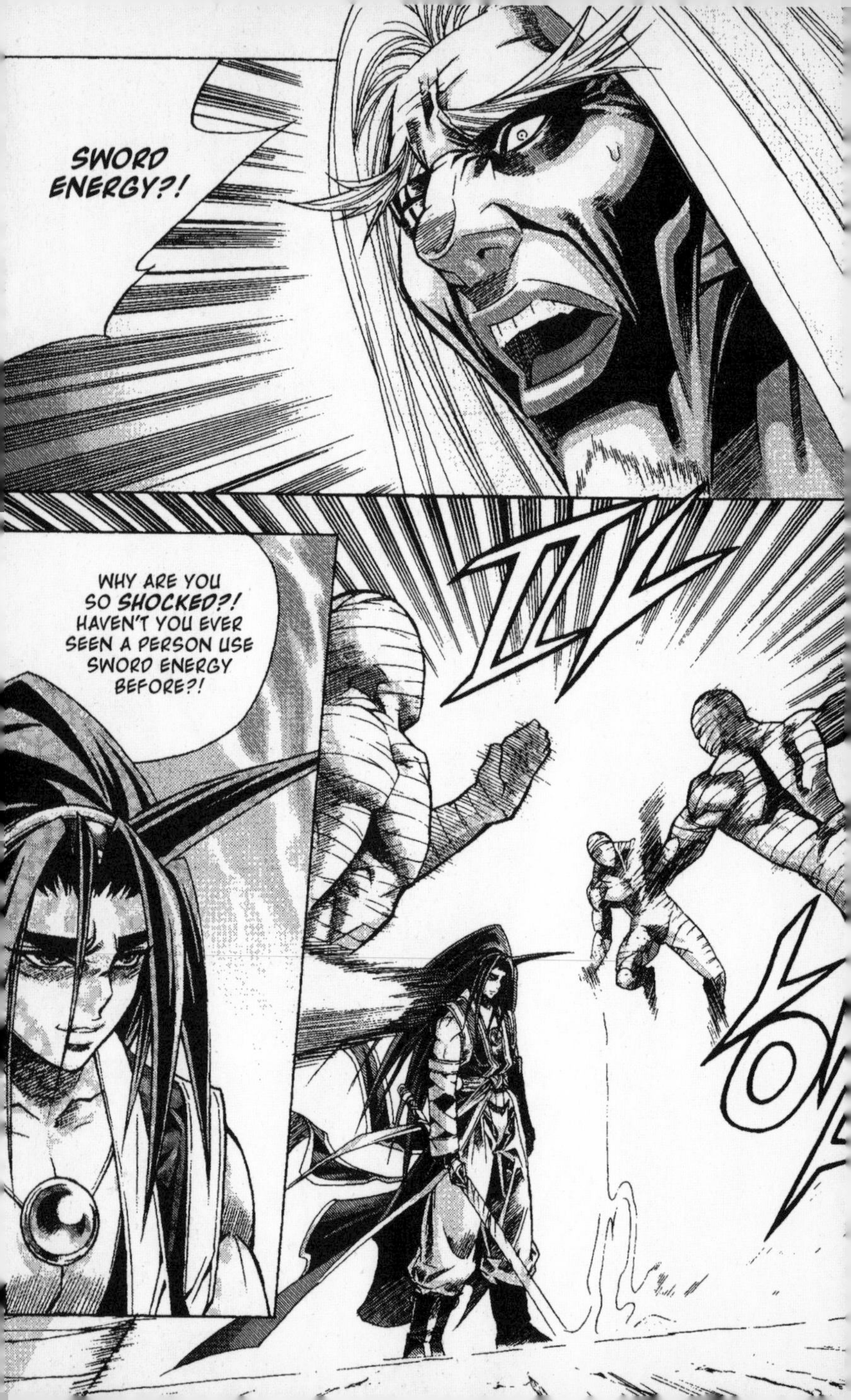
SWORD ENERGY?!
WHY ARE YOU SO SHOCKED?! HAVEN'T YOU EVER SEEN A PERSON USE SWORD ENERGY BEFORE?!

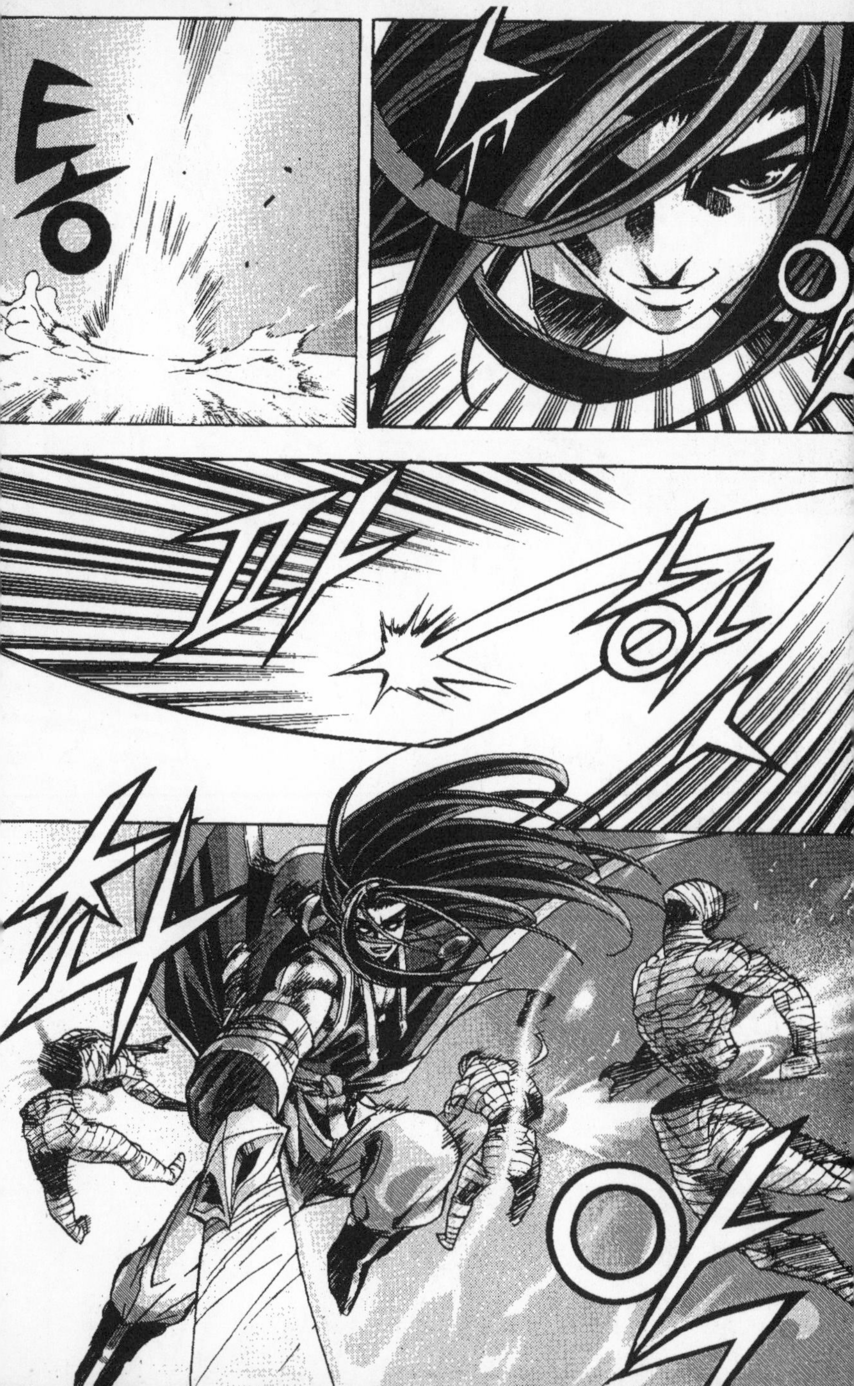

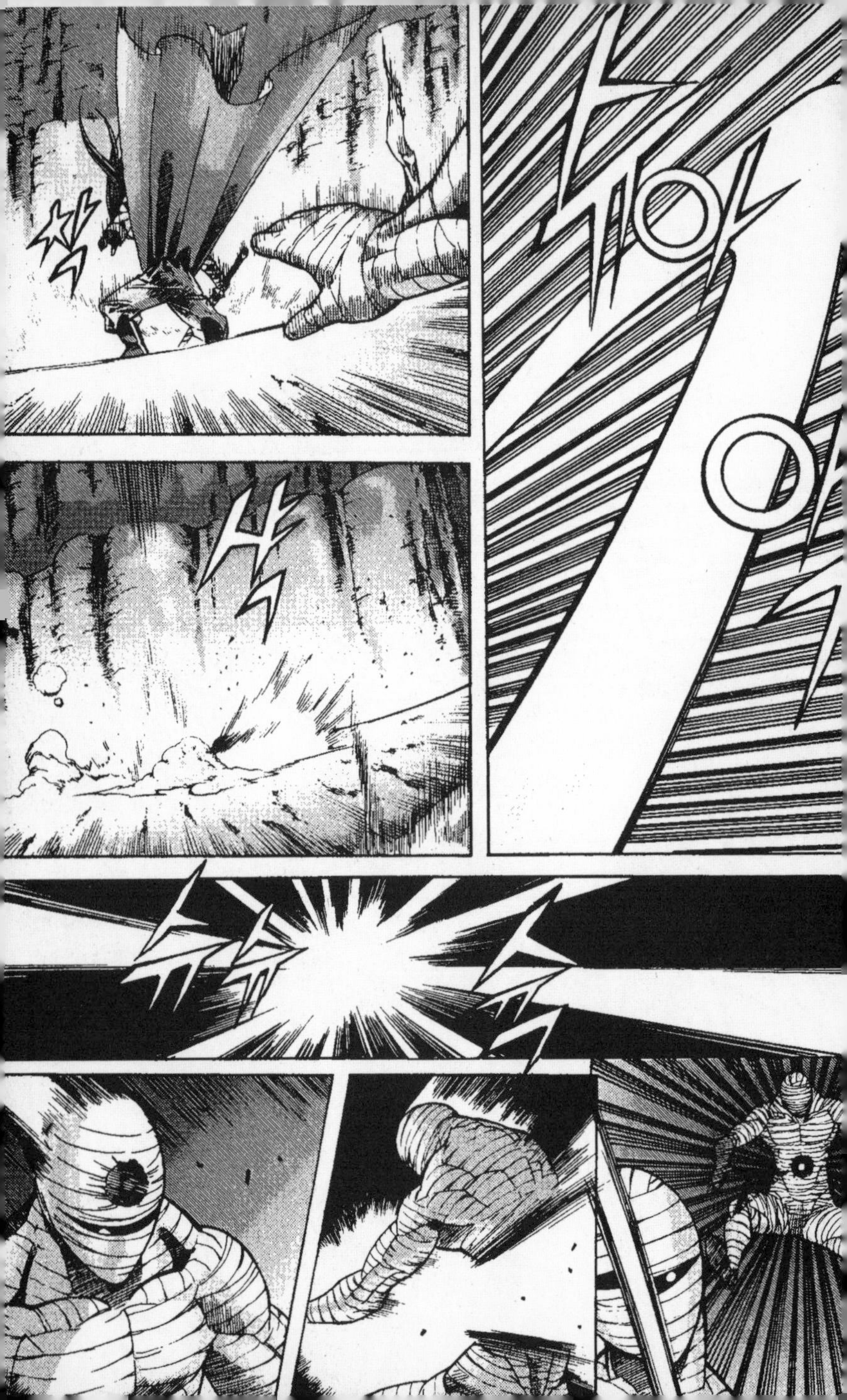

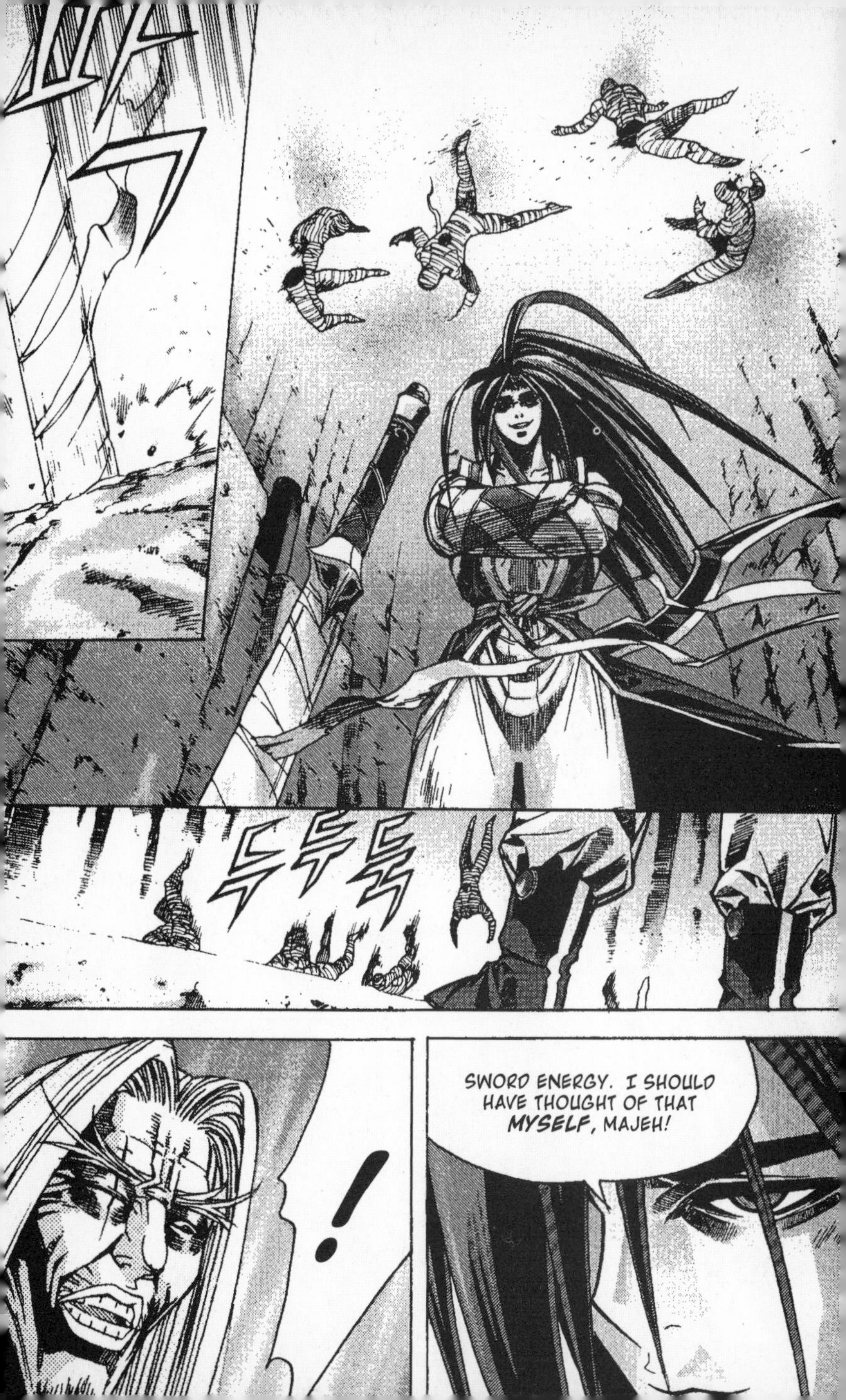
SWORD ENERGY. I SHOULD HAVE THOUGHT OF THAT *MYSELF*, MAJEH!

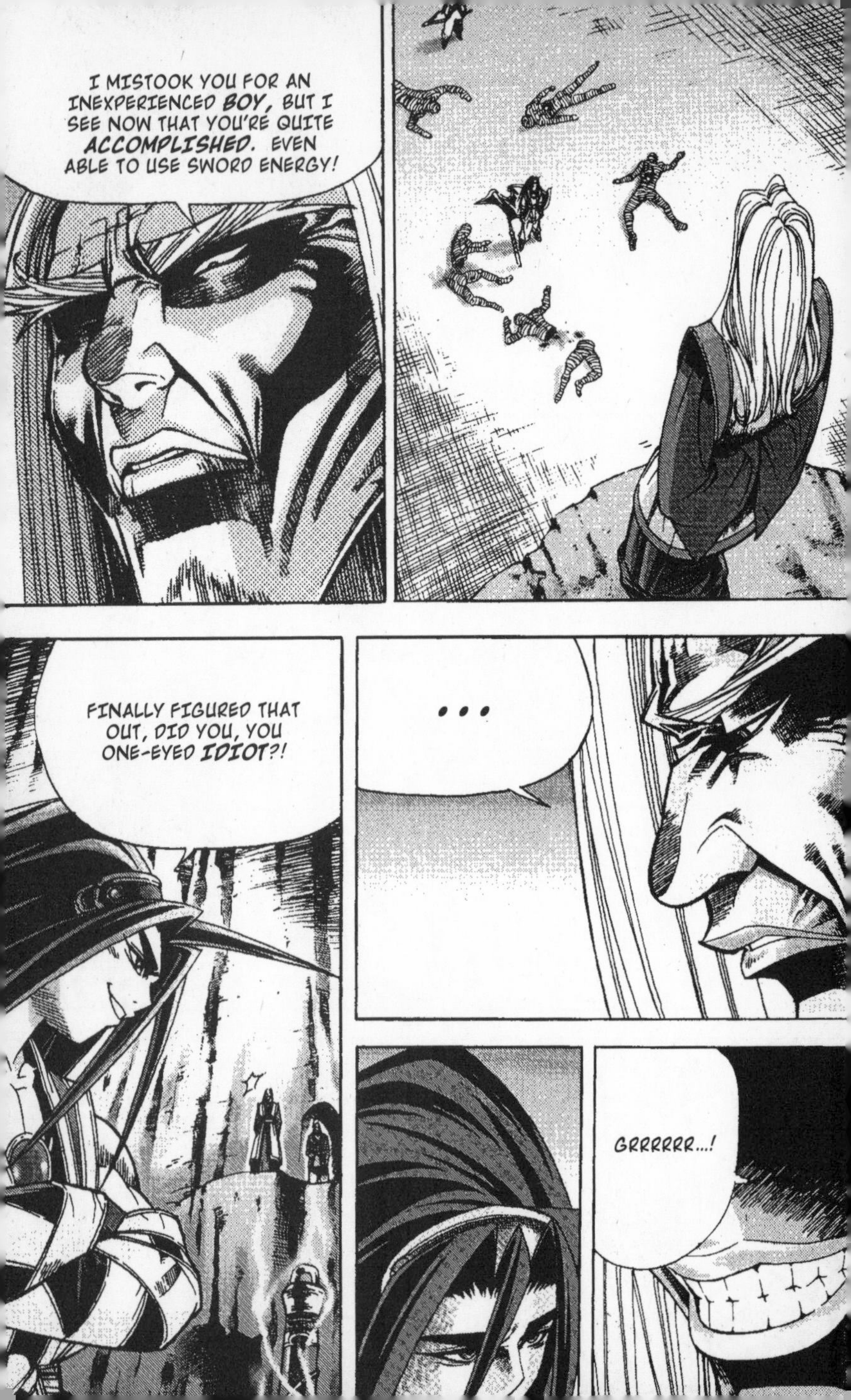
I MISTOOK YOU FOR AN INEXPERIENCED BOY, BUT I SEE NOW THAT YOU'RE QUITE ACCOMPLISHED. EVEN ABLE TO USE SWORD ENERGY!
FINALLY FIGURED THAT OUT, DID YOU, YOU ONE-EYED IDIOT?!
...
GRRRRRR...!

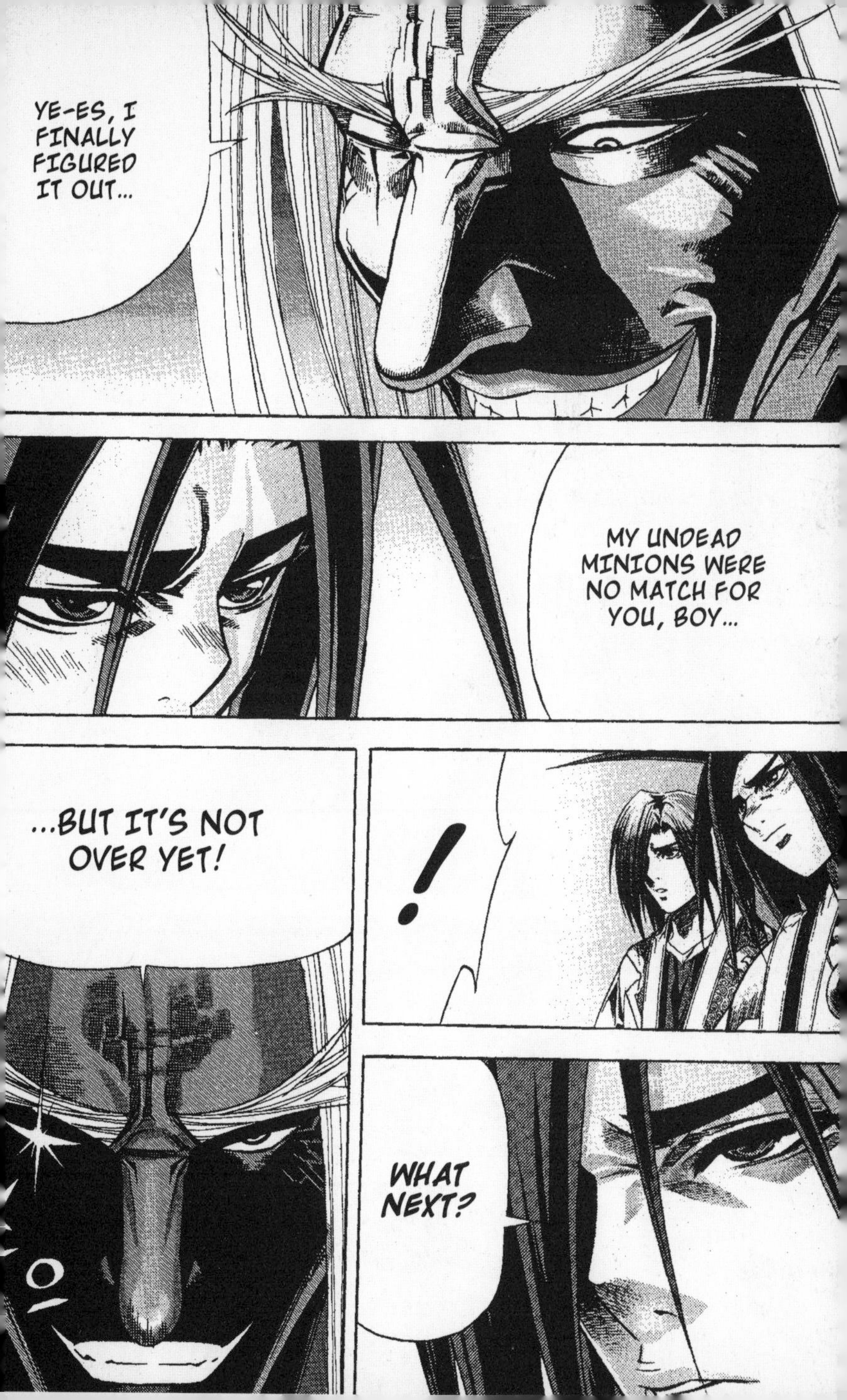
YE-ES, I FINALLY FIGURED IT OUT...
MY UNDEAD MINIONS WERE NO MATCH FOR YOU, BOY...
...BUT IT'S NOT OVER YET!
!
WHAT NEXT?

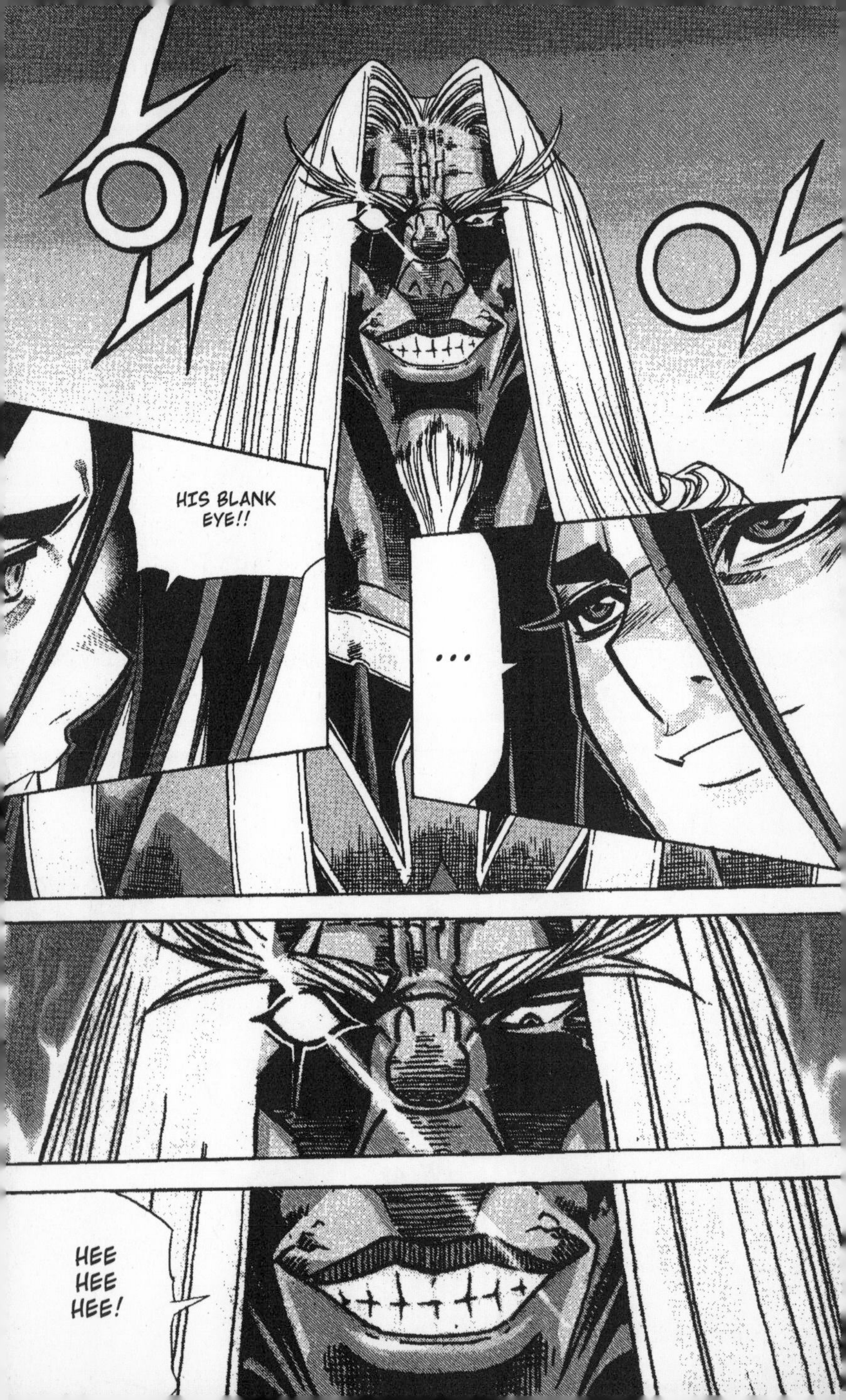
HIS BLANK EYE!!
...
HEE HEE HEE!

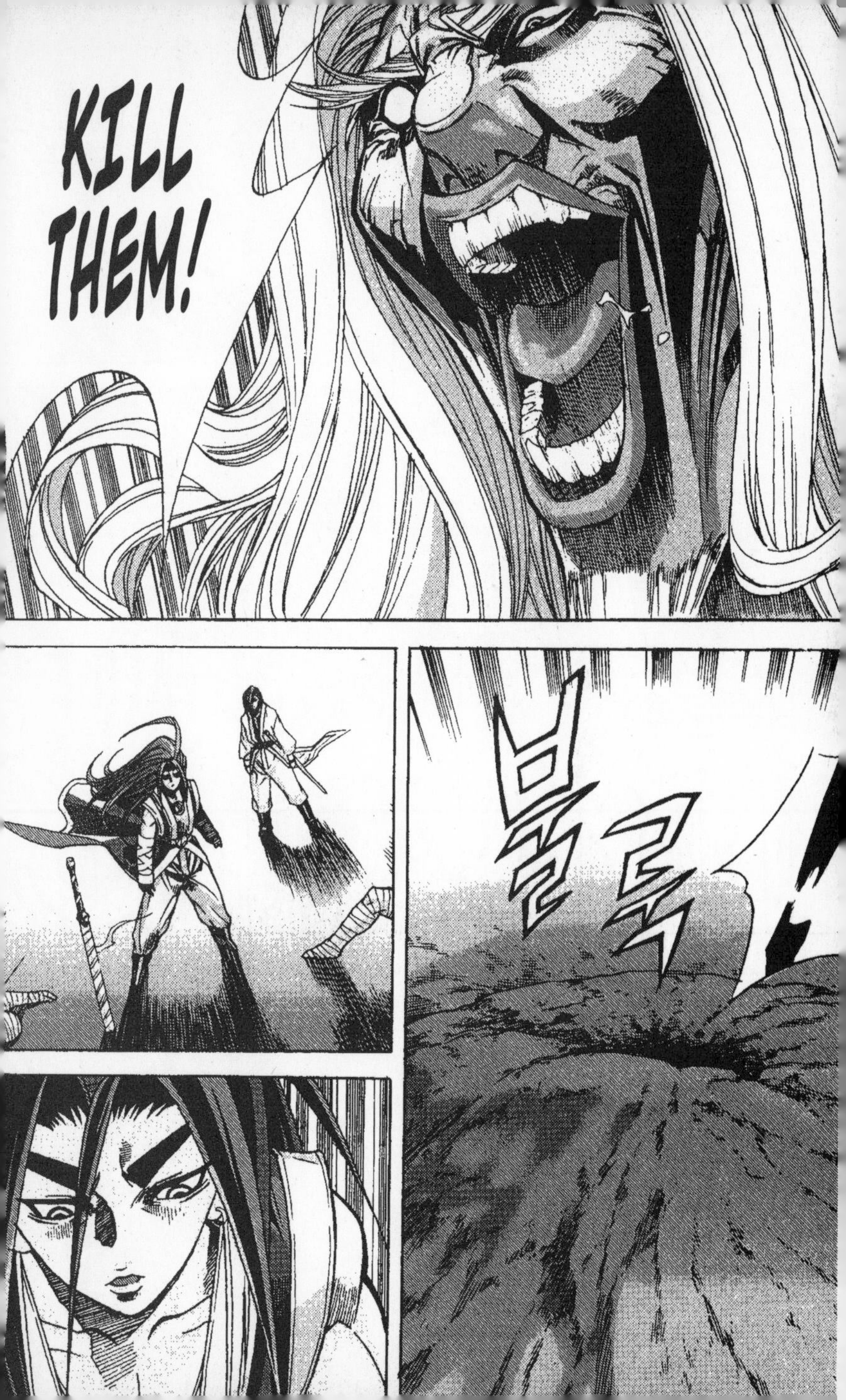
KILL THEM!

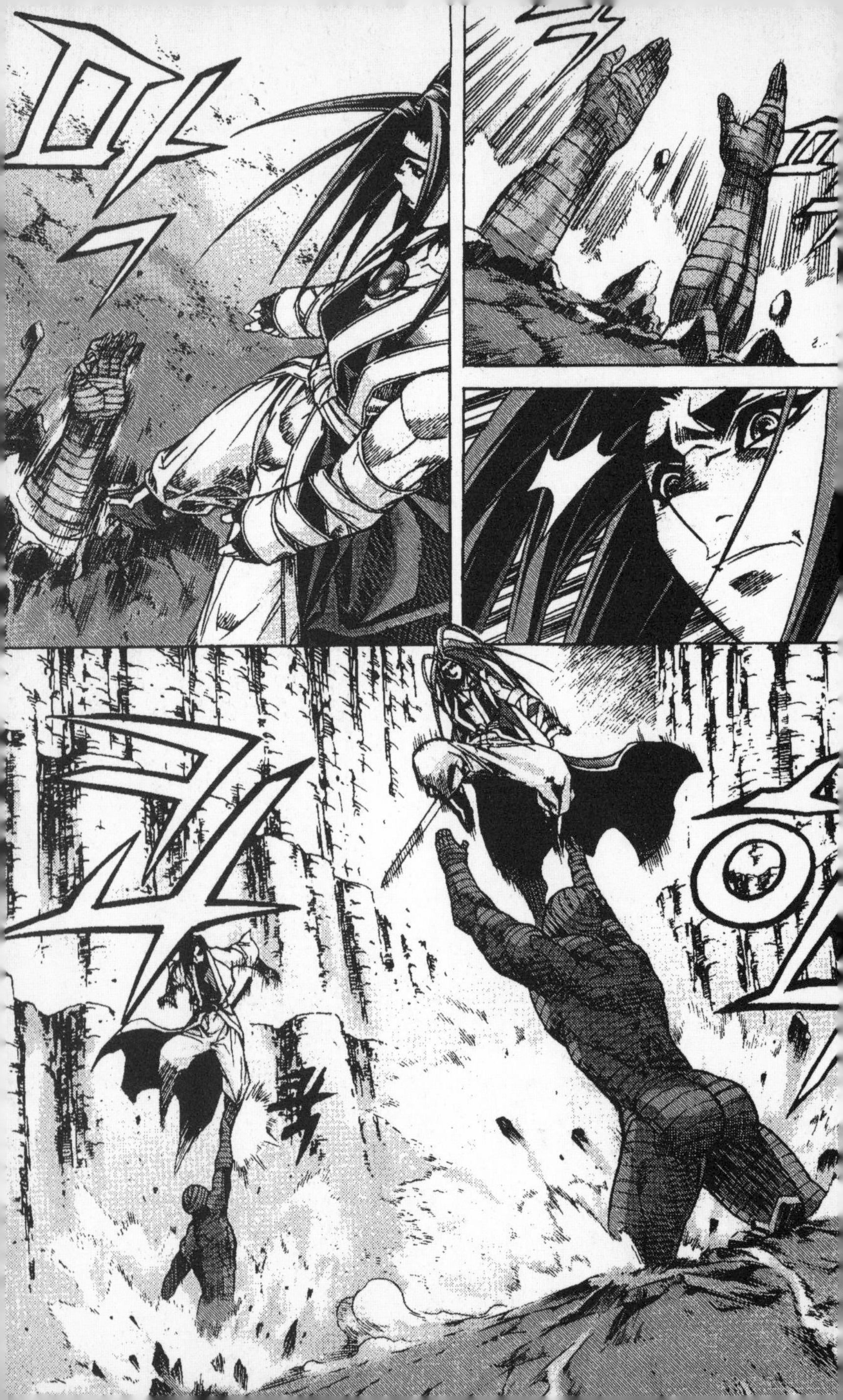

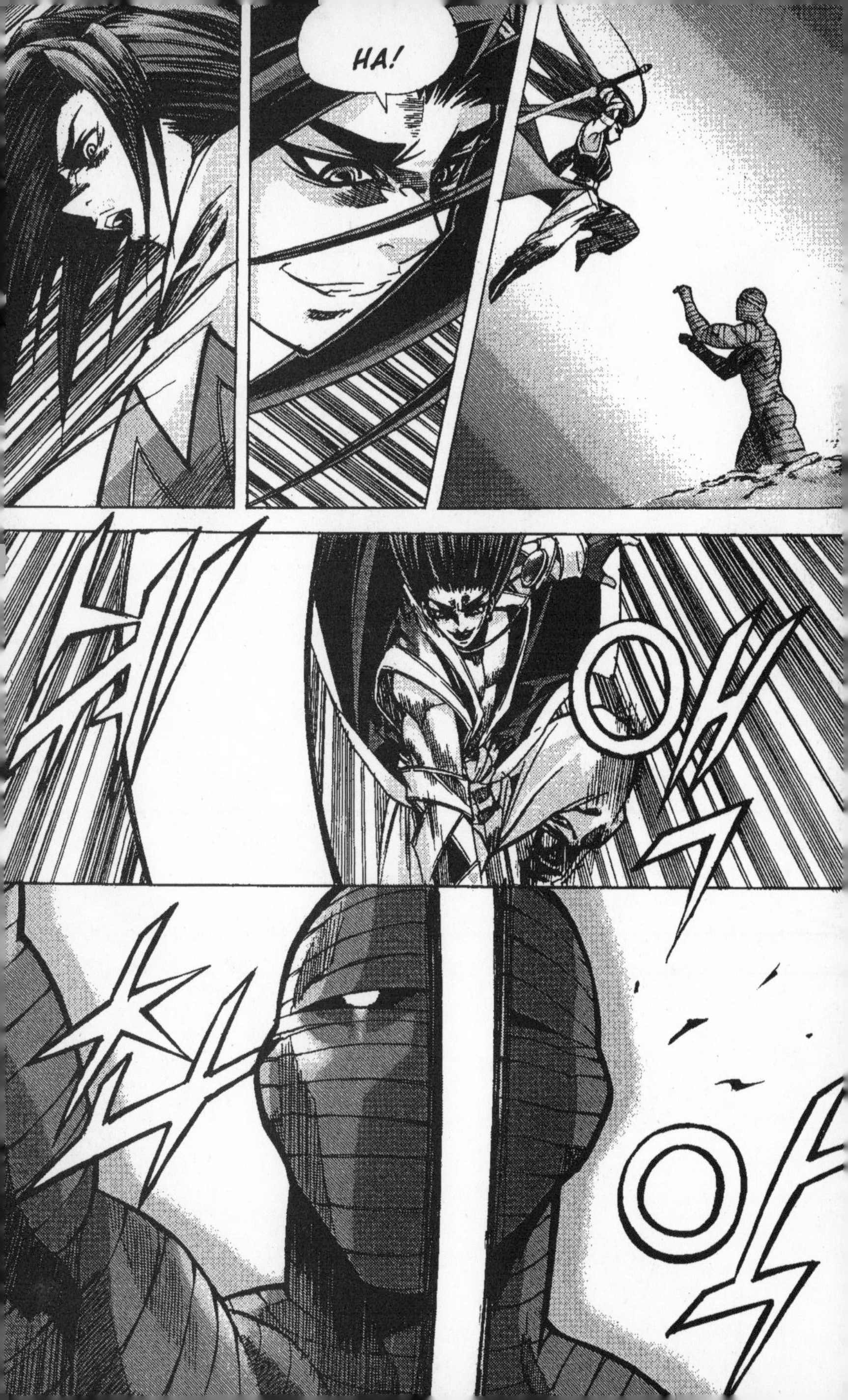
HA!

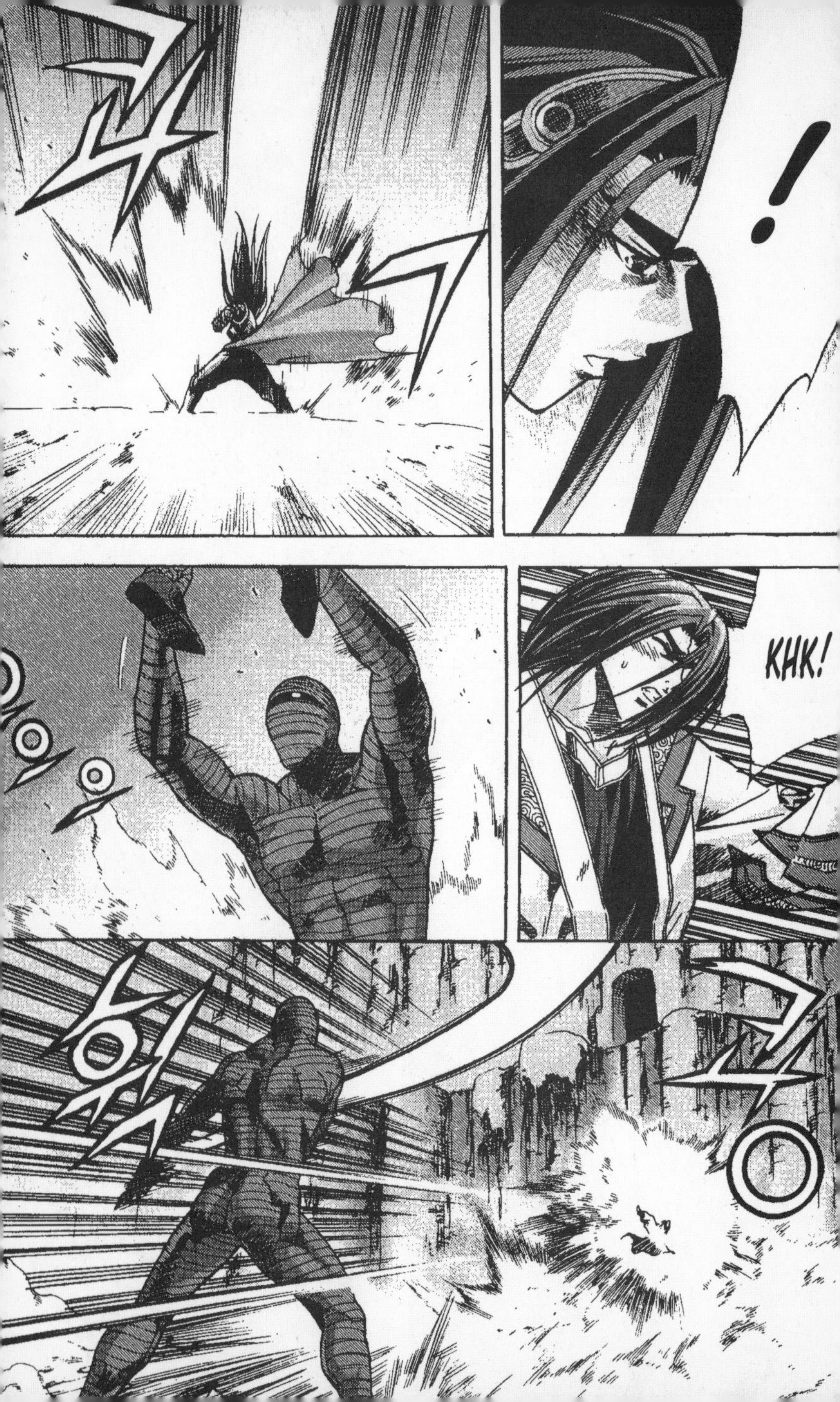
!
KHK!

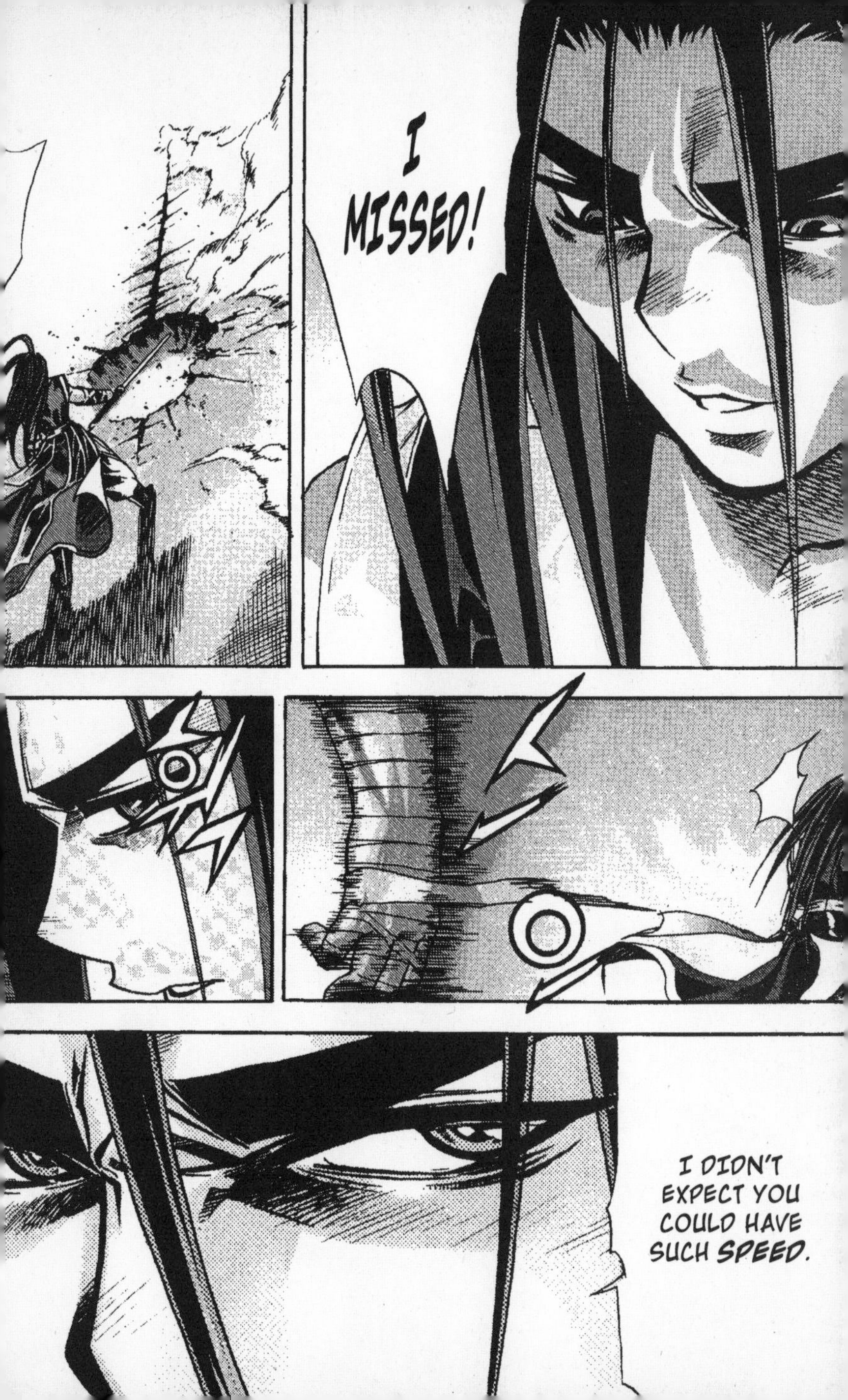
I MISSED!
I DIDN'T EXPECT YOU COULD HAVE SUCH SPEED.

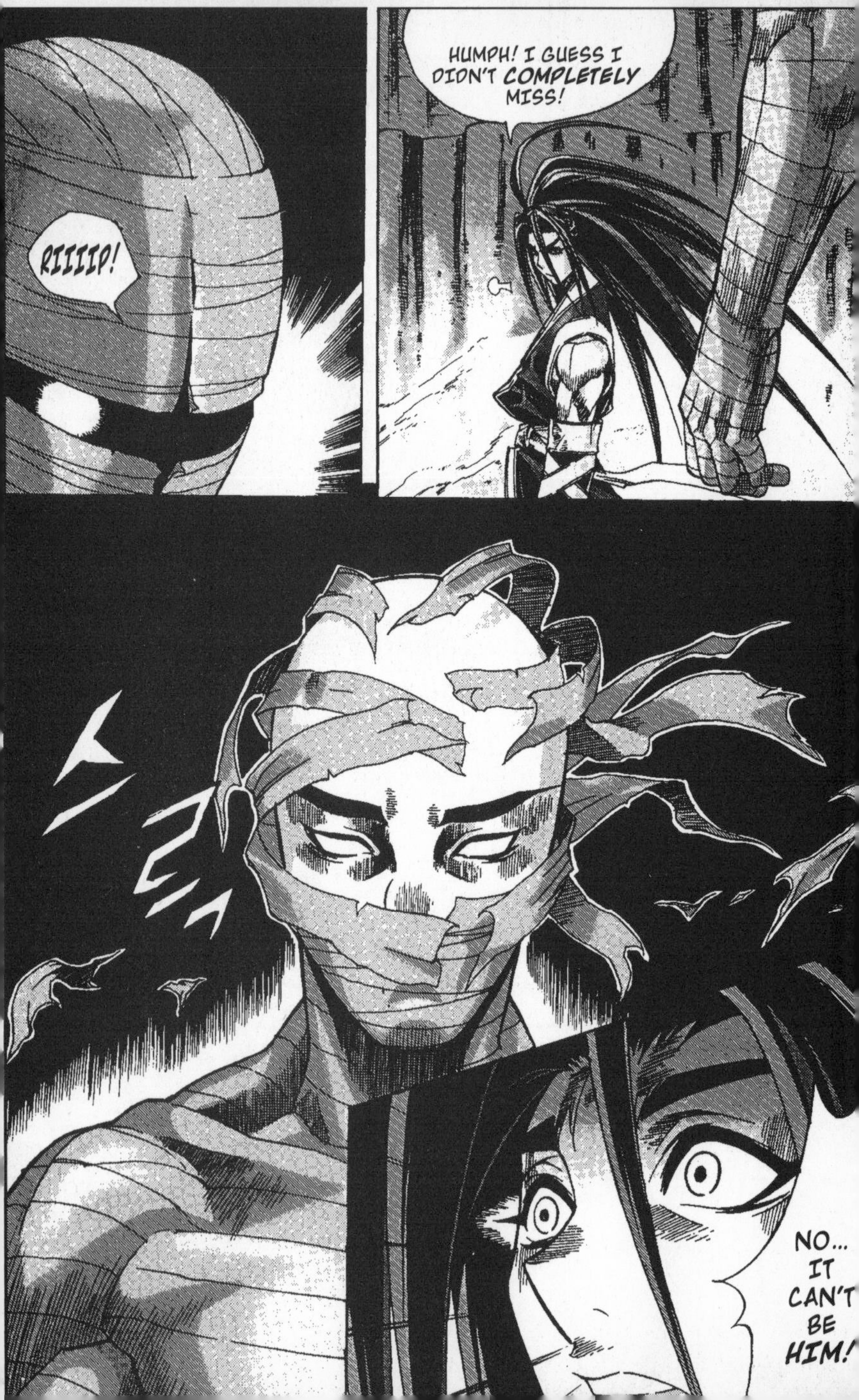
RIIIIP!
HUMPH! I GUESS I DIDN'T COMPLETELY MISS!
NO... IT CAN'T BE HIM!

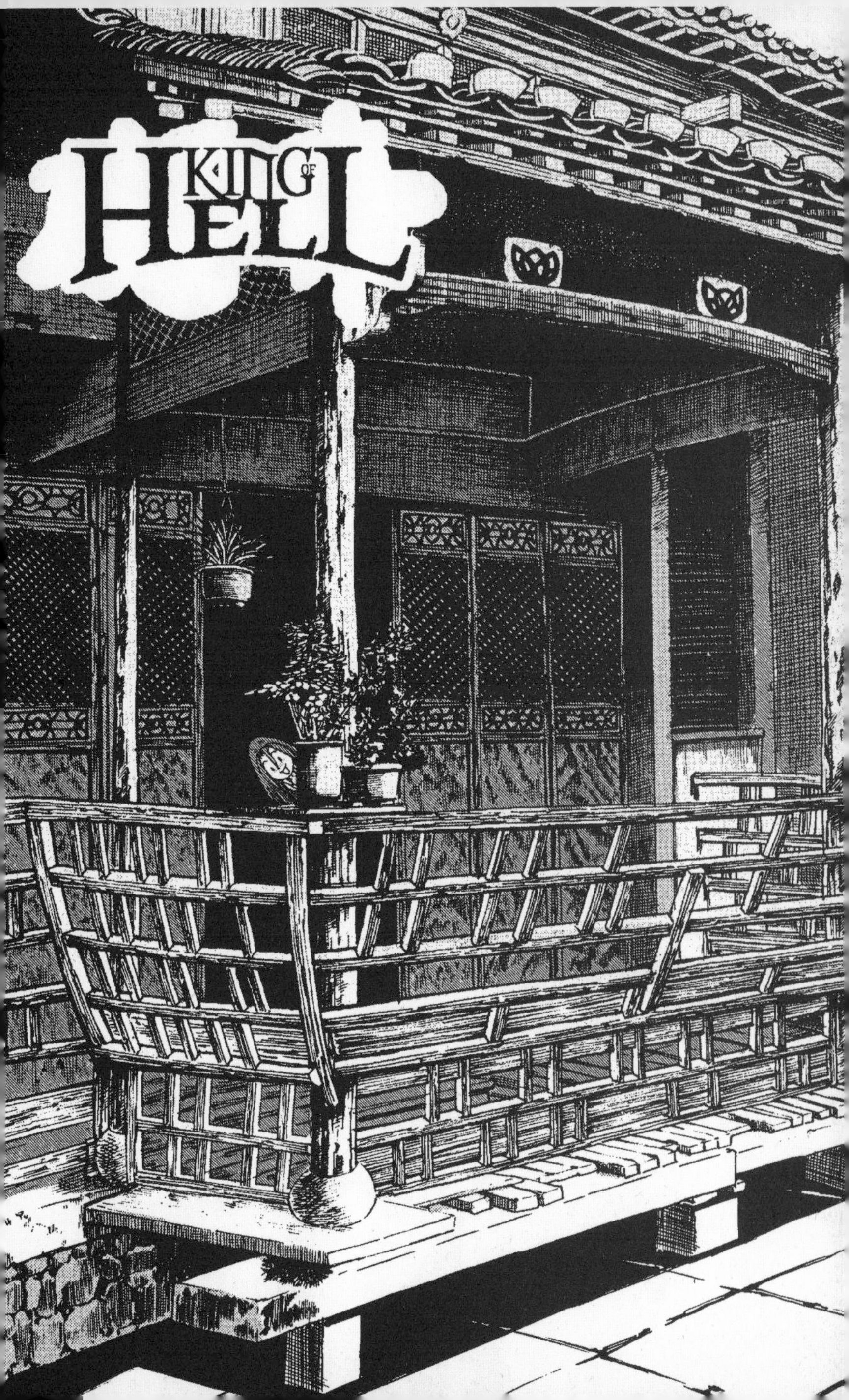
KING OF HELL

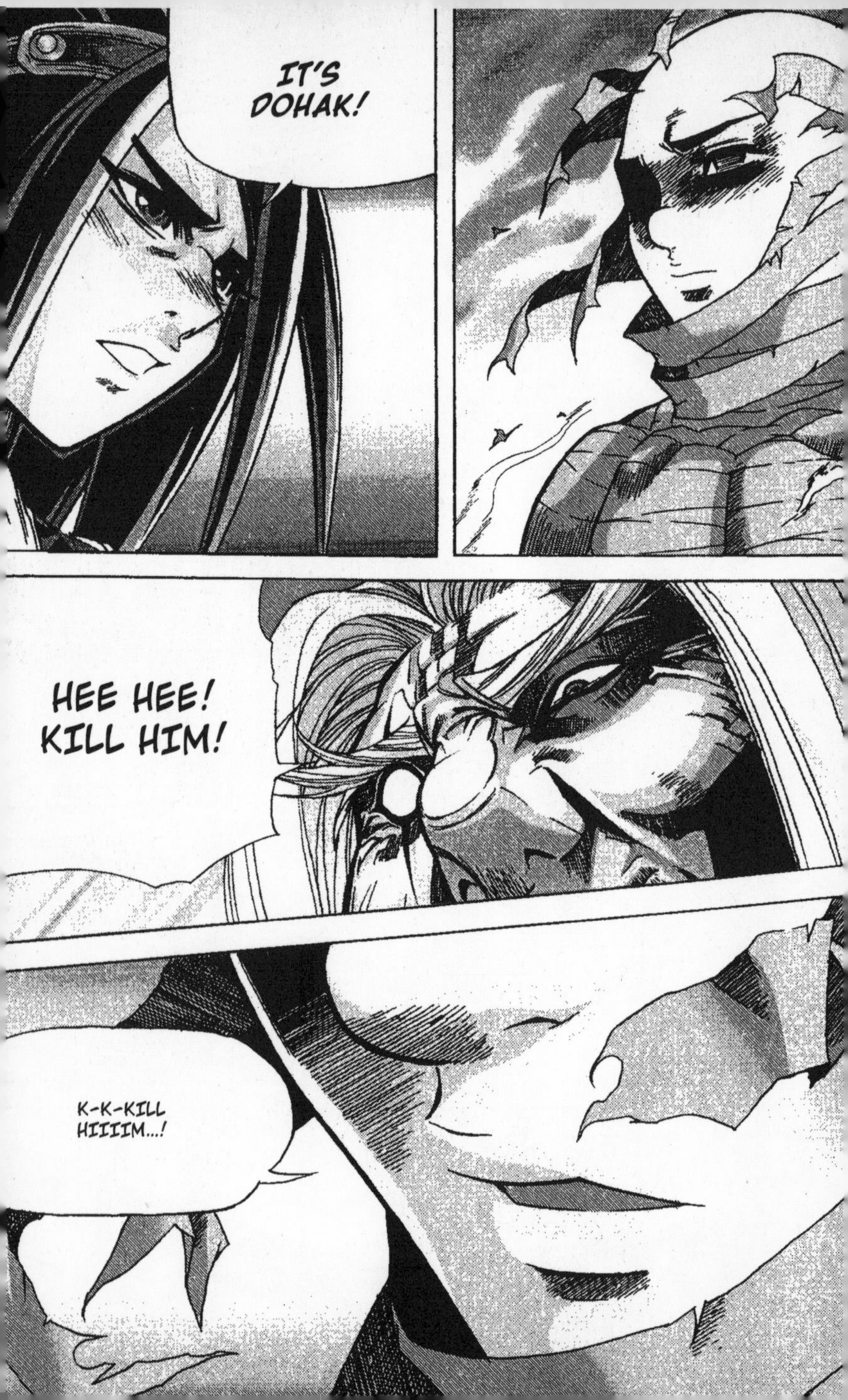
IT'S DOHAK!
HEE HEE! KILL HIM!
K-K-KILL HIIIIM...!

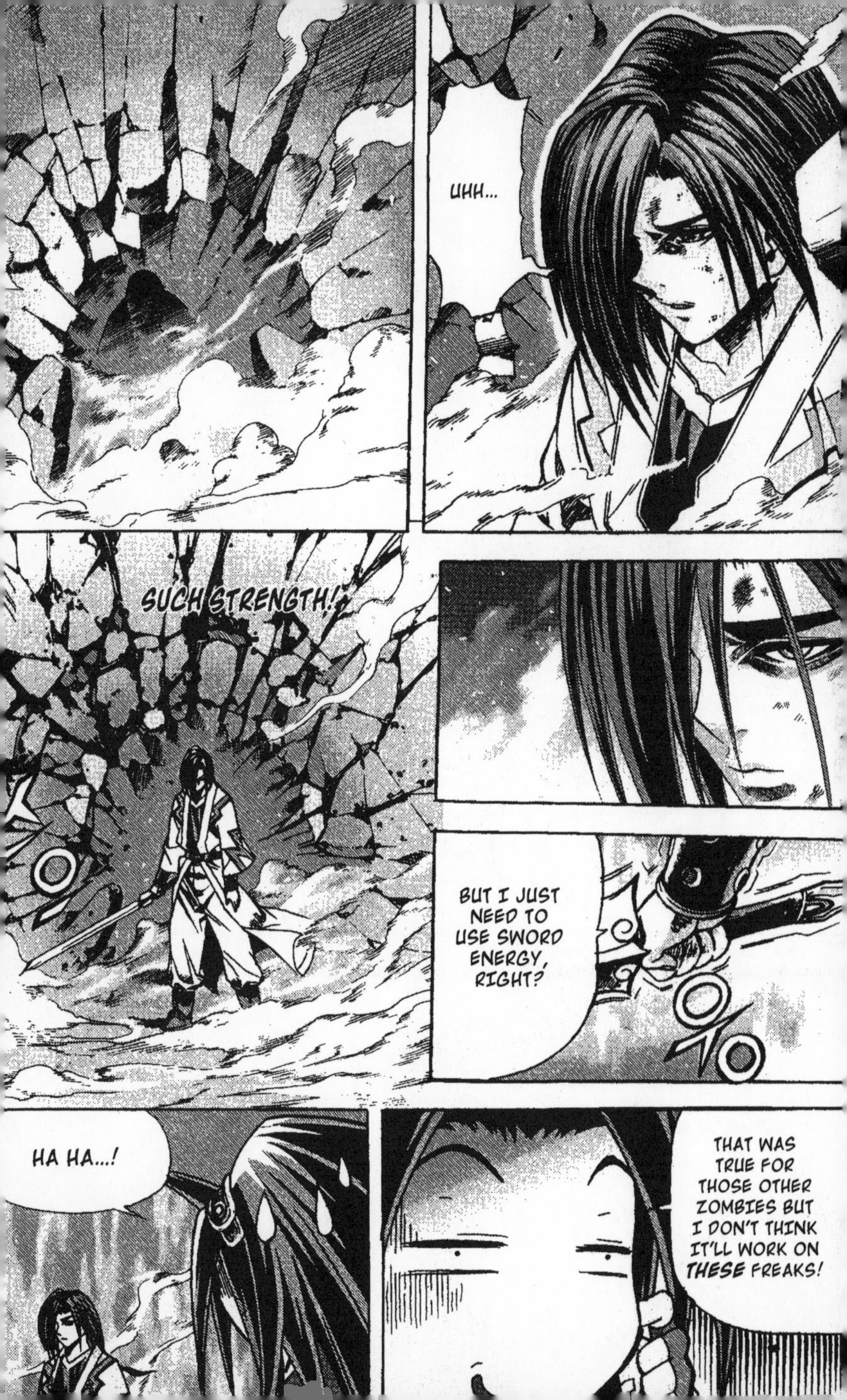
UHH...
SUCH STRENGTH!
BUT I JUST NEED TO USE SWORD ENERGY, RIGHT?
HA HA...!
THAT WAS TRUE FOR THOSE OTHER ZOMBIES BUT I DON'T THINK IT'LL WORK ON *THESE* FREAKS!

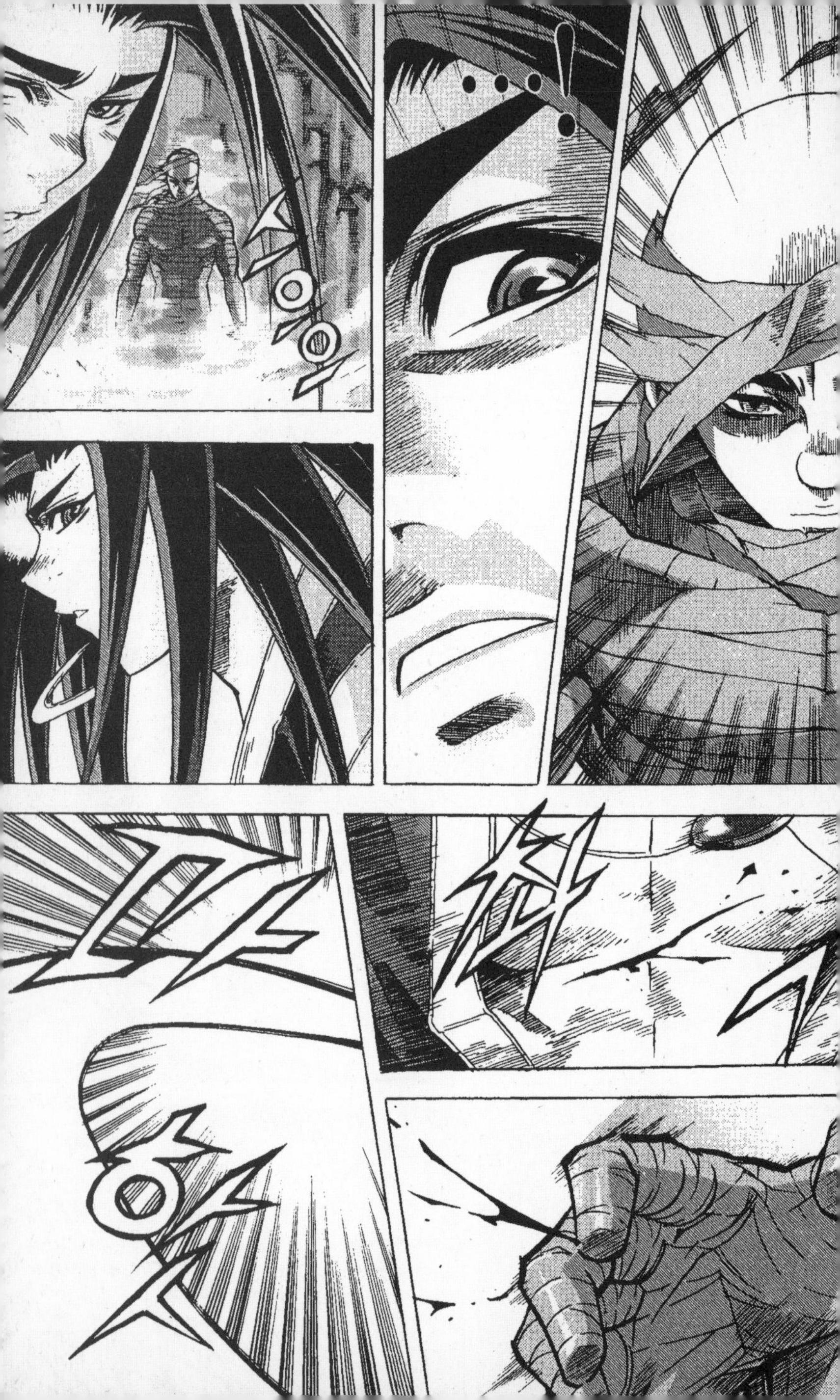
...!!

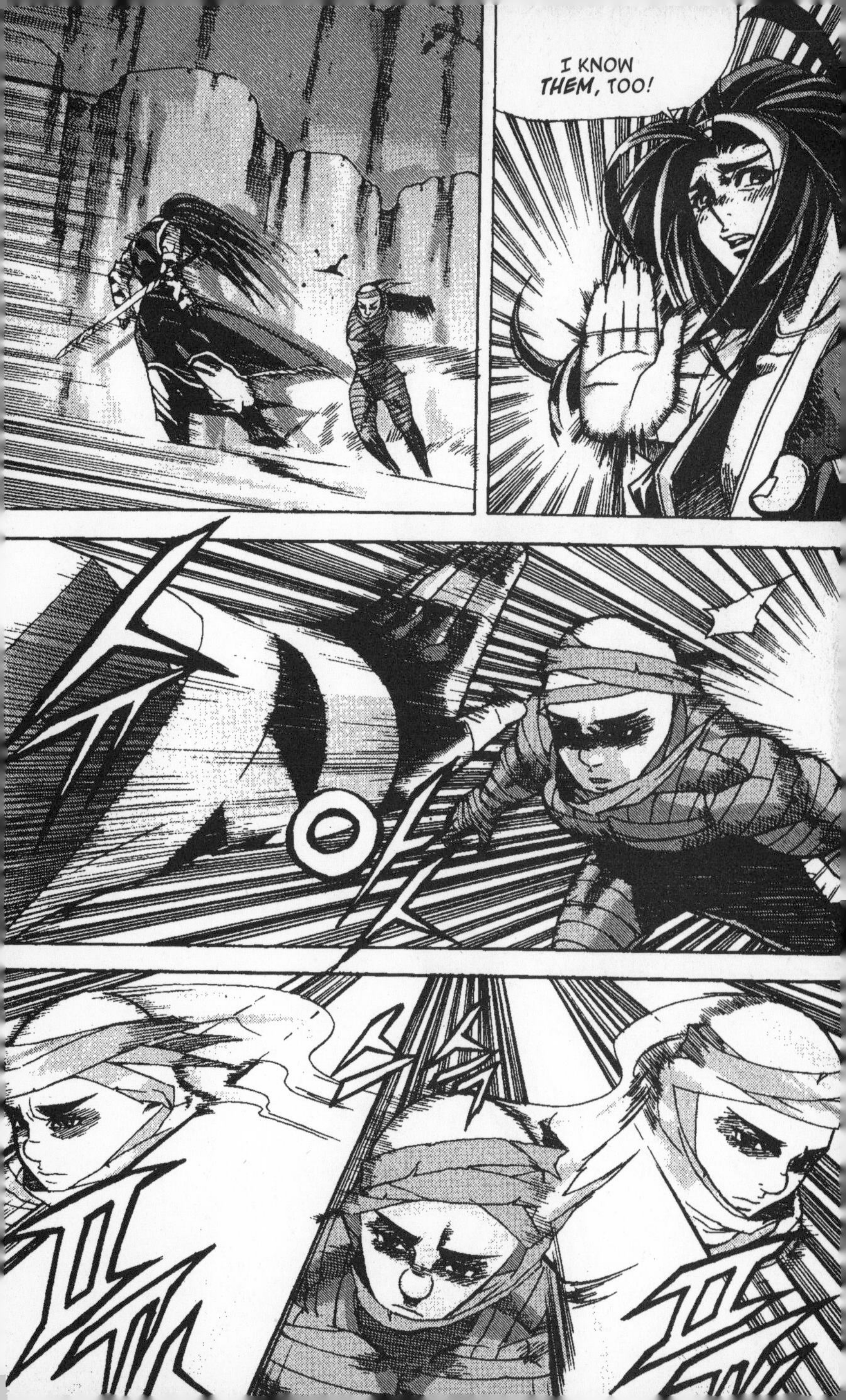
I KNOW THEM, TOO!

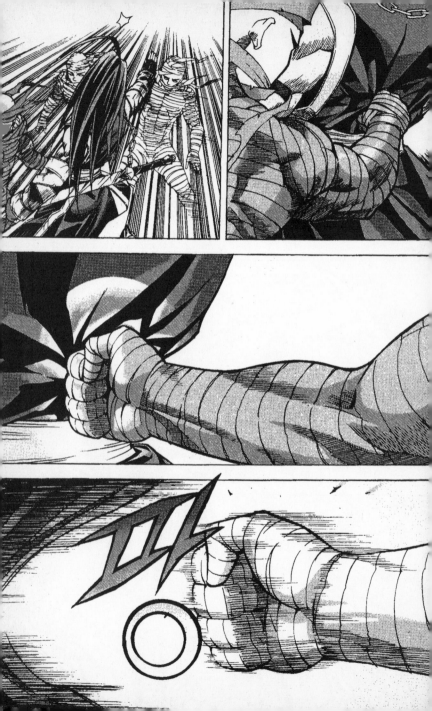

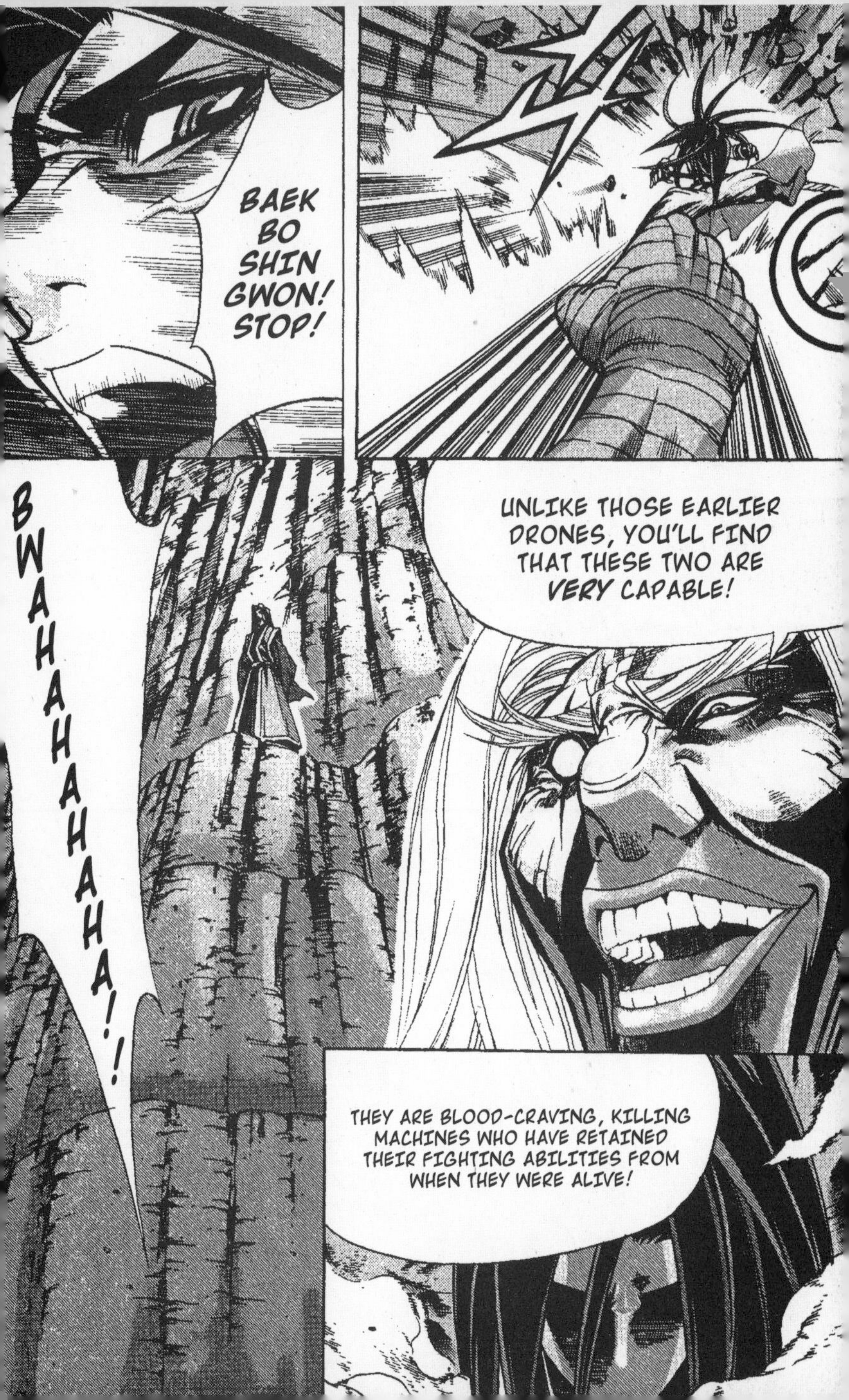
BAEK BO SHIN GWON! STOP!
BWAHAHAHAHAHA!!!
UNLIKE THOSE EARLIER DRONES, YOU'LL FIND THAT THESE TWO ARE VERY CAPABLE!
THEY ARE BLOOD-CRAVING, KILLING MACHINES WHO HAVE RETAINED THEIR FIGHTING ABILITIES FROM WHEN THEY WERE ALIVE!

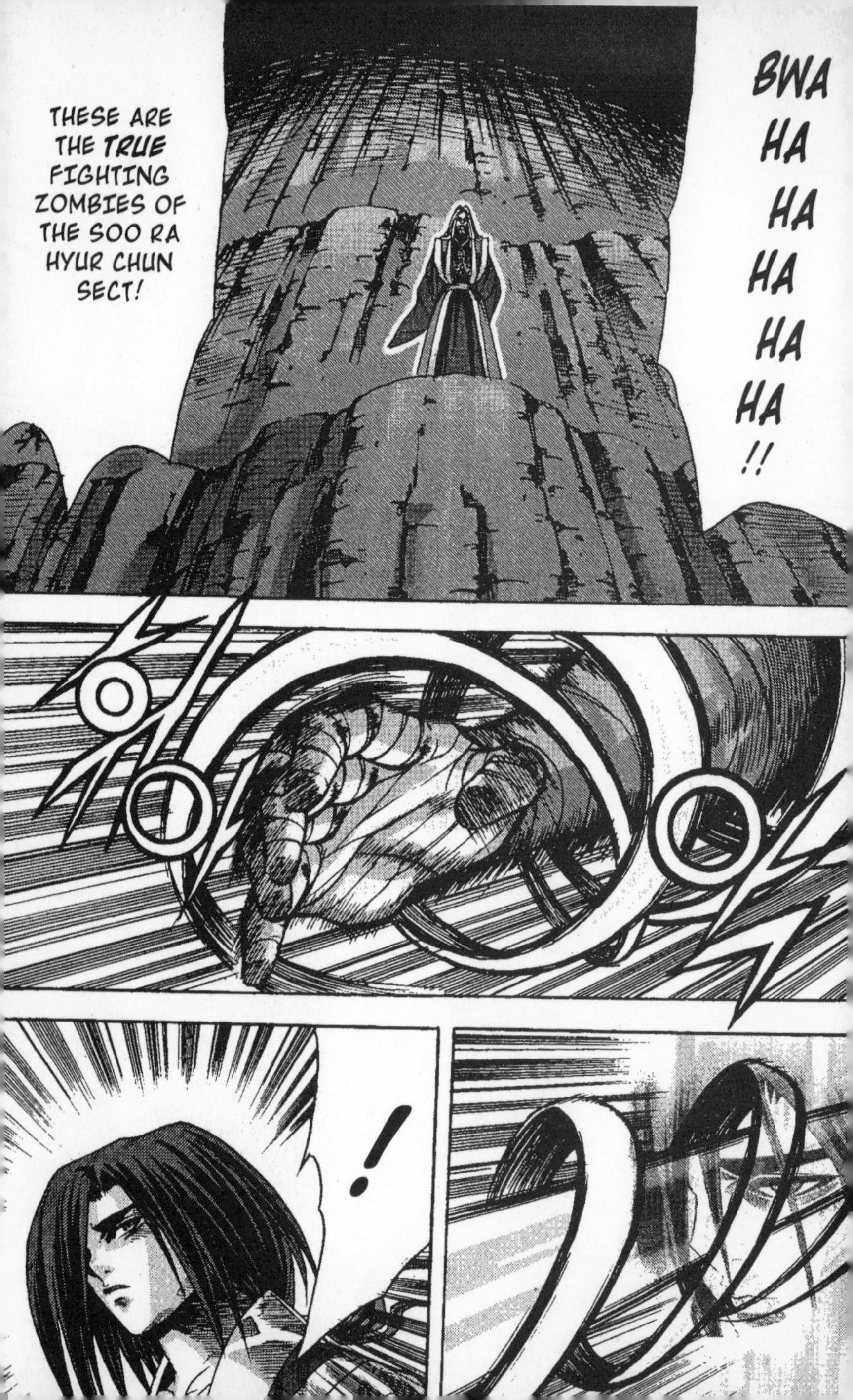
THESE ARE THE TRUE FIGHTING ZOMBIES OF THE SOO RA HYUR CHUN SECT!
BWA HA HA HA HA HA!!
!

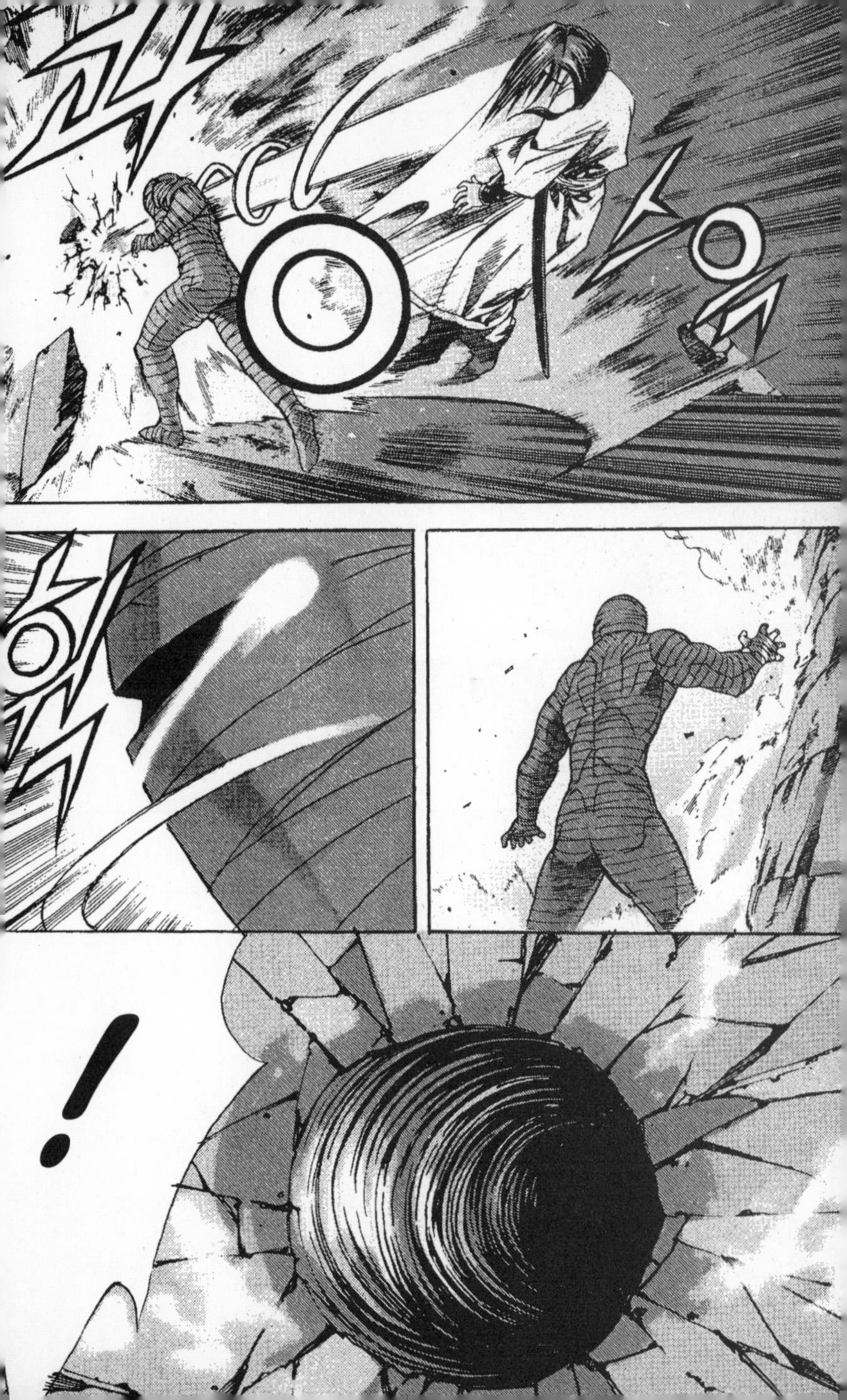
!

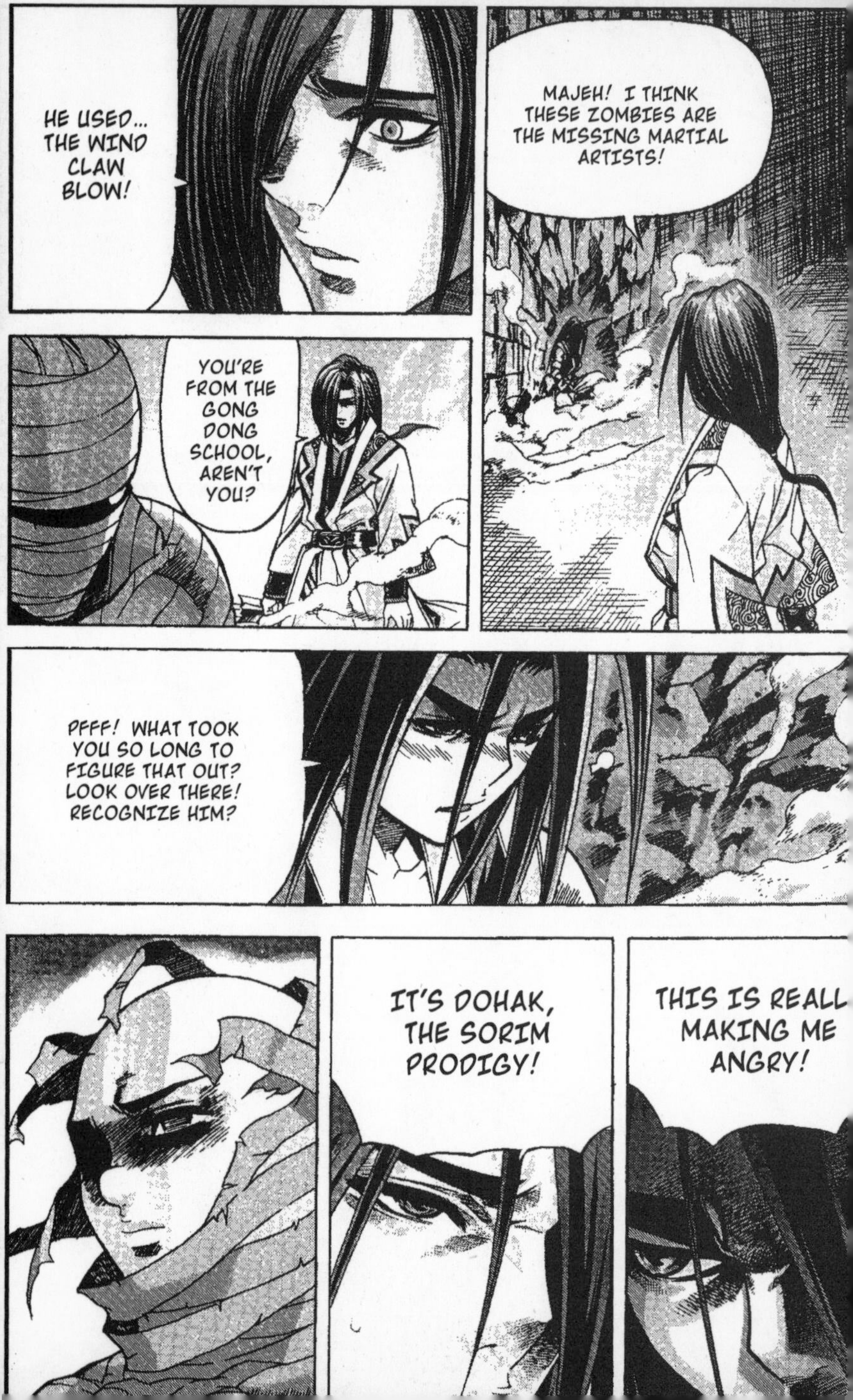
HE USED... THE WIND CLAW BLOW!
MAJEH! I THINK THESE ZOMBIES ARE THE MISSING MARTIAL ARTISTS!
YOU'RE FROM THE GONG DONG SCHOOL, AREN'T YOU?
PFFF! WHAT TOOK YOU SO LONG TO FIGURE THAT OUT? LOOK OVER THERE! RECOGNIZE HIM?
IT'S DOHAK, THE SORIM PRODIGY!
THIS IS REALL MAKING ME ANGRY!

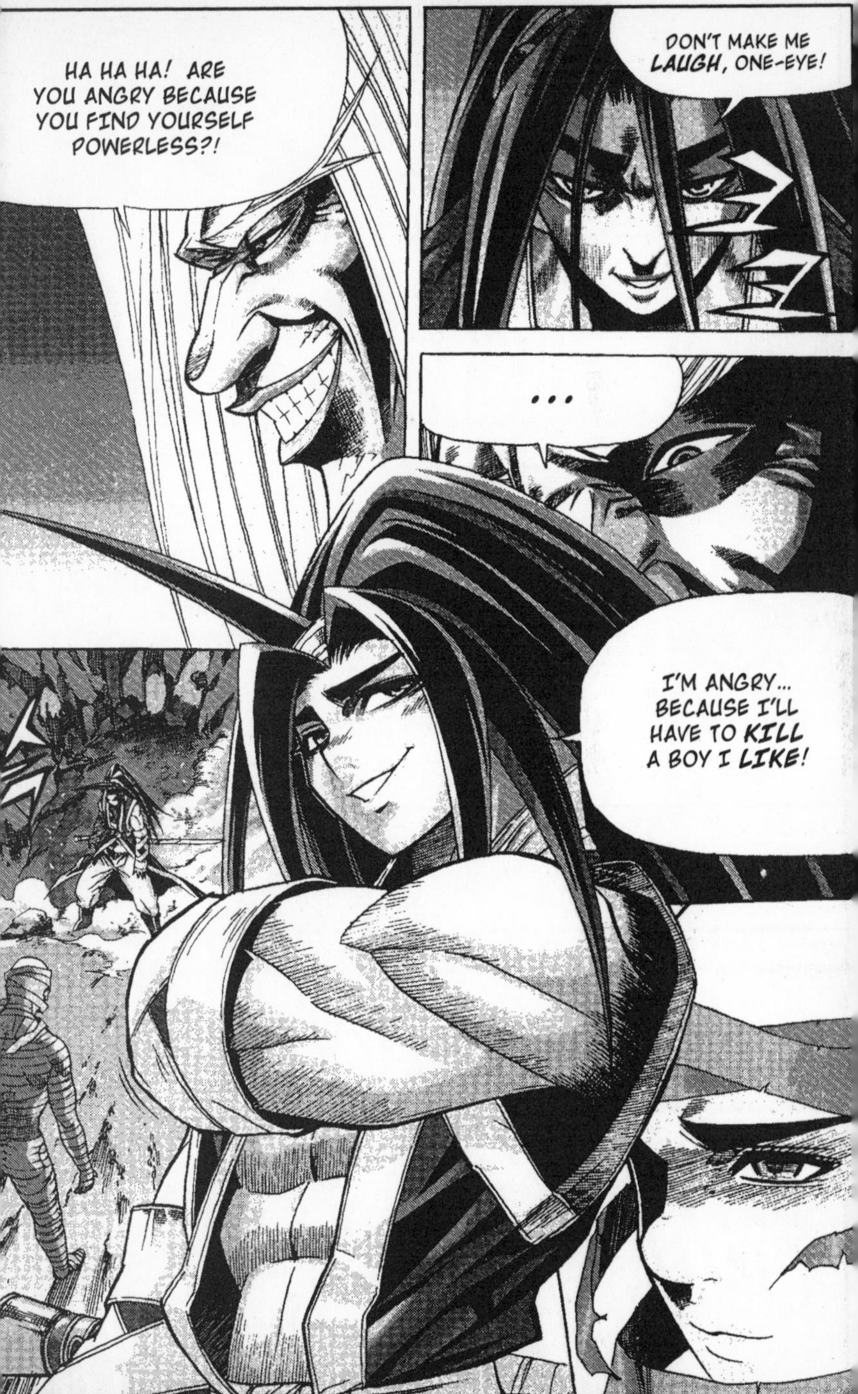
HA HA HA! ARE YOU ANGRY BECAUSE YOU FIND YOURSELF POWERLESS?!
DON'T MAKE ME LAUGH, ONE-EYE!
...
I'M ANGRY... BECAUSE I'LL HAVE TO KILL A BOY I LIKE!

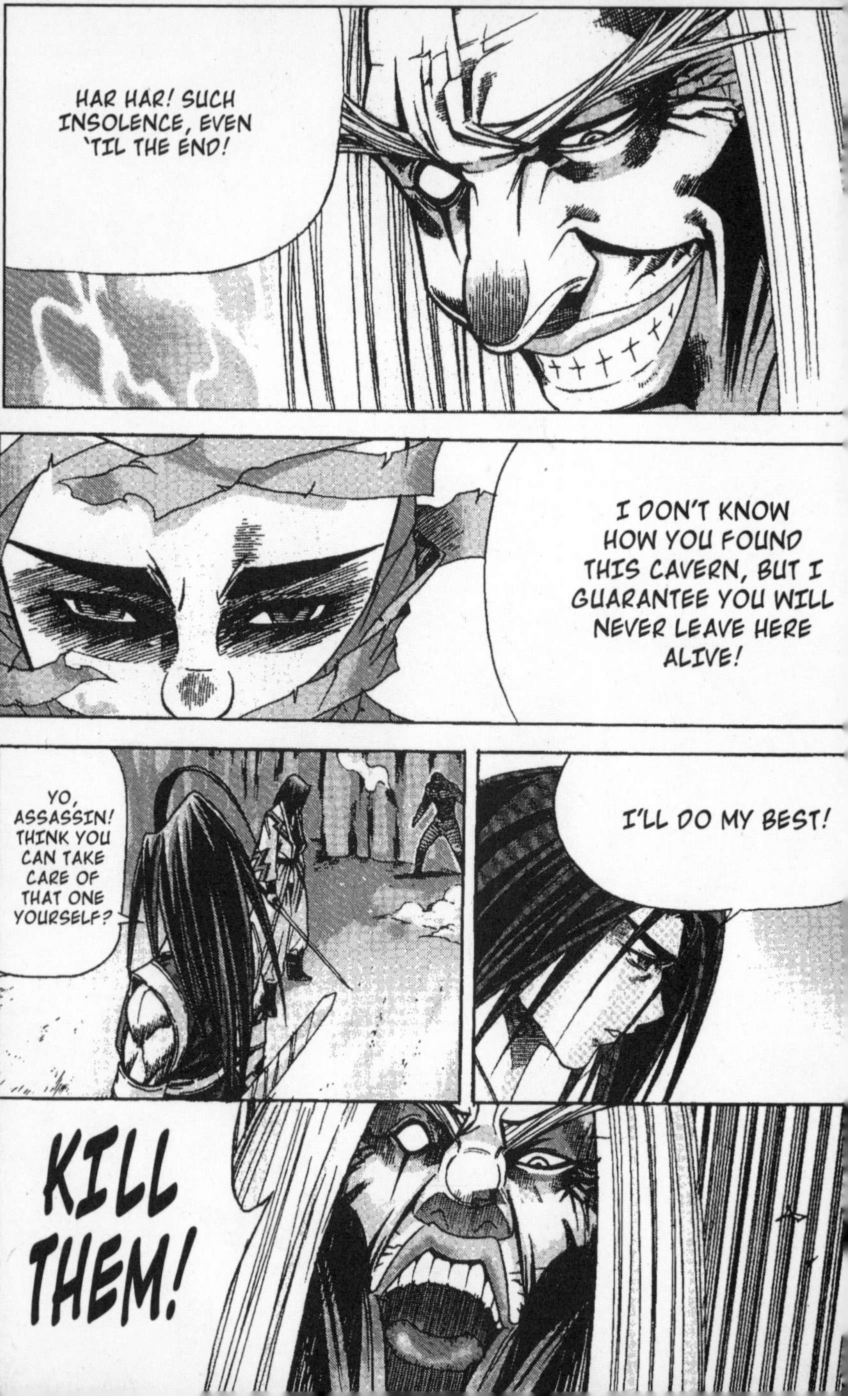
HAR HAR! SUCH INSOLENCE, EVEN 'TIL THE END!
I DON'T KNOW HOW YOU FOUND THIS CAVERN, BUT I GUARANTEE YOU WILL NEVER LEAVE HERE ALIVE!
YO, ASSASSIN! THINK YOU CAN TAKE CARE OF THAT ONE YOURSELF?
I'LL DO MY BEST!
KILL THEM!

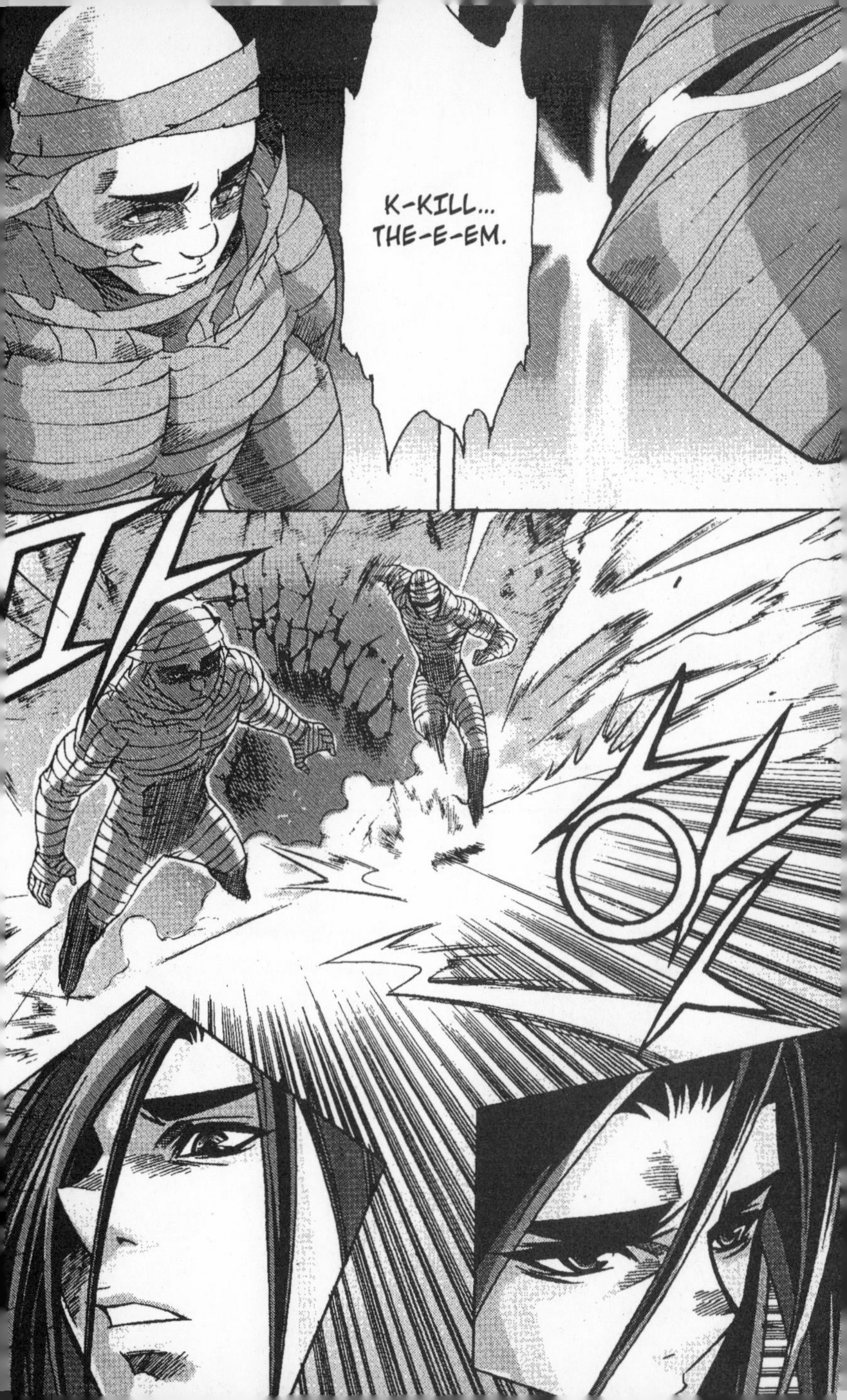
K-KILL...
THE-E-EM.

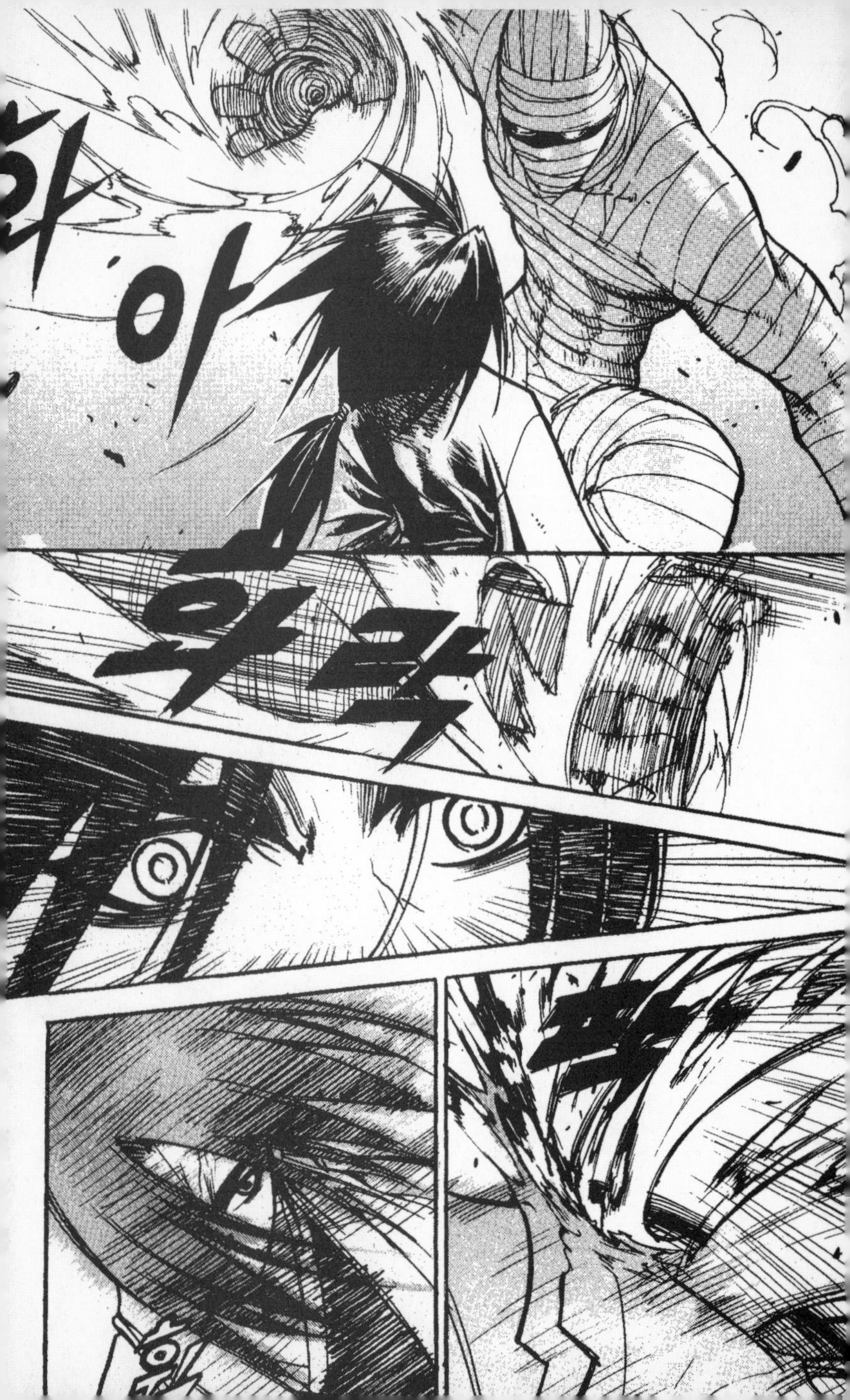
아

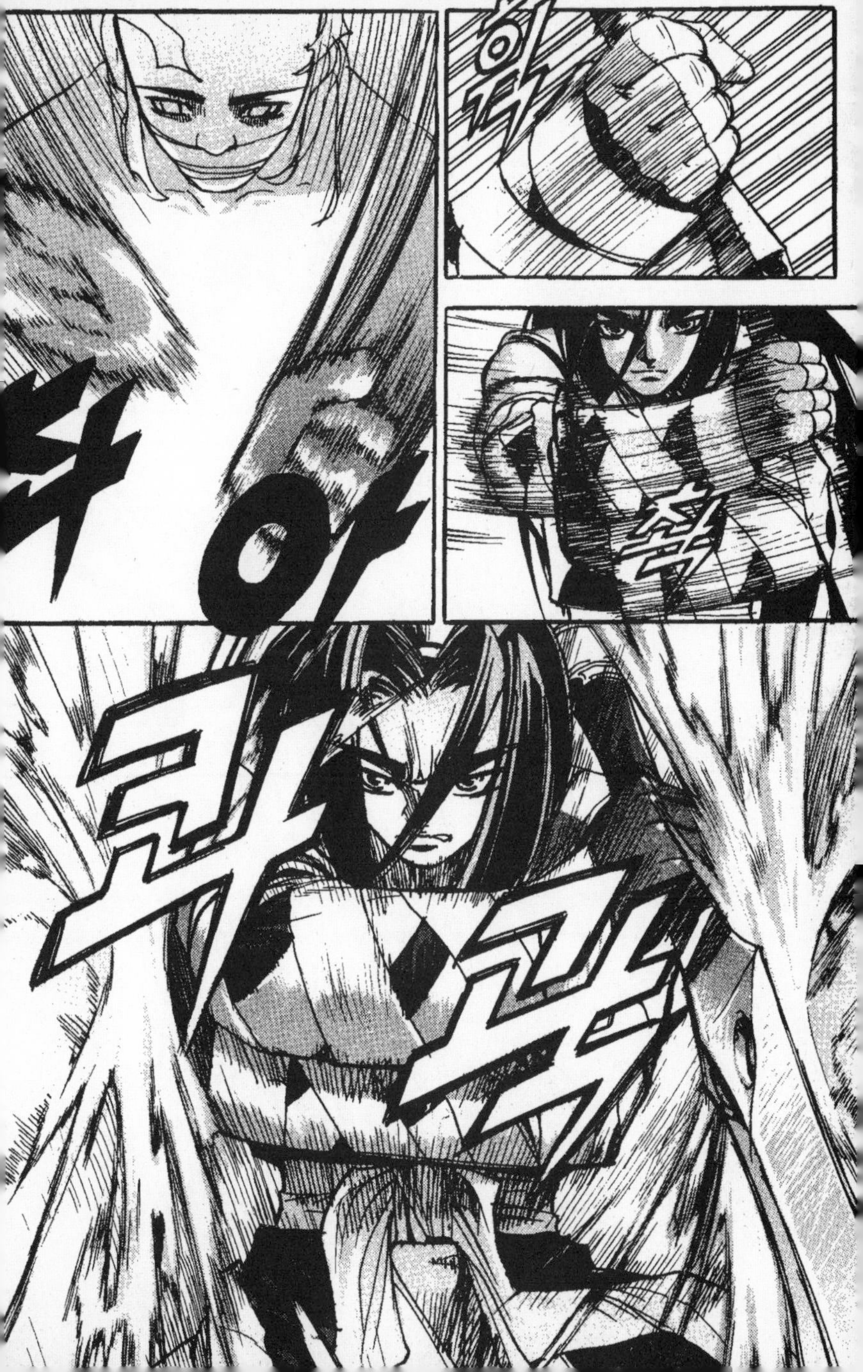

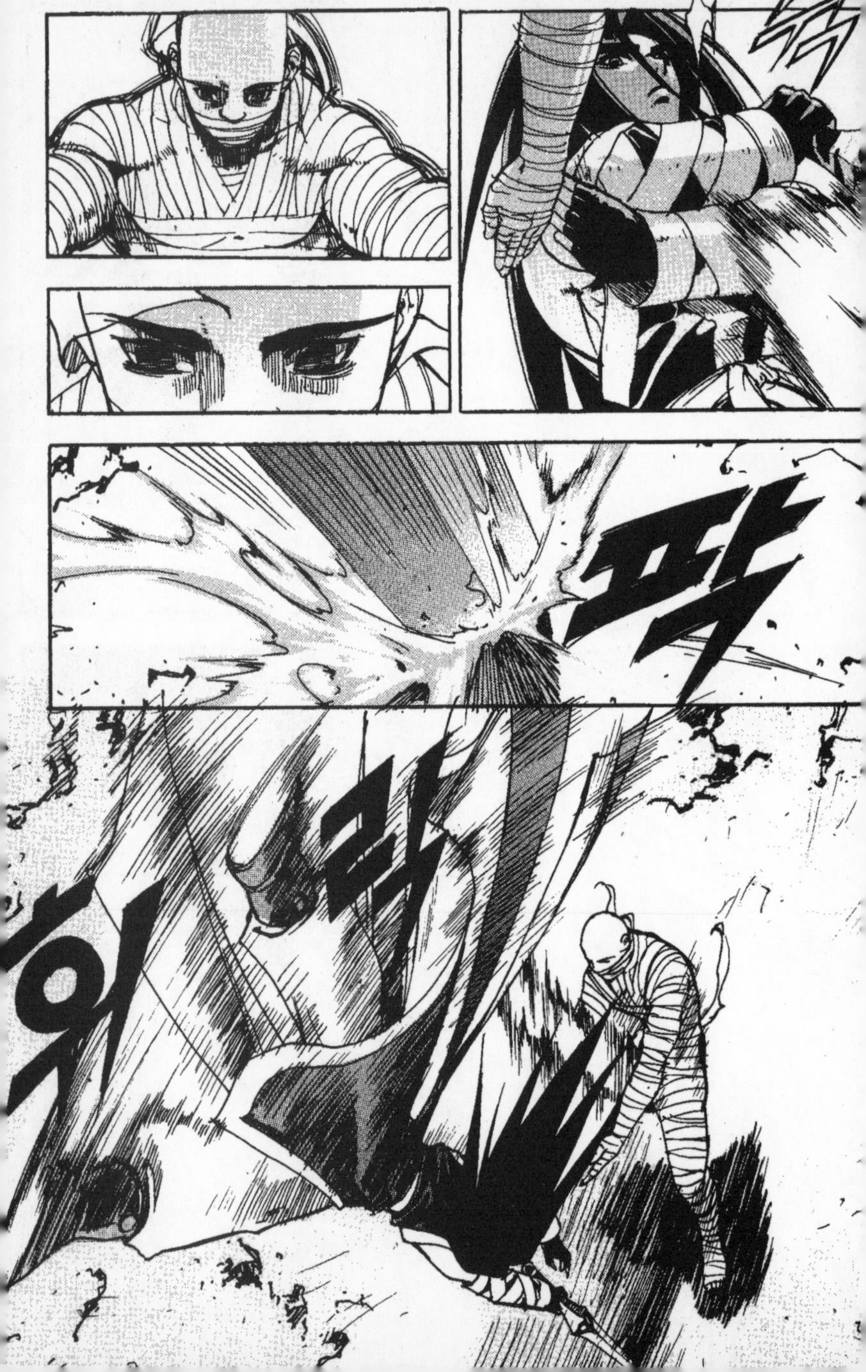
팍

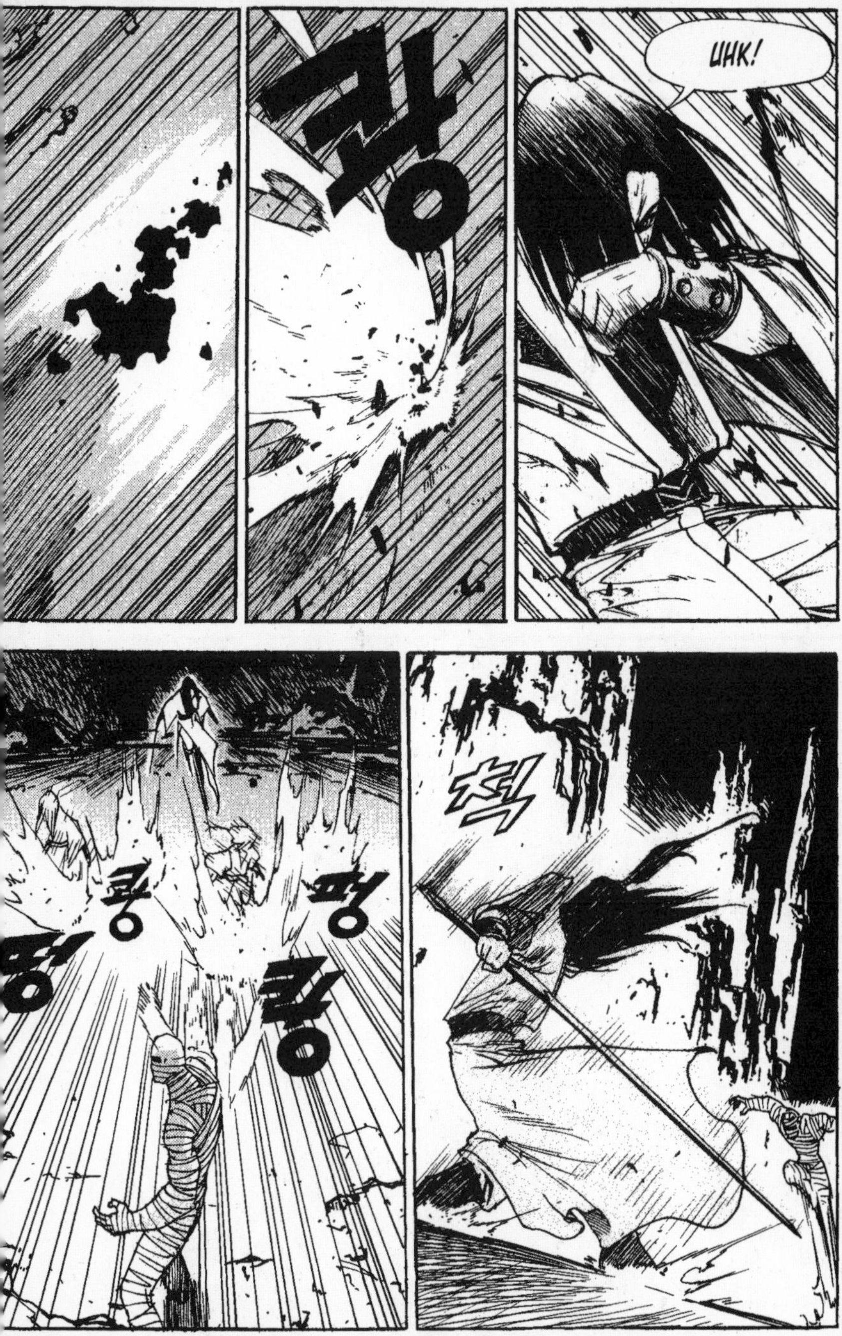
쾅
UHK!

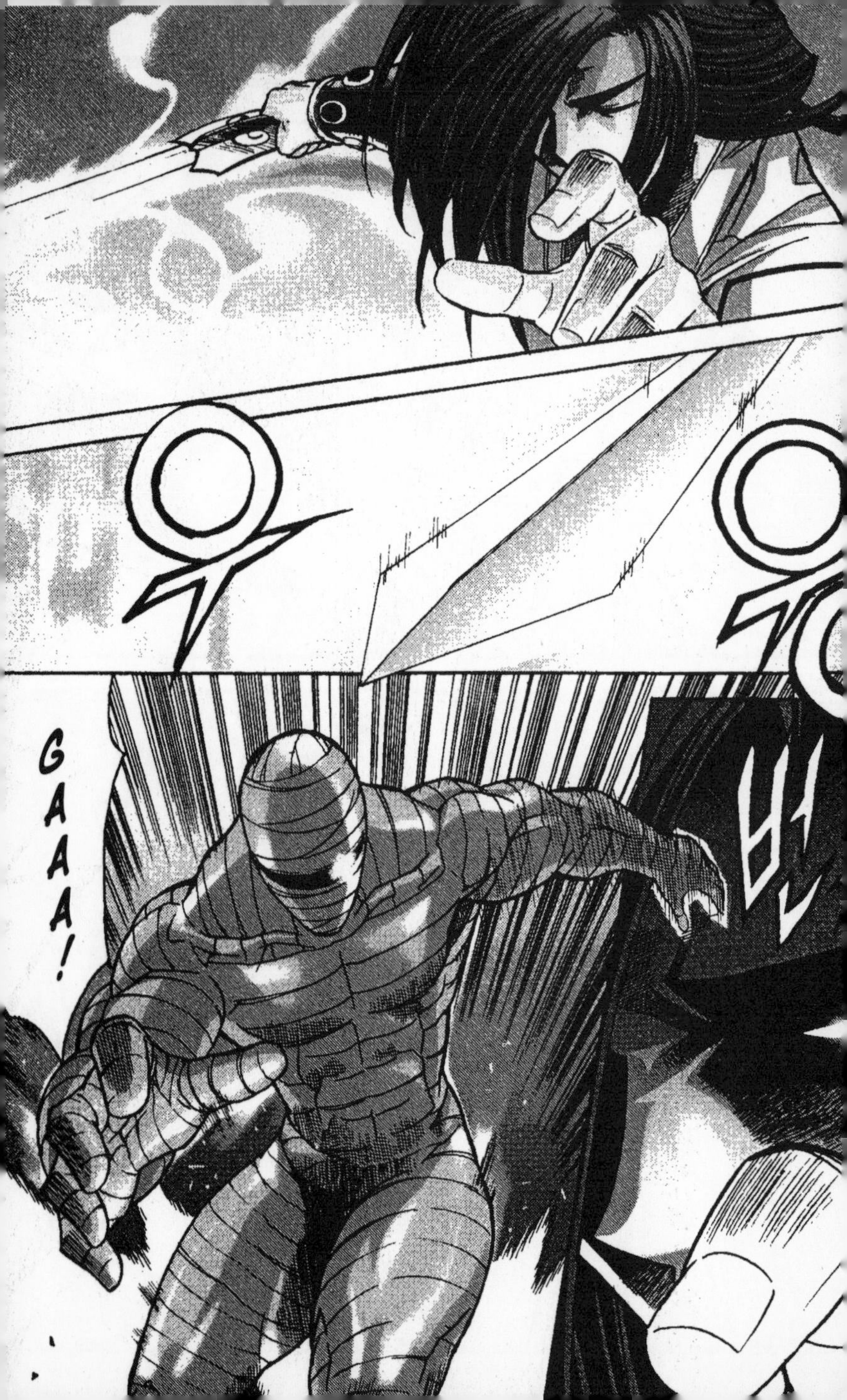
GAAAA!

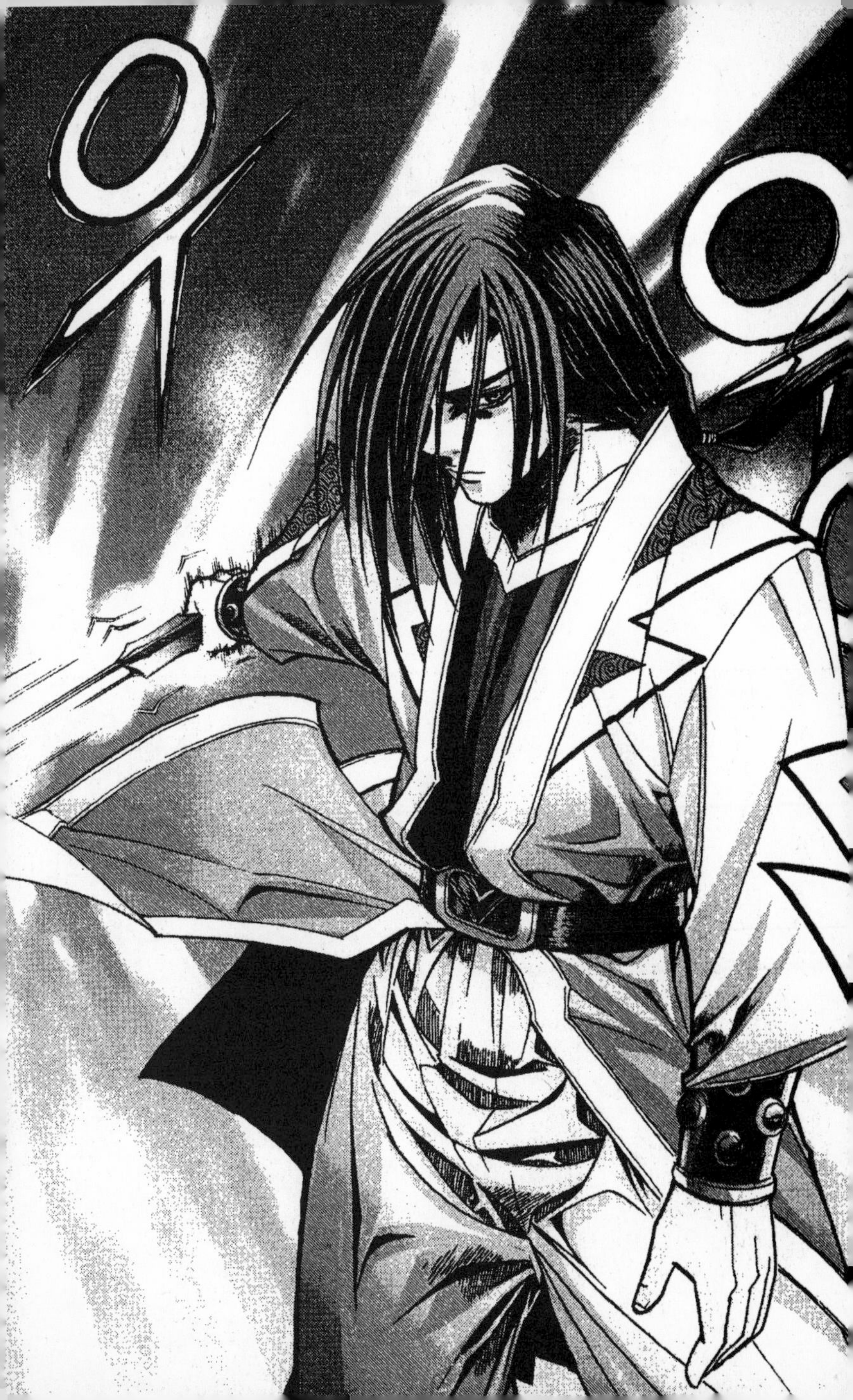

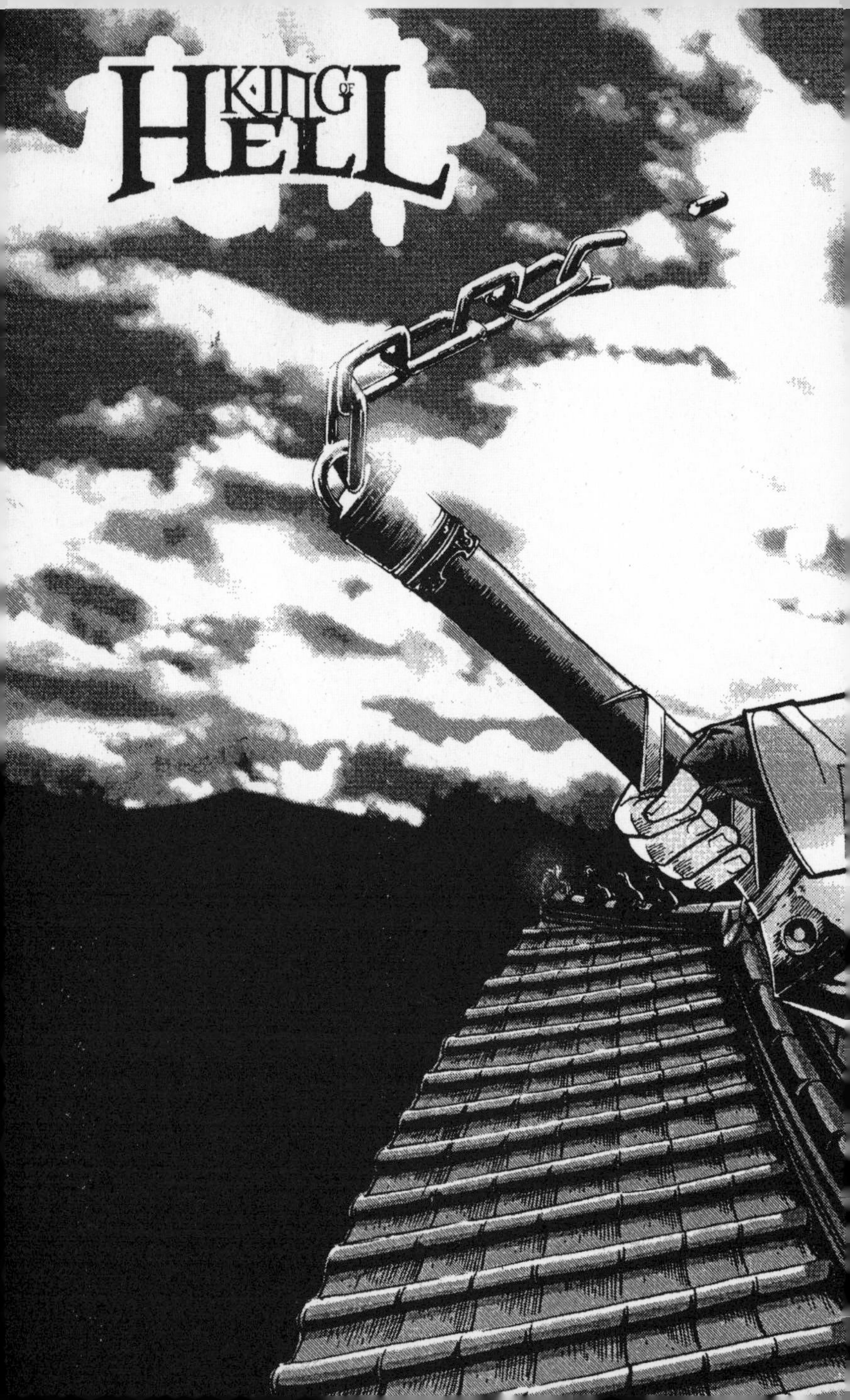
KING OF HELL

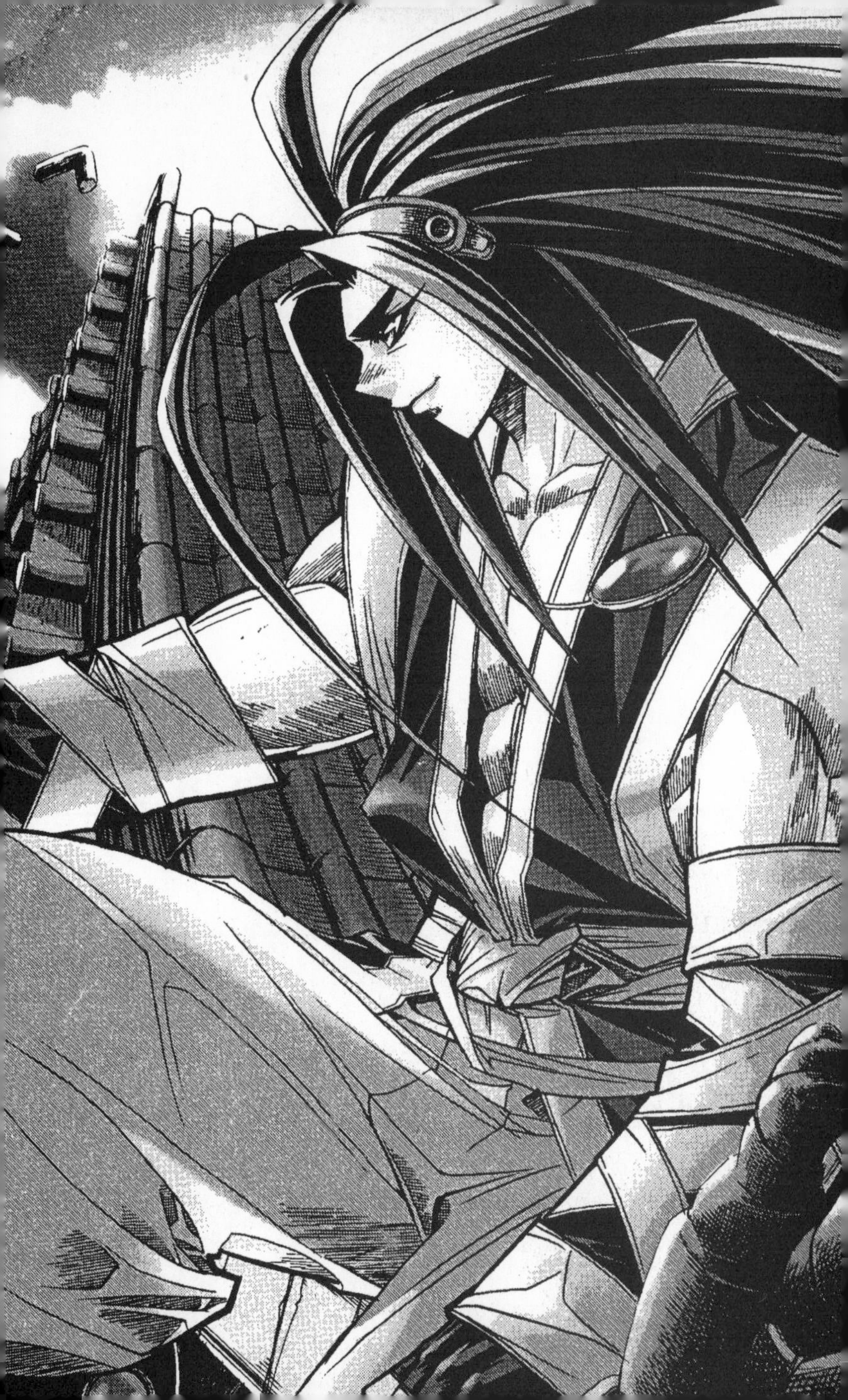

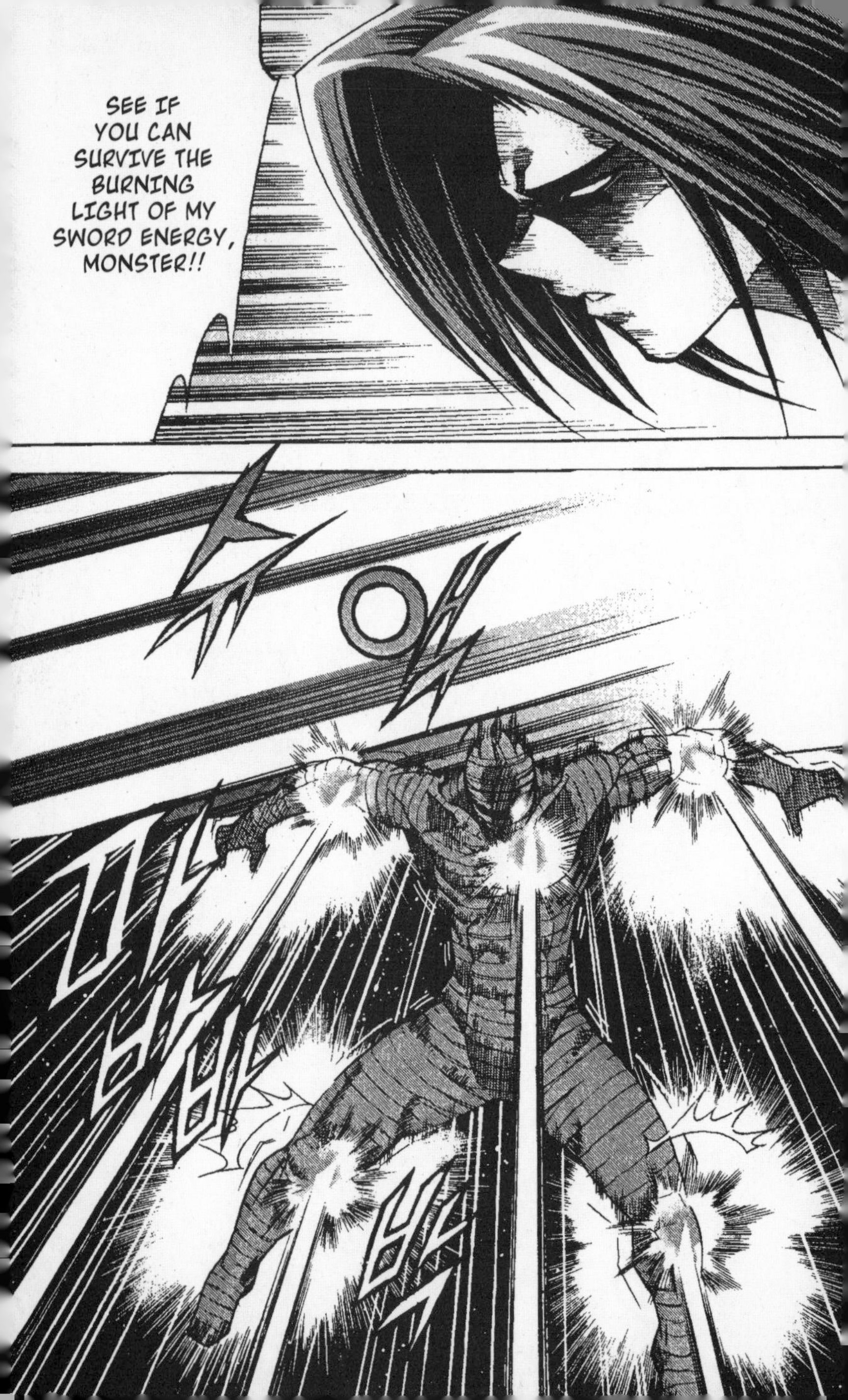
SEE IF YOU CAN SURVIVE THE BURNING LIGHT OF MY SWORD ENERGY, MONSTER!!

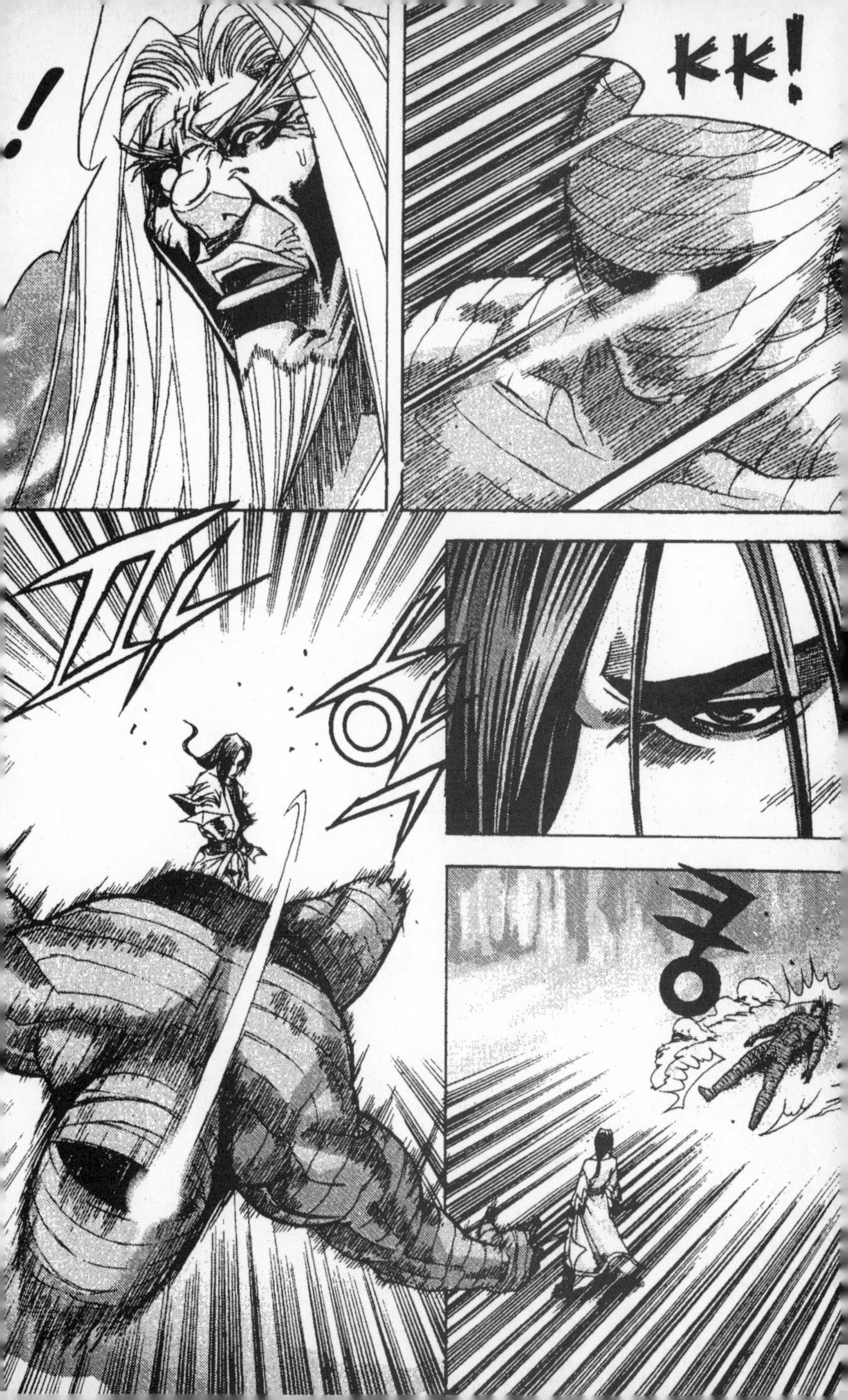
!
KK!

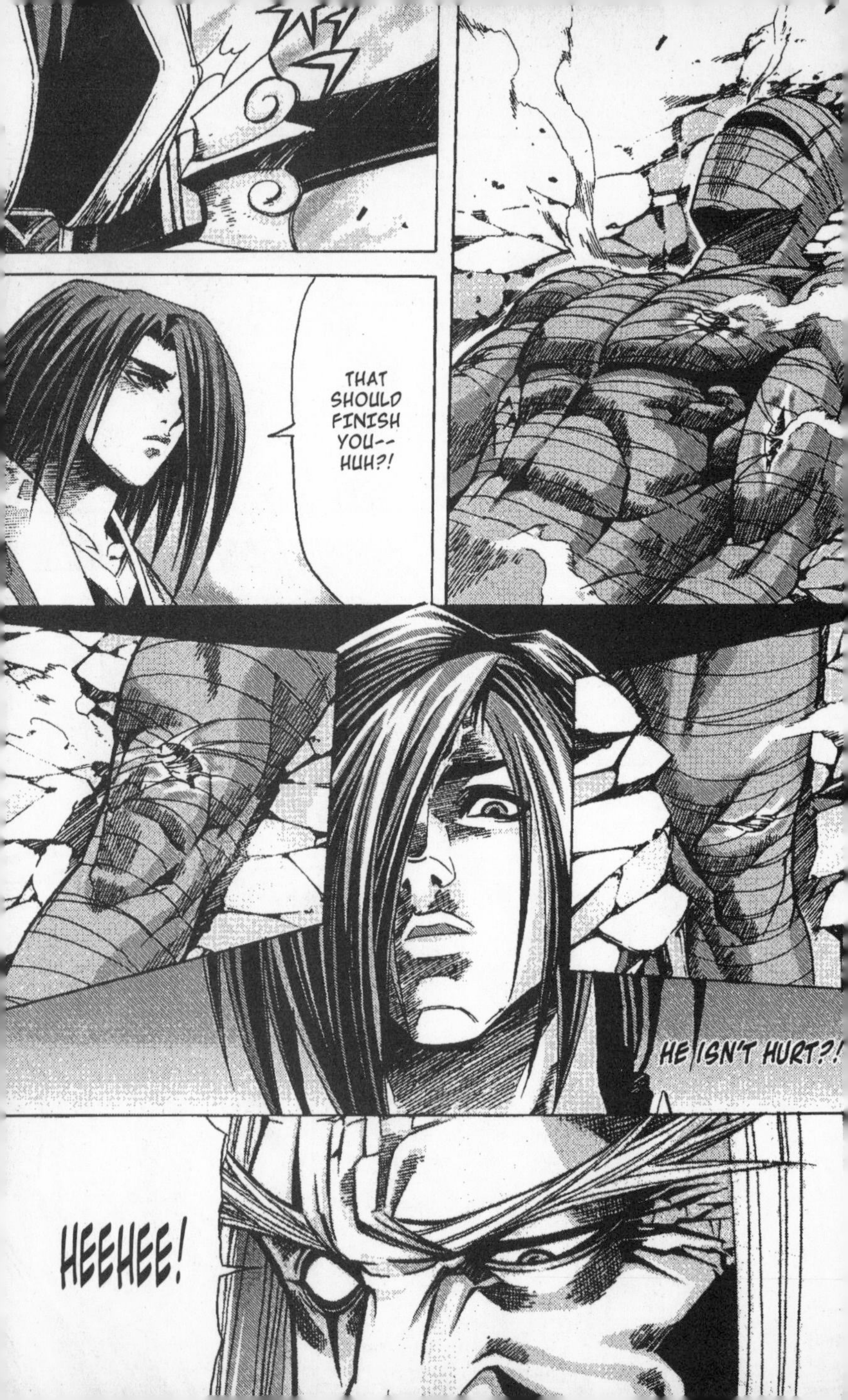
THAT SHOULD FINISH YOU-- HUH?!
HE ISN'T HURT?!
HEEHEE!

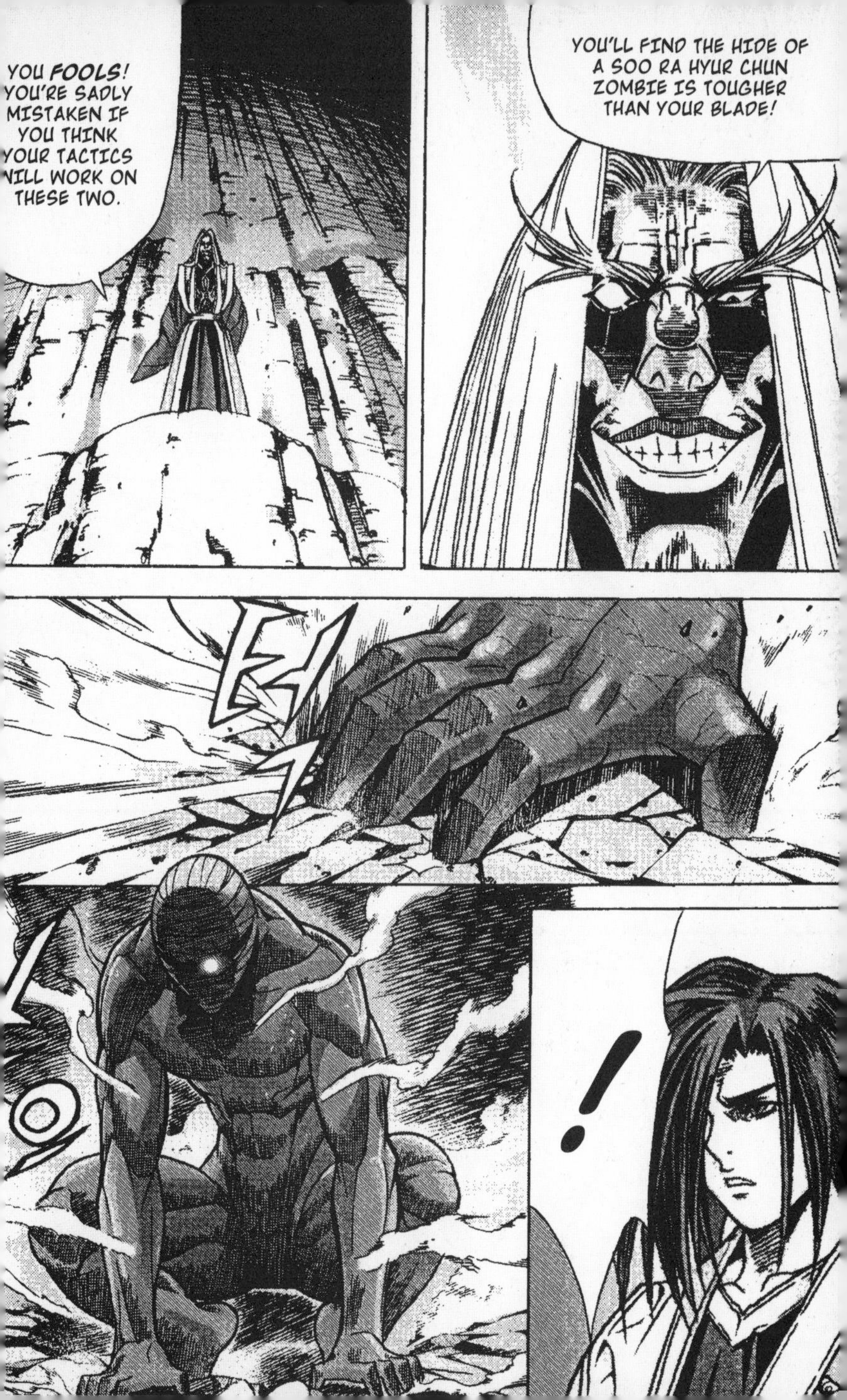
YOU **FOOLS**! YOU'RE SADLY MISTAKEN IF YOU THINK YOUR TACTICS WILL WORK ON THESE TWO.
YOU'LL FIND THE HIDE OF A SOO RA HYUR CHUN ZOMBIE IS TOUGHER THAN YOUR BLADE!
!

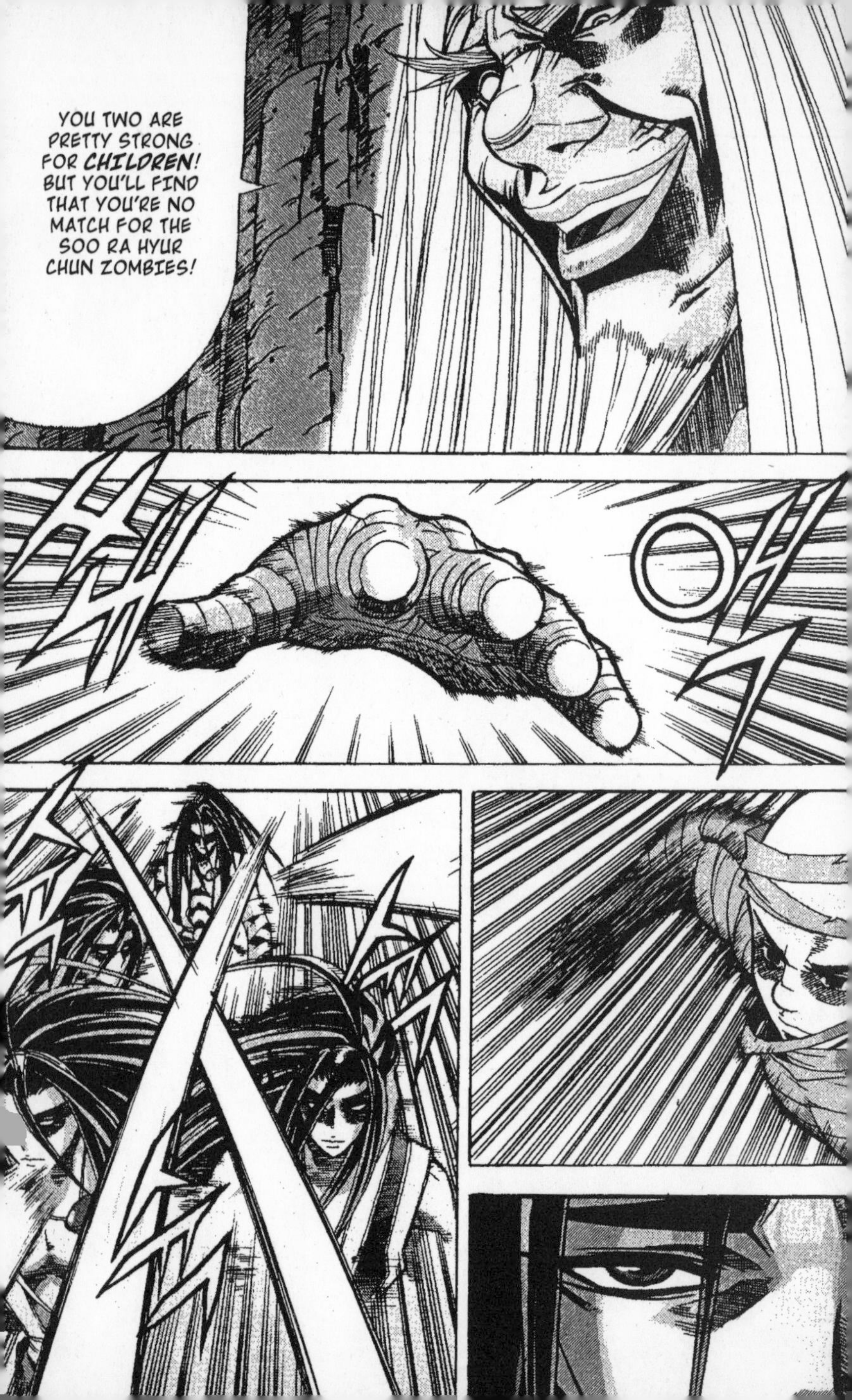
YOU TWO ARE PRETTY STRONG FOR **CHILDREN**! BUT YOU'LL FIND THAT YOU'RE NO MATCH FOR THE SOO RA HYUR CHUN ZOMBIES!
HHH
OHA

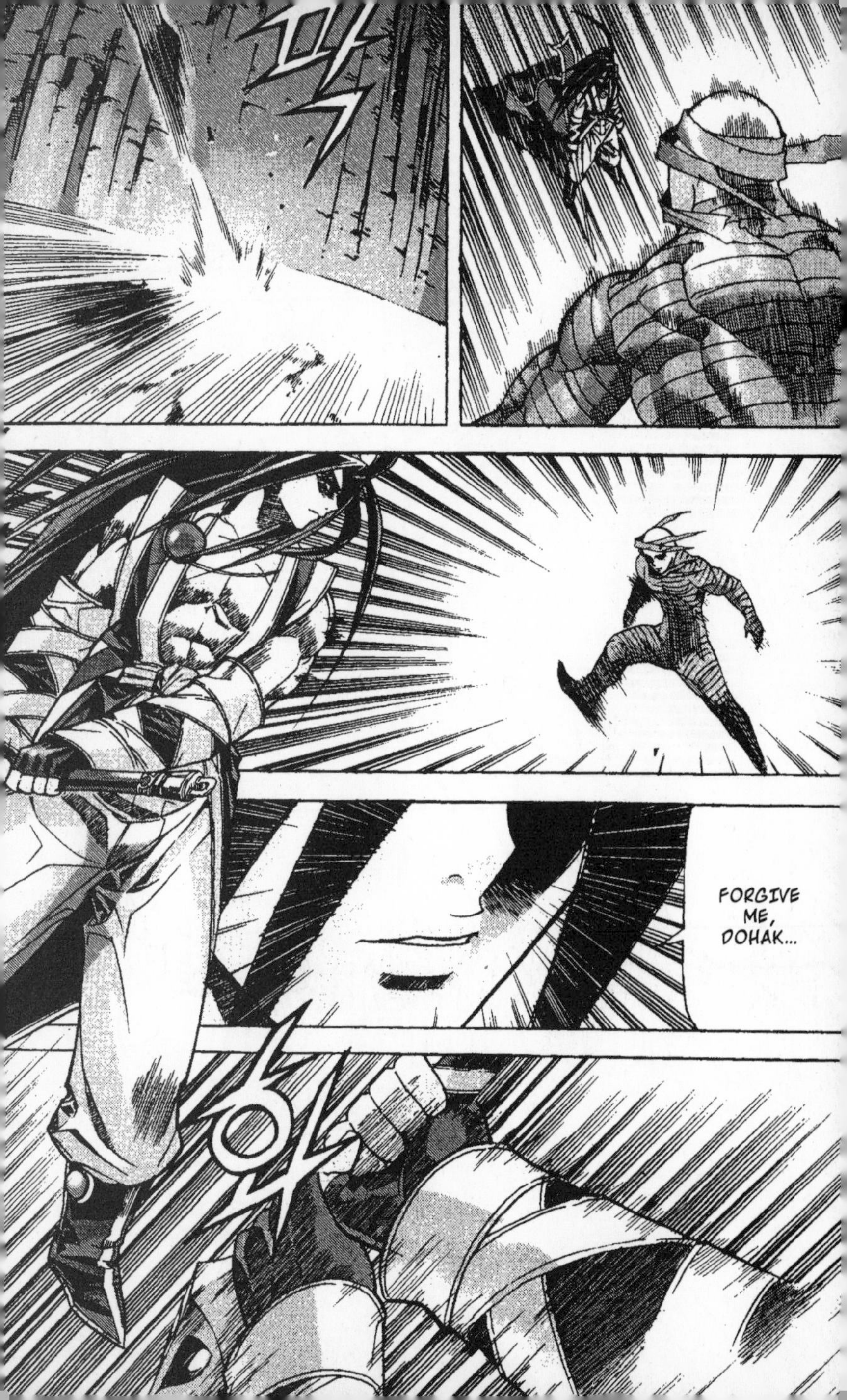
FORGIVE ME, DOHAK...

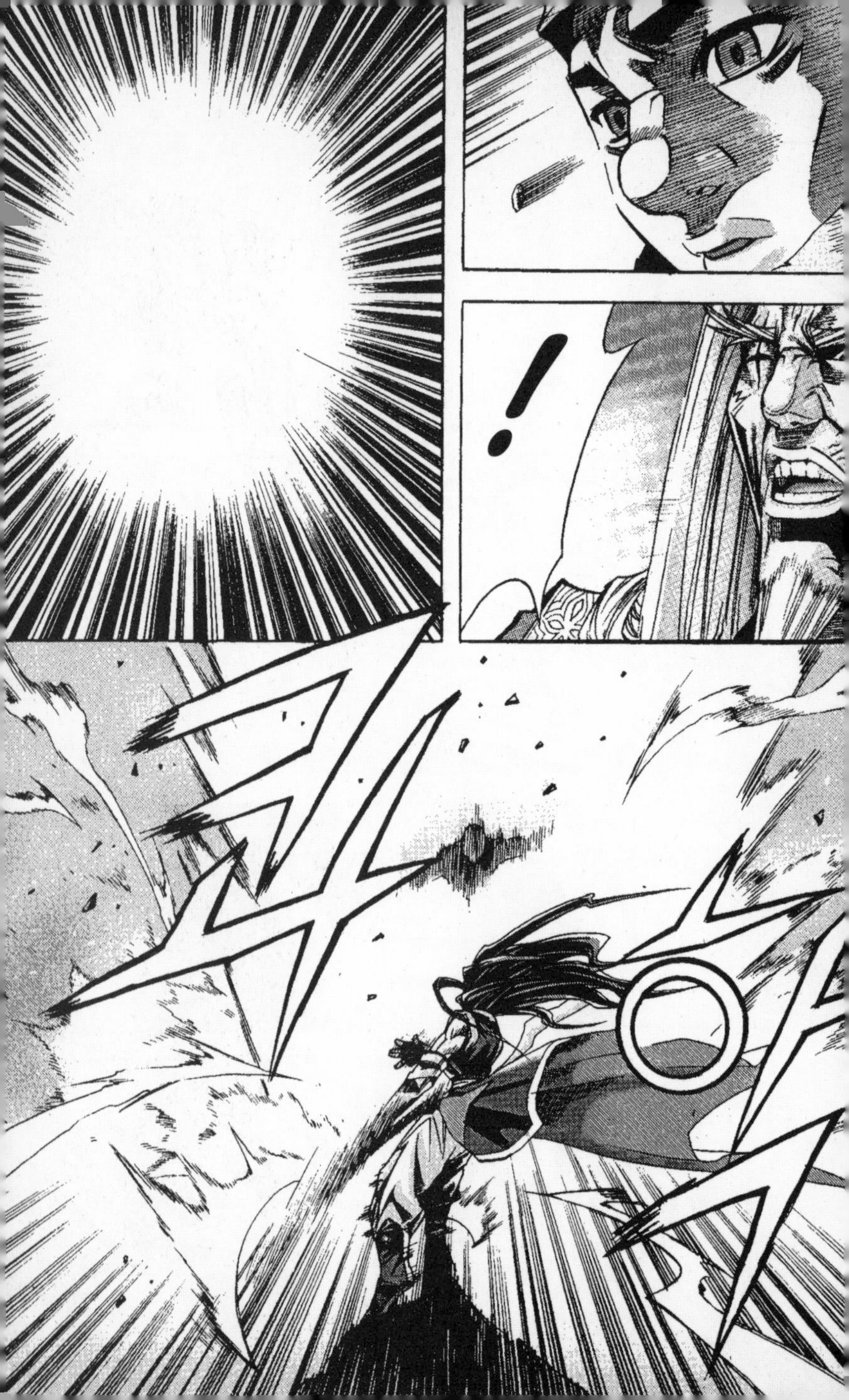
!

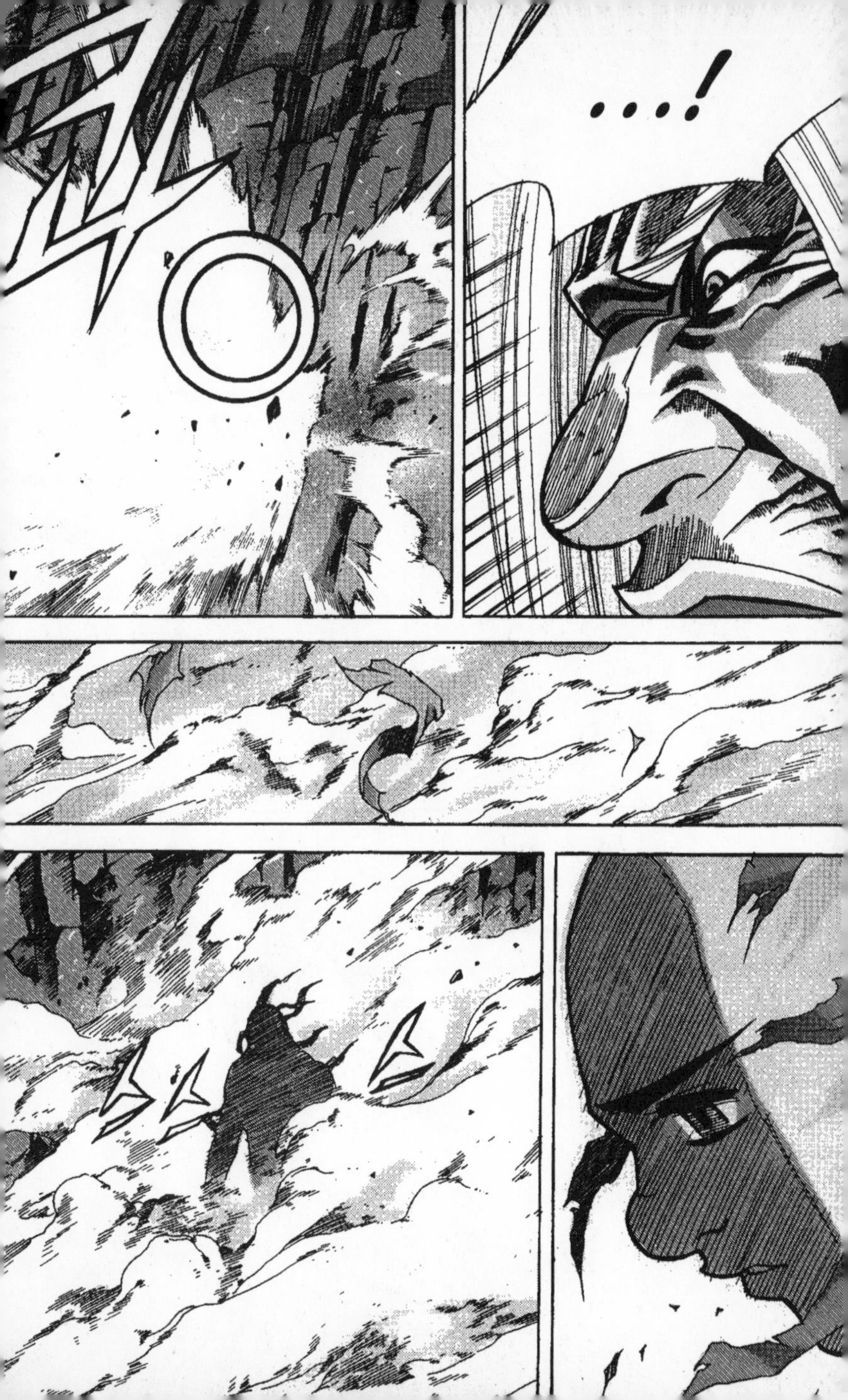
...!

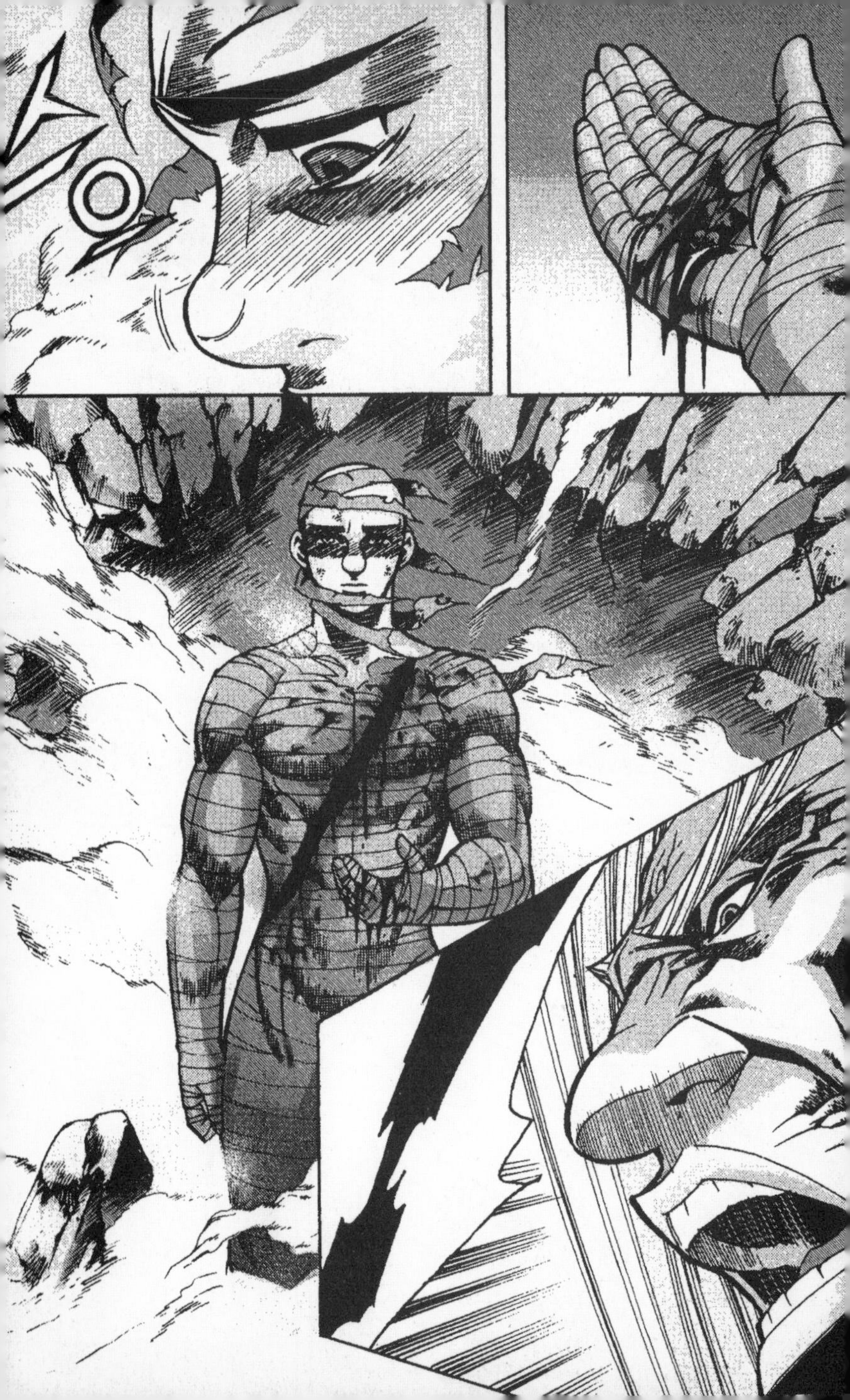

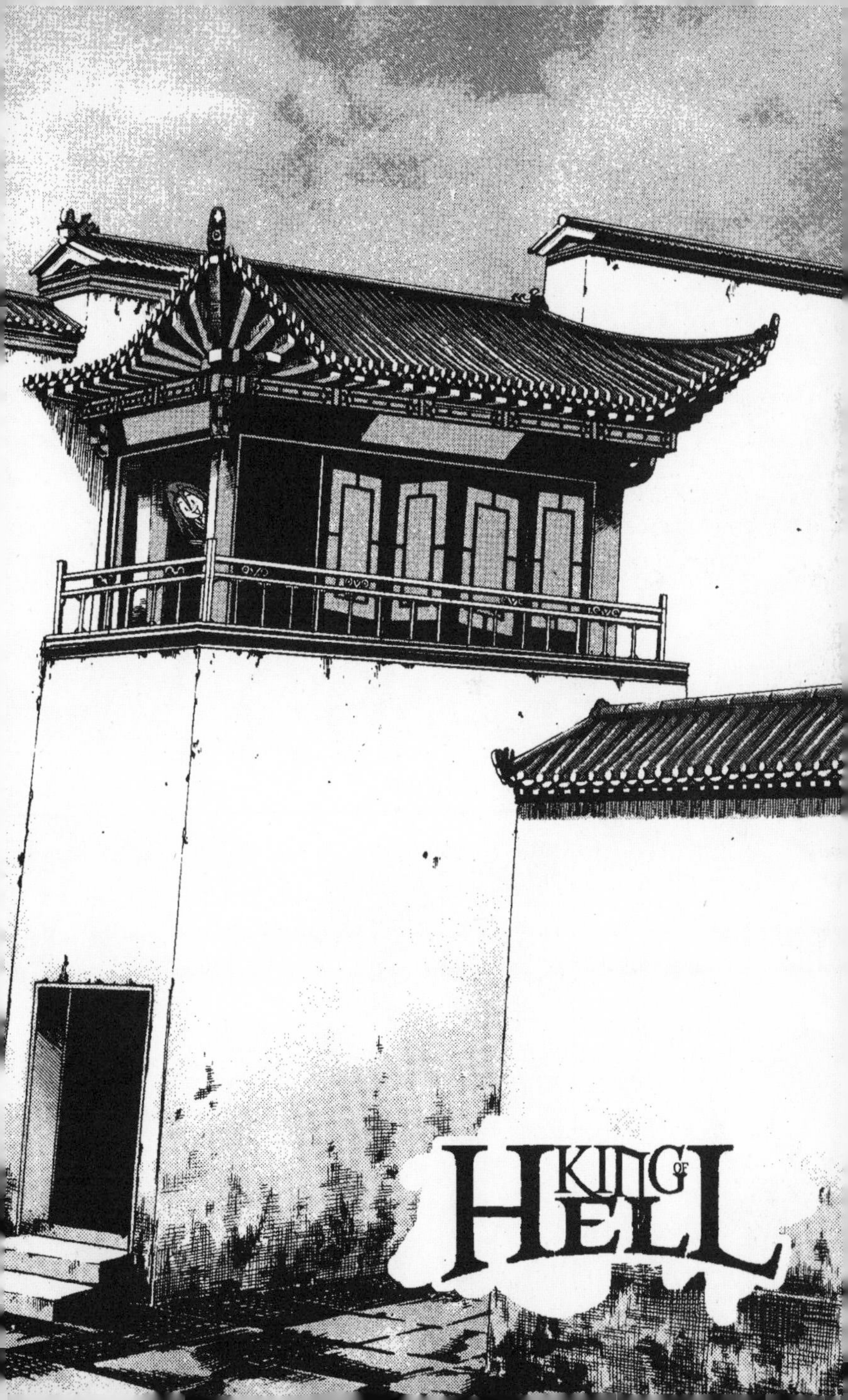
KING OF HELL

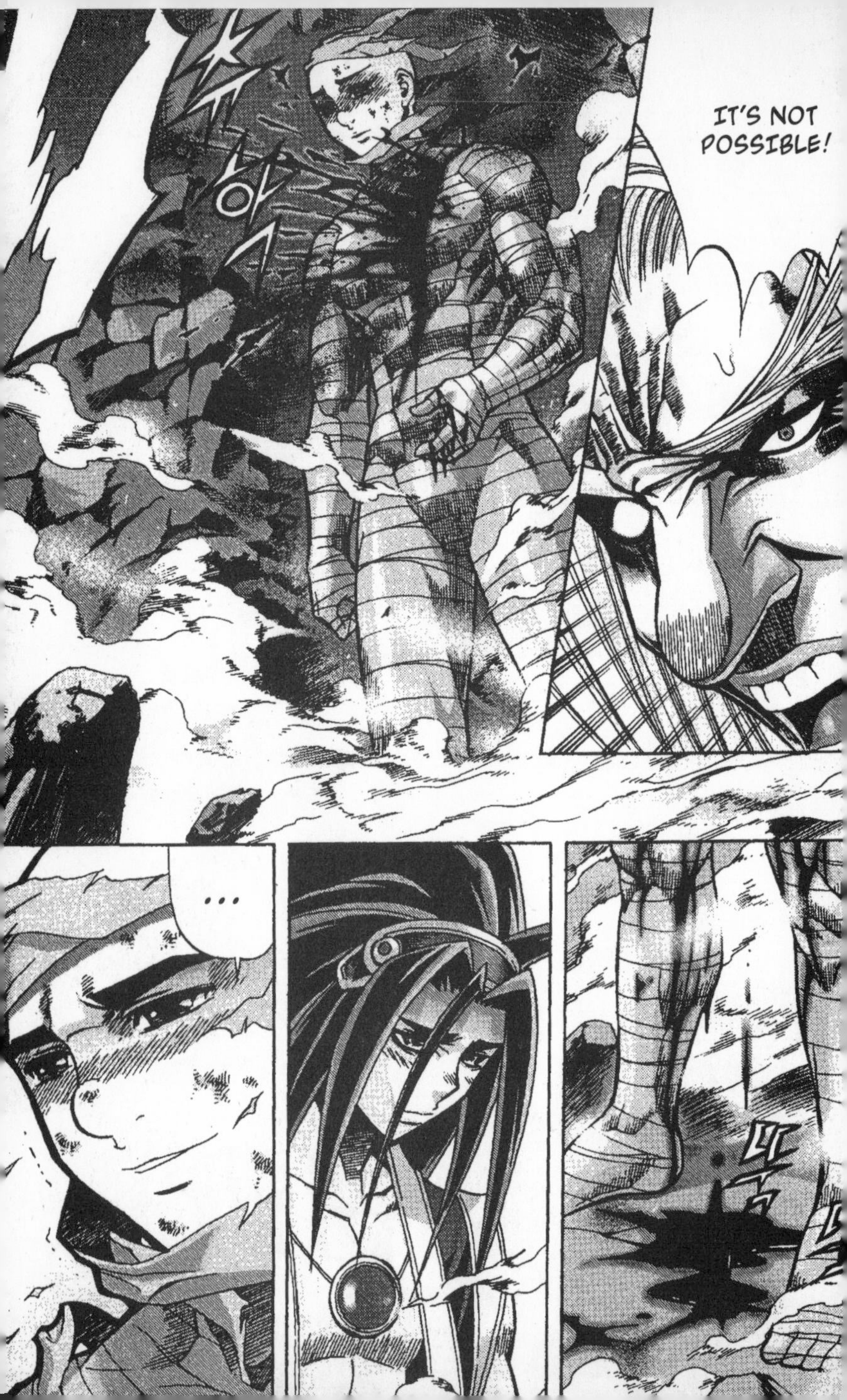
IT'S NOT POSSIBLE!
...

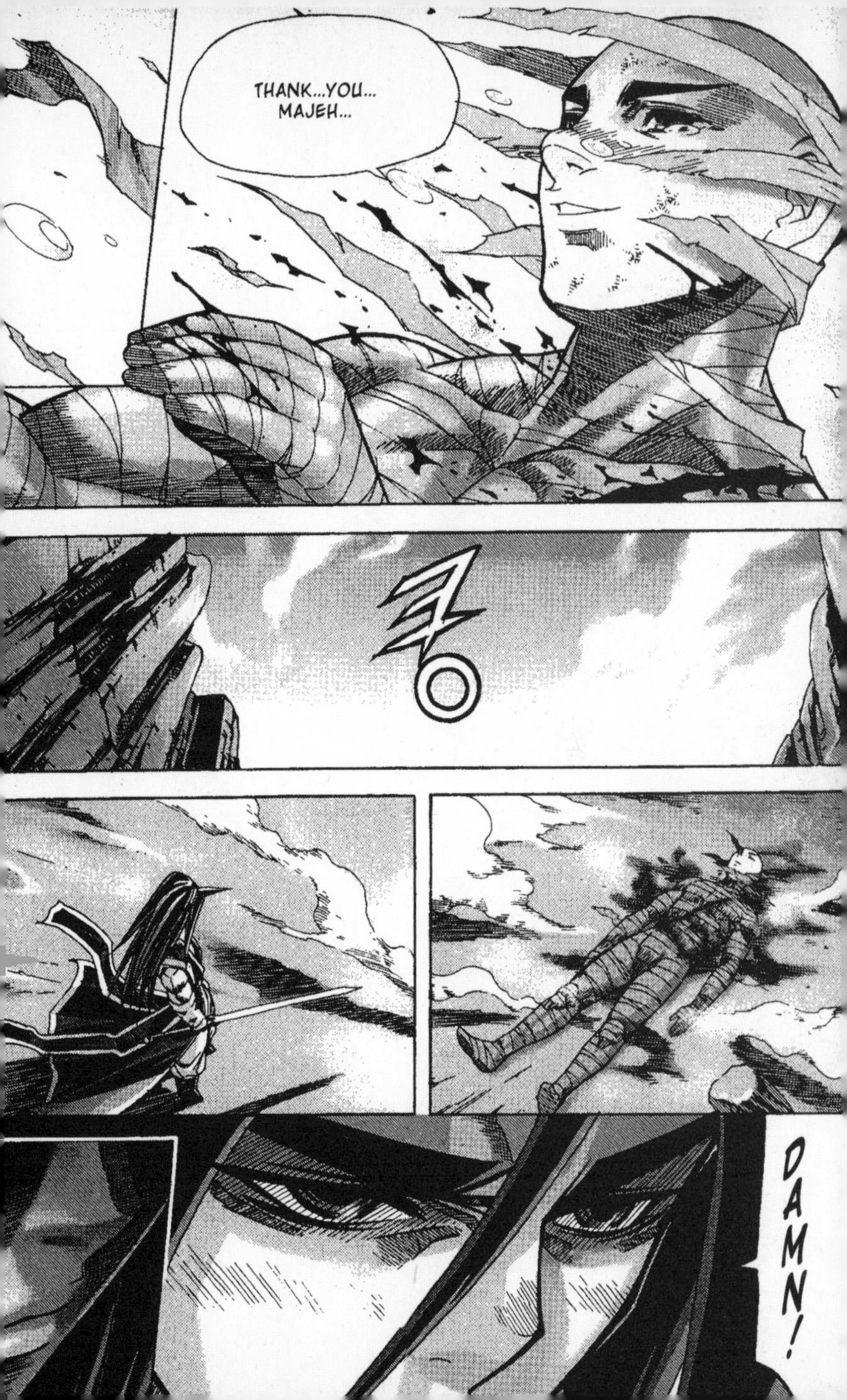
THANK...YOU...
MAJEH...
DAMN!

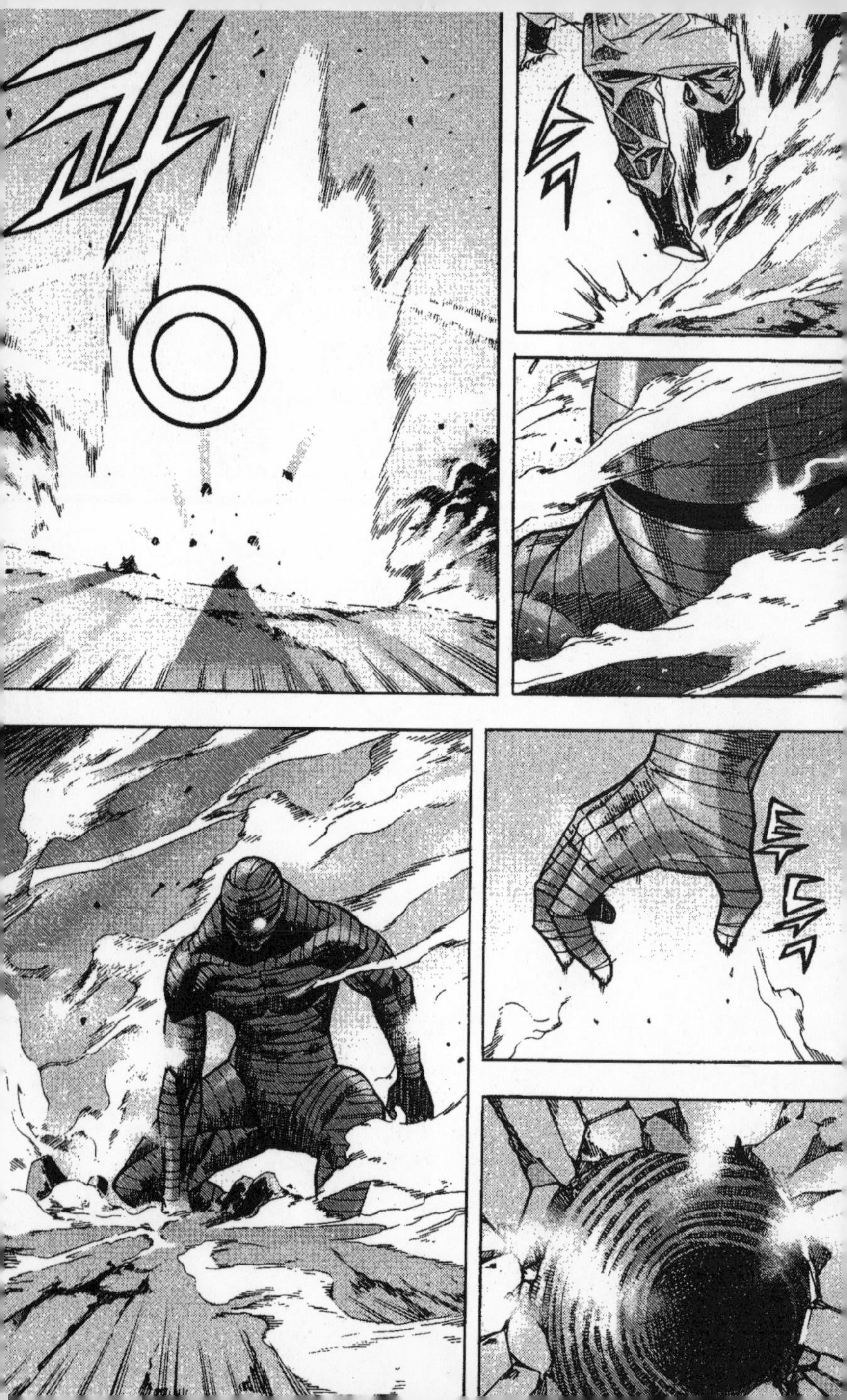

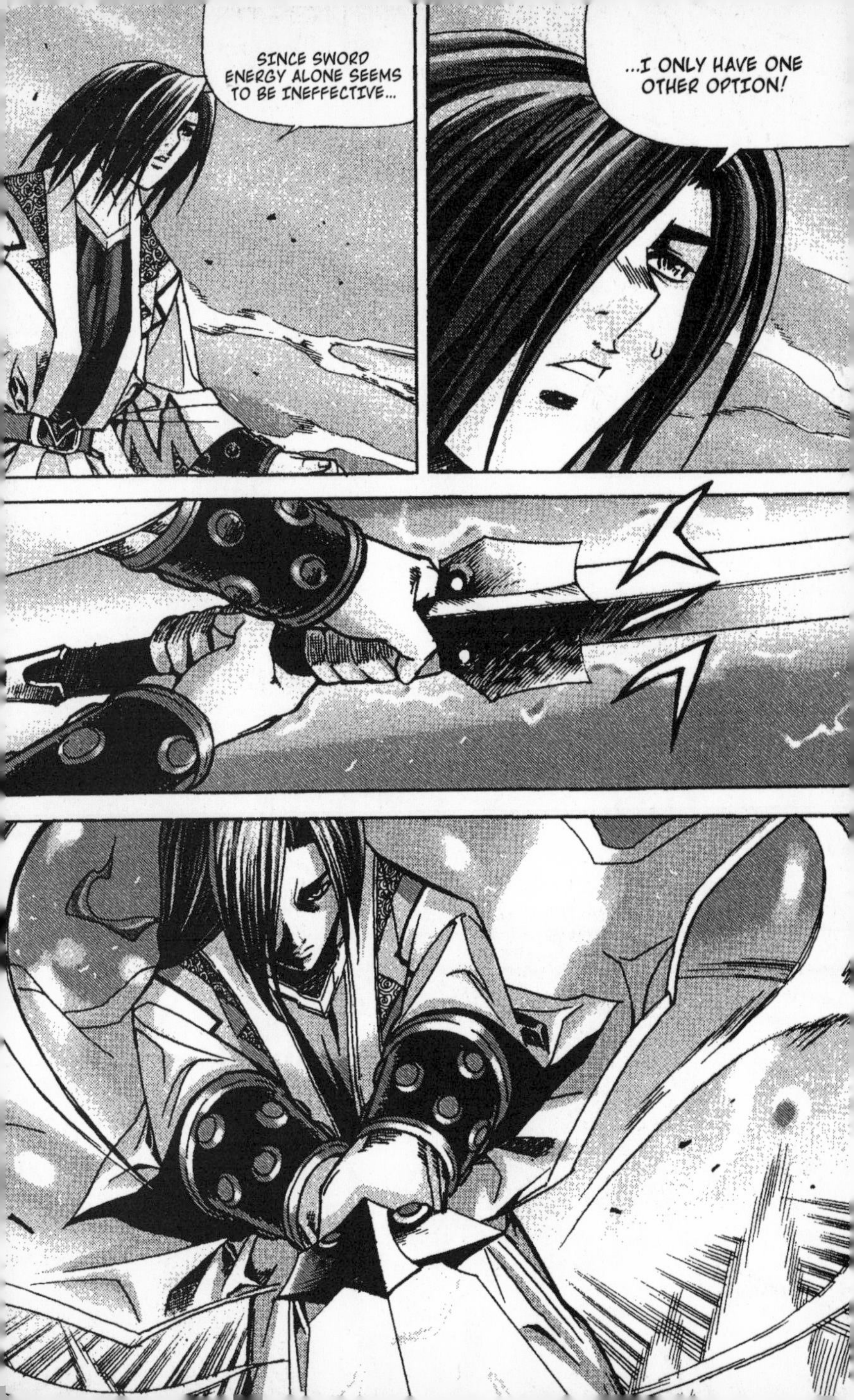
SINCE SWORD ENERGY ALONE SEEMS TO BE INEFFECTIVE...
...I ONLY HAVE ONE OTHER OPTION!

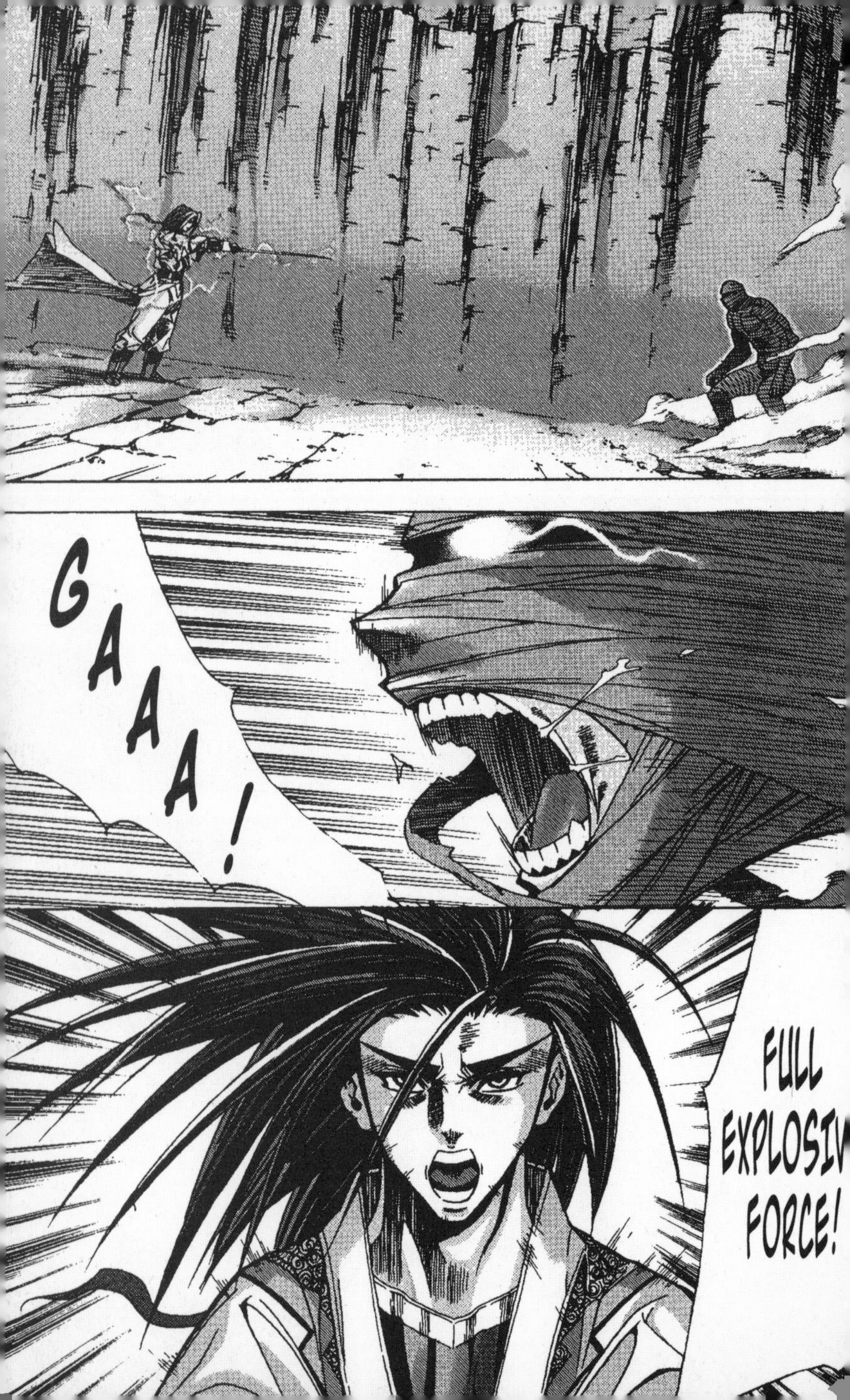
GAAA!
FULL EXPLOSIV FORCE!

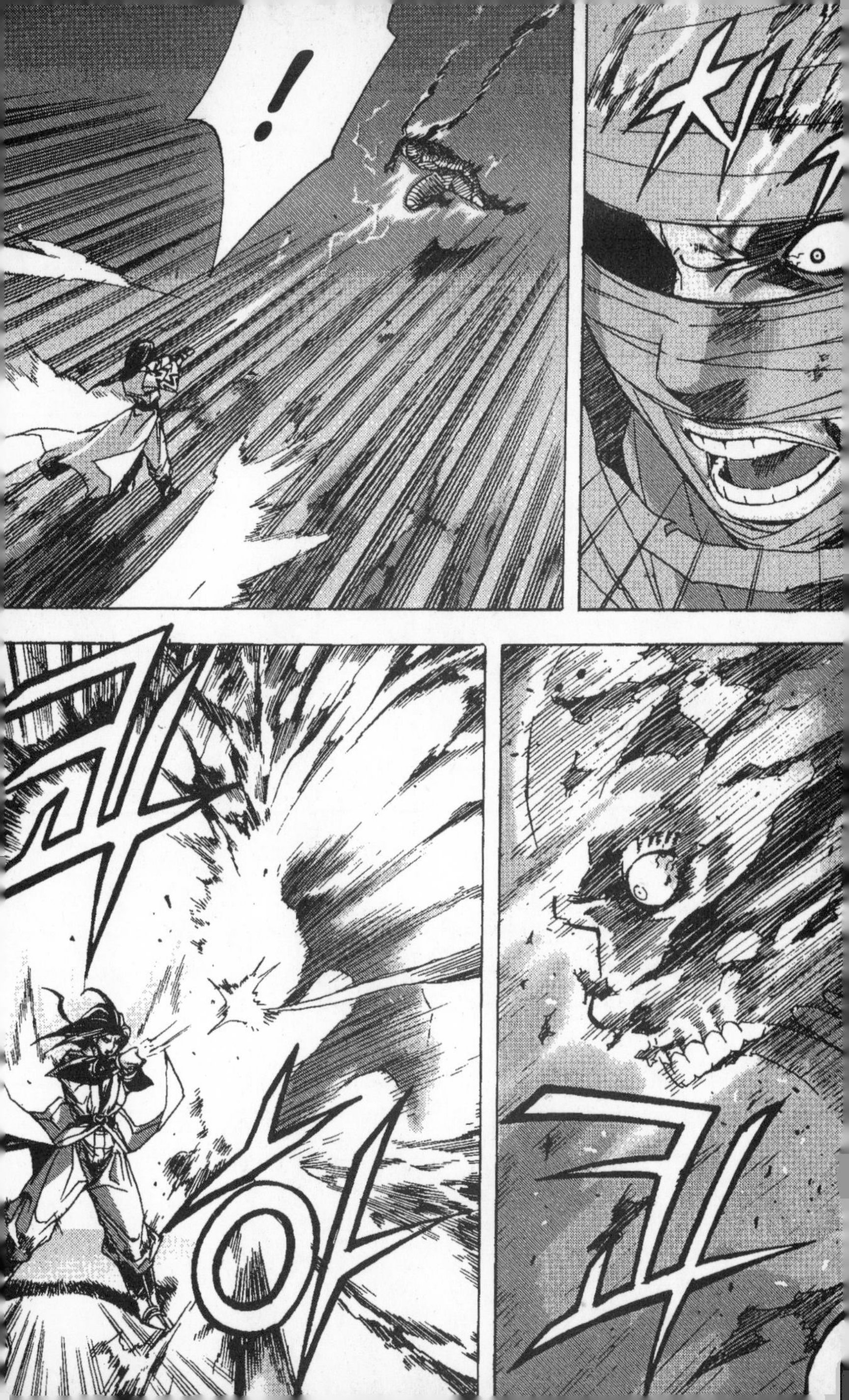
!

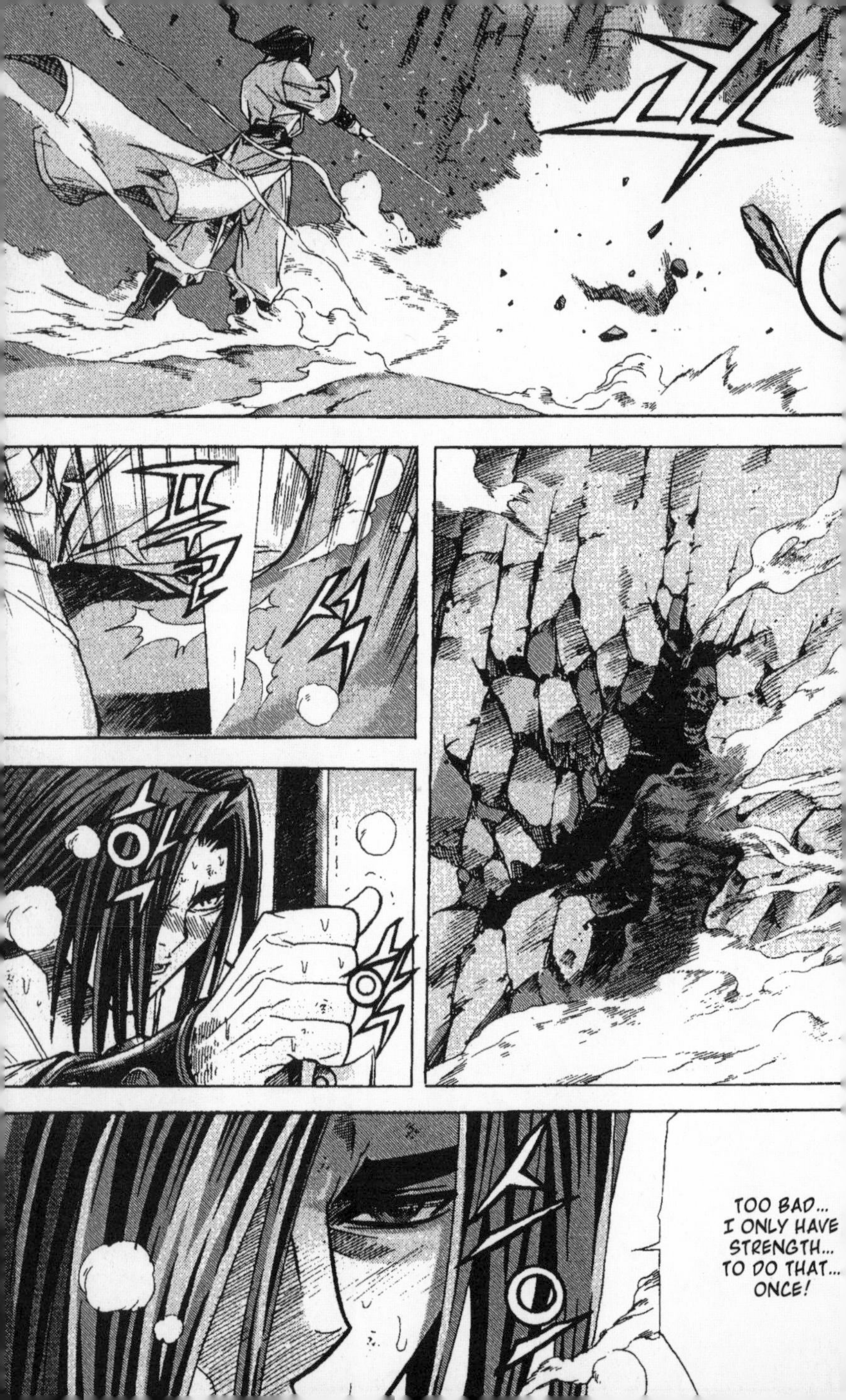
TOO BAD...
I ONLY HAVE
STRENGTH...
TO DO THAT...
ONCE!

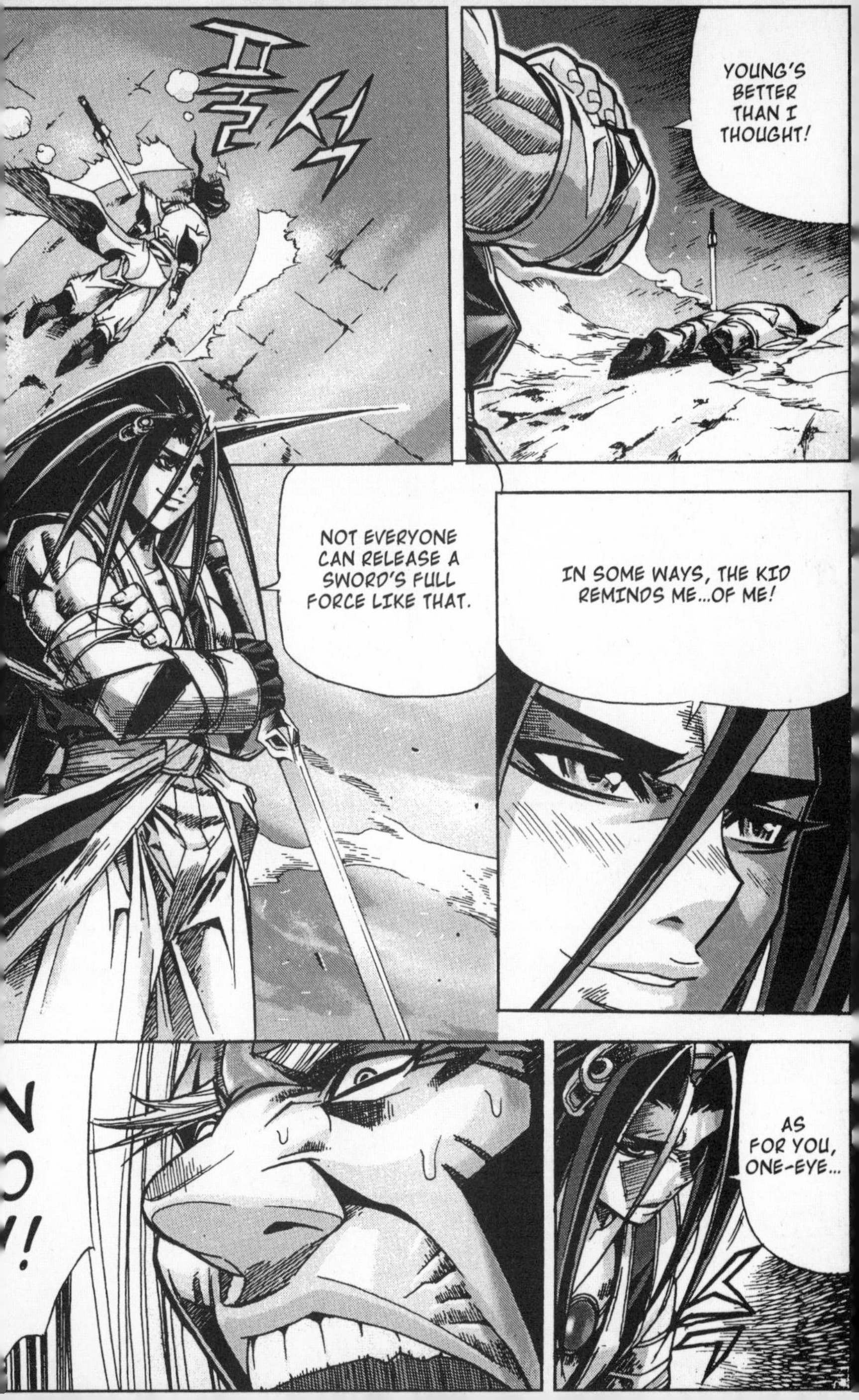
YOUNG'S BETTER THAN I THOUGHT!
NOT EVERYONE CAN RELEASE A SWORD'S FULL FORCE LIKE THAT.
IN SOME WAYS, THE KID REMINDS ME...OF ME!
NO!!
AS FOR YOU, ONE-EYE...

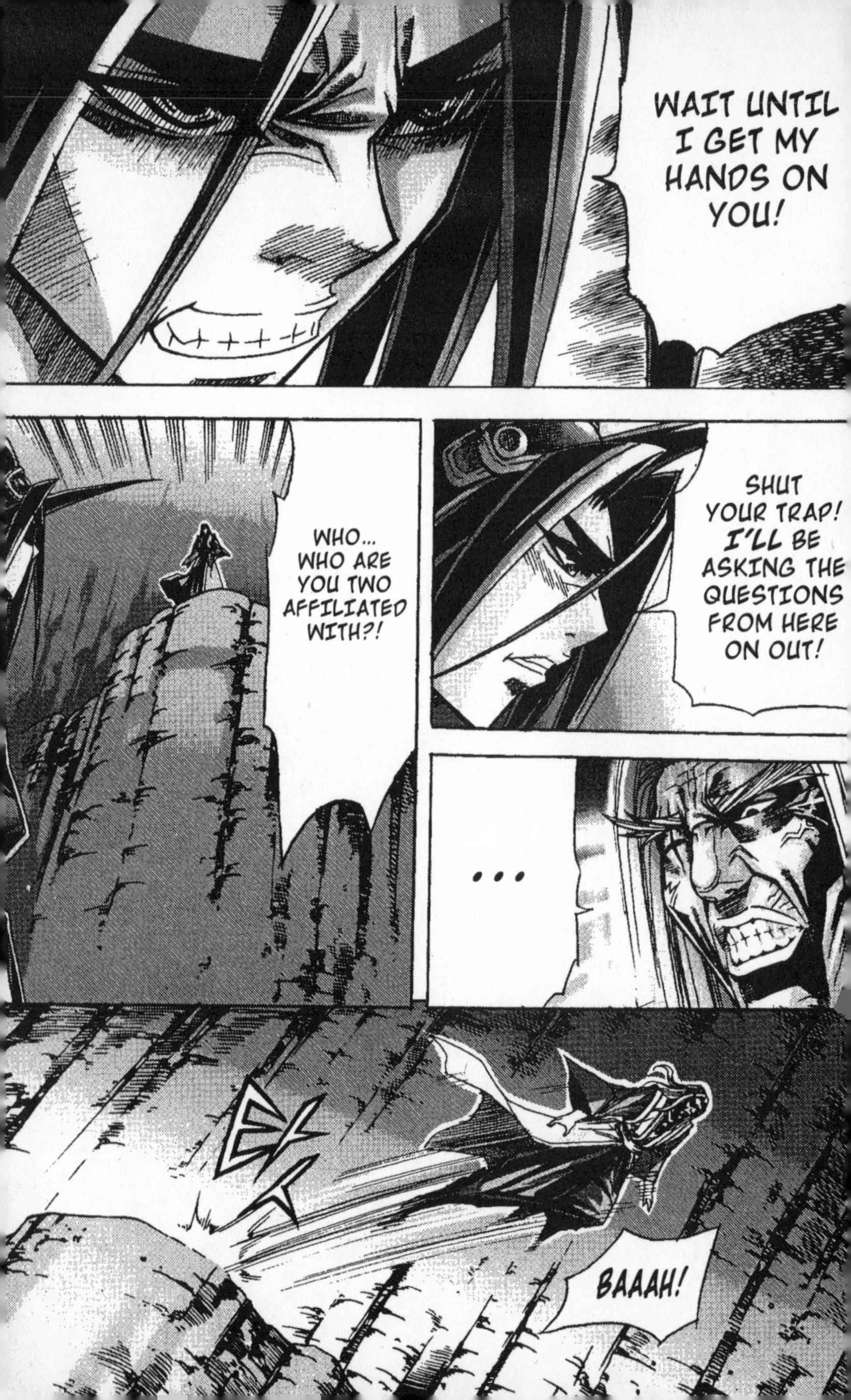
WAIT UNTIL I GET MY HANDS ON YOU!
WHO... WHO ARE YOU TWO AFFILIATED WITH?!
SHUT YOUR TRAP! I'LL BE ASKING THE QUESTIONS FROM HERE ON OUT!
...
BAAAH!

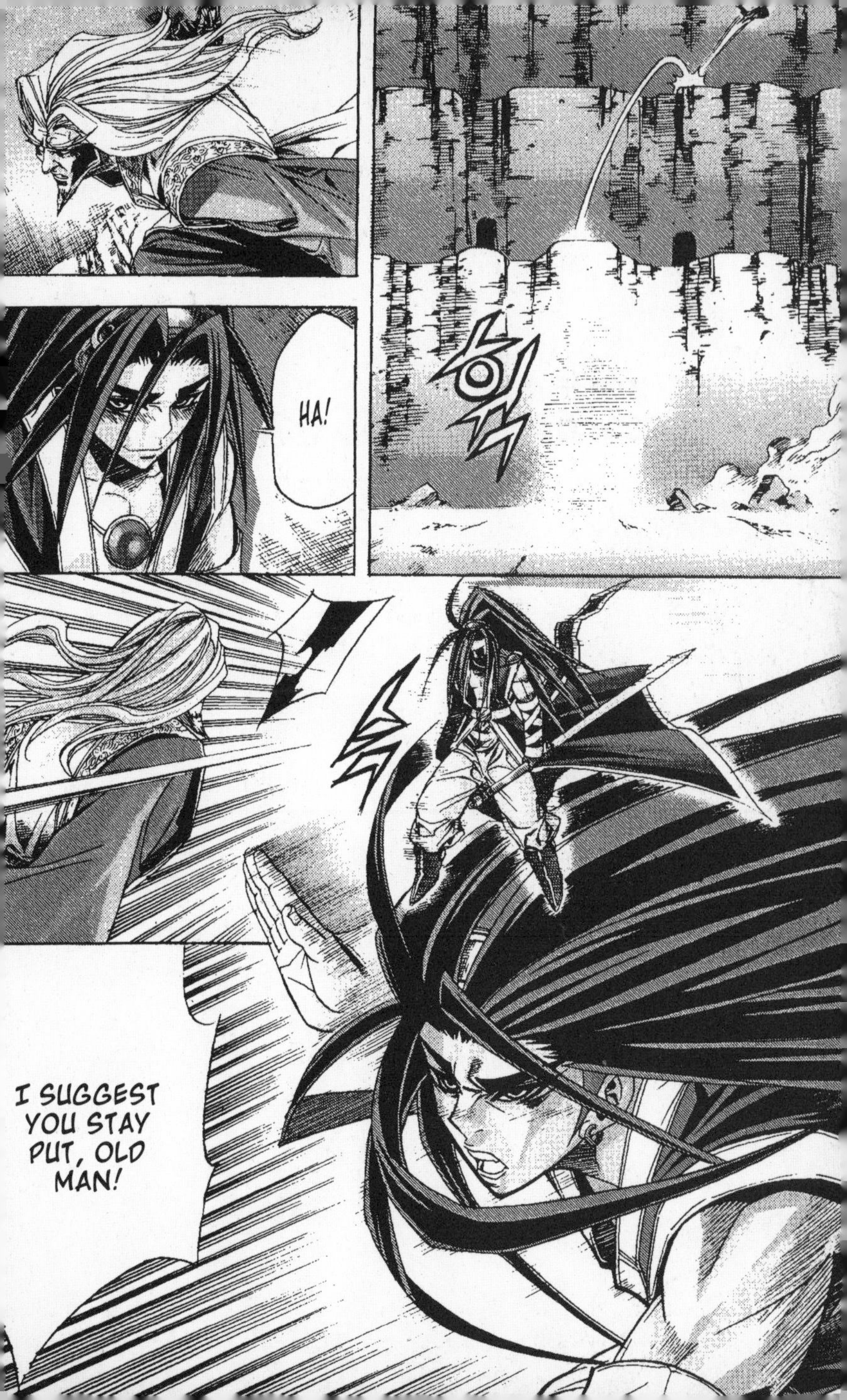
HA!
I SUGGEST YOU STAY PUT, OLD MAN!

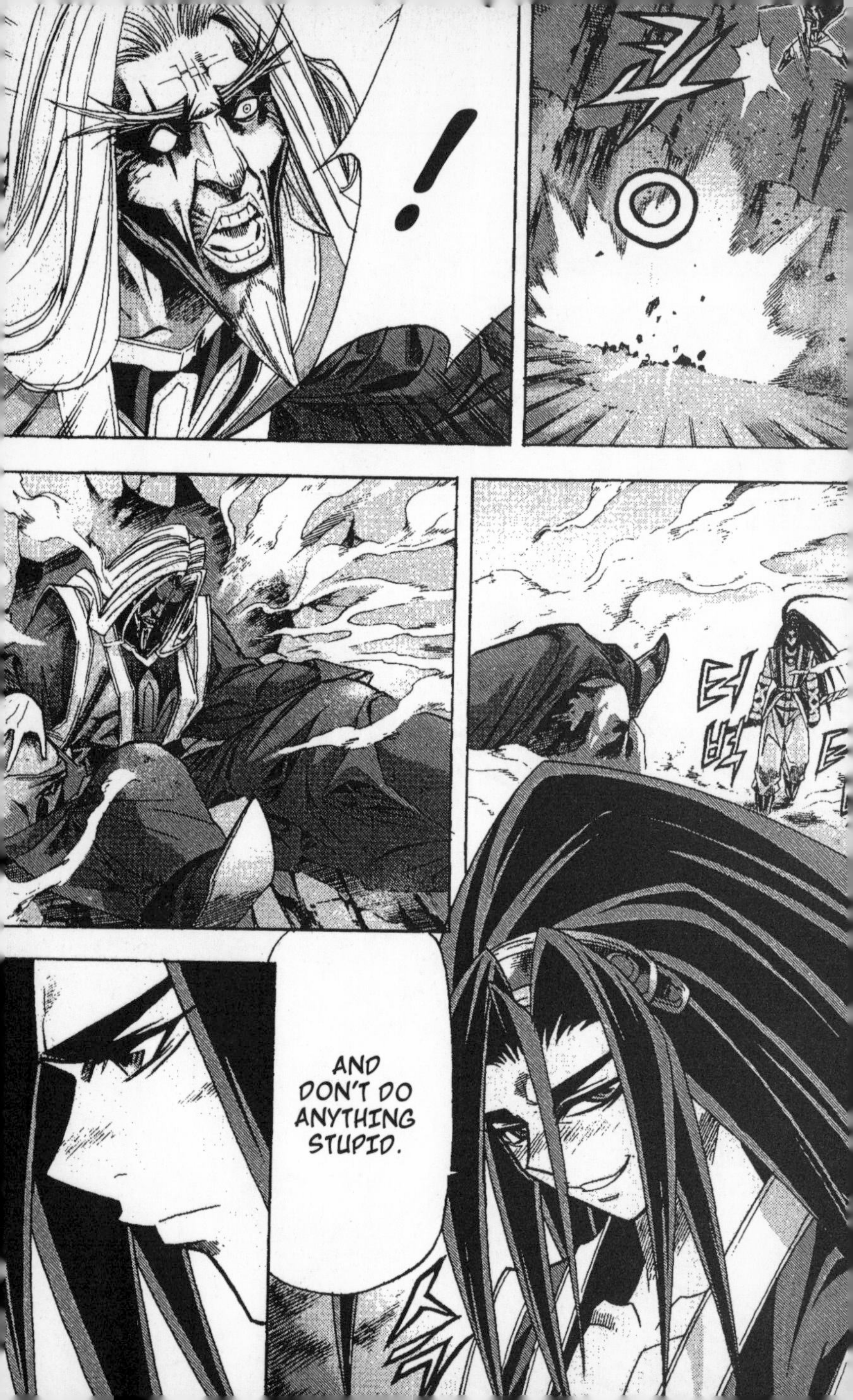
AND DON'T DO ANYTHING STUPID.

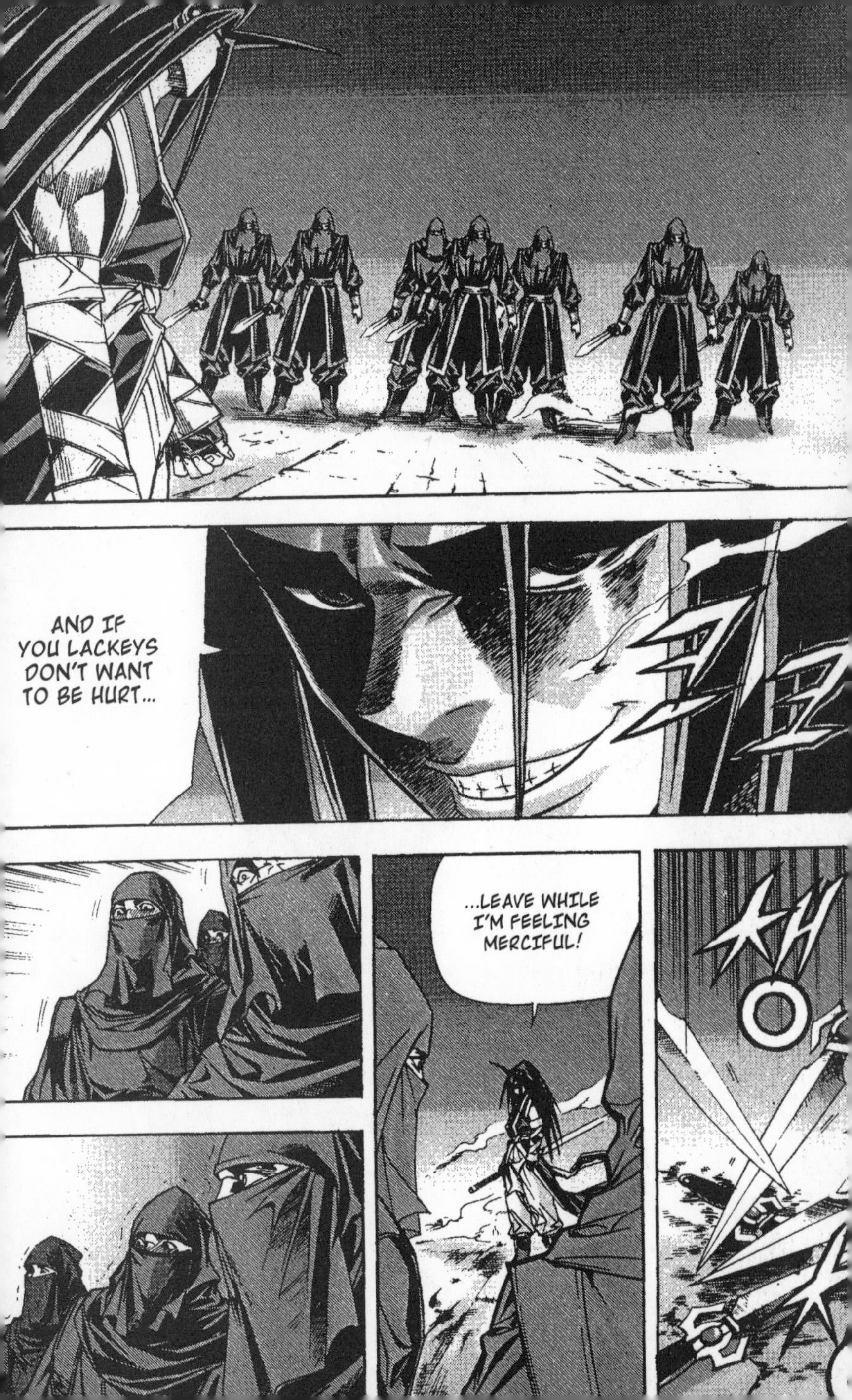
AND IF YOU LACKEYS DON'T WANT TO BE HURT...
...LEAVE WHILE I'M FEELING MERCIFUL!

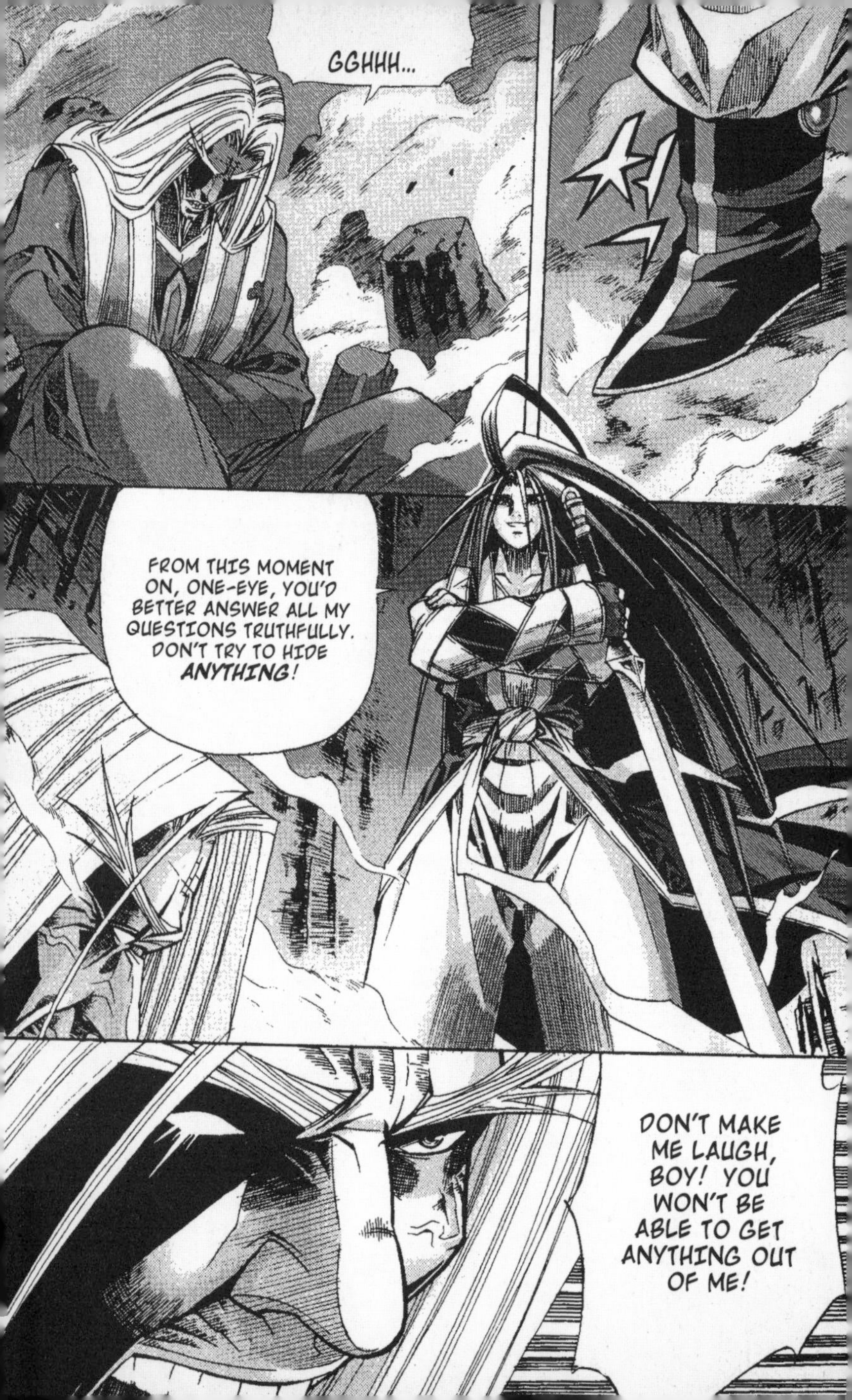
GGHHH...
FROM THIS MOMENT ON, ONE-EYE, YOU'D BETTER ANSWER ALL MY QUESTIONS TRUTHFULLY. DON'T TRY TO HIDE ANYTHING!
DON'T MAKE ME LAUGH, BOY! YOU WON'T BE ABLE TO GET ANYTHING OUT OF ME!

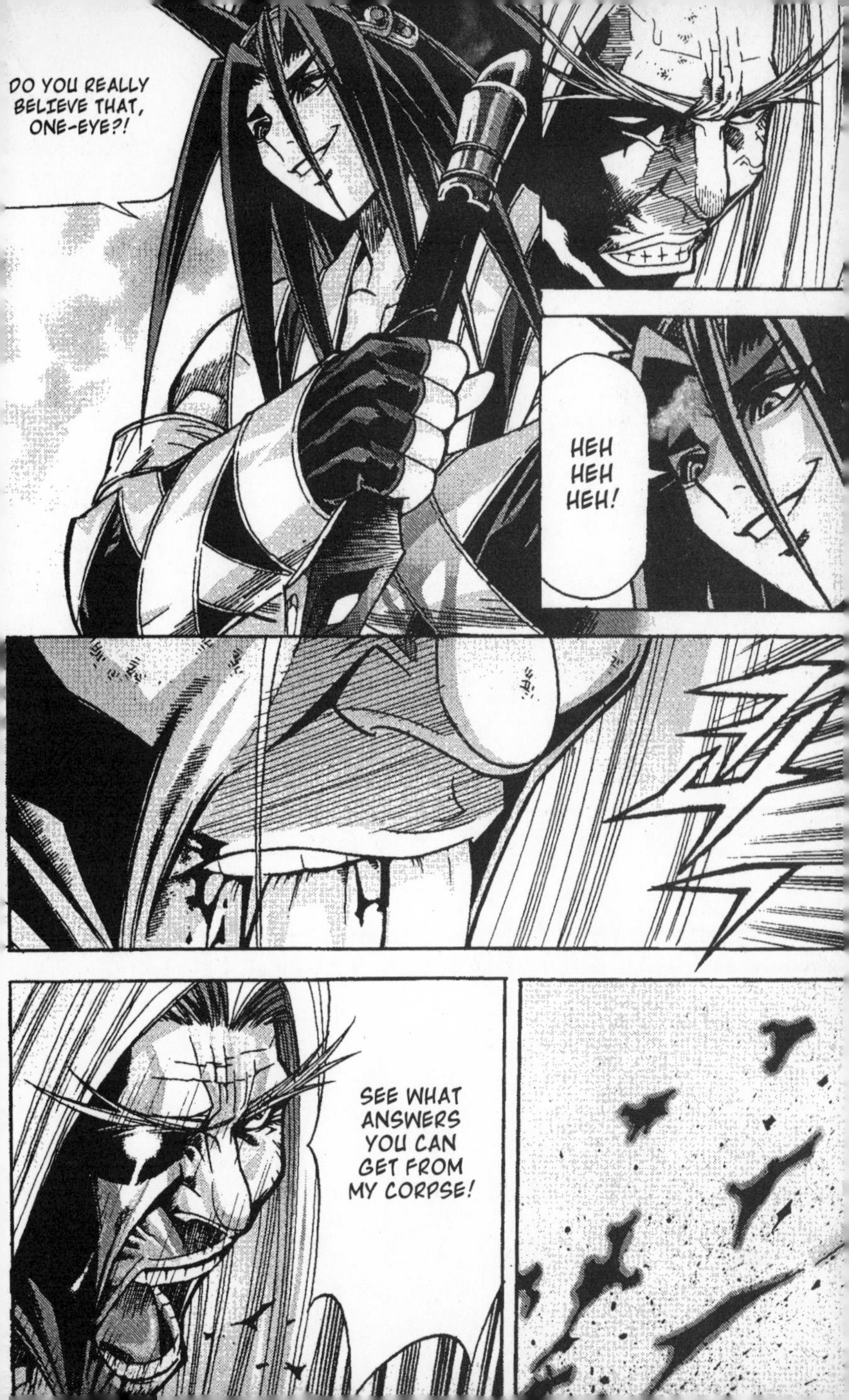
DO YOU REALLY BELIEVE THAT, ONE-EYE?!
HEH HEH HEH!
SEE WHAT ANSWERS YOU CAN GET FROM MY CORPSE!

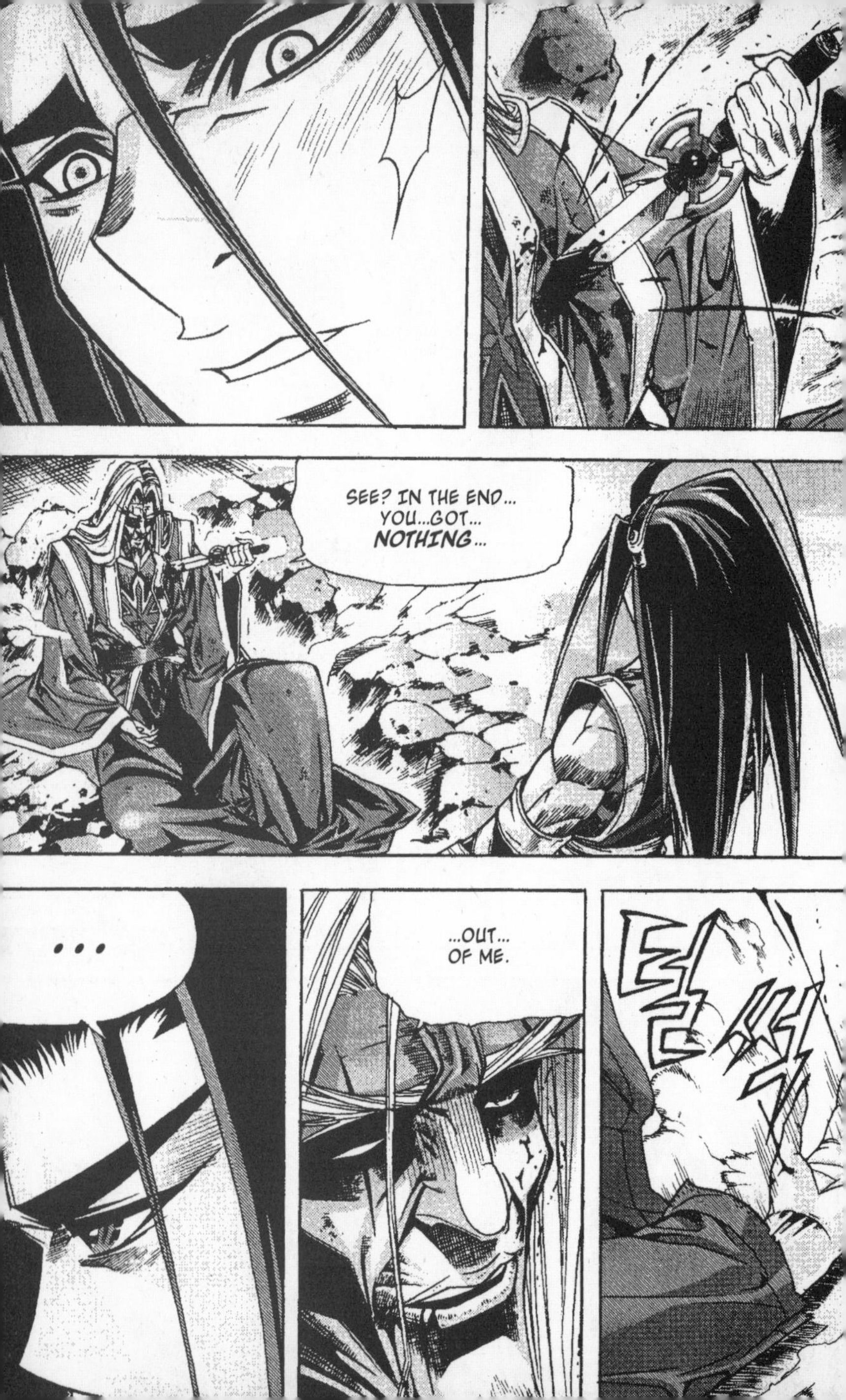
SEE? IN THE END... YOU...GOT... NOTHING...
...
...OUT... OF ME.

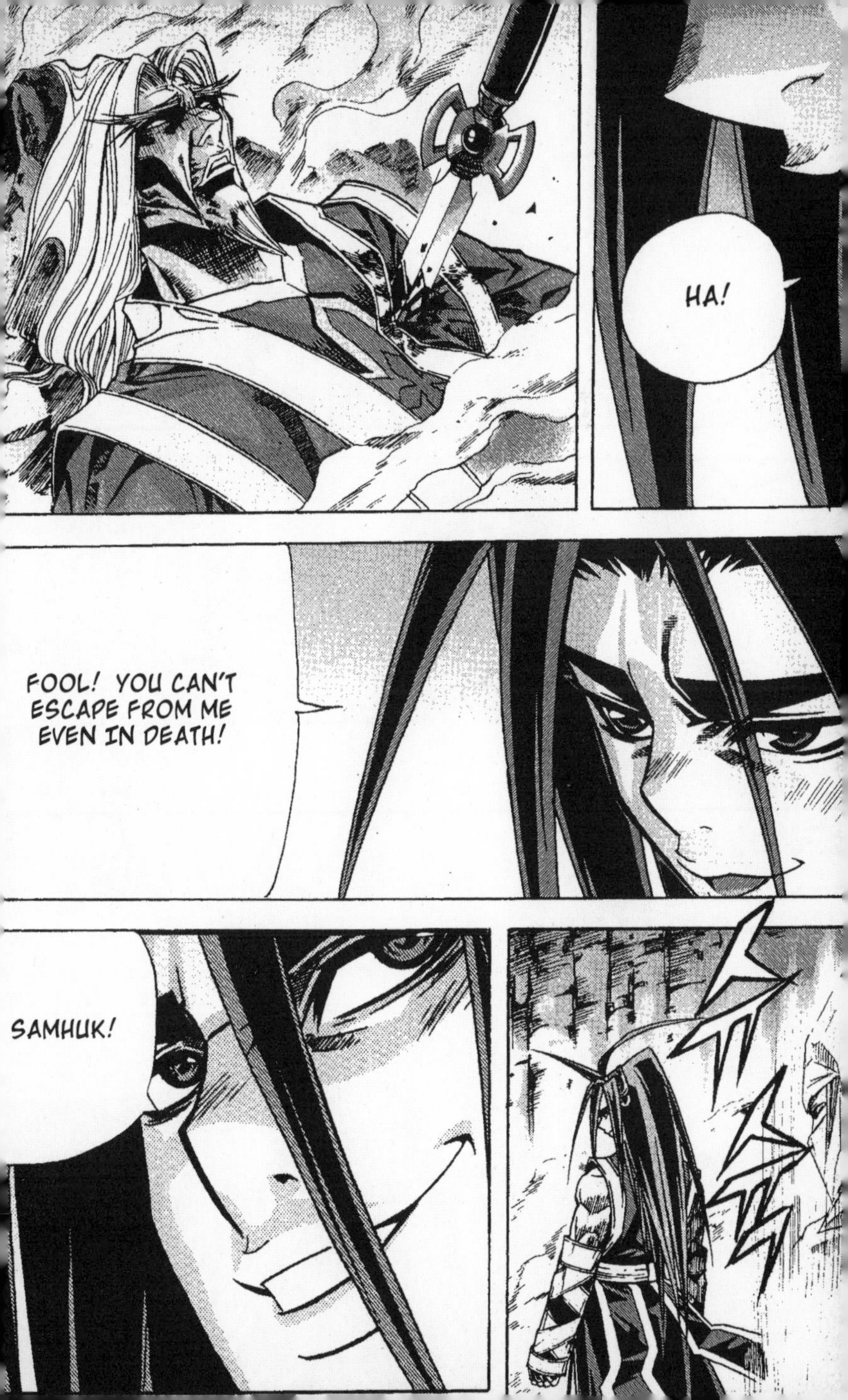
HA!
FOOL! YOU CAN'T ESCAPE FROM ME EVEN IN DEATH!
SAMHUK!

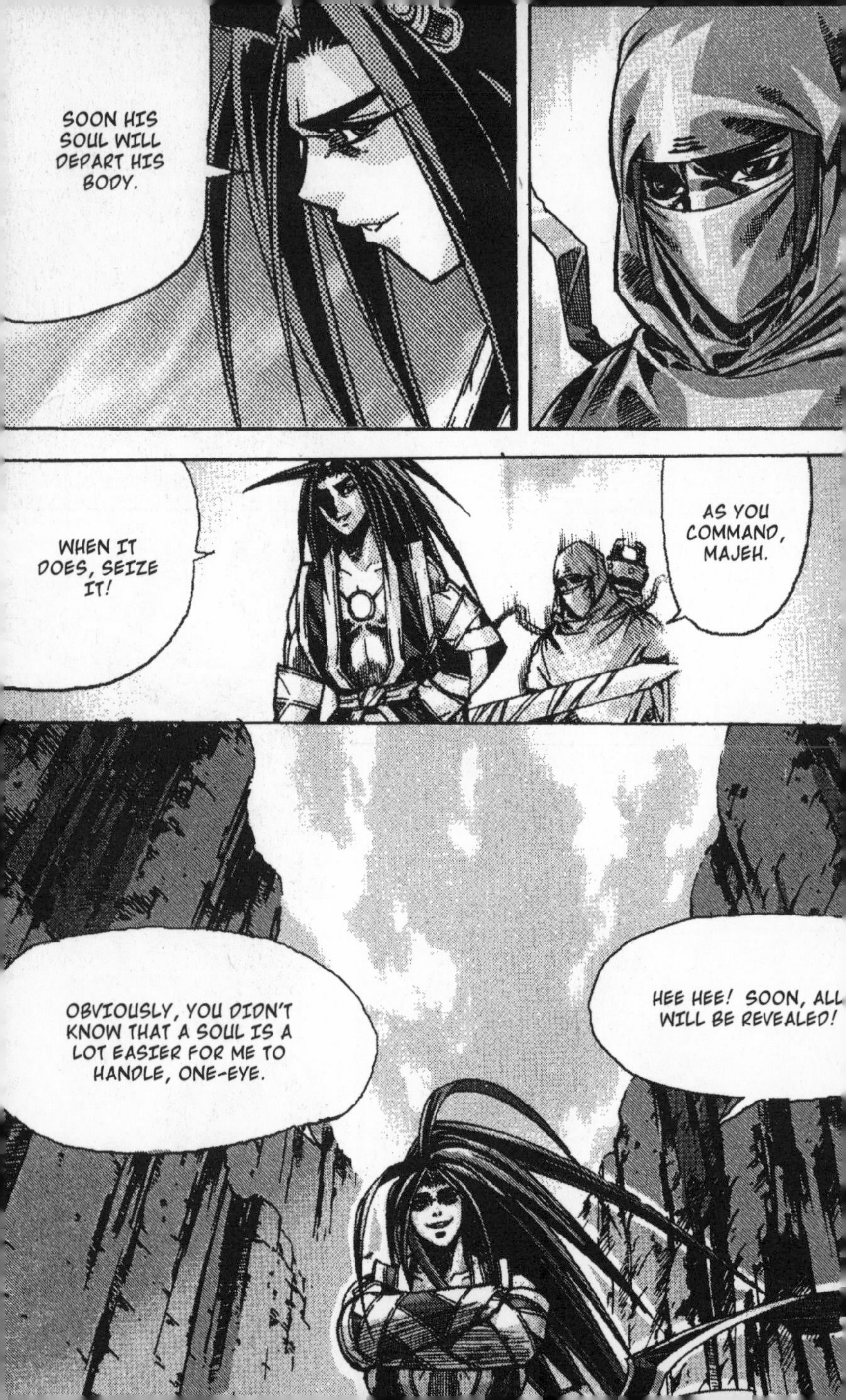
SOON HIS SOUL WILL DEPART HIS BODY.
WHEN IT DOES, SEIZE IT!
AS YOU COMMAND, MAJEH.
OBVIOUSLY, YOU DIDN'T KNOW THAT A SOUL IS A LOT EASIER FOR ME TO HANDLE, ONE-EYE.
HEE HEE! SOON, ALL WILL BE REVEALED!

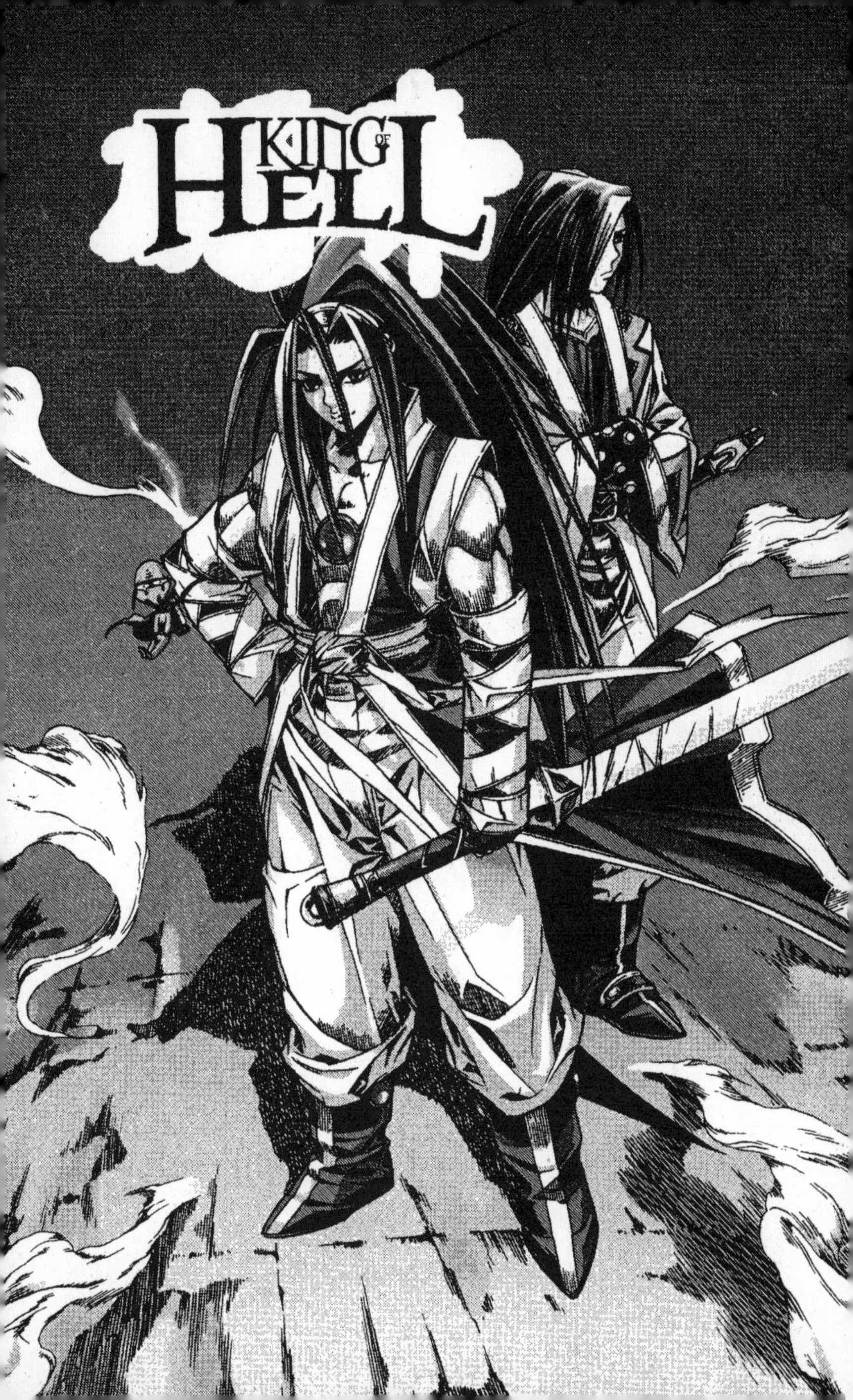
KING OF HELL

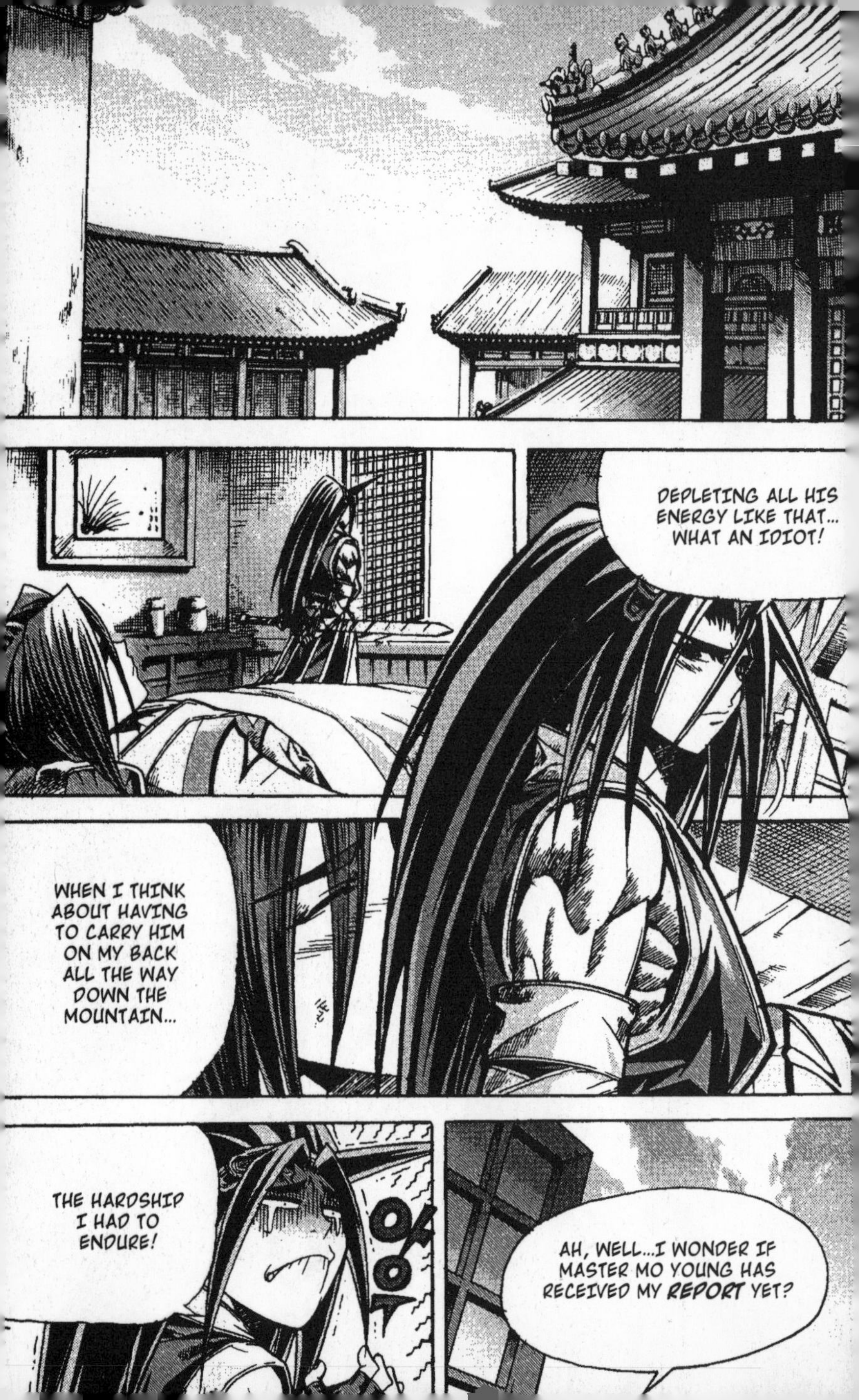
DEPLETING ALL HIS ENERGY LIKE THAT... WHAT AN IDIOT!
WHEN I THINK ABOUT HAVING TO CARRY HIM ON MY BACK ALL THE WAY DOWN THE MOUNTAIN...
THE HARDSHIP I HAD TO ENDURE!
AH, WELL...I WONDER IF MASTER MO YOUNG HAS RECEIVED MY REPORT YET?

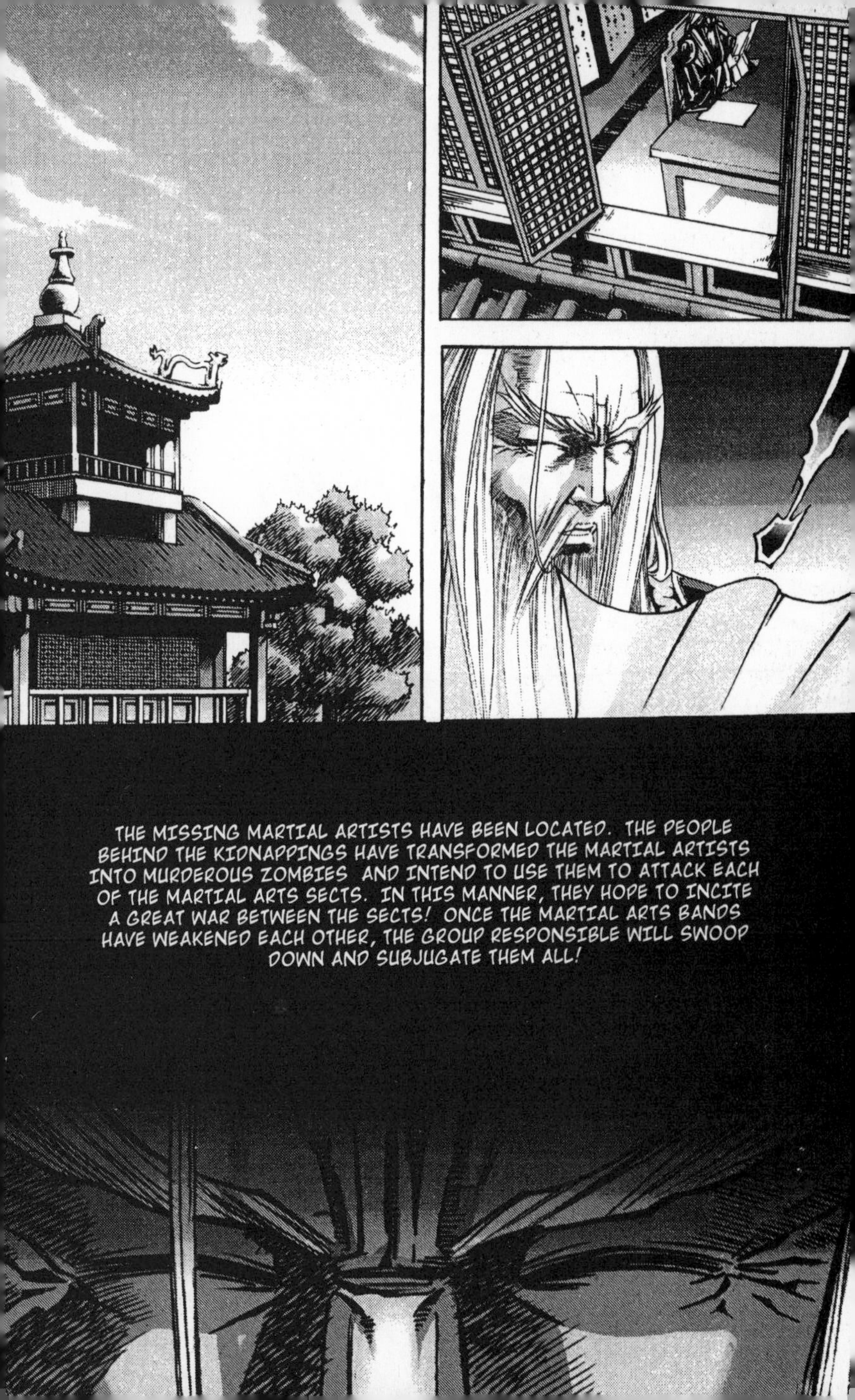
THE MISSING MARTIAL ARTISTS HAVE BEEN LOCATED. THE PEOPLE BEHIND THE KIDNAPPINGS HAVE TRANSFORMED THE MARTIAL ARTISTS INTO MURDEROUS ZOMBIES AND INTEND TO USE THEM TO ATTACK EACH OF THE MARTIAL ARTS SECTS. IN THIS MANNER, THEY HOPE TO INCITE A GREAT WAR BETWEEN THE SECTS! ONCE THE MARTIAL ARTS BANDS HAVE WEAKENED EACH OTHER, THE GROUP RESPONSIBLE WILL SWOOP DOWN AND SUBJUGATE THEM ALL!

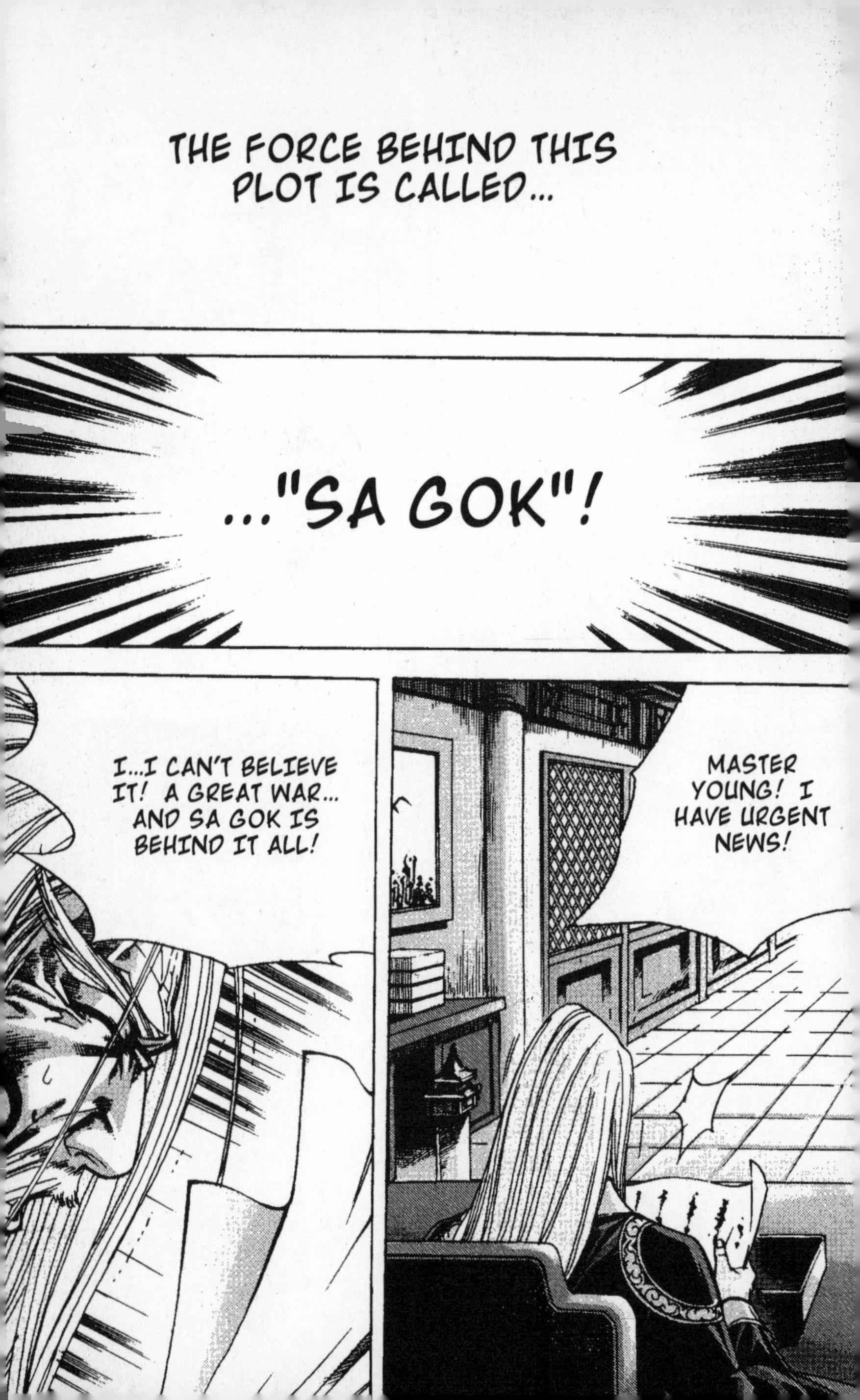
THE FORCE BEHIND THIS PLOT IS CALLED...
..."SA GOK"!
I...I CAN'T BELIEVE IT! A GREAT WAR... AND SA GOK IS BEHIND IT ALL!
MASTER YOUNG! I HAVE URGENT NEWS!

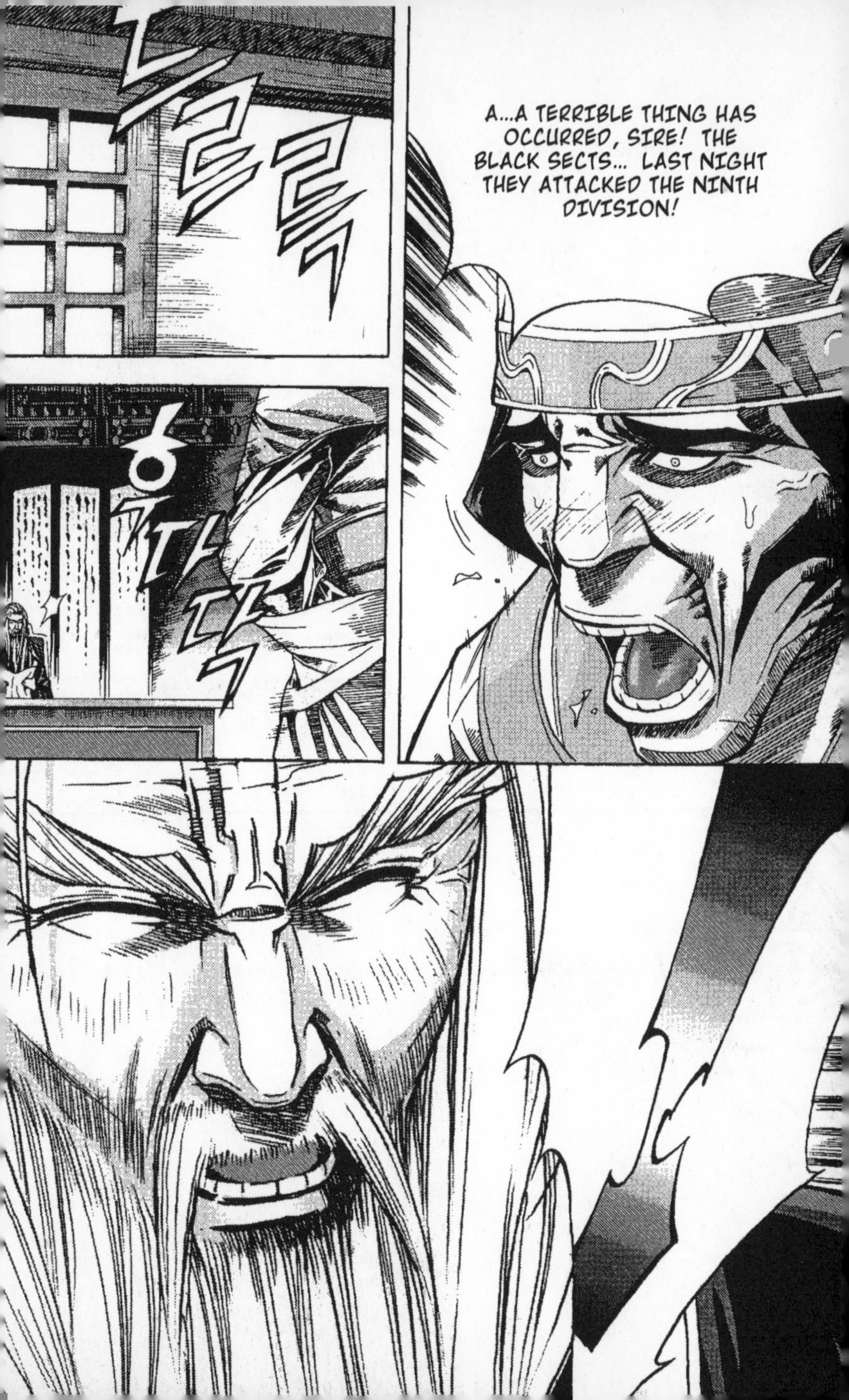
A...A TERRIBLE THING HAS OCCURRED, SIRE! THE BLACK SECTS... LAST NIGHT THEY ATTACKED THE NINTH DIVISION!

A GREAT WAR BETWEEN THE SECTS...

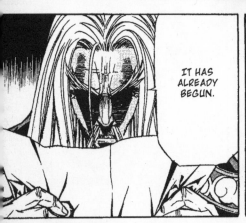

IT HAS ALREADY BEGUN.

INFORM ALL THE SCHOOLS THAT WE WILL HOLD AN EMERGENCY MEETING IMMEDIATELY!

YES, SIRE! AS YOU COMMAND!

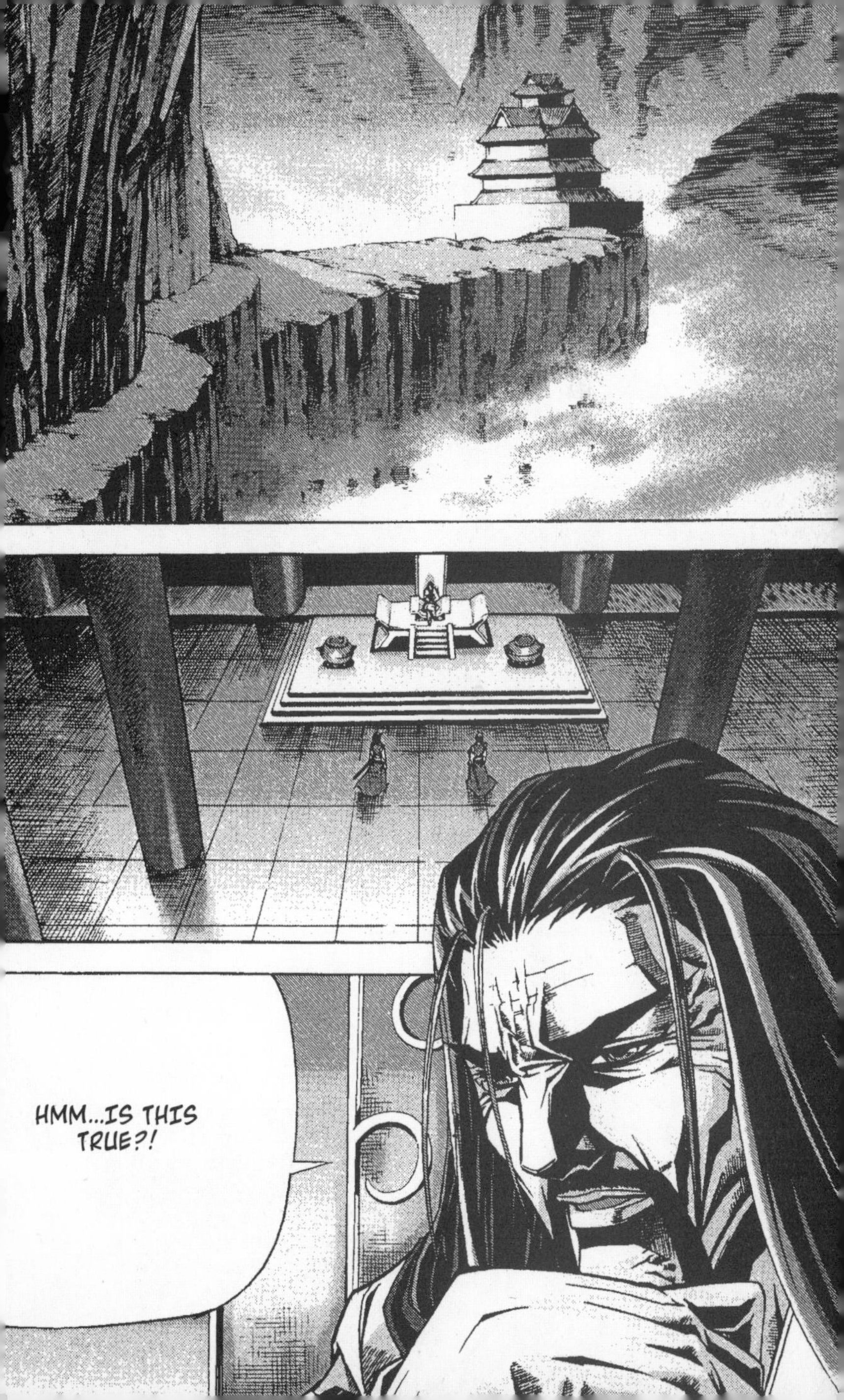
HMM...IS THIS TRUE?!

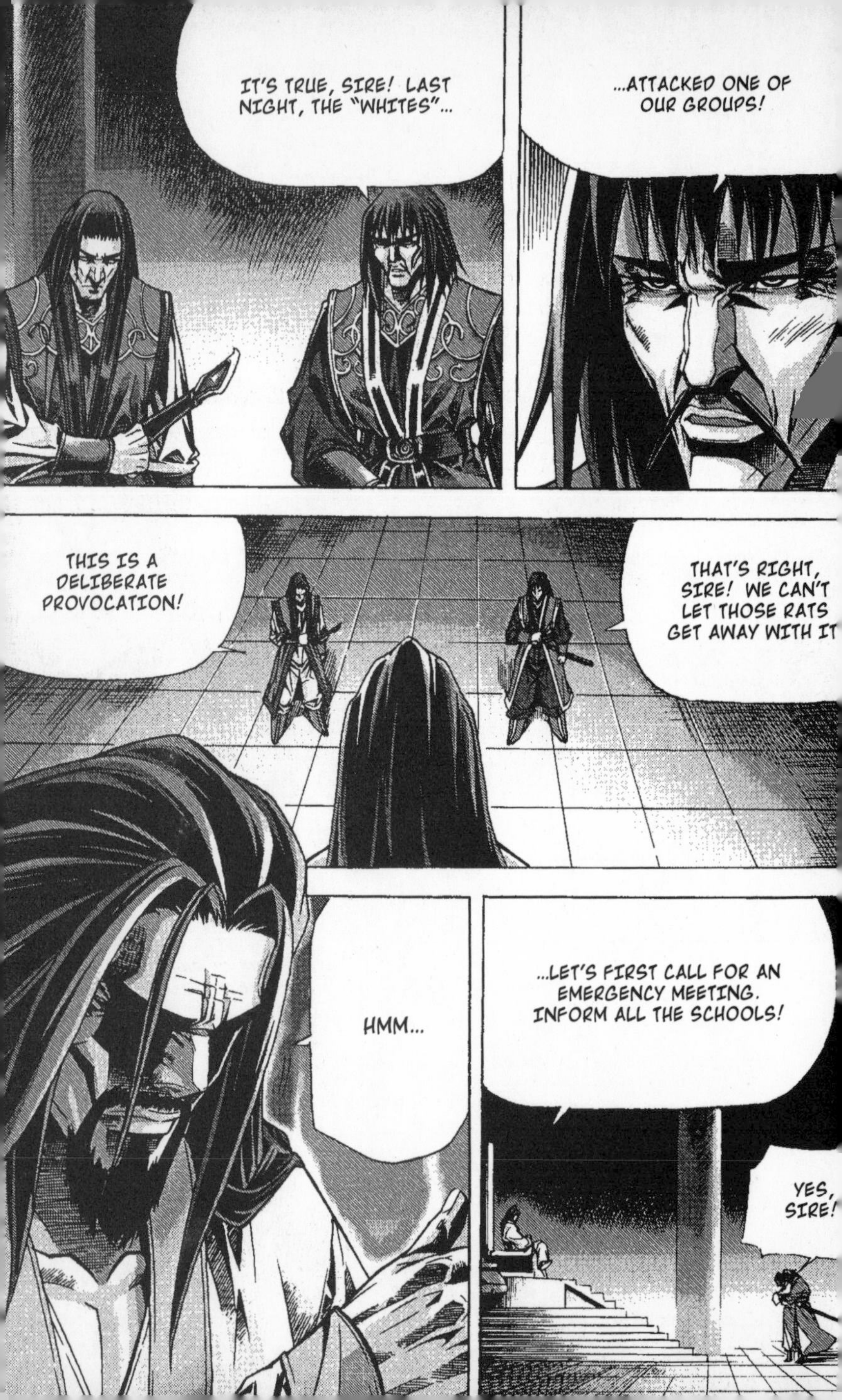
IT'S TRUE, SIRE! LAST NIGHT, THE "WHITES"...
...ATTACKED ONE OF OUR GROUPS!
THIS IS A DELIBERATE PROVOCATION!
THAT'S RIGHT, SIRE! WE CAN'T LET THOSE RATS GET AWAY WITH IT
HMM...
...LET'S FIRST CALL FOR AN EMERGENCY MEETING. INFORM ALL THE SCHOOLS!
YES, SIRE!

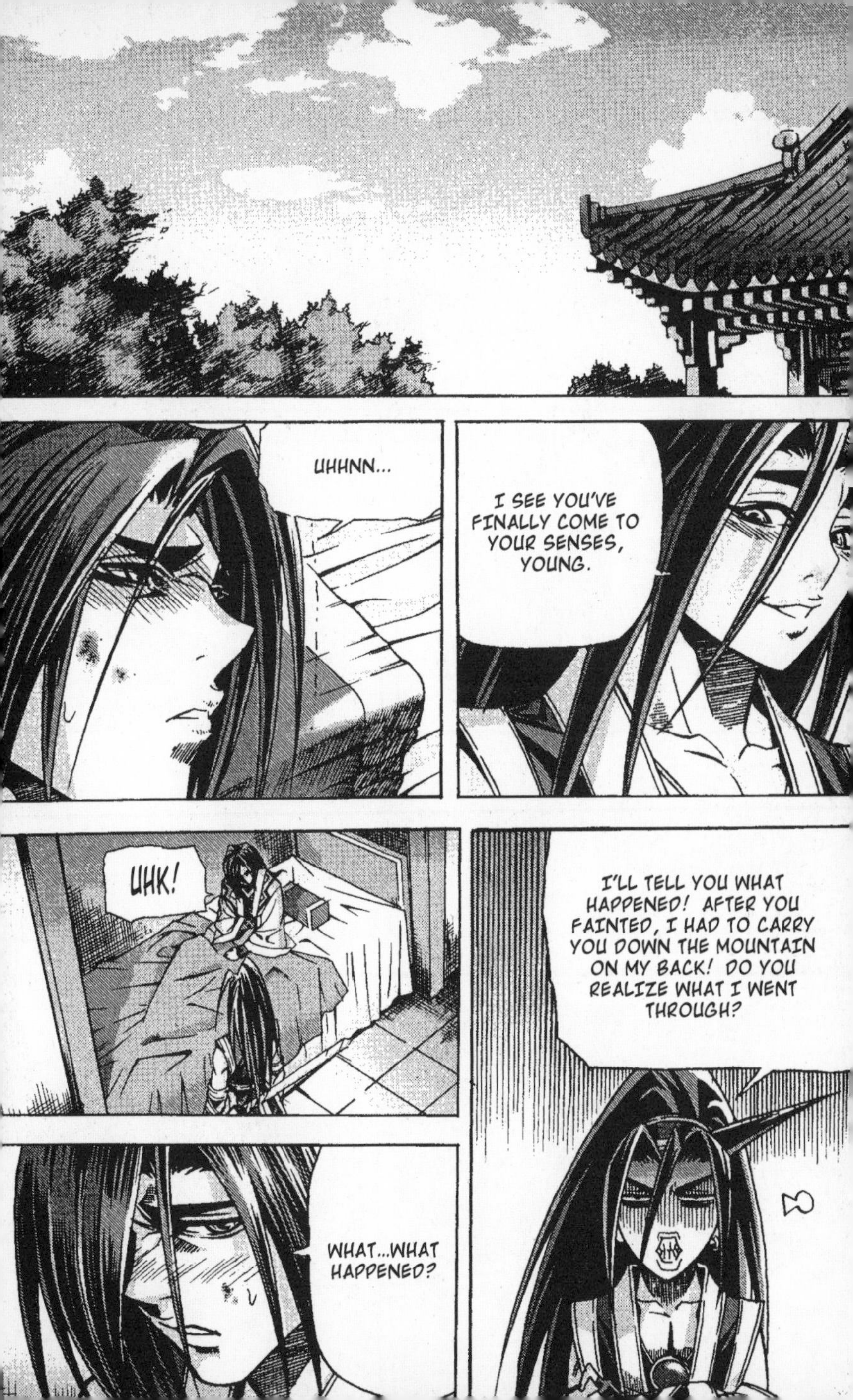

UHHNN...
I SEE YOU'VE FINALLY COME TO YOUR SENSES, YOUNG.
UHK!
I'LL TELL YOU WHAT HAPPENED! AFTER YOU FAINTED, I HAD TO CARRY YOU DOWN THE MOUNTAIN ON MY BACK! DO YOU REALIZE WHAT I WENT THROUGH?
WHAT...WHAT HAPPENED?

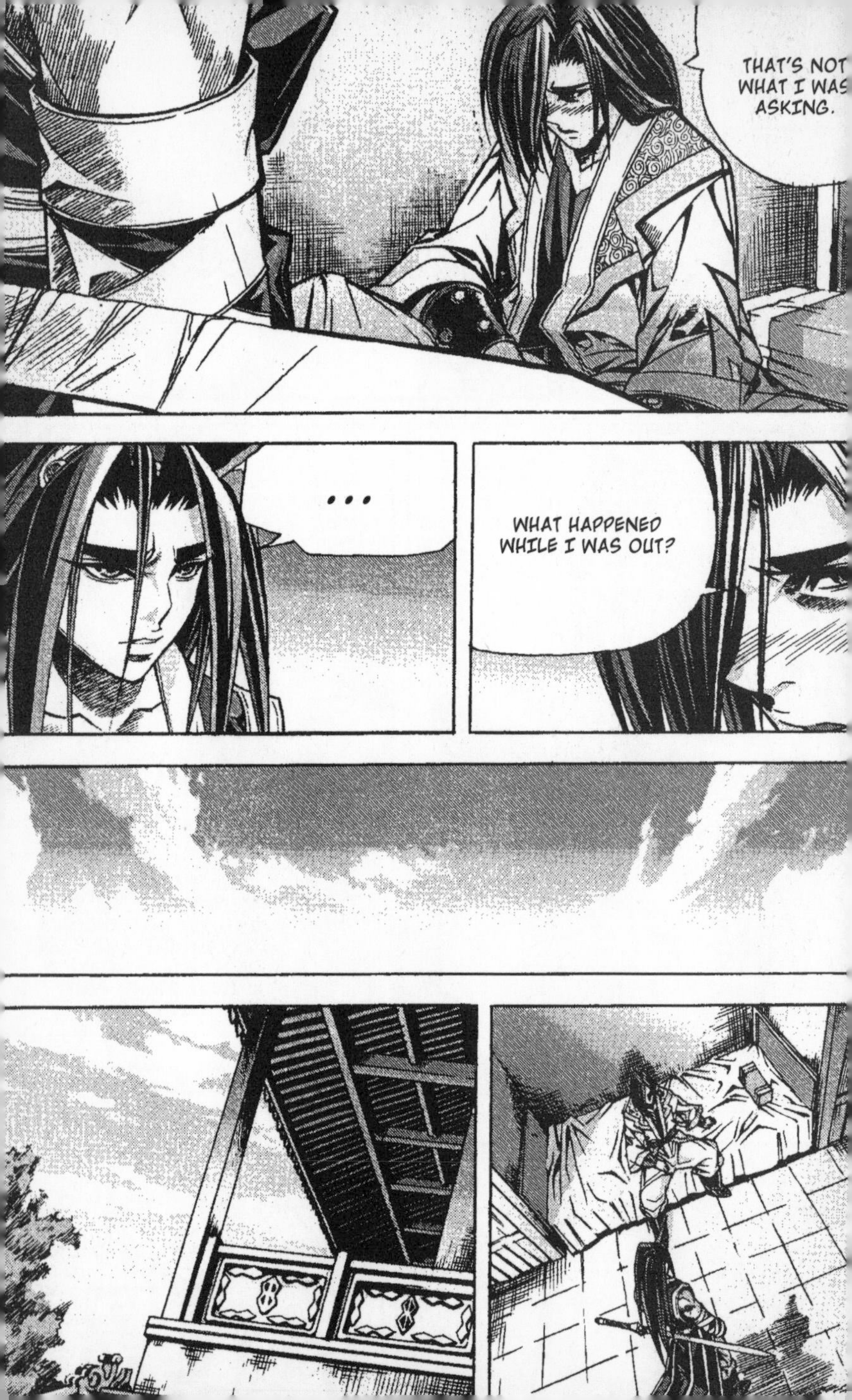
THAT'S NOT WHAT I WAS ASKING.
...
WHAT HAPPENED WHILE I WAS OUT?

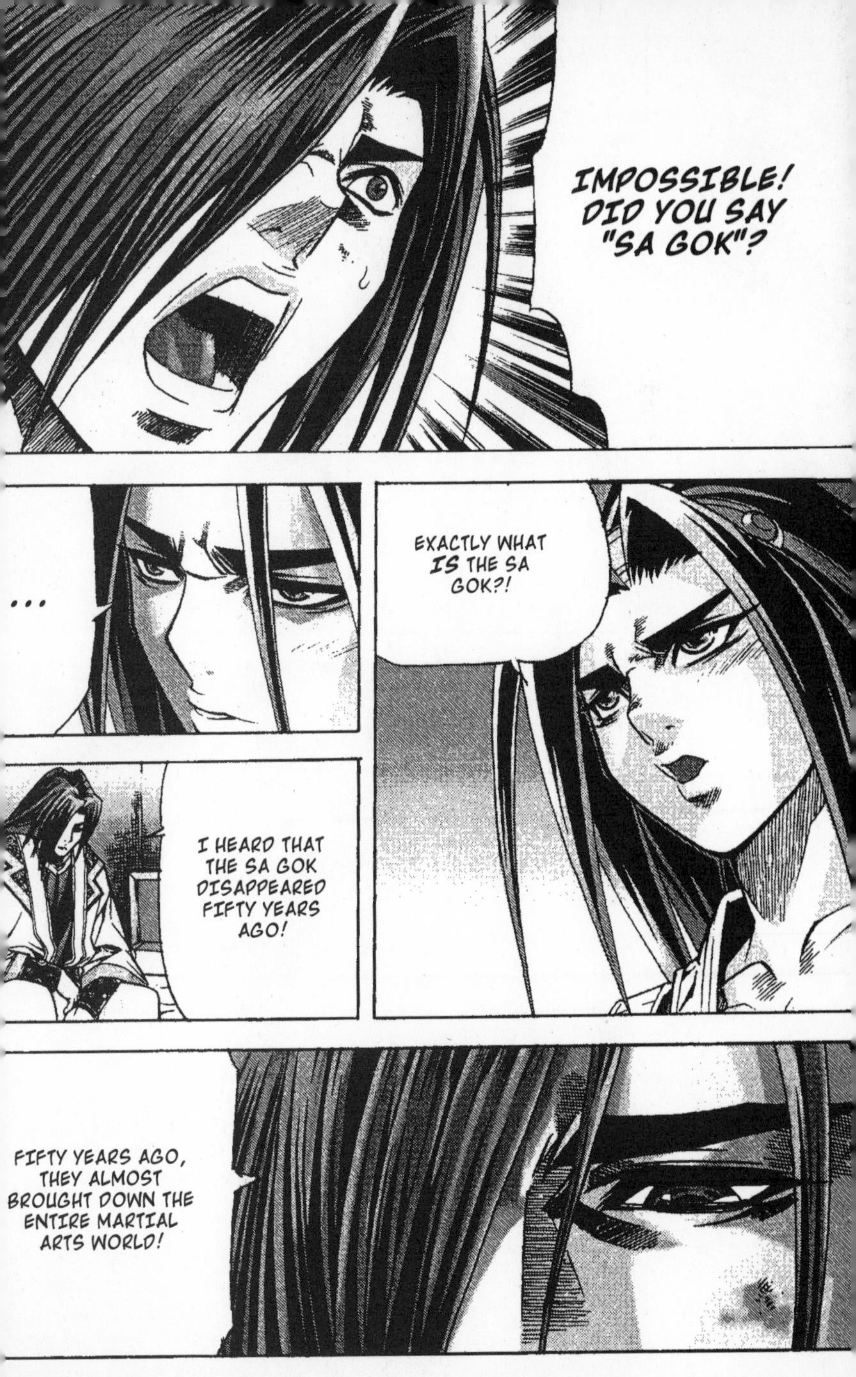
IMPOSSIBLE! DID YOU SAY "SA GOK"?
...
EXACTLY WHAT IS THE SA GOK?!
I HEARD THAT THE SA GOK DISAPPEARED FIFTY YEARS AGO!
FIFTY YEARS AGO, THEY ALMOST BROUGHT DOWN THE ENTIRE MARTIAL ARTS WORLD!

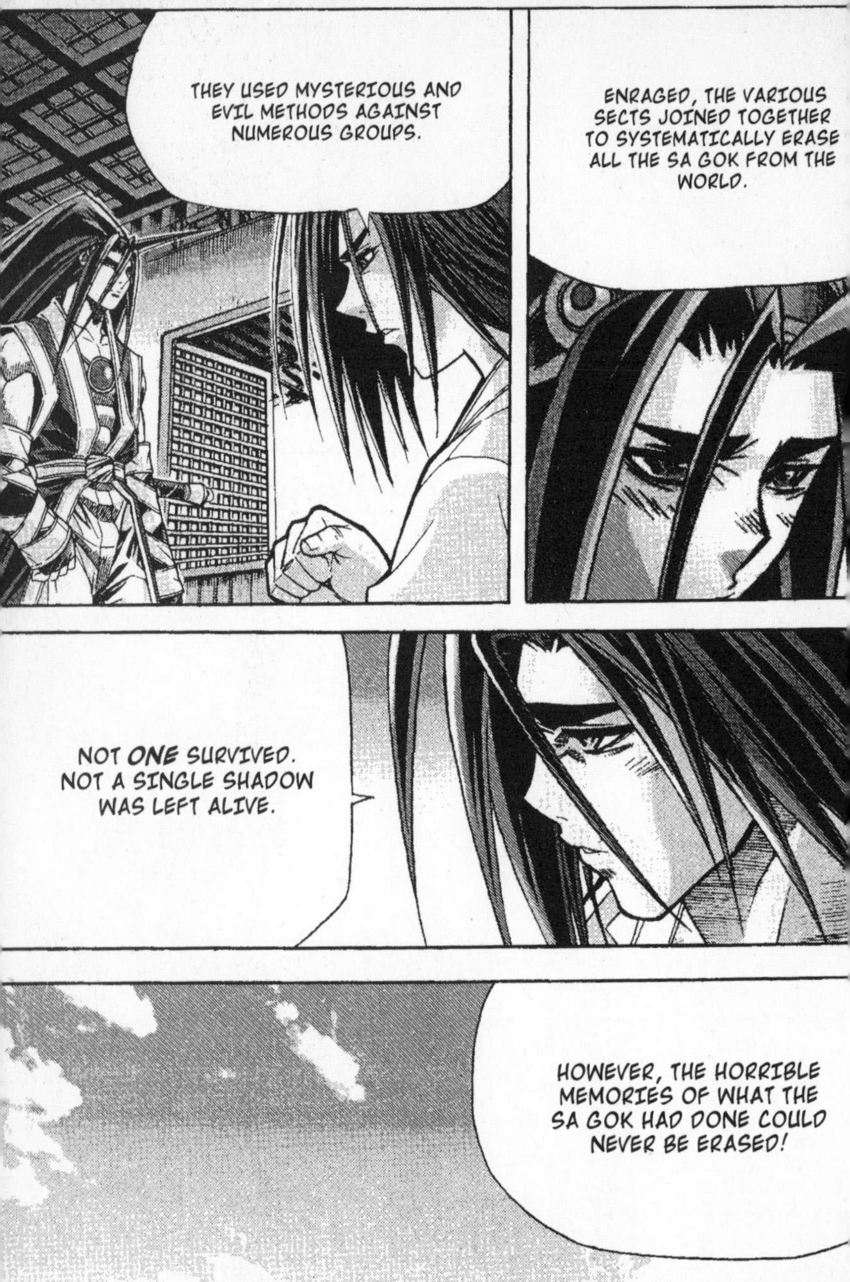
THEY USED MYSTERIOUS AND EVIL METHODS AGAINST NUMEROUS GROUPS.
ENRAGED, THE VARIOUS SECTS JOINED TOGETHER TO SYSTEMATICALLY ERASE ALL THE SA GOK FROM THE WORLD.
NOT *ONE* SURVIVED. NOT A SINGLE SHADOW WAS LEFT ALIVE.
HOWEVER, THE HORRIBLE MEMORIES OF WHAT THE SA GOK HAD DONE COULD NEVER BE ERASED!

PEOPLE STILL REMEMBER AND TREMBLE IN FEAR OF THE SA GOK'S POWERFUL AND EVIL TACTICS.

...

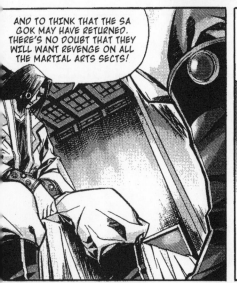

AND TO THINK THAT THE SA GOK MAY HAVE RETURNED. THERE'S NO DOUBT THAT THEY WILL WANT REVENGE ON ALL THE MARTIAL ARTS SECTS!

I BELIEVE THEY'VE ALREADY SET THAT PLAN INTO MOTION!

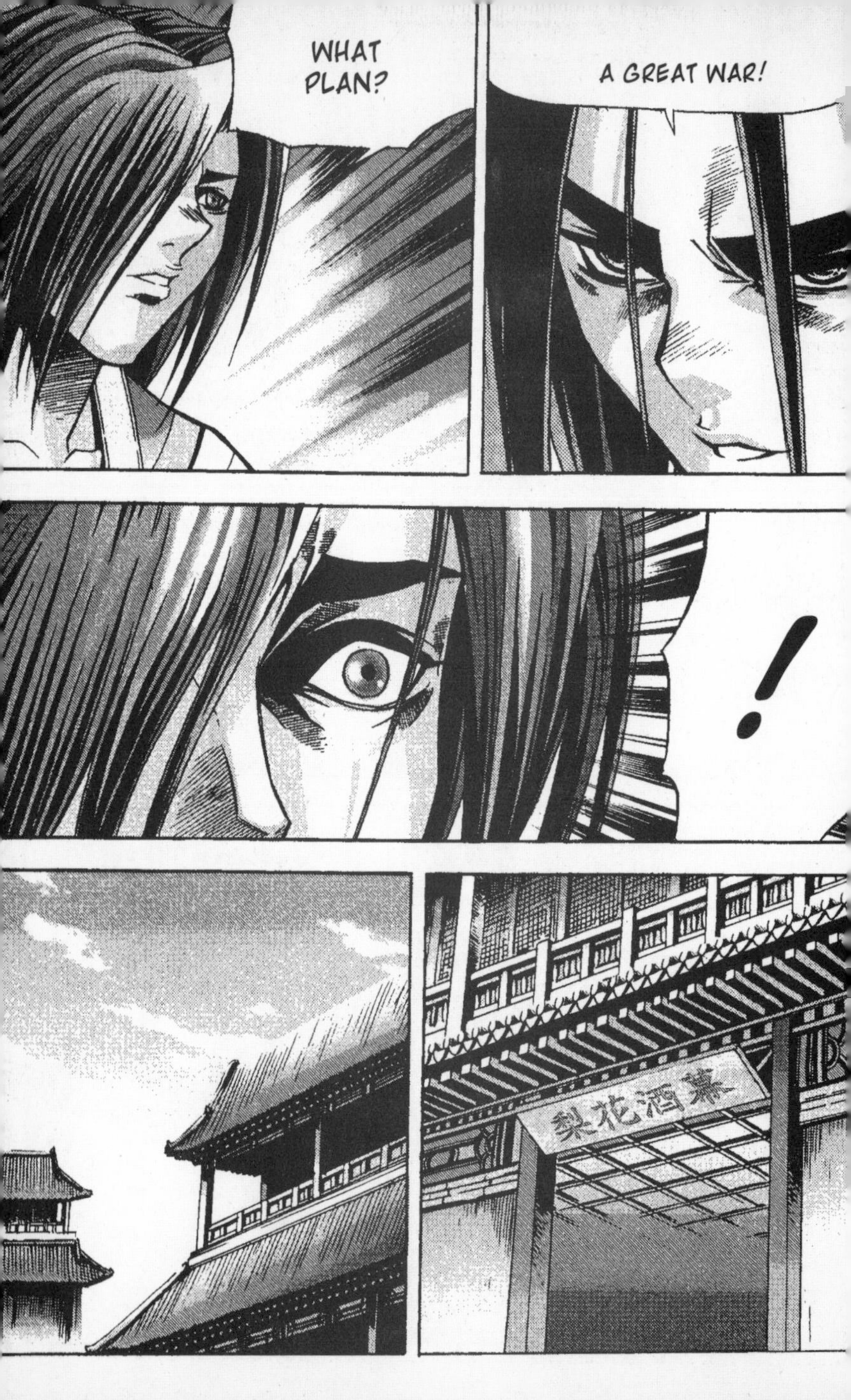
WHAT PLAN?
A GREAT WAR!
!

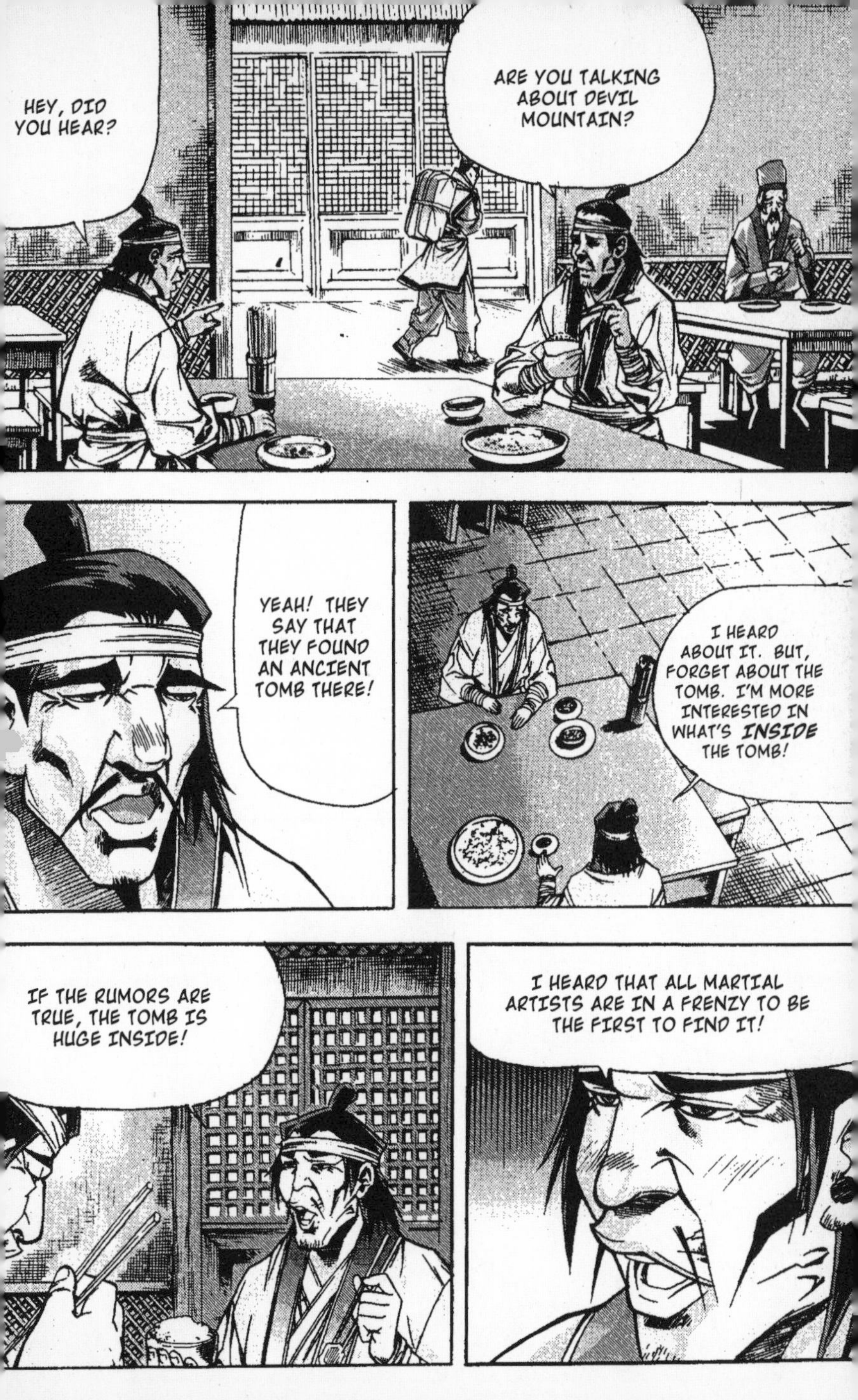
HEY, DID YOU HEAR?
ARE YOU TALKING ABOUT DEVIL MOUNTAIN?
YEAH! THEY SAY THAT THEY FOUND AN ANCIENT TOMB THERE!
I HEARD ABOUT IT. BUT, FORGET ABOUT THE TOMB. I'M MORE INTERESTED IN WHAT'S *INSIDE* THE TOMB!
IF THE RUMORS ARE TRUE, THE TOMB IS HUGE INSIDE!
I HEARD THAT ALL MARTIAL ARTISTS ARE IN A FRENZY TO BE THE FIRST TO FIND IT!

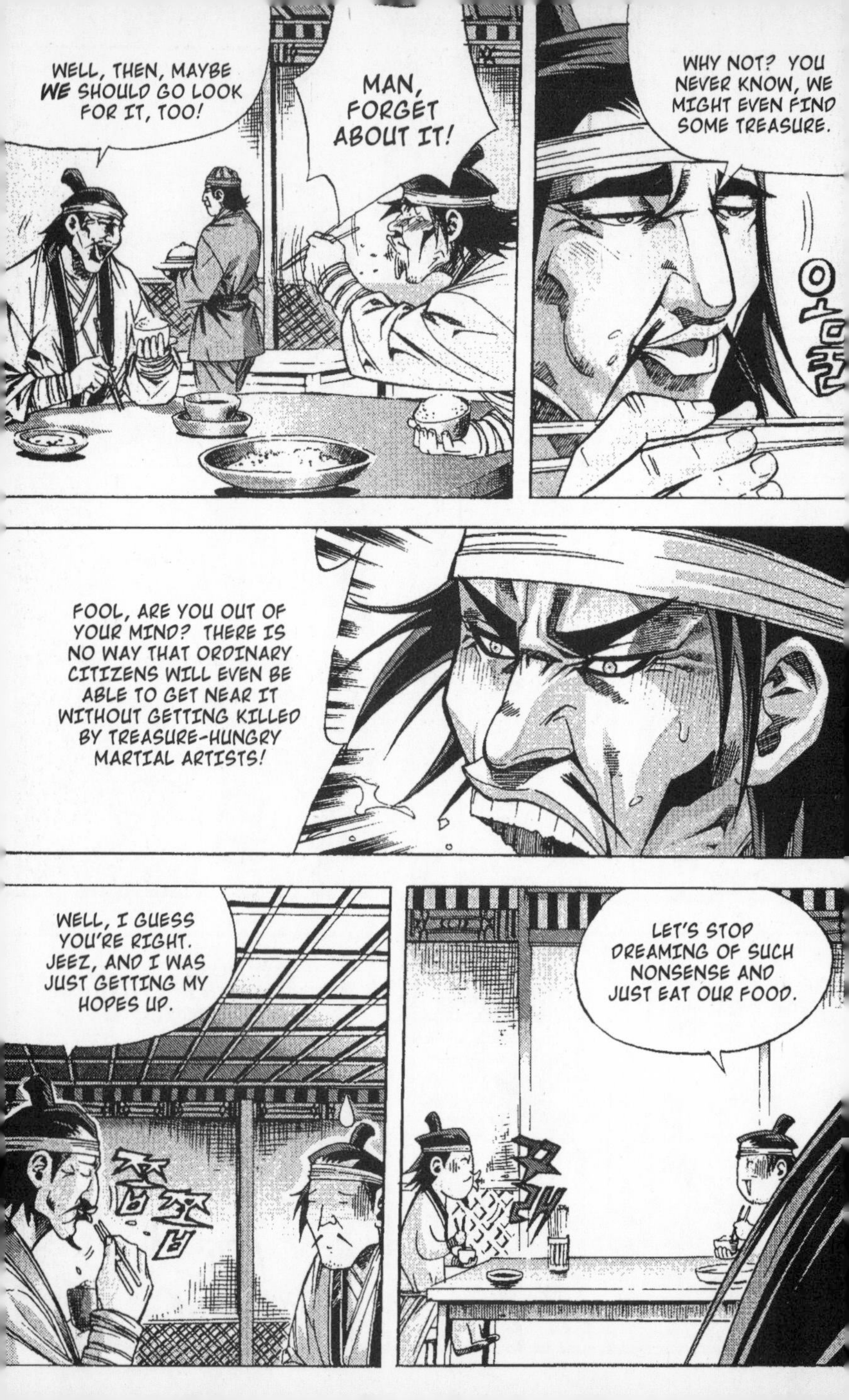

WELL, THEN, MAYBE WE SHOULD GO LOOK FOR IT, TOO!
MAN, FORGET ABOUT IT!
WHY NOT? YOU NEVER KNOW, WE MIGHT EVEN FIND SOME TREASURE.
FOOL, ARE YOU OUT OF YOUR MIND? THERE IS NO WAY THAT ORDINARY CITIZENS WILL EVEN BE ABLE TO GET NEAR IT WITHOUT GETTING KILLED BY TREASURE-HUNGRY MARTIAL ARTISTS!
WELL, I GUESS YOU'RE RIGHT. JEEZ, AND I WAS JUST GETTING MY HOPES UP.
LET'S STOP DREAMING OF SUCH NONSENSE AND JUST EAT OUR FOOD.

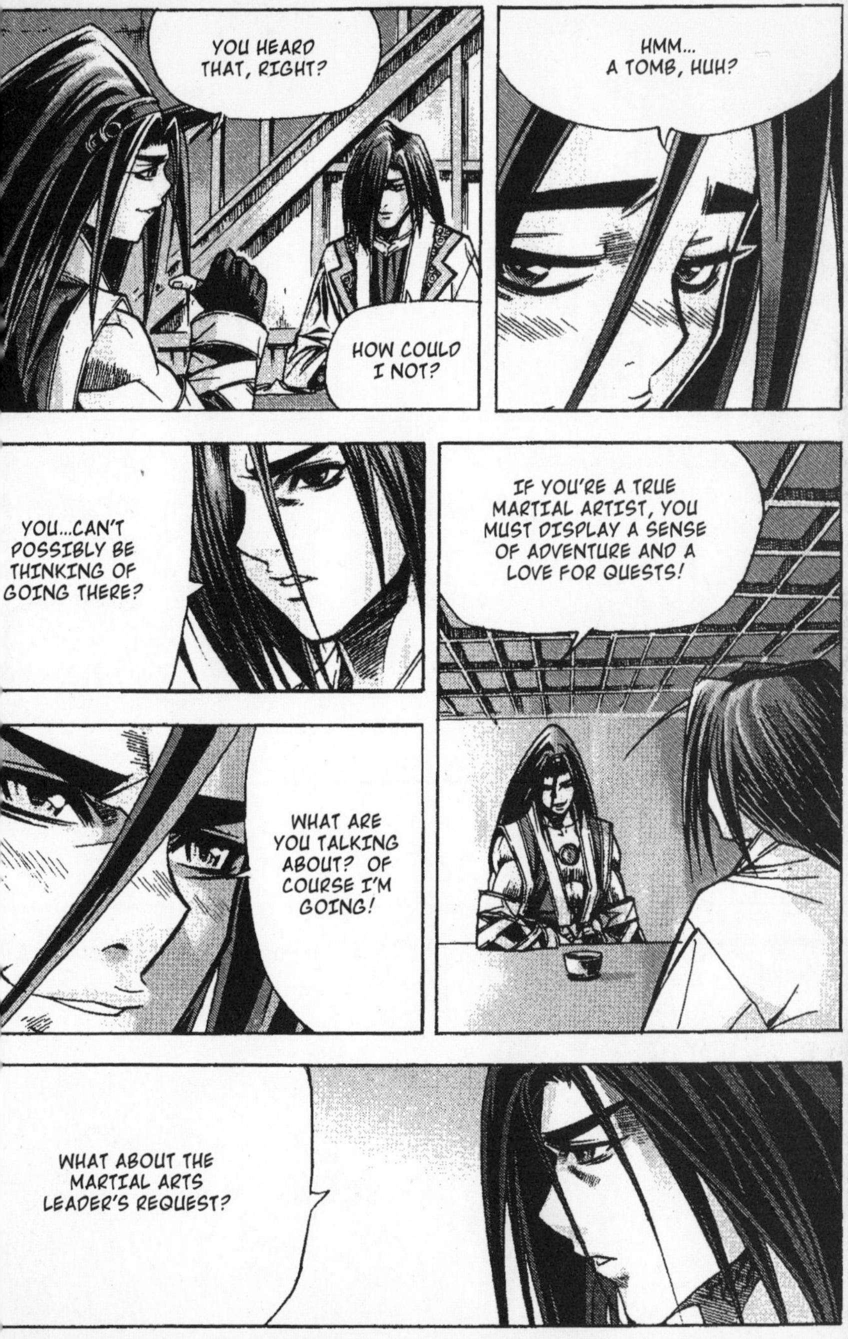
YOU HEARD THAT, RIGHT?
HOW COULD I NOT?
HMM... A TOMB, HUH?
YOU...CAN'T POSSIBLY BE THINKING OF GOING THERE?
IF YOU'RE A TRUE MARTIAL ARTIST, YOU MUST DISPLAY A SENSE OF ADVENTURE AND A LOVE FOR QUESTS!
WHAT ARE YOU TALKING ABOUT? OF COURSE I'M GOING!
WHAT ABOUT THE MARTIAL ARTS LEADER'S REQUEST?

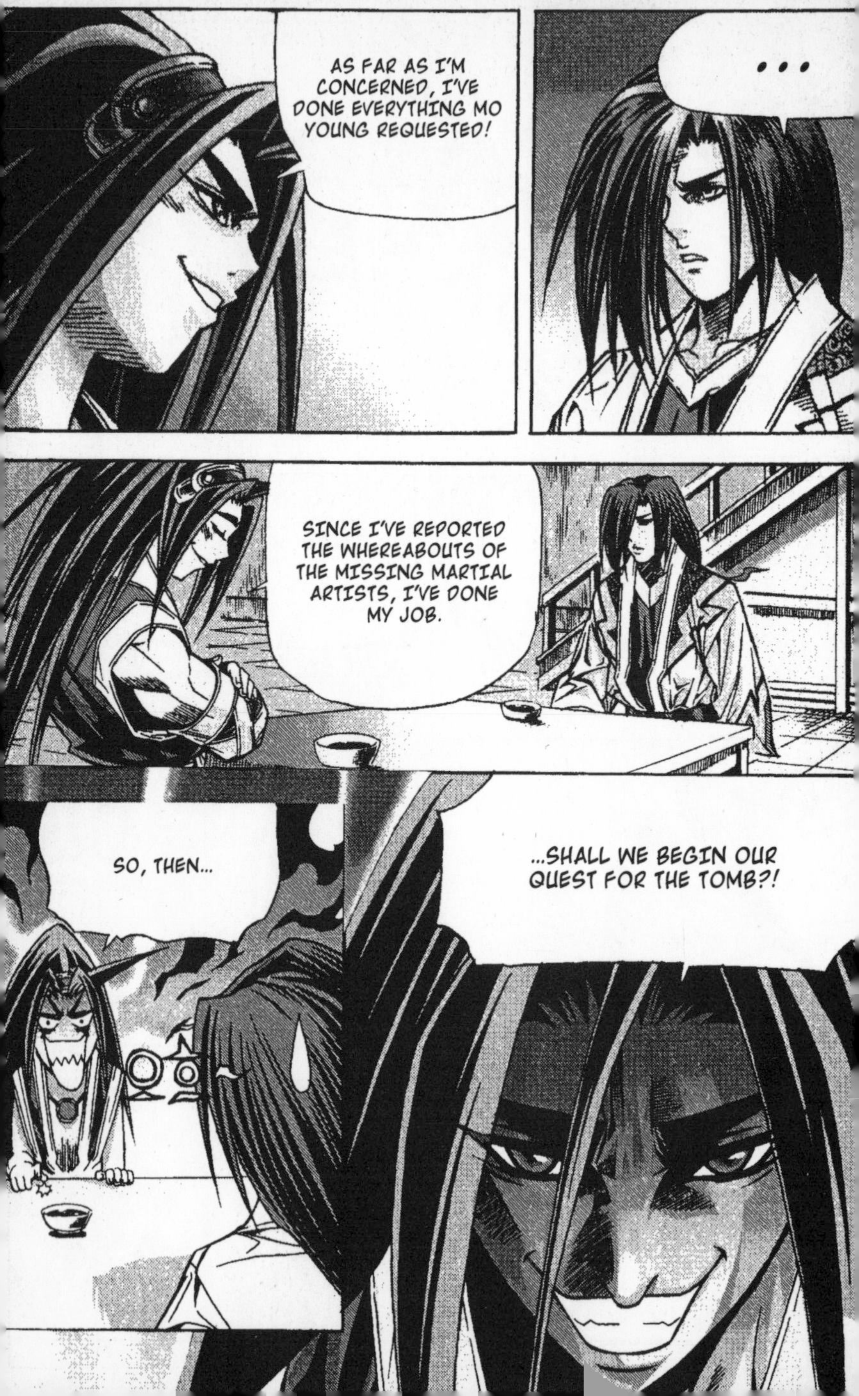
AS FAR AS I'M CONCERNED, I'VE DONE EVERYTHING MO YOUNG REQUESTED!
...
SINCE I'VE REPORTED THE WHEREABOUTS OF THE MISSING MARTIAL ARTISTS, I'VE DONE MY JOB.
SO, THEN...
...SHALL WE BEGIN OUR QUEST FOR THE TOMB?!

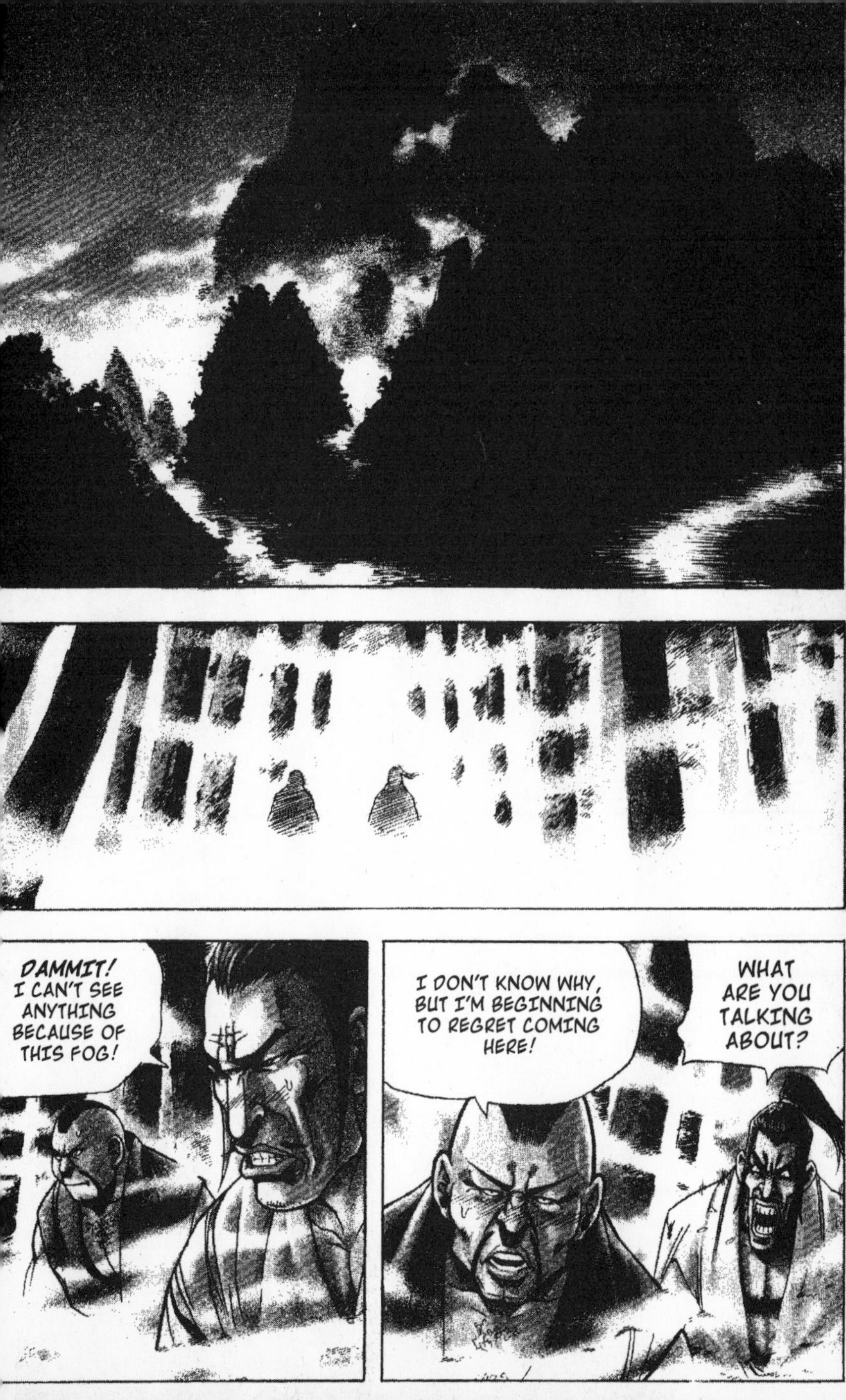
DAMMIT! I CAN'T SEE ANYTHING BECAUSE OF THIS FOG!
I DON'T KNOW WHY, BUT I'M BEGINNING TO REGRET COMING HERE!
WHAT ARE YOU TALKING ABOUT?

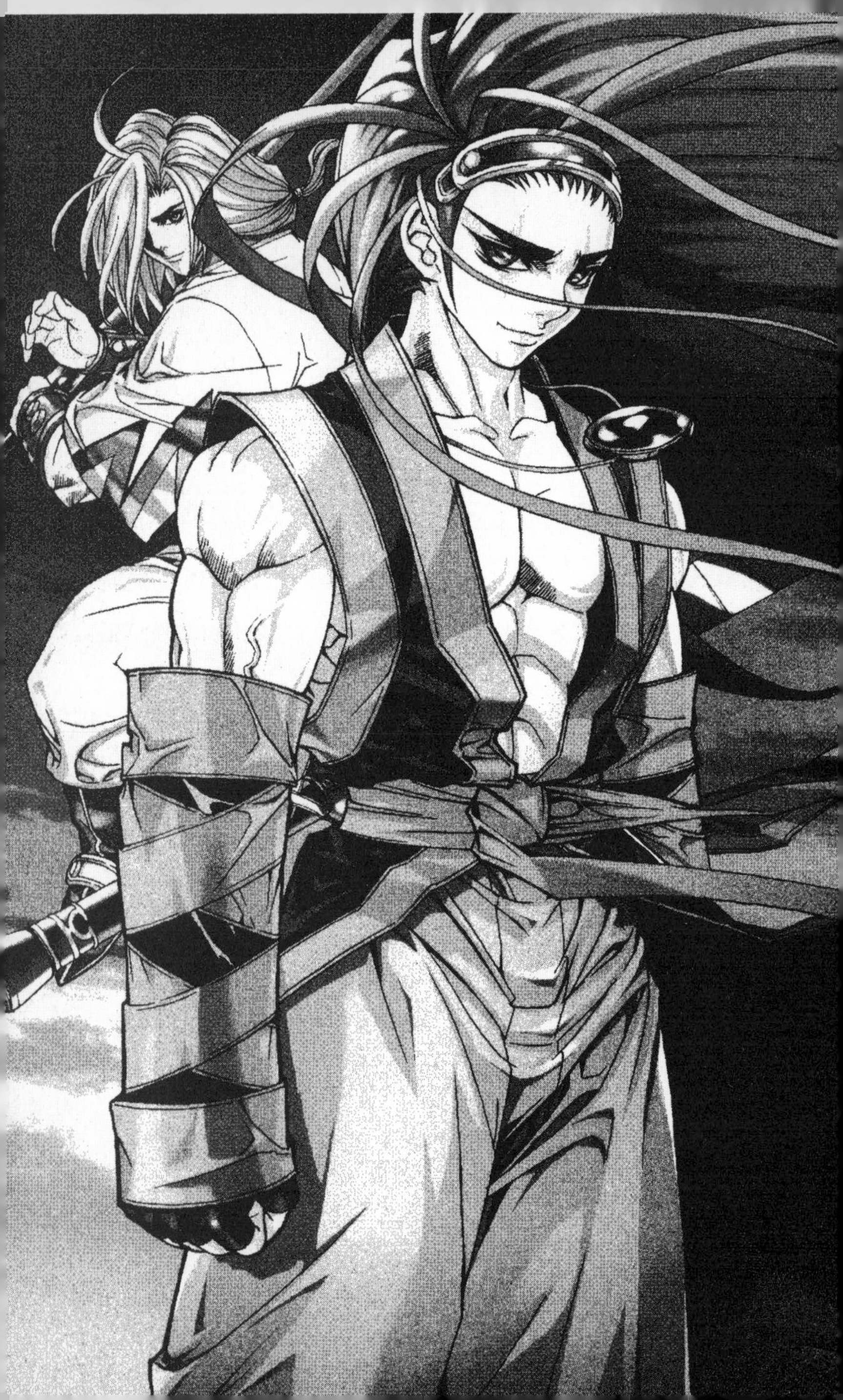

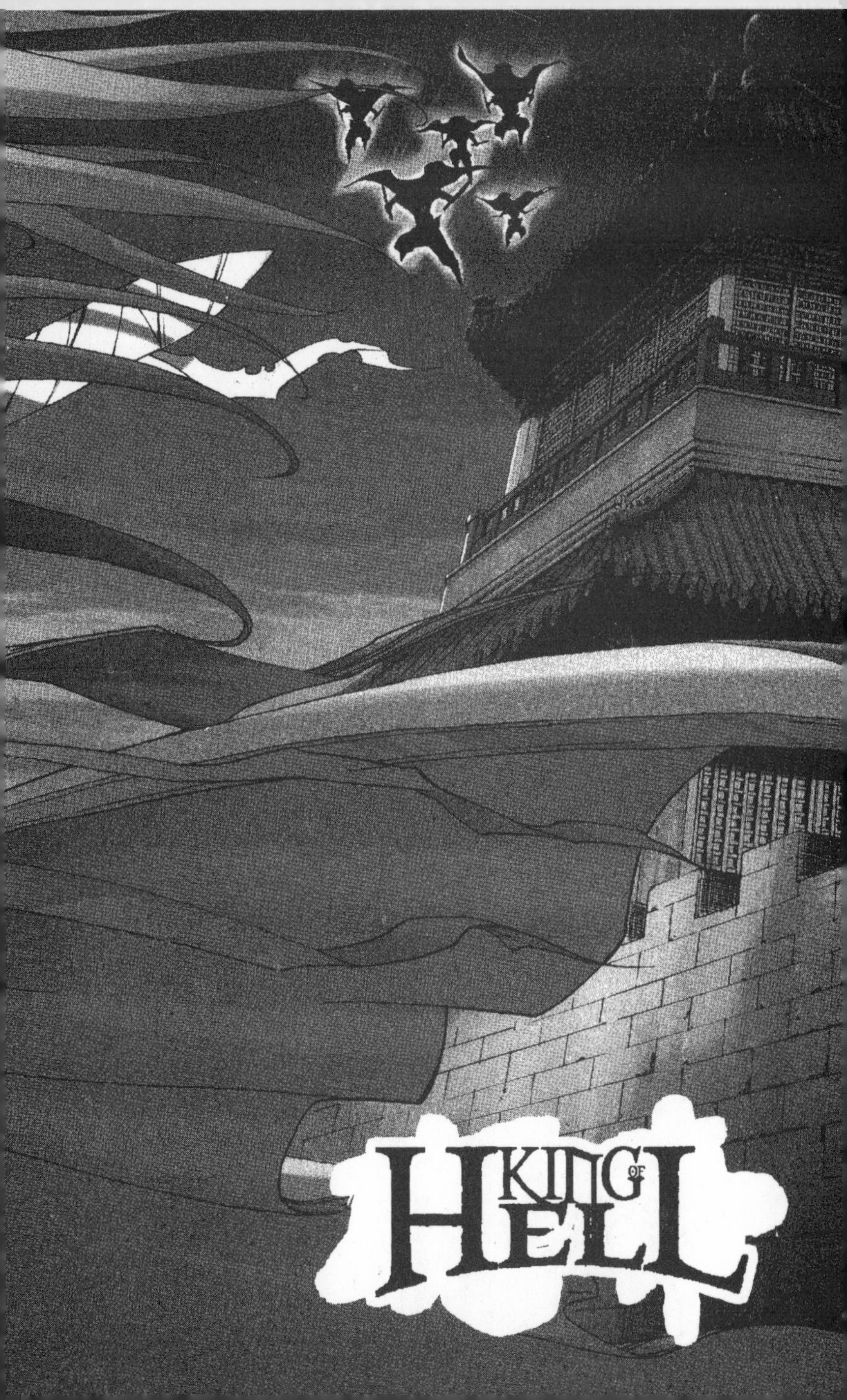
KING OF HELL

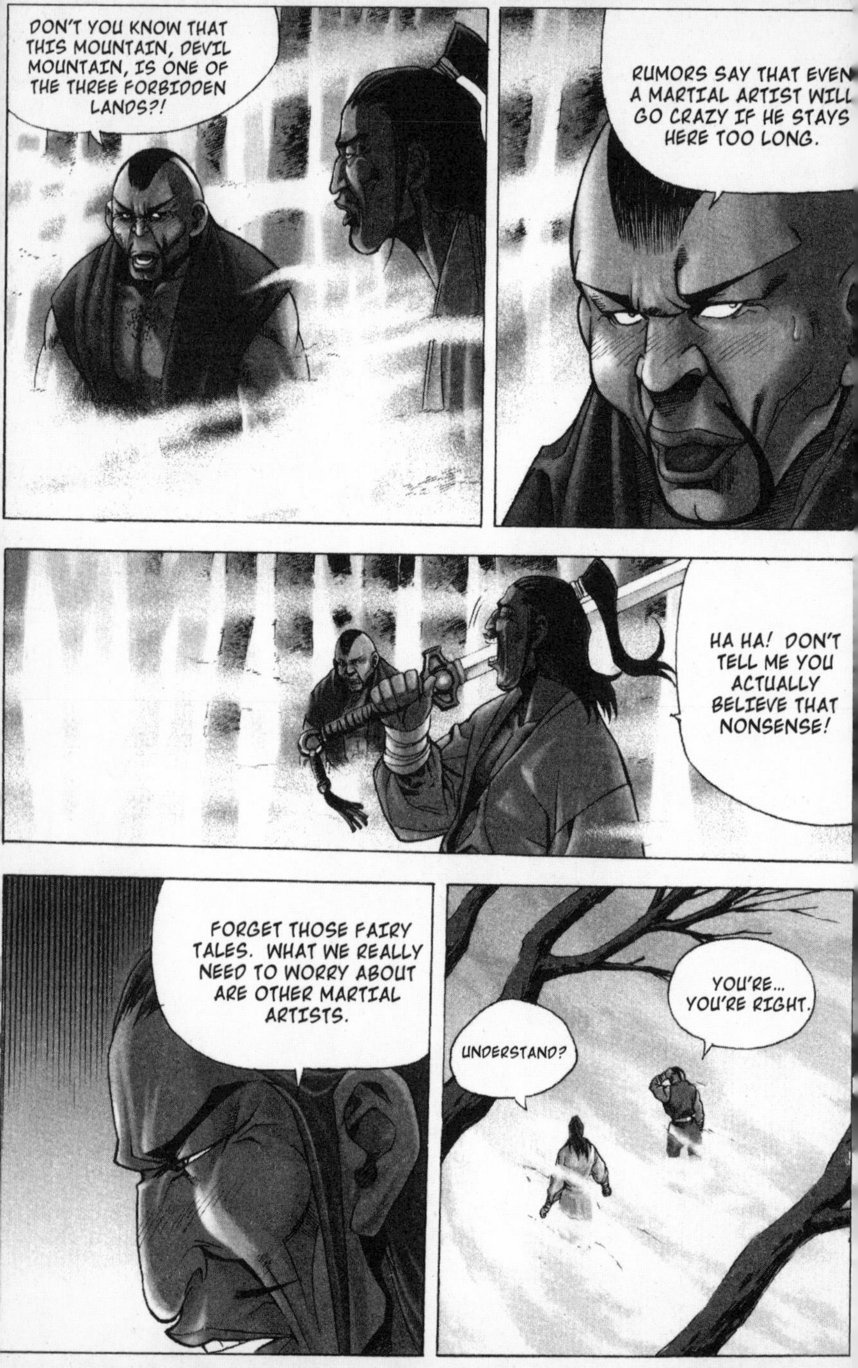
DON'T YOU KNOW THAT THIS MOUNTAIN, DEVIL MOUNTAIN, IS ONE OF THE THREE FORBIDDEN LANDS?!
RUMORS SAY THAT EVEN A MARTIAL ARTIST WILL GO CRAZY IF HE STAYS HERE TOO LONG.
HA HA! DON'T TELL ME YOU ACTUALLY BELIEVE THAT NONSENSE!
FORGET THOSE FAIRY TALES. WHAT WE REALLY NEED TO WORRY ABOUT ARE OTHER MARTIAL ARTISTS.
UNDERSTAND?
YOU'RE... YOU'RE RIGHT.

FOR WORKING WARRIORS LIKE US, A MARTIAL ARTIST, HUNGRY FOR TREASURE IS MORE DANGEROUS THAN ANYTHING.

THAT'S TRUE. WE SHOULD BE ON OUR GUARD. IF WE'RE NOT CAREFUL, WE MIGHT BE IN DANGER OF BECOMING LIKE TWO FLIES ON A FLY SWATTER!

WHAT'S THIS? IS IT BEGINNING TO RAIN?

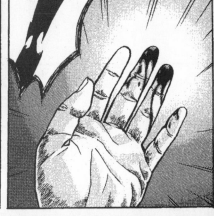

BLOOD!

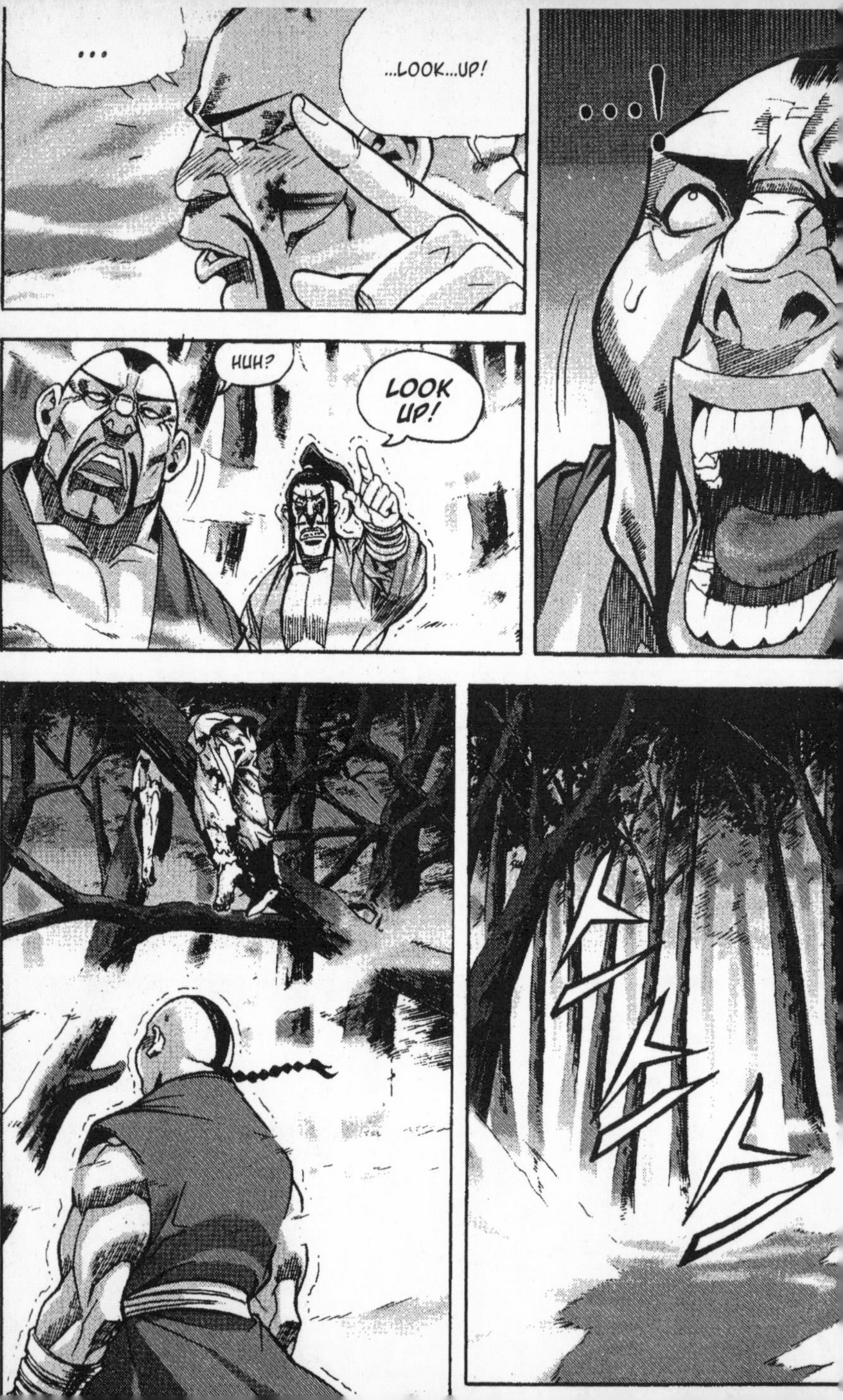
...
...LOOK...UP!
HUH?
LOOK UP!
...!

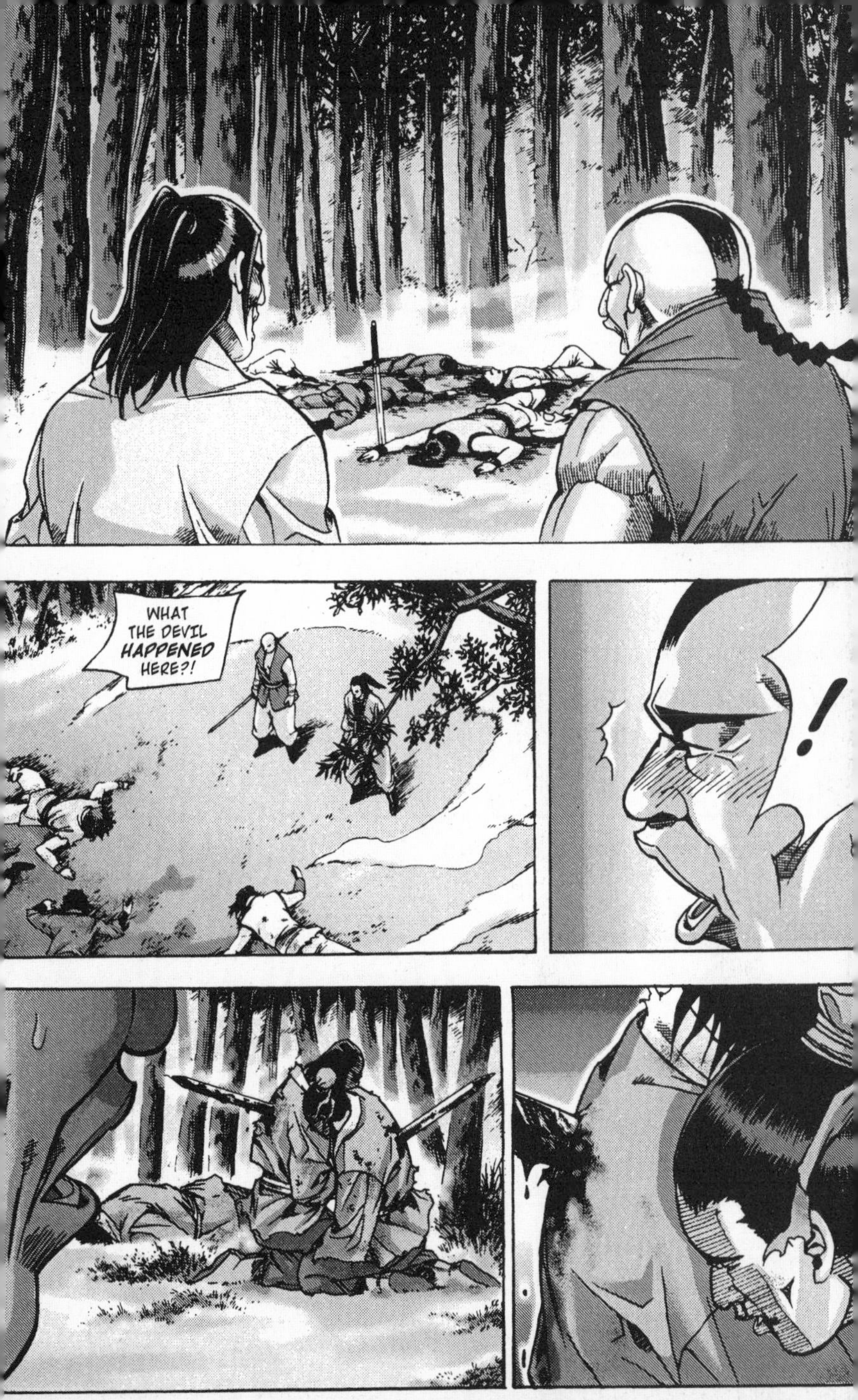
WHAT THE DEVIL HAPPENED HERE?!
!

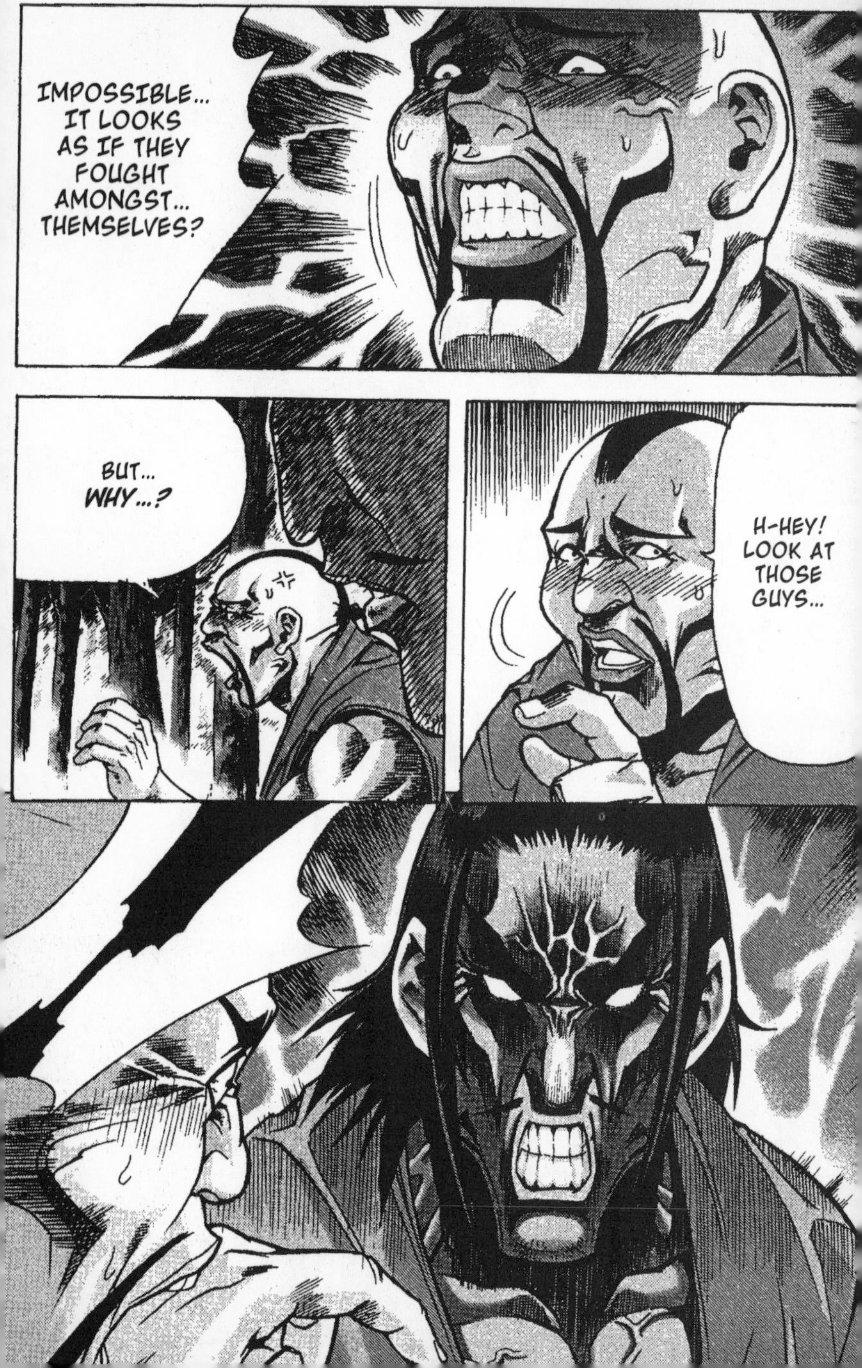
IMPOSSIBLE... IT LOOKS AS IF THEY FOUGHT AMONGST... THEMSELVES?
BUT... WHY...?
H-HEY! LOOK AT THOSE GUYS...

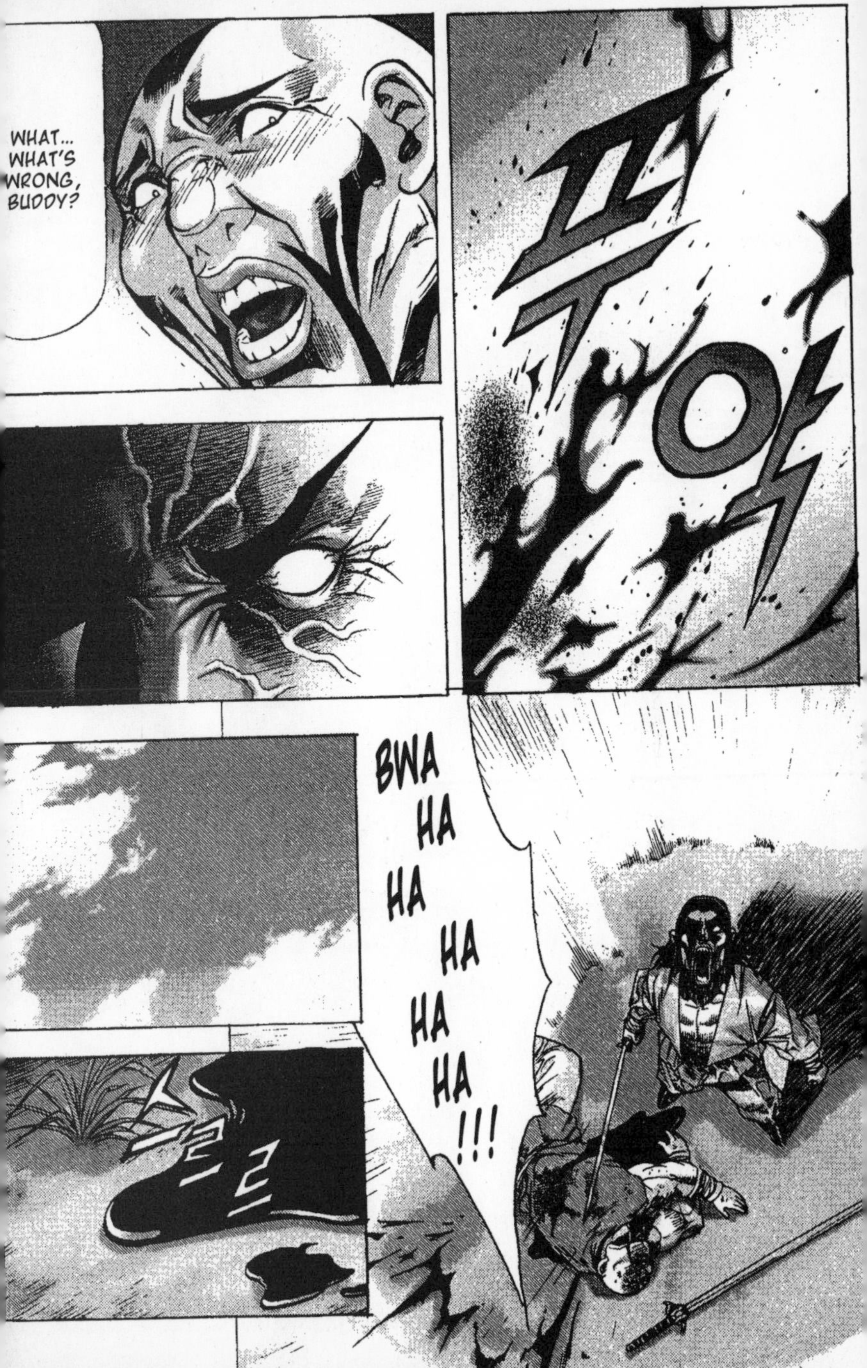
WHAT... WHAT'S WRONG, BUDDY?
BWA HA HA HA HA HA!!!

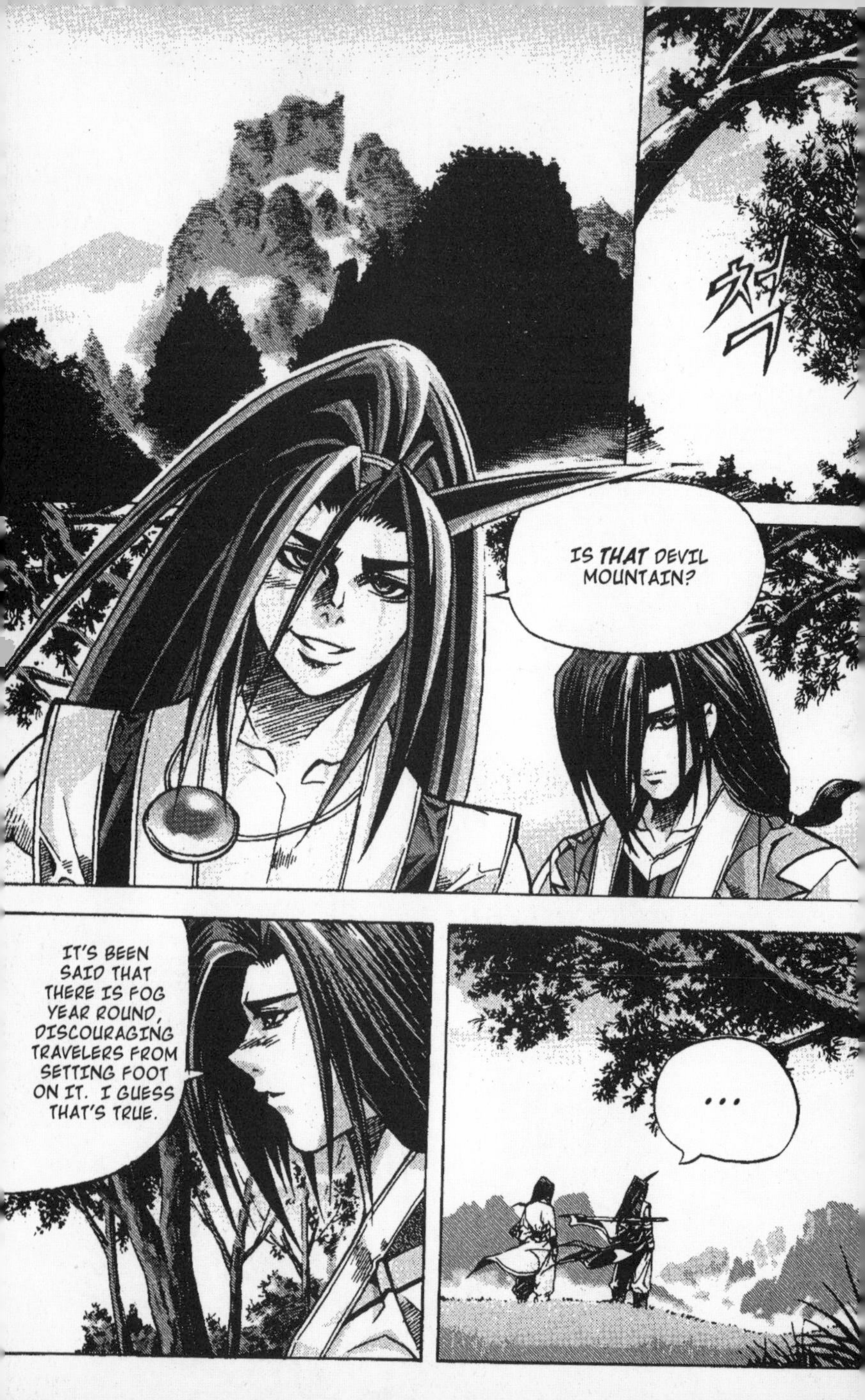
IS THAT DEVIL MOUNTAIN?
IT'S BEEN SAID THAT THERE IS FOG YEAR ROUND, DISCOURAGING TRAVELERS FROM SETTING FOOT ON IT. I GUESS THAT'S TRUE.
...

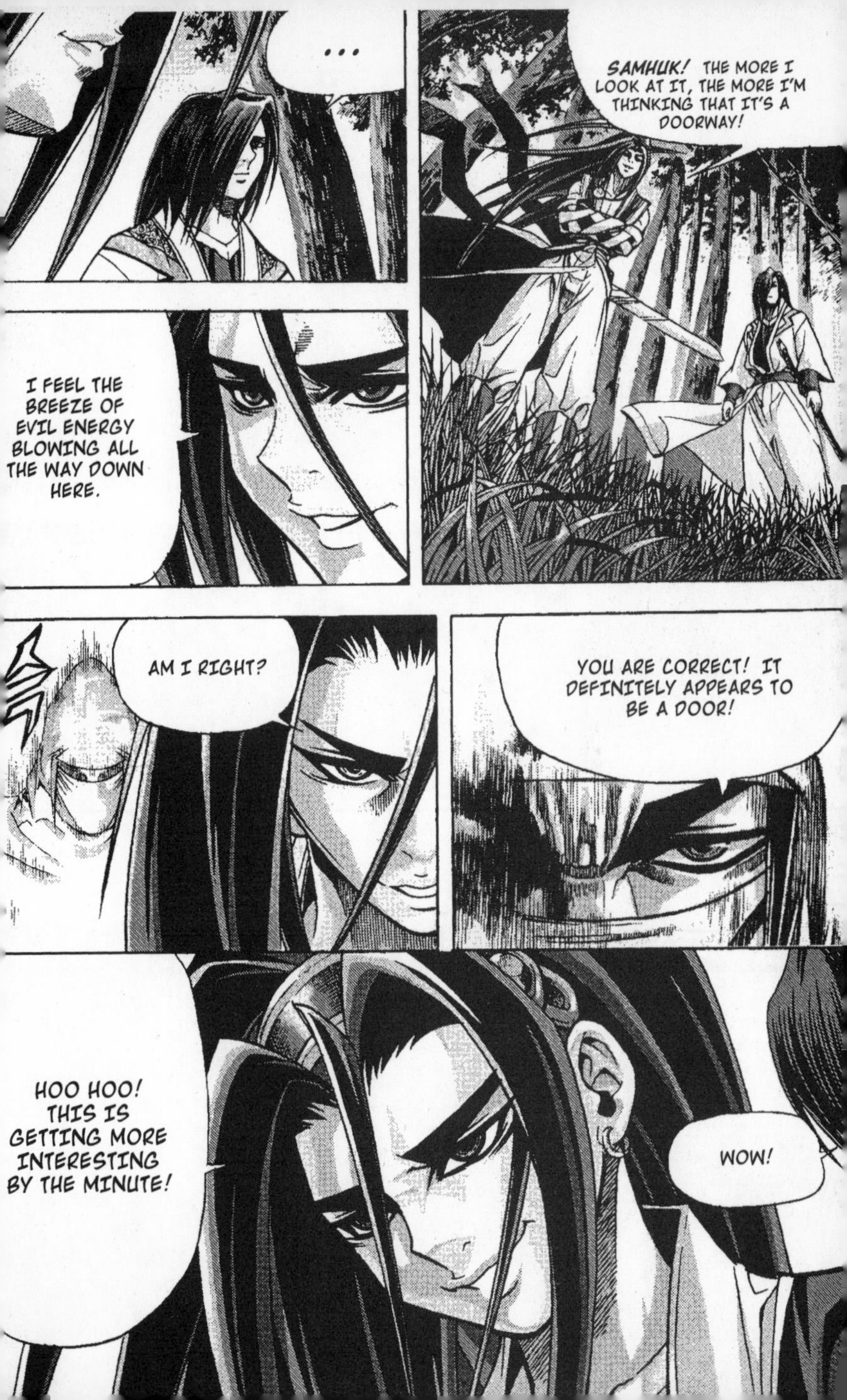
...
SAMHUK! THE MORE I LOOK AT IT, THE MORE I'M THINKING THAT IT'S A DOORWAY!
I FEEL THE BREEZE OF EVIL ENERGY BLOWING ALL THE WAY DOWN HERE.
AM I RIGHT?
YOU ARE CORRECT! IT DEFINITELY APPEARS TO BE A DOOR!
HOO HOO! THIS IS GETTING MORE INTERESTING BY THE MINUTE!
WOW!

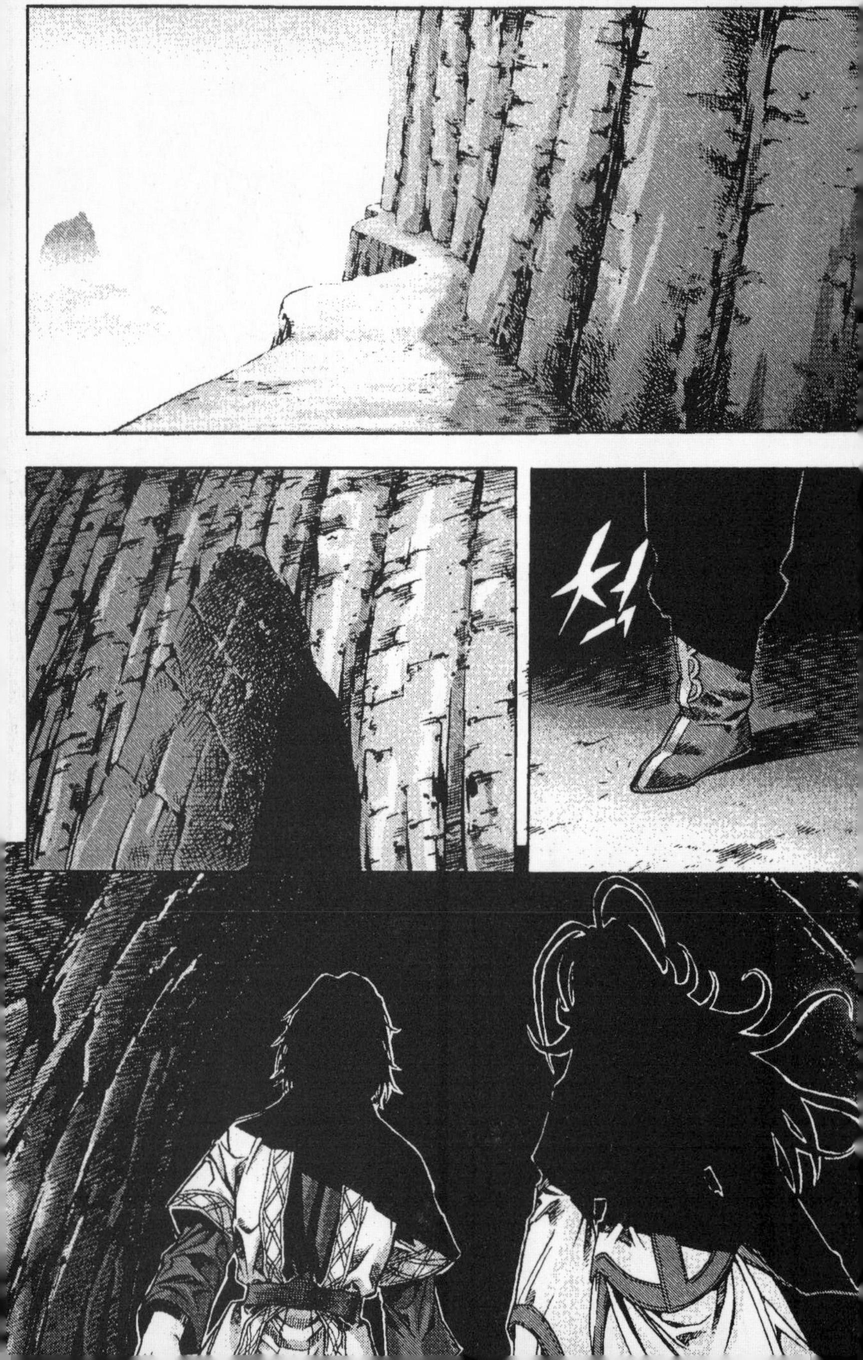

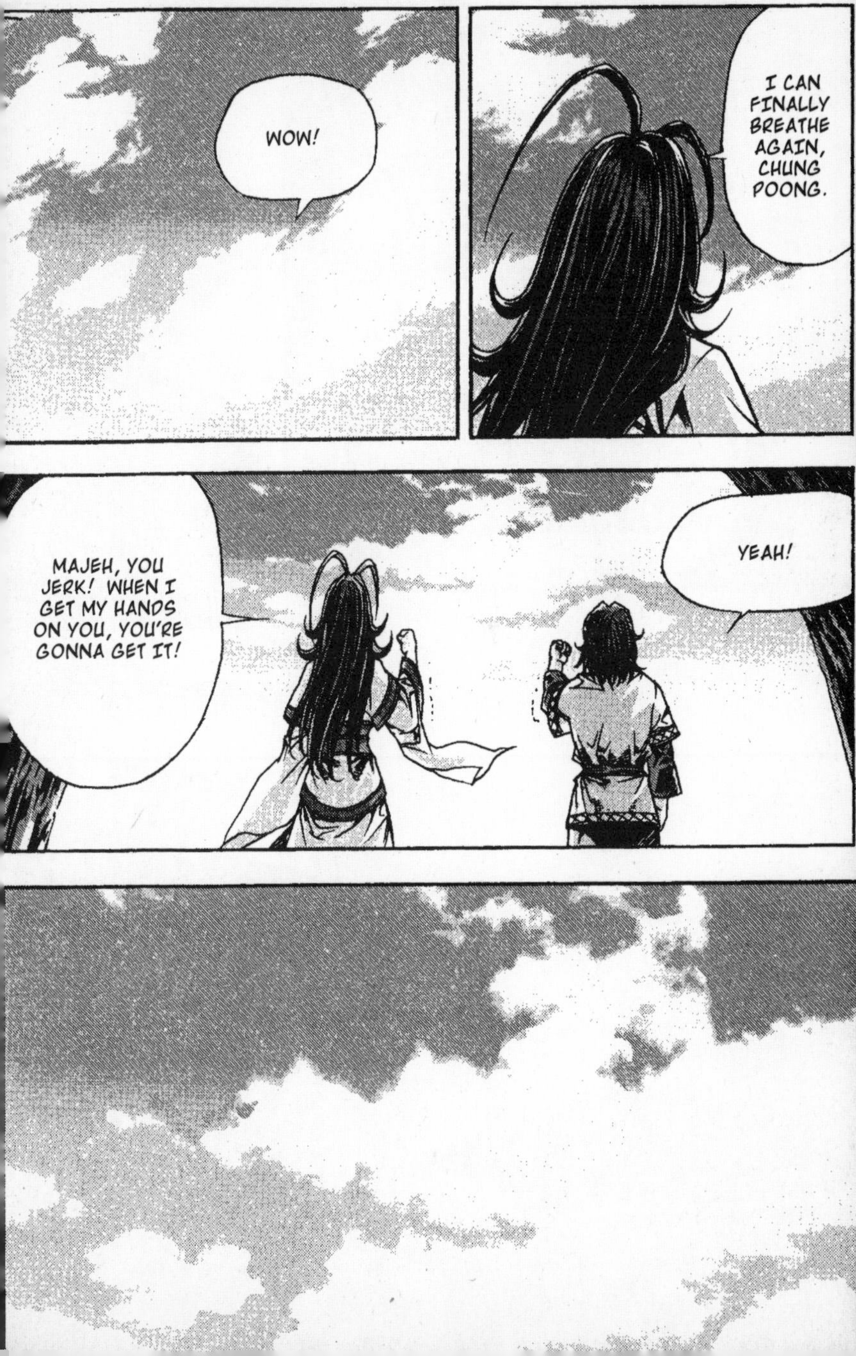
WOW!
I CAN FINALLY BREATHE AGAIN, CHUNG POONG.
MAJEH, YOU JERK! WHEN I GET MY HANDS ON YOU, YOU'RE GONNA GET IT!
YEAH!

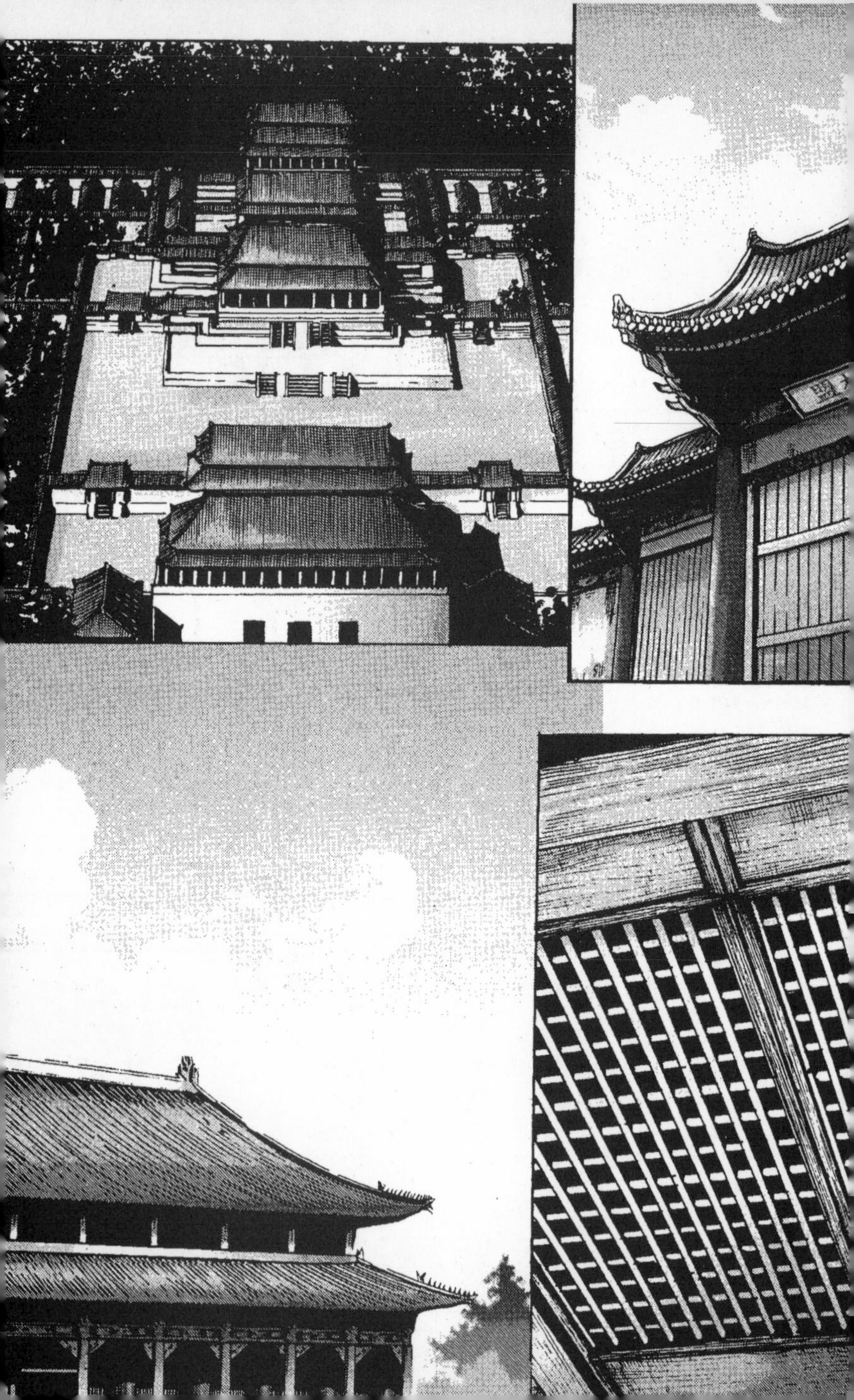

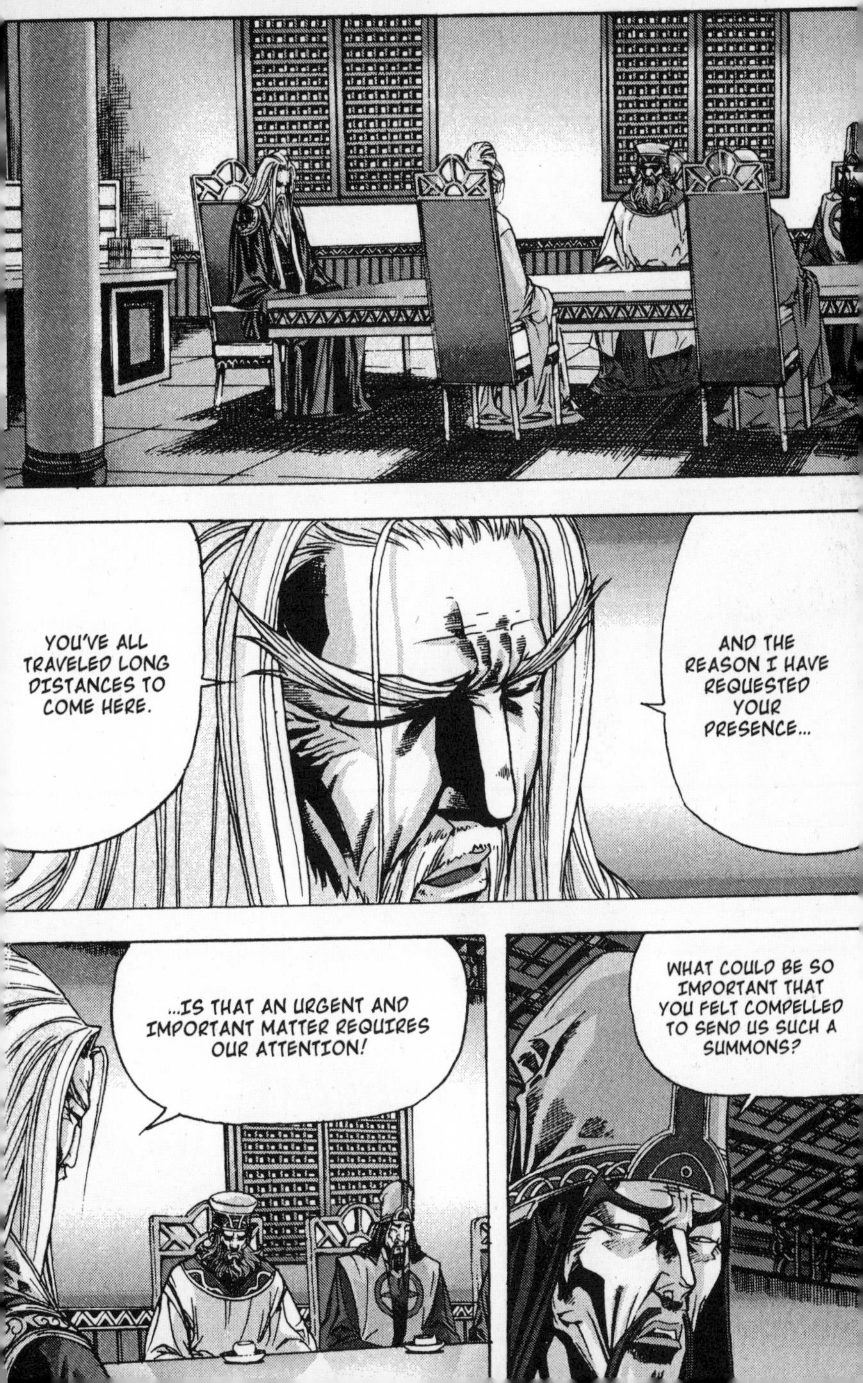
YOU'VE ALL TRAVELED LONG DISTANCES TO COME HERE.
AND THE REASON I HAVE REQUESTED YOUR PRESENCE...
...IS THAT AN URGENT AND IMPORTANT MATTER REQUIRES OUR ATTENTION!
WHAT COULD BE SO IMPORTANT THAT YOU FELT COMPELLED TO SEND US SUCH A SUMMONS?

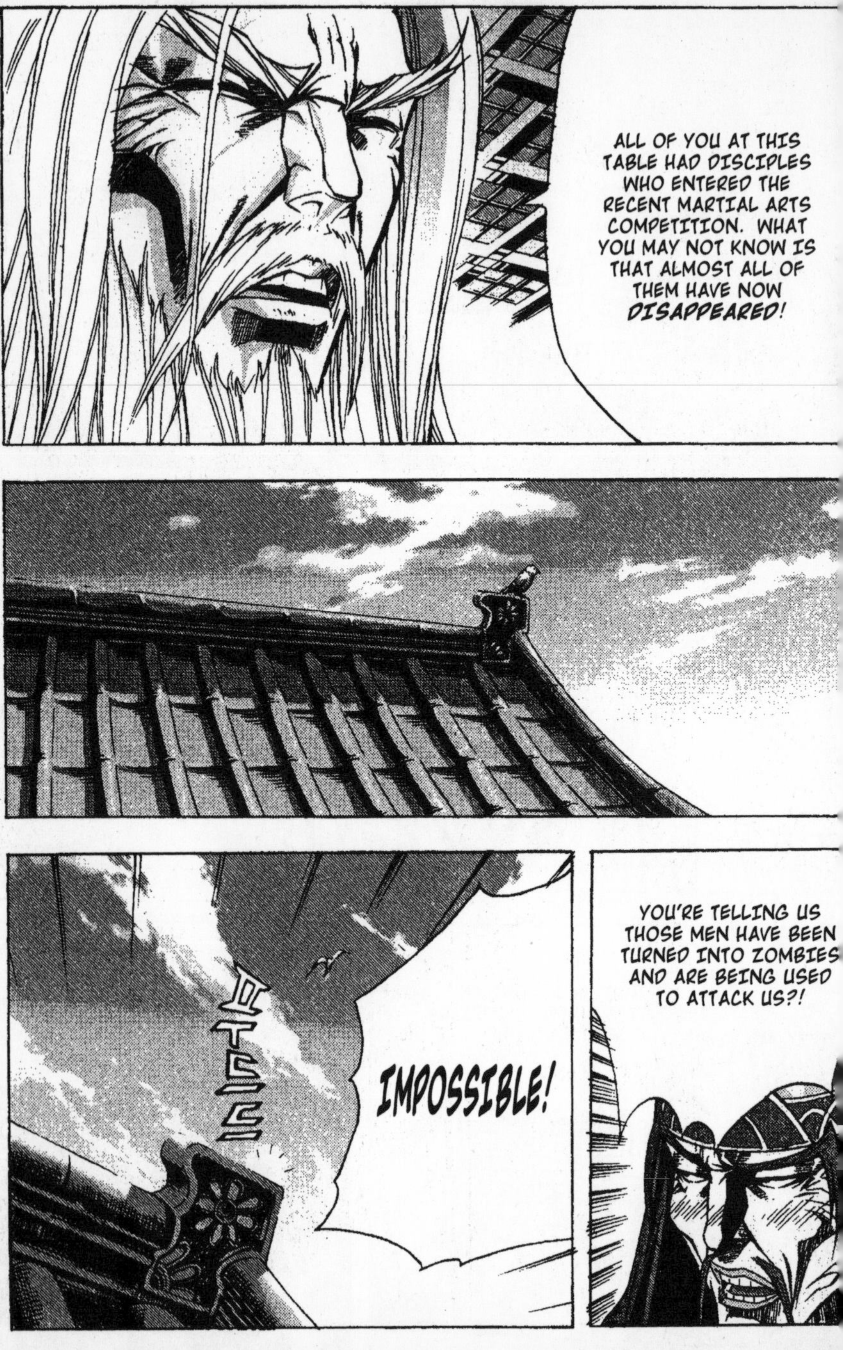
ALL OF YOU AT THIS TABLE HAD DISCIPLES WHO ENTERED THE RECENT MARTIAL ARTS COMPETITION. WHAT YOU MAY NOT KNOW IS THAT ALMOST ALL OF THEM HAVE NOW DISAPPEARED!
IMPOSSIBLE!
YOU'RE TELLING US THOSE MEN HAVE BEEN TURNED INTO ZOMBIES AND ARE BEING USED TO ATTACK US?!

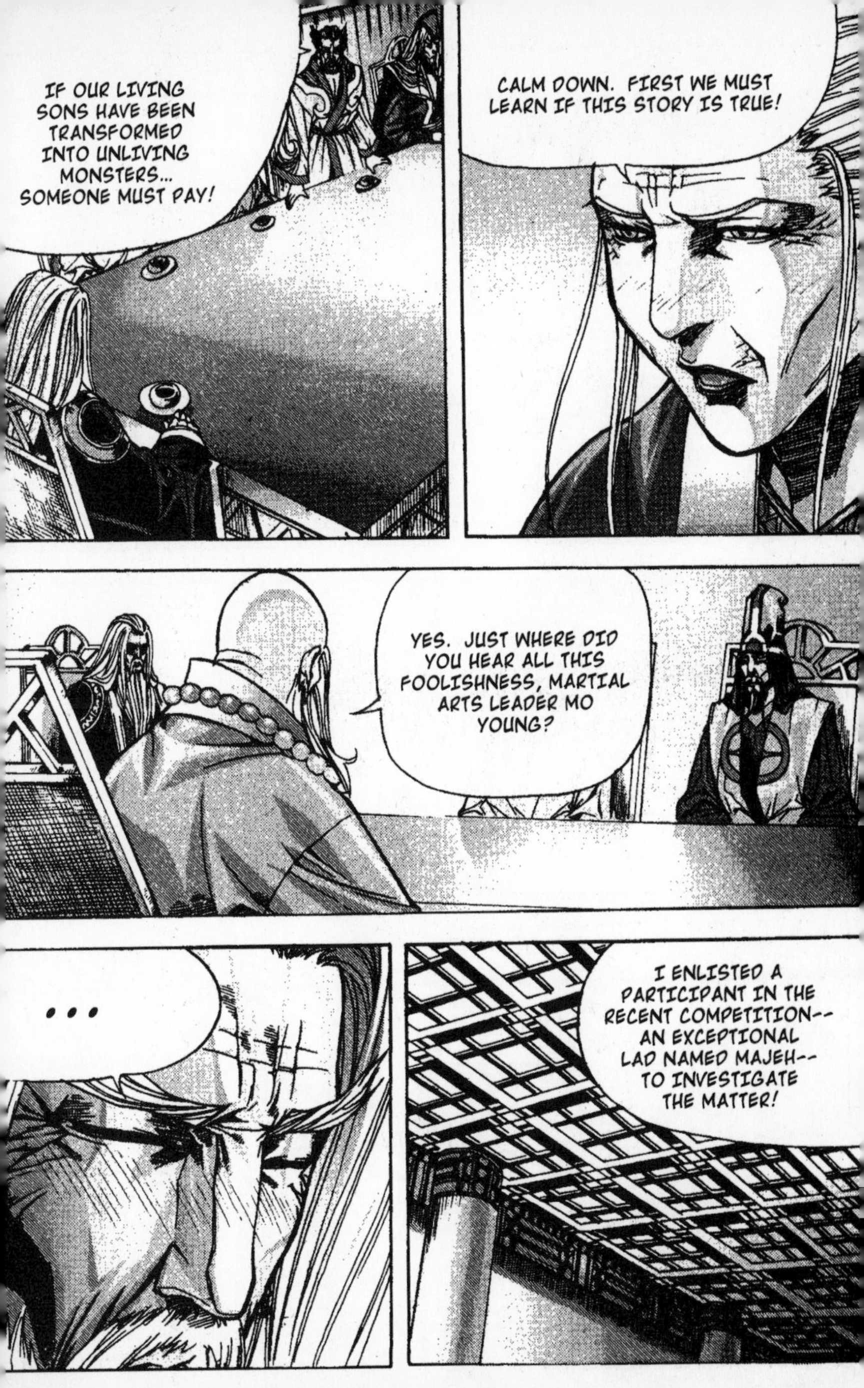
IF OUR LIVING SONS HAVE BEEN TRANSFORMED INTO UNLIVING MONSTERS... SOMEONE MUST PAY!
CALM DOWN. FIRST WE MUST LEARN IF THIS STORY IS TRUE!
YES. JUST WHERE DID YOU HEAR ALL THIS FOOLISHNESS, MARTIAL ARTS LEADER MO YOUNG?
...
I ENLISTED A PARTICIPANT IN THE RECENT COMPETITION--AN EXCEPTIONAL LAD NAMED MAJEH--TO INVESTIGATE THE MATTER!

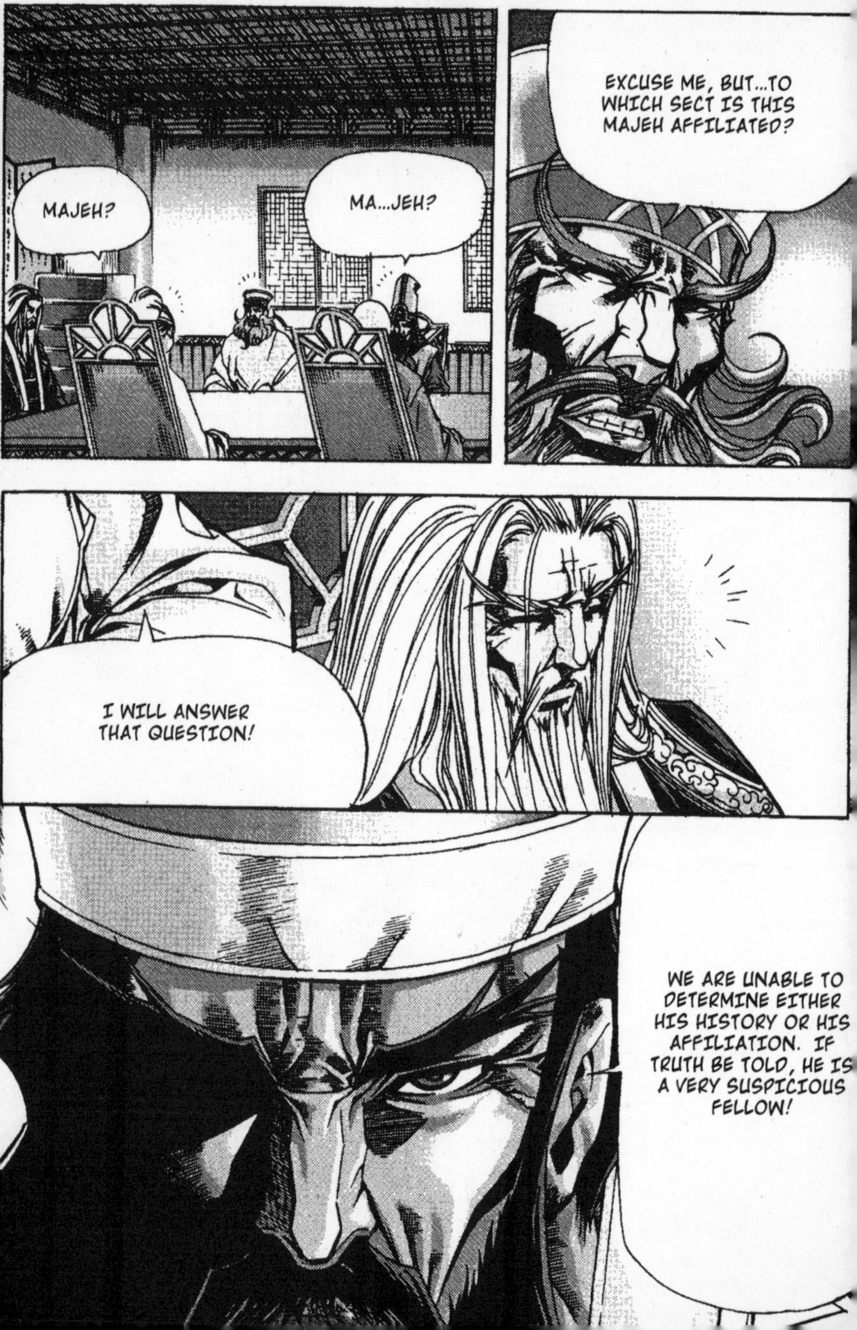
MAJEH?
MA...JEH?
EXCUSE ME, BUT...TO WHICH SECT IS THIS MAJEH AFFILIATED?
I WILL ANSWER THAT QUESTION!
WE ARE UNABLE TO DETERMINE EITHER HIS HISTORY OR HIS AFFILIATION. IF TRUTH BE TOLD, HE IS A VERY SUSPICIOUS FELLOW!

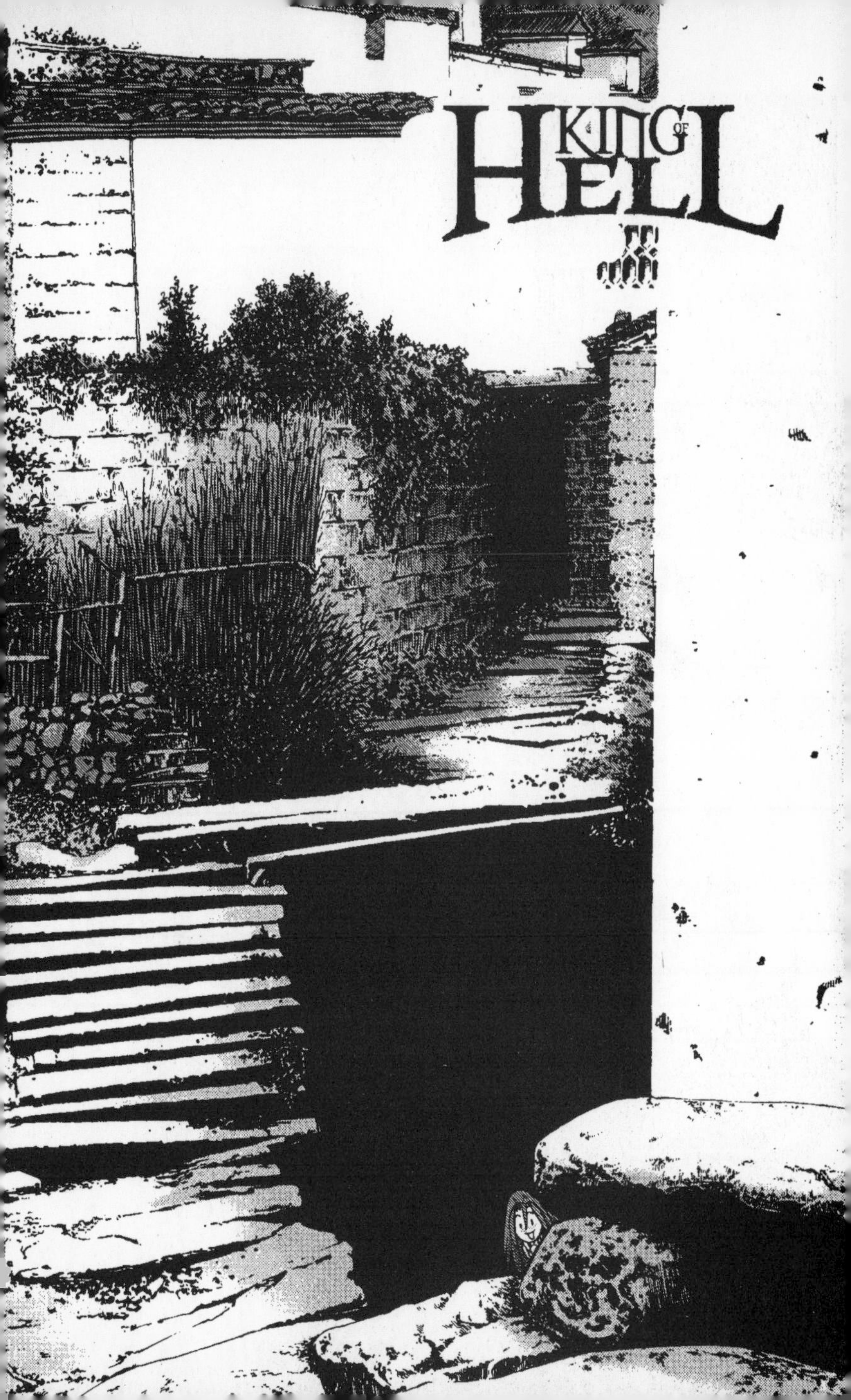
KING OF HELL

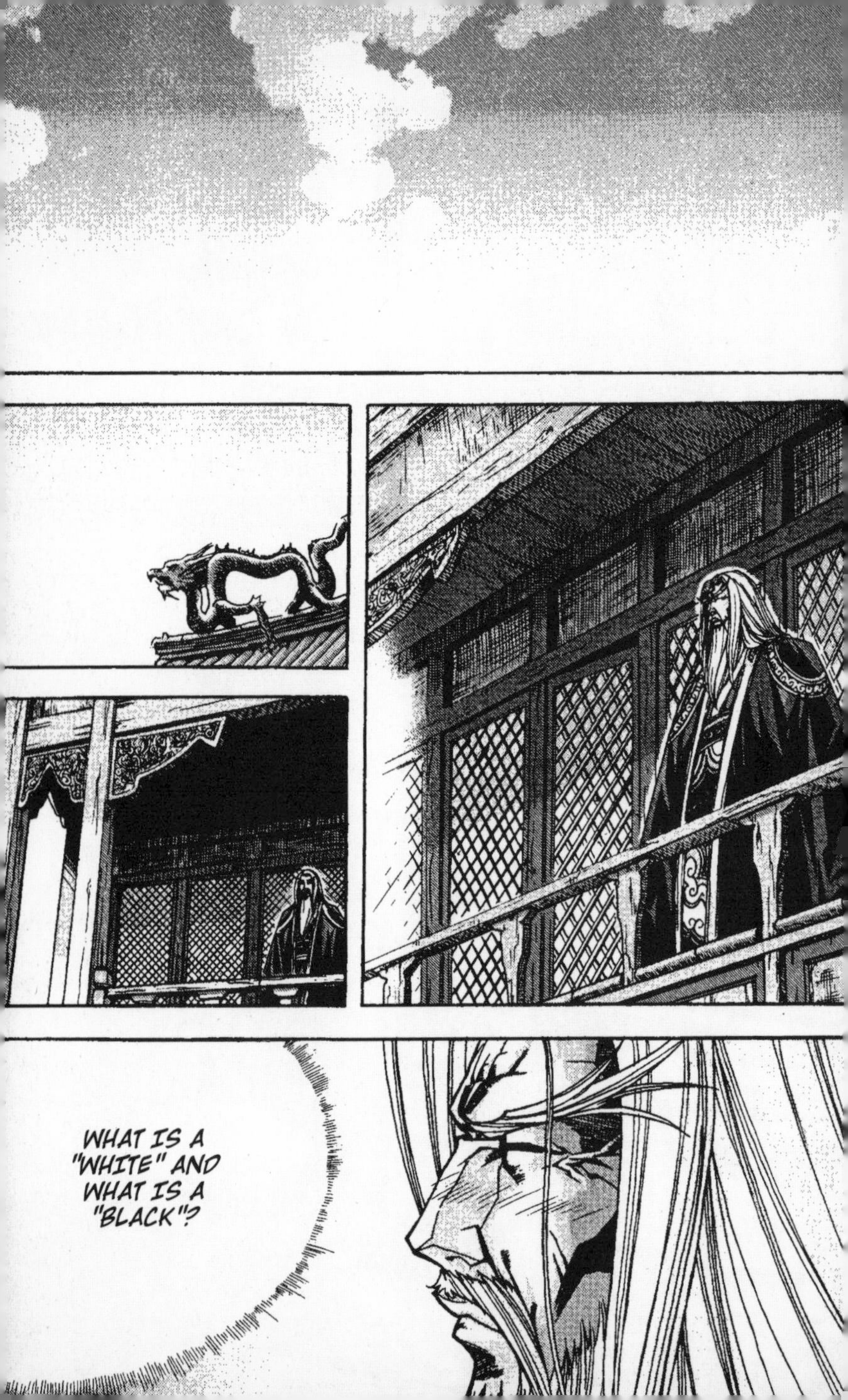
WHAT IS A "WHITE" AND WHAT IS A "BLACK"?

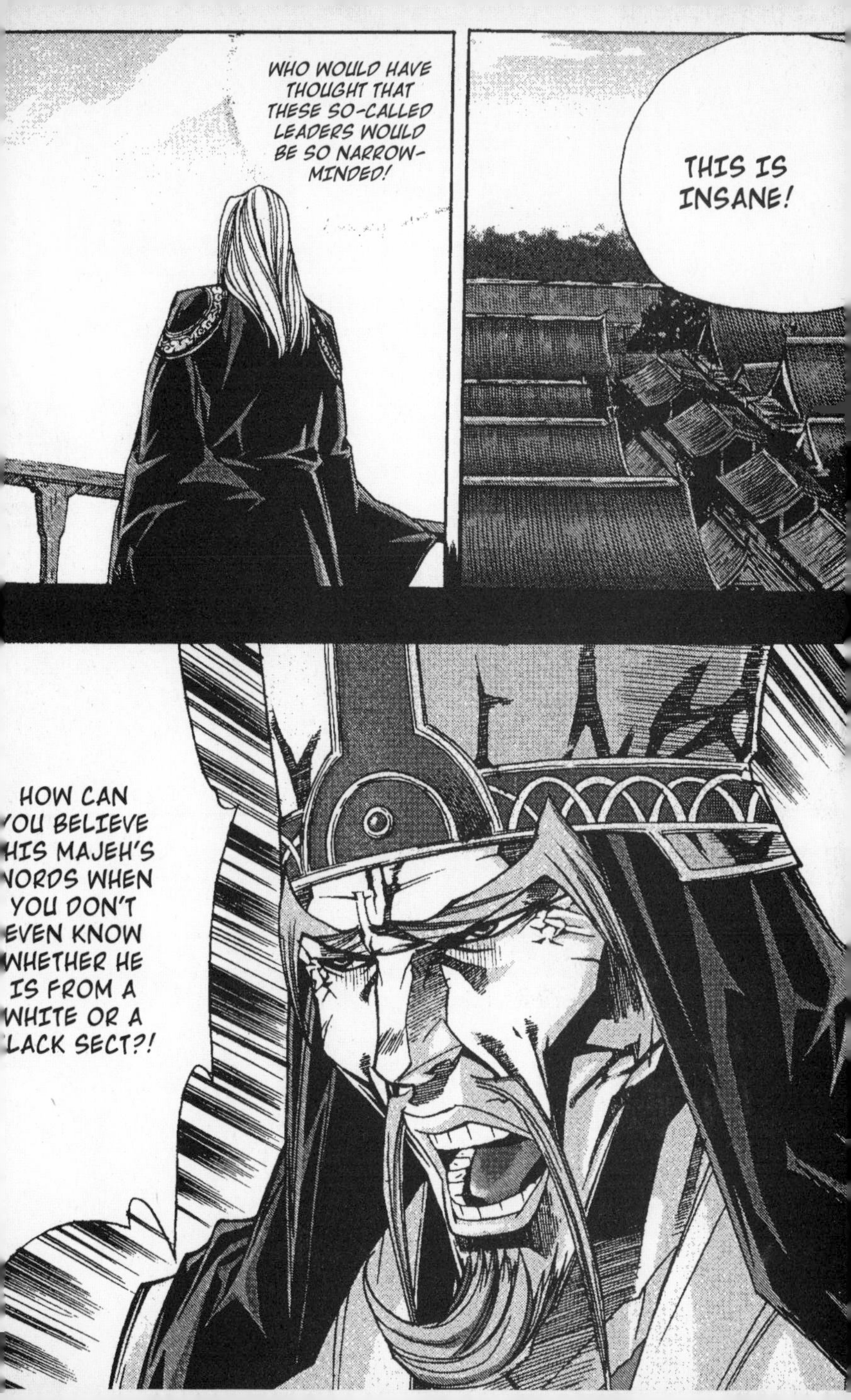
THIS IS INSANE!
WHO WOULD HAVE THOUGHT THAT THESE SO-CALLED LEADERS WOULD BE SO NARROW-MINDED!
HOW CAN 'OU BELIEVE HIS MAJEH'S VORDS WHEN YOU DON'T EVEN KNOW WHETHER HE IS FROM A WHITE OR A LACK SECT?!

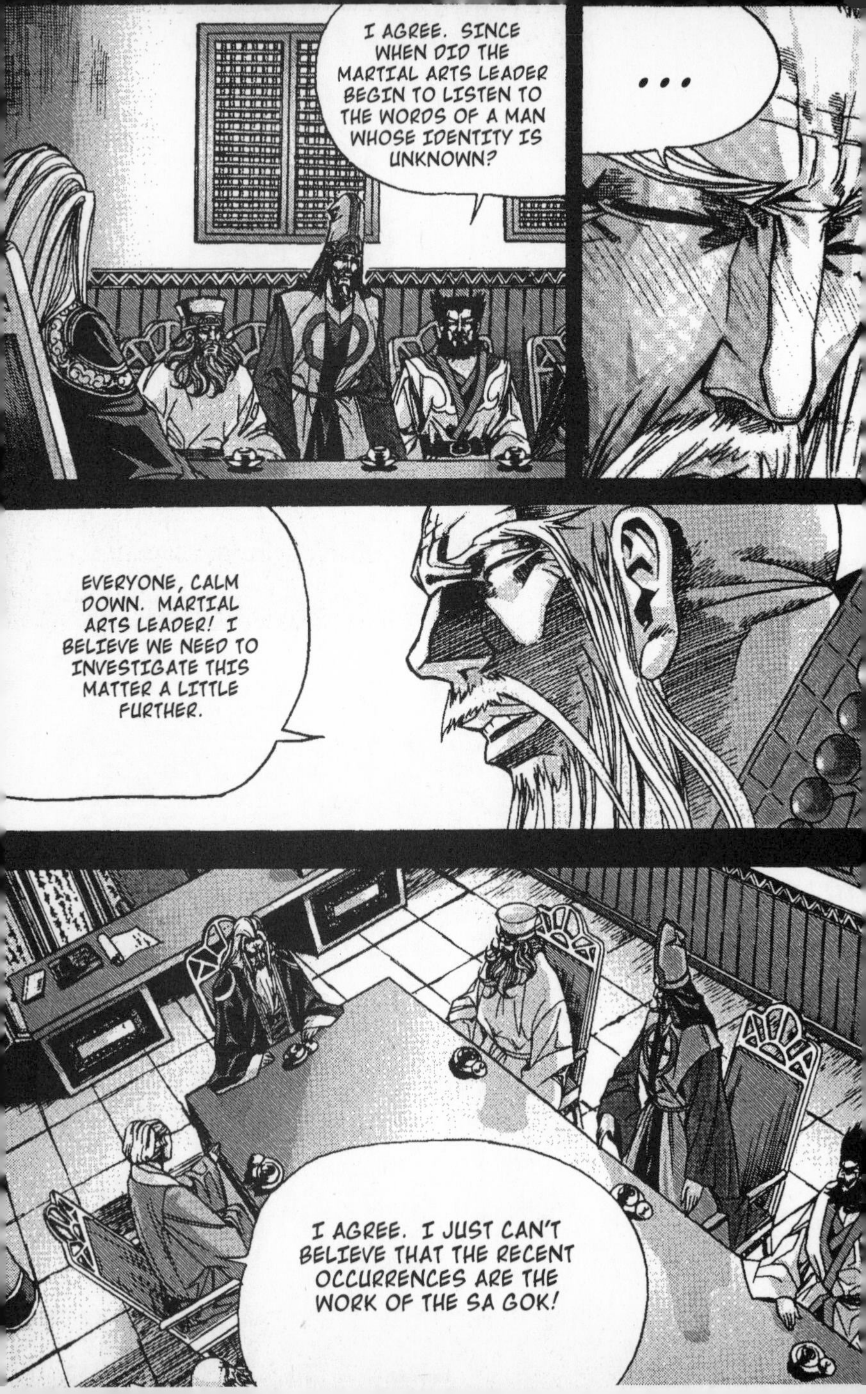
I AGREE. SINCE WHEN DID THE MARTIAL ARTS LEADER BEGIN TO LISTEN TO THE WORDS OF A MAN WHOSE IDENTITY IS UNKNOWN?
...
EVERYONE, CALM DOWN. MARTIAL ARTS LEADER! I BELIEVE WE NEED TO INVESTIGATE THIS MATTER A LITTLE FURTHER.
I AGREE. I JUST CAN'T BELIEVE THAT THE RECENT OCCURRENCES ARE THE WORK OF THE SA GOK!

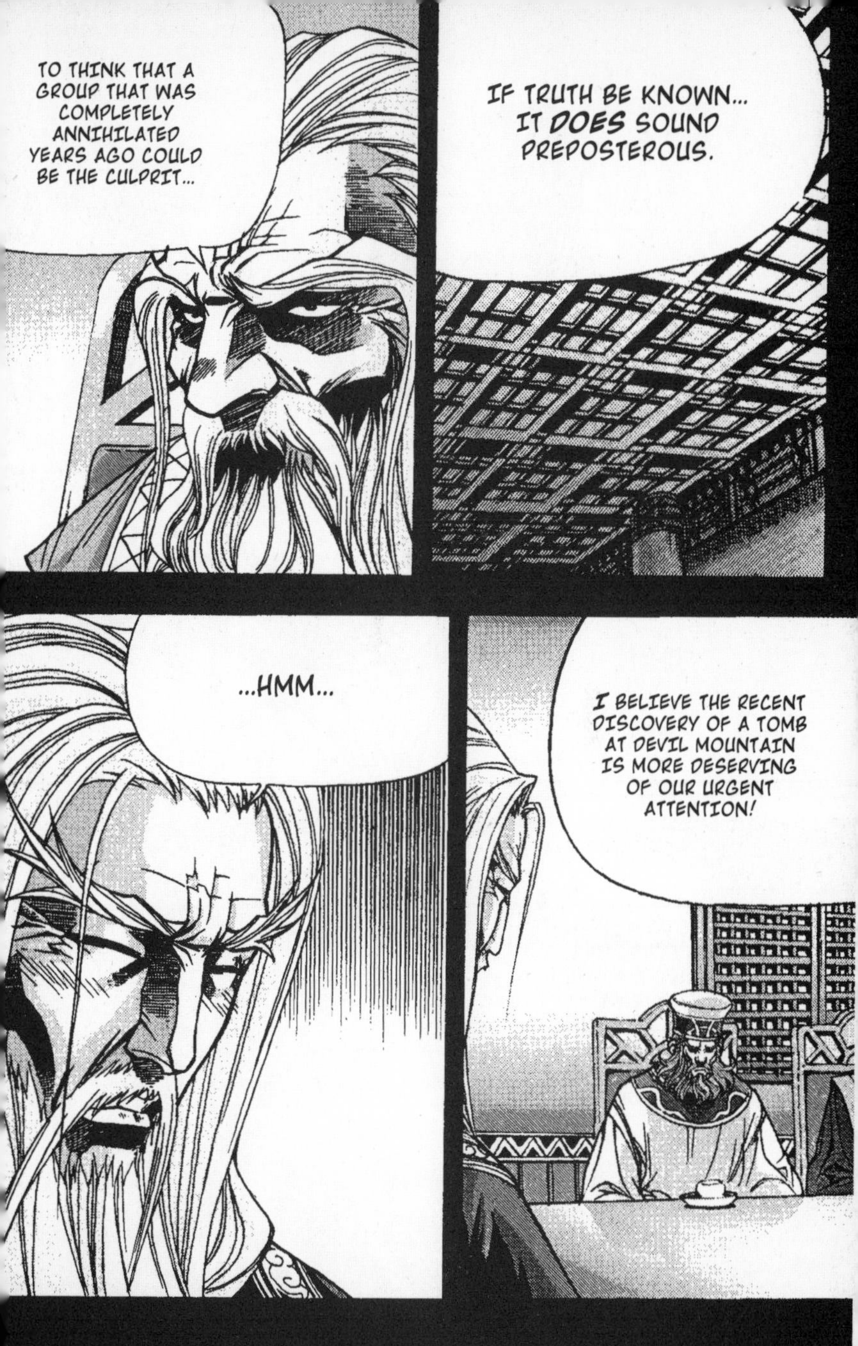
TO THINK THAT A GROUP THAT WAS COMPLETELY ANNIHILATED YEARS AGO COULD BE THE CULPRIT...
IF TRUTH BE KNOWN... IT *DOES* SOUND PREPOSTEROUS.
...HMM...
I BELIEVE THE RECENT DISCOVERY OF A TOMB AT DEVIL MOUNTAIN IS MORE DESERVING OF OUR URGENT ATTENTION!

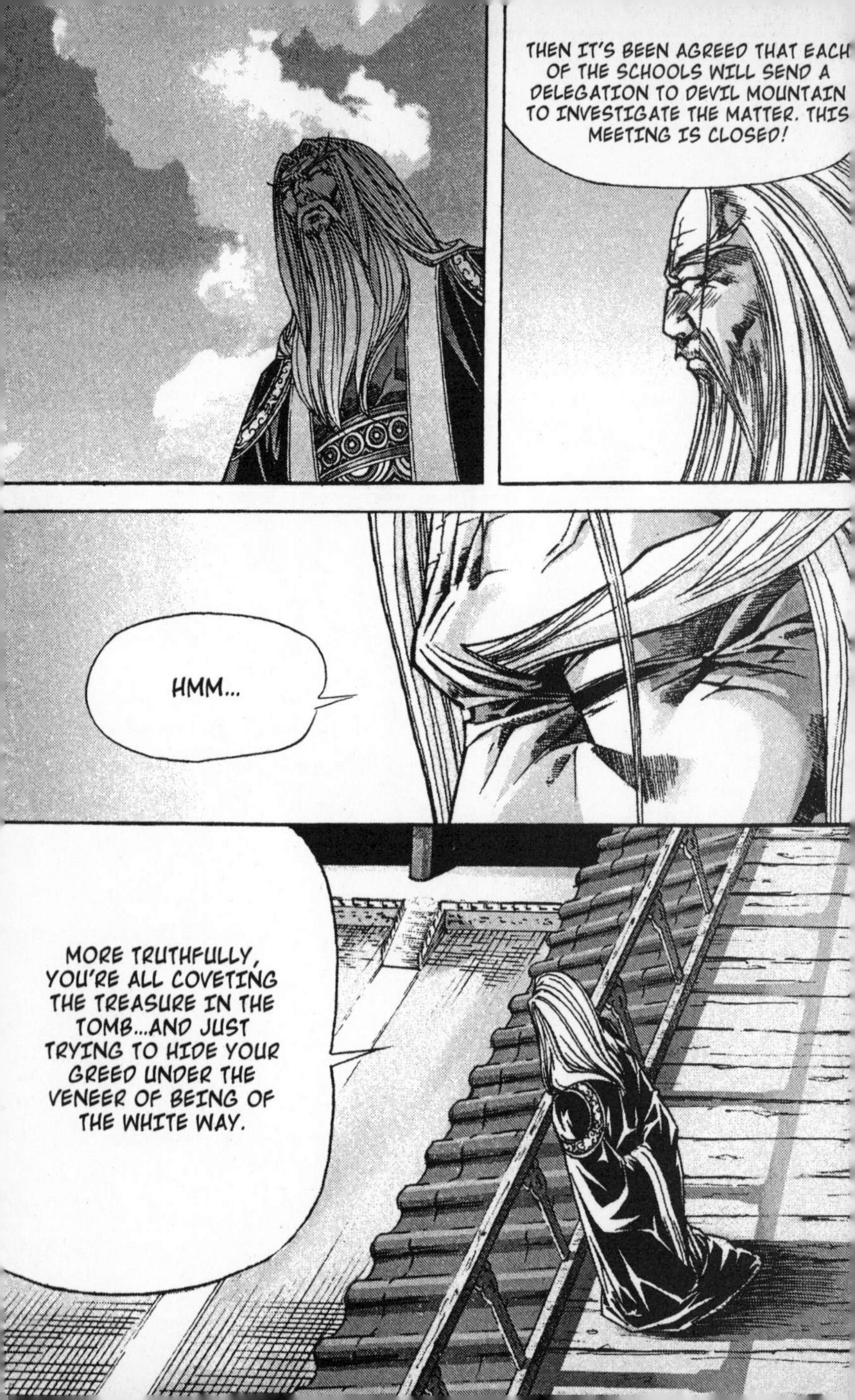
THEN IT'S BEEN AGREED THAT EACH OF THE SCHOOLS WILL SEND A DELEGATION TO DEVIL MOUNTAIN TO INVESTIGATE THE MATTER. THIS MEETING IS CLOSED!
HMM...
MORE TRUTHFULLY, YOU'RE ALL COVETING THE TREASURE IN THE TOMB...AND JUST TRYING TO HIDE YOUR GREED UNDER THE VENEER OF BEING OF THE WHITE WAY.

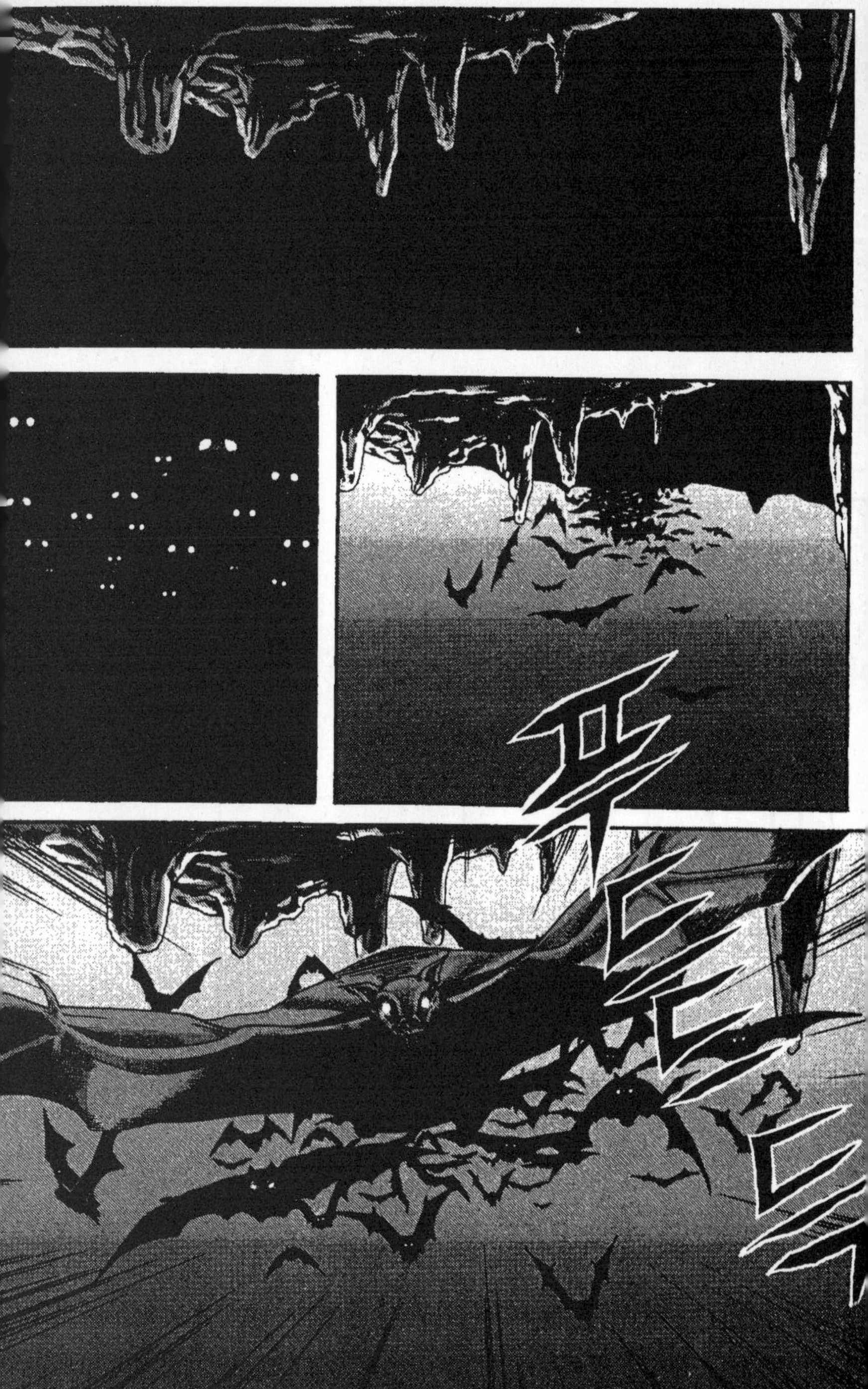

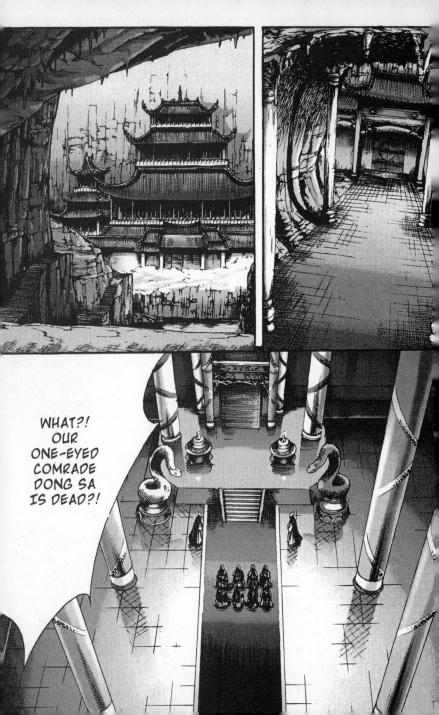

WHAT?!
OUR
ONE-EYED
COMRADE
DONG SA
IS DEAD?!

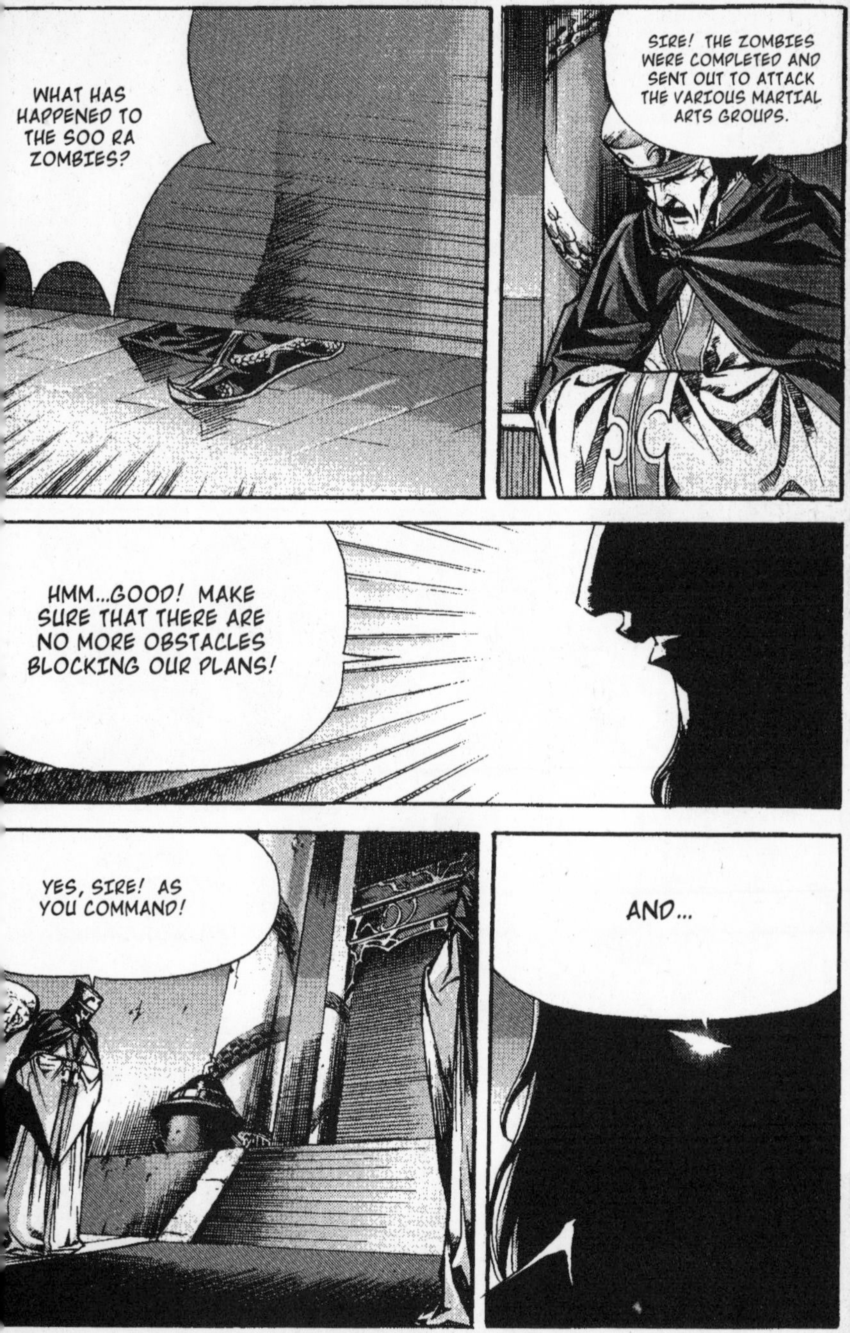
WHAT HAS HAPPENED TO THE SOO RA ZOMBIES?
SIRE! THE ZOMBIES WERE COMPLETED AND SENT OUT TO ATTACK THE VARIOUS MARTIAL ARTS GROUPS.
HMM...GOOD! MAKE SURE THAT THERE ARE NO MORE OBSTACLES BLOCKING OUR PLANS!
YES, SIRE! AS YOU COMMAND!
AND...

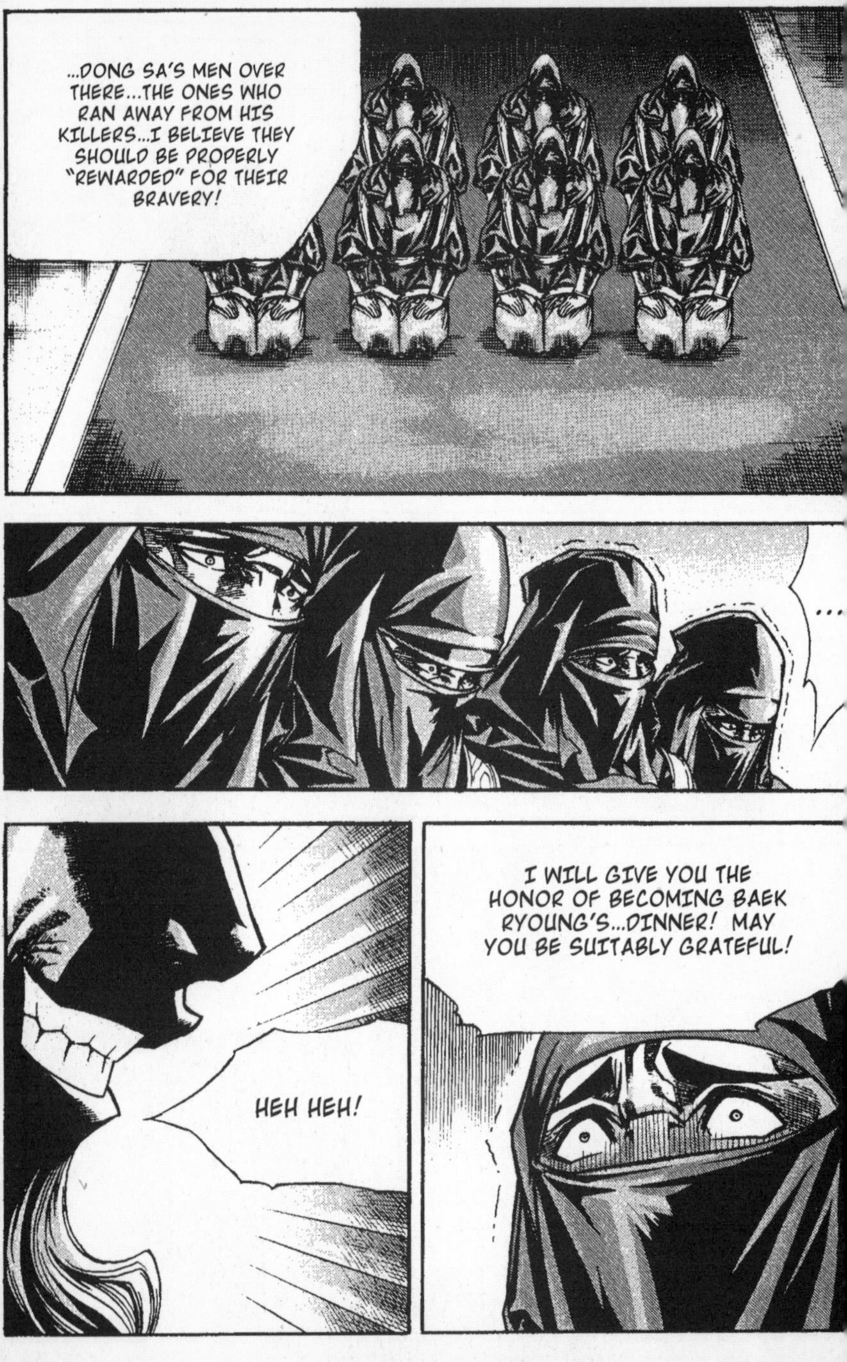

...DONG SA'S MEN OVER THERE...THE ONES WHO RAN AWAY FROM HIS KILLERS...I BELIEVE THEY SHOULD BE PROPERLY "REWARDED" FOR THEIR BRAVERY!
...
HEH HEH!
I WILL GIVE YOU THE HONOR OF BECOMING BAEK RYOUNG'S...DINNER! MAY YOU BE SUITABLY GRATEFUL!

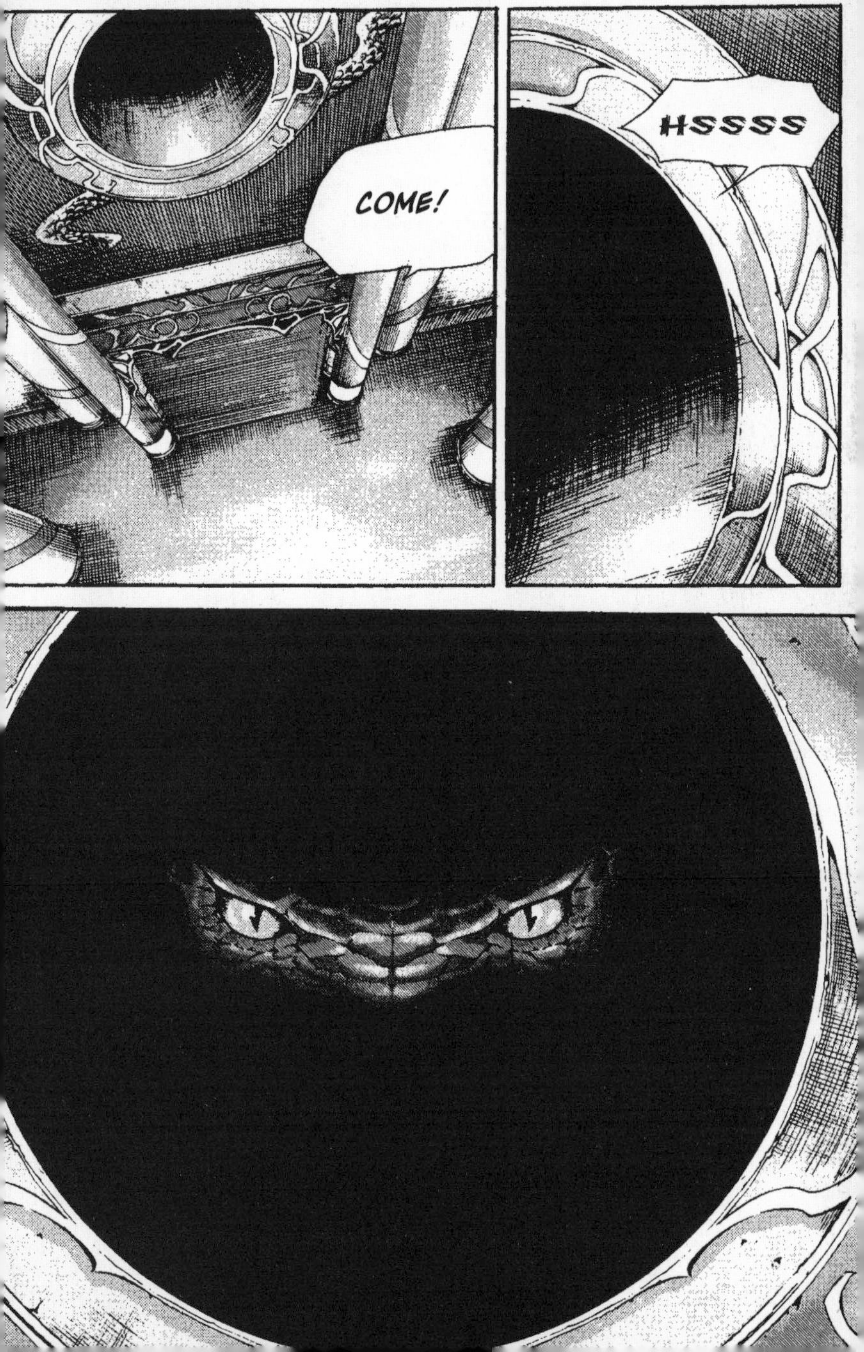
COME!
HSSSS

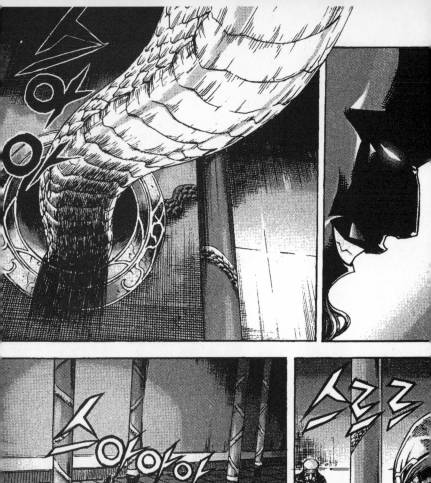

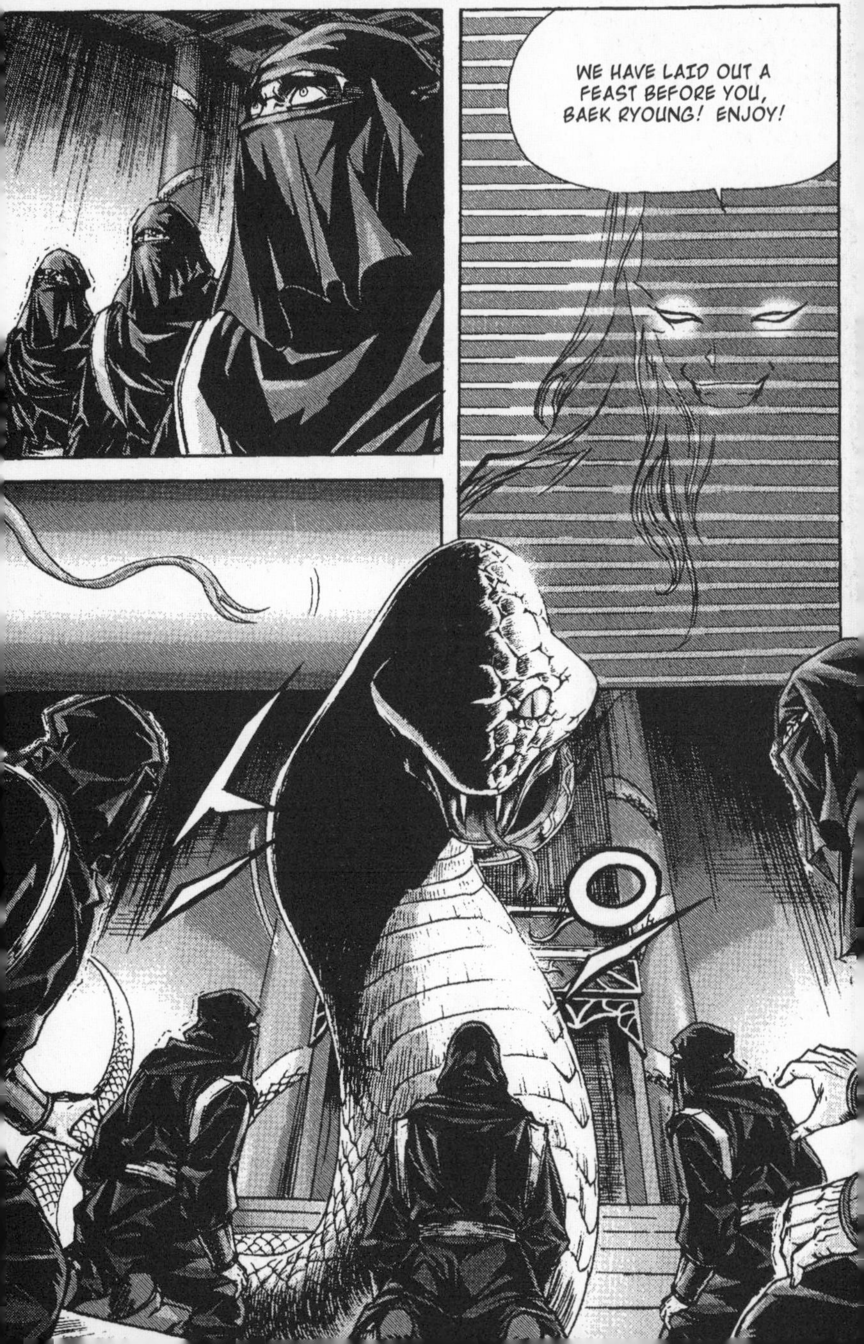
WE HAVE LAID OUT A FEAST BEFORE YOU, BAEK RYOUNG! ENJOY!

...N-NO!

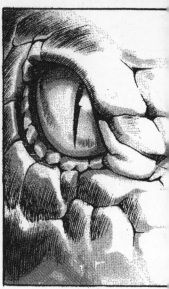

UU...AH!

...AH...AH!

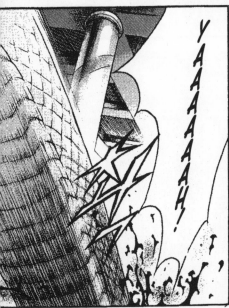

YAAAAAAH!

HMM...JUST WHO EXACTLY ARE THOSE MEN WHO KILLED DONG SA?! HE MAY NOT HAVE BEEN OUR BEST FIGHTER, BUT AS LONG AS HE HAD HIS ZOMBIES, HE WOULDN'T HAVE BEEN EASY TO KILL...

COULD HIS KILLER HAVE BEEN MARTIAL ARTS LEADER MO YOUNG HIMSELF?

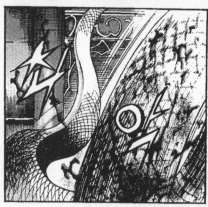

BAEK RYOUNG! DID YOU ENJOY YOUR MEAL?!

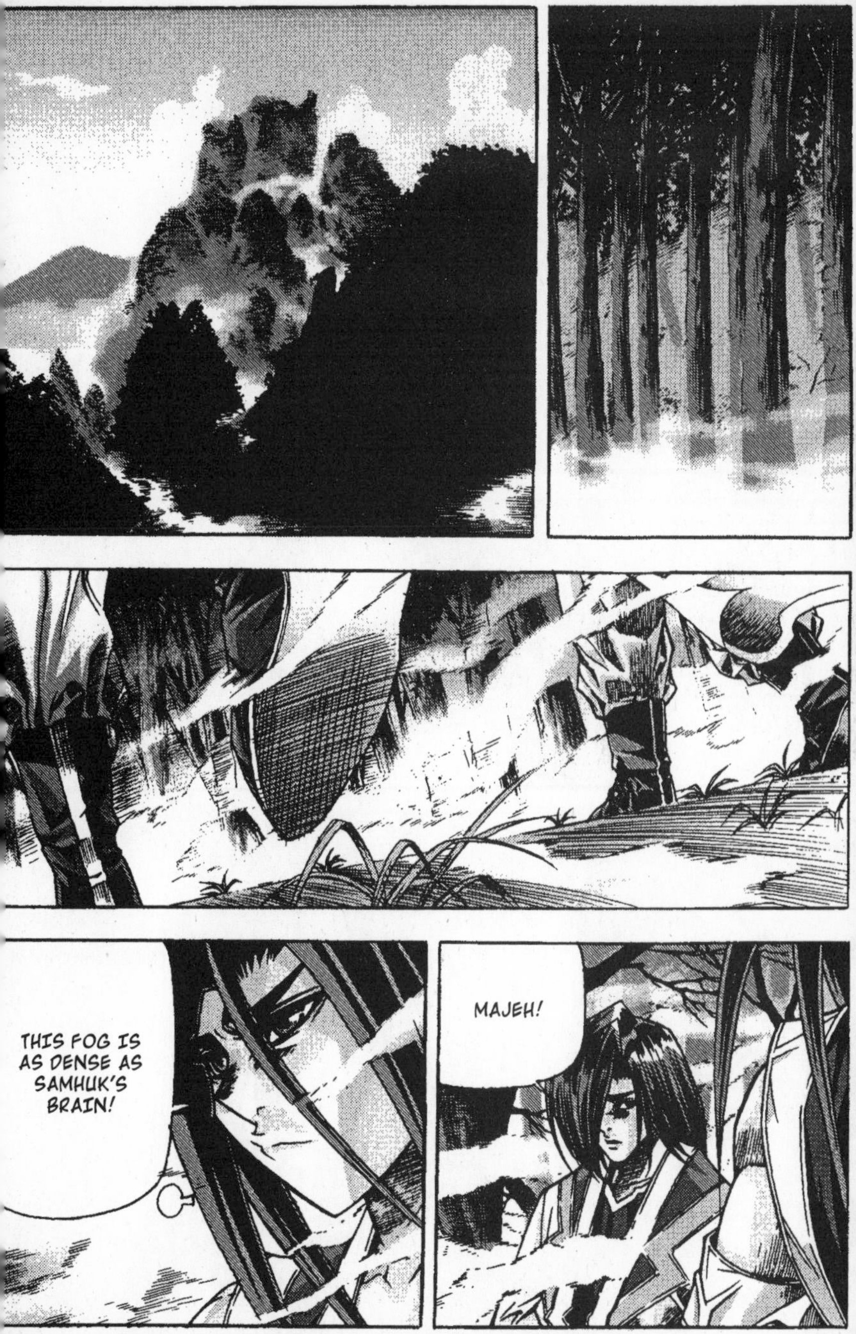
THIS FOG IS AS DENSE AS SAMHUK'S BRAIN!
MAJEH!

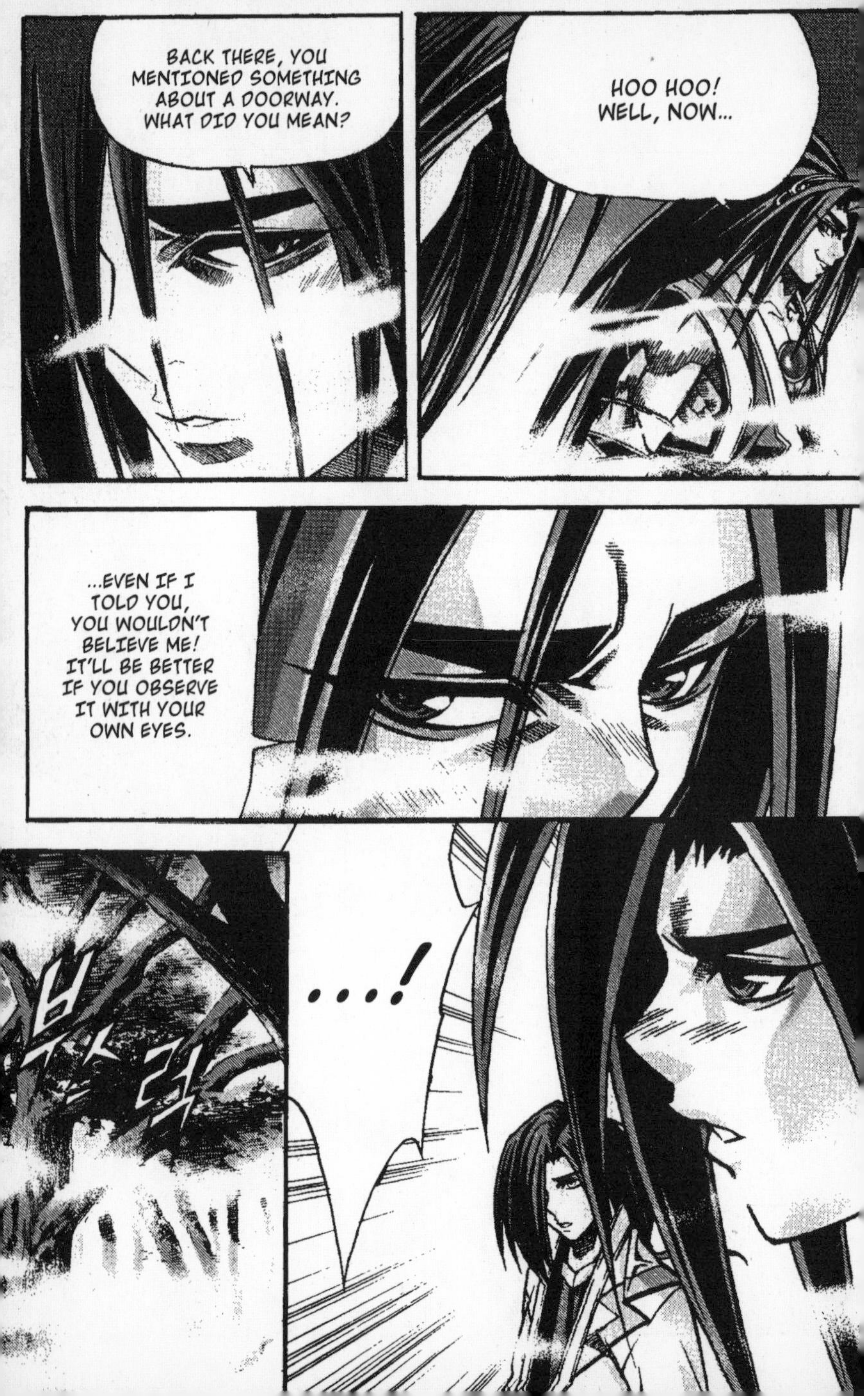
BACK THERE, YOU MENTIONED SOMETHING ABOUT A DOORWAY. WHAT DID YOU MEAN?
HOO HOO! WELL, NOW...
...EVEN IF I TOLD YOU, YOU WOULDN'T BELIEVE ME! IT'LL BE BETTER IF YOU OBSERVE IT WITH YOUR OWN EYES.
...!

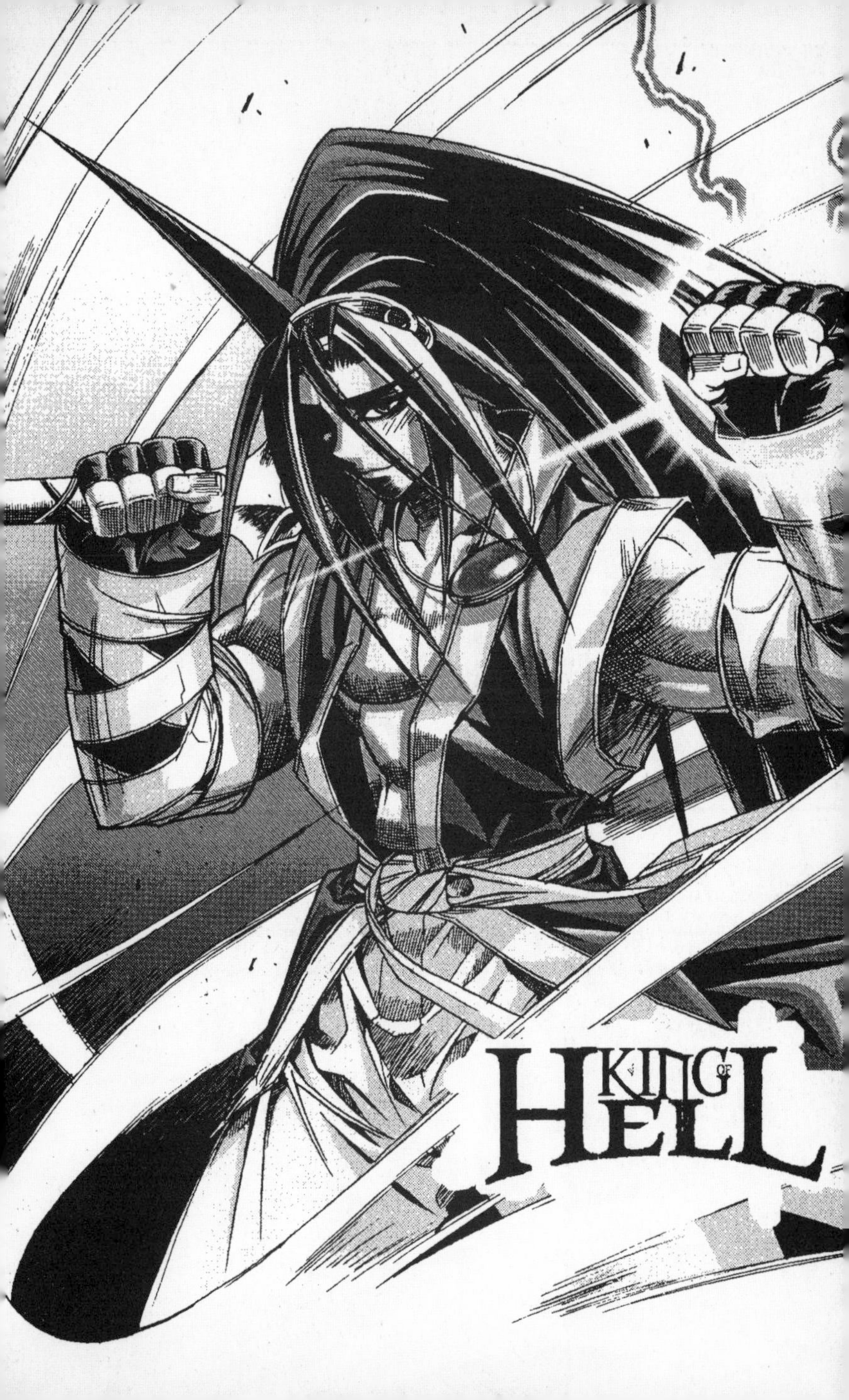
KING OF HELL

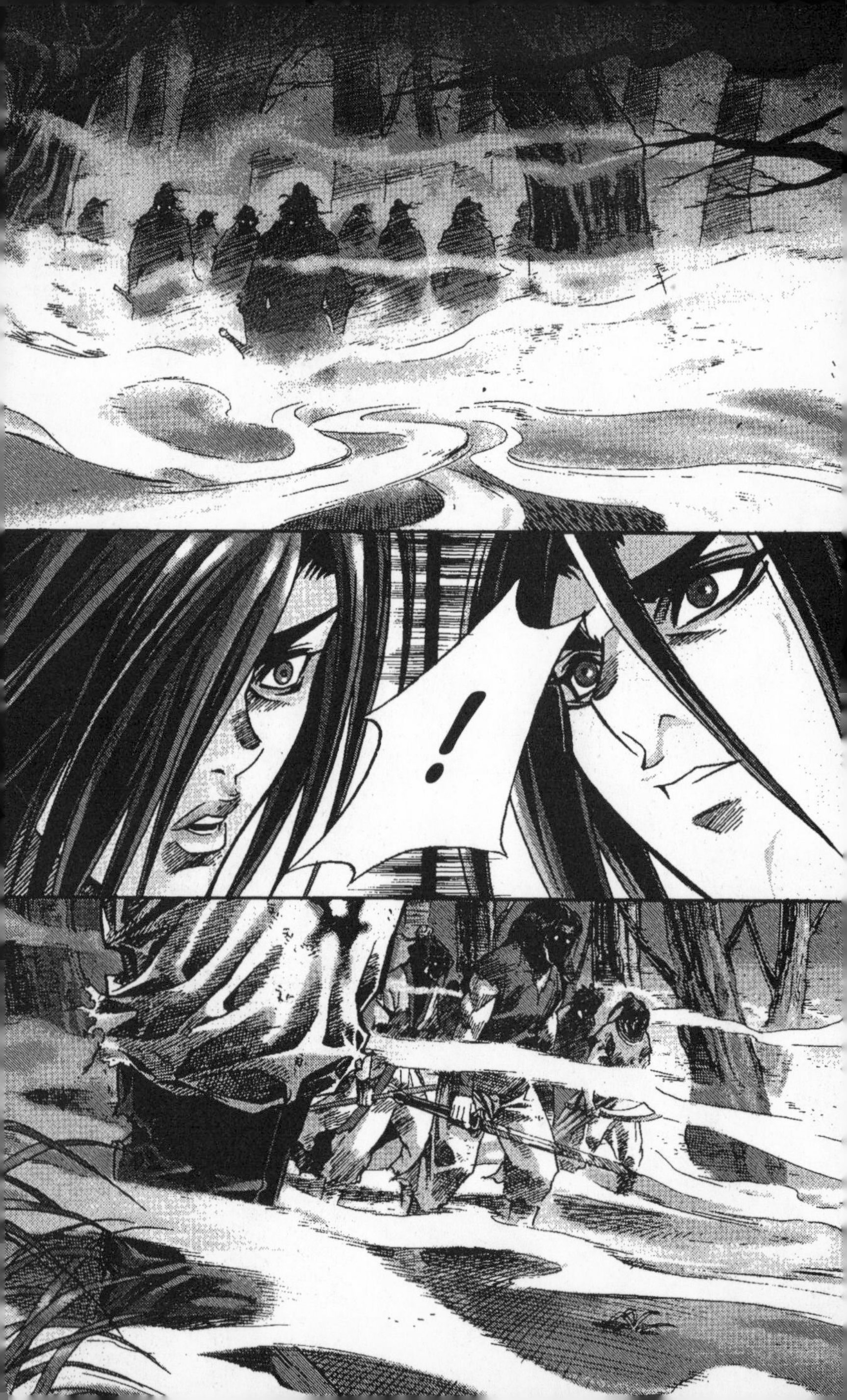
!

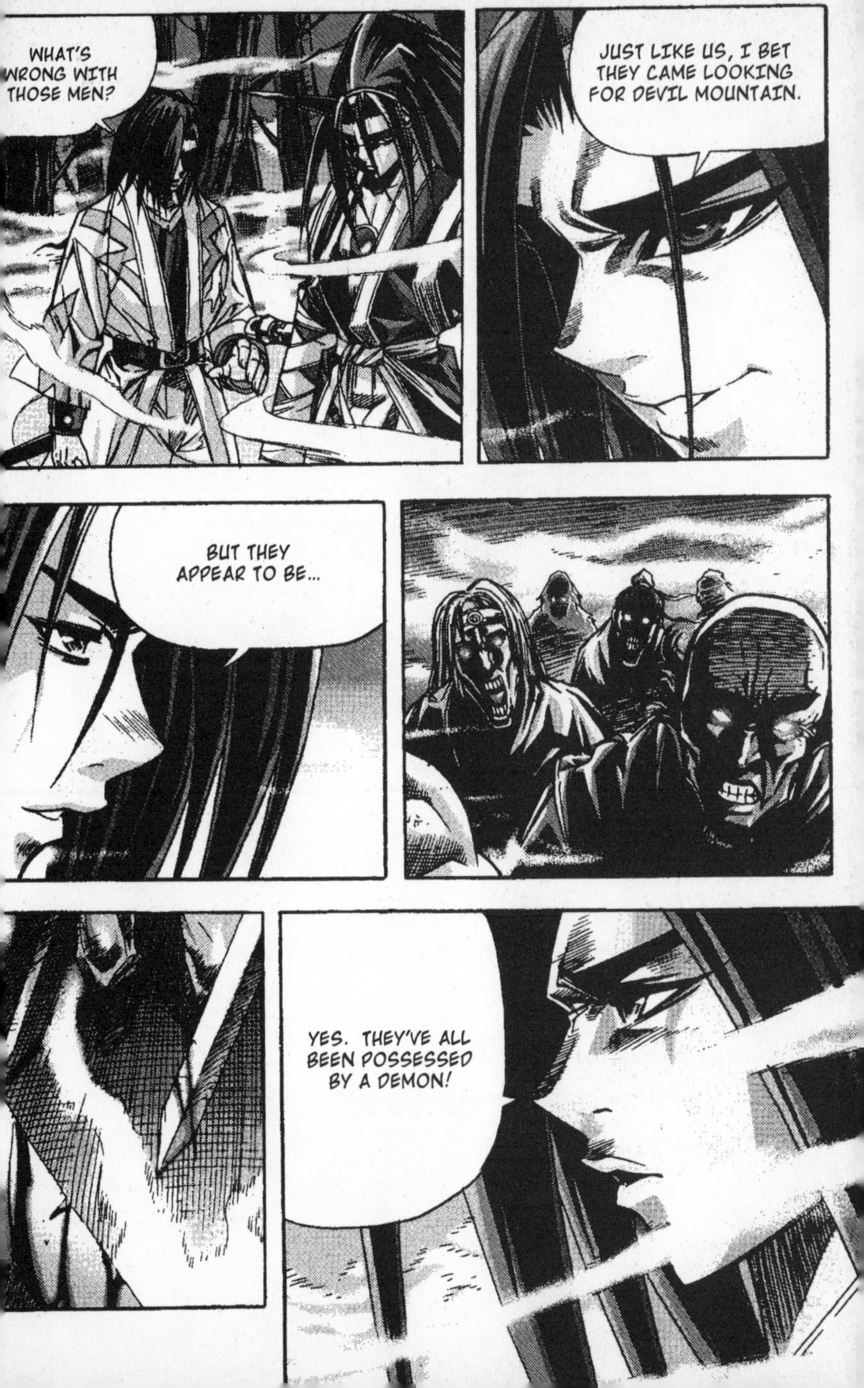
WHAT'S WRONG WITH THOSE MEN?
JUST LIKE US, I BET THEY CAME LOOKING FOR DEVIL MOUNTAIN.
BUT THEY APPEAR TO BE...
YES. THEY'VE ALL BEEN POSSESSED BY A DEMON!

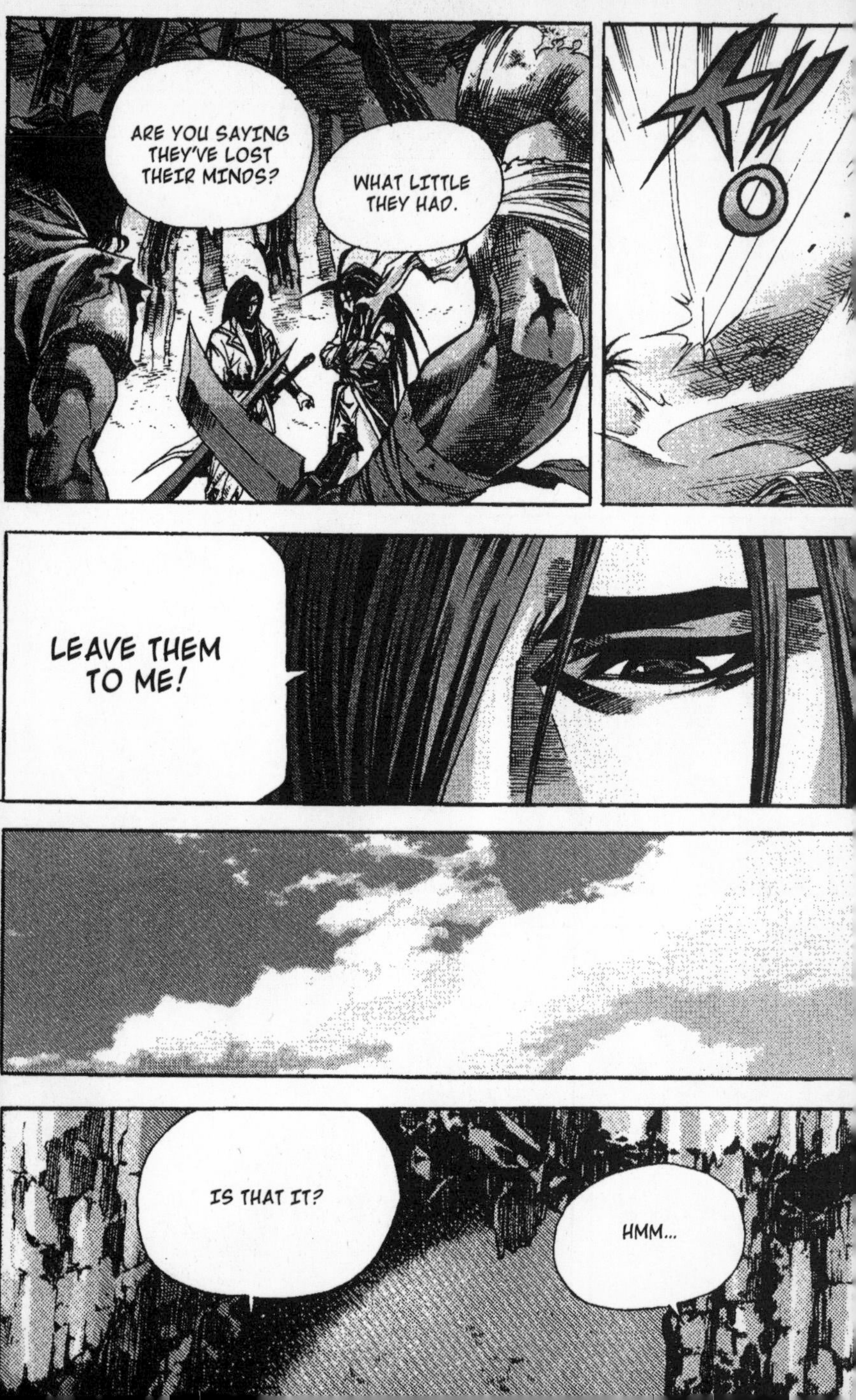
ARE YOU SAYING THEY'VE LOST THEIR MINDS?
WHAT LITTLE THEY HAD.
KHN
LEAVE THEM TO ME!
IS THAT IT?
HMM...

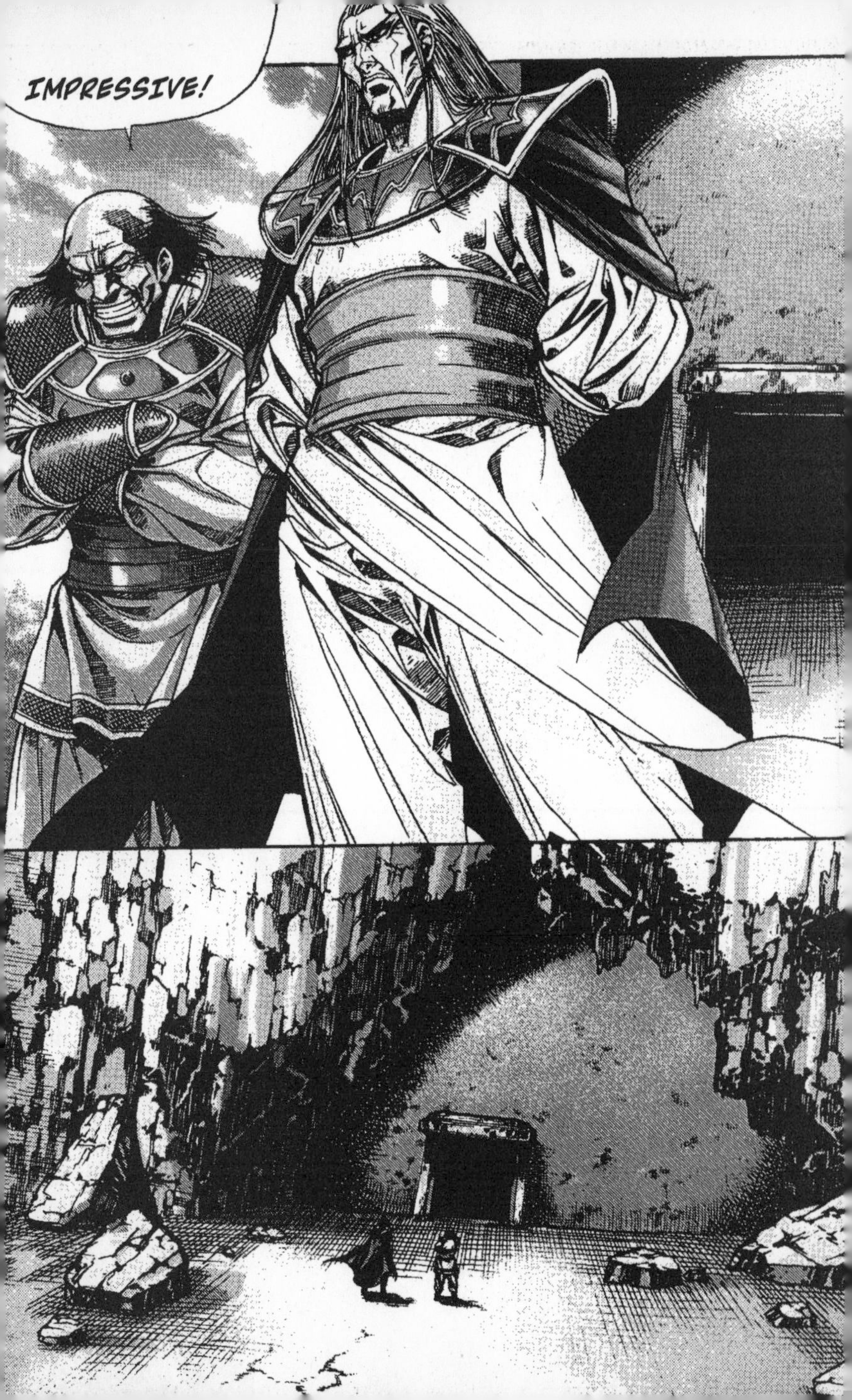
IMPRESSIVE!

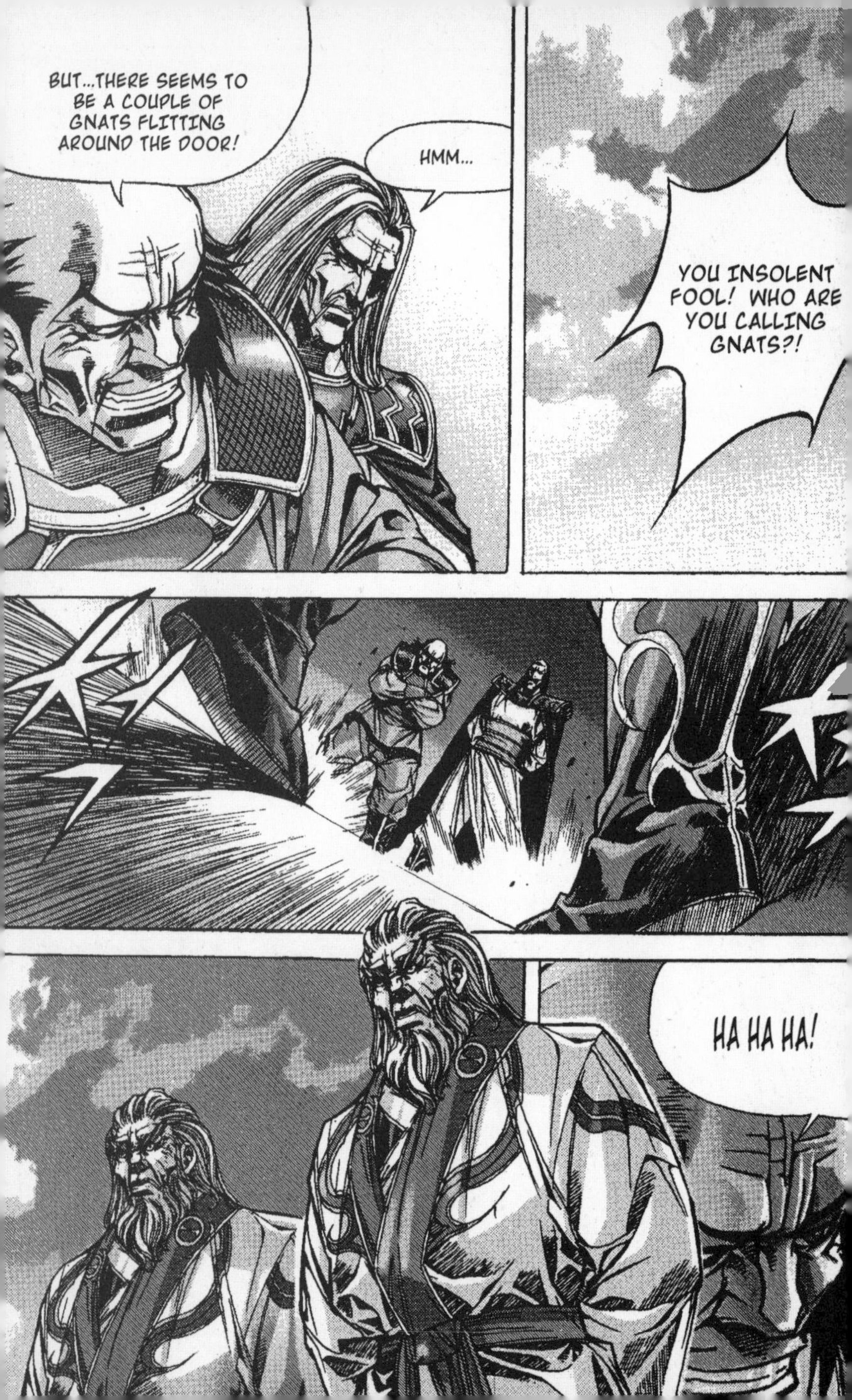
BUT...THERE SEEMS TO BE A COUPLE OF GNATS FLITTING AROUND THE DOOR!
HMM...
YOU INSOLENT FOOL! WHO ARE YOU CALLING GNATS?!
HA HA HA!

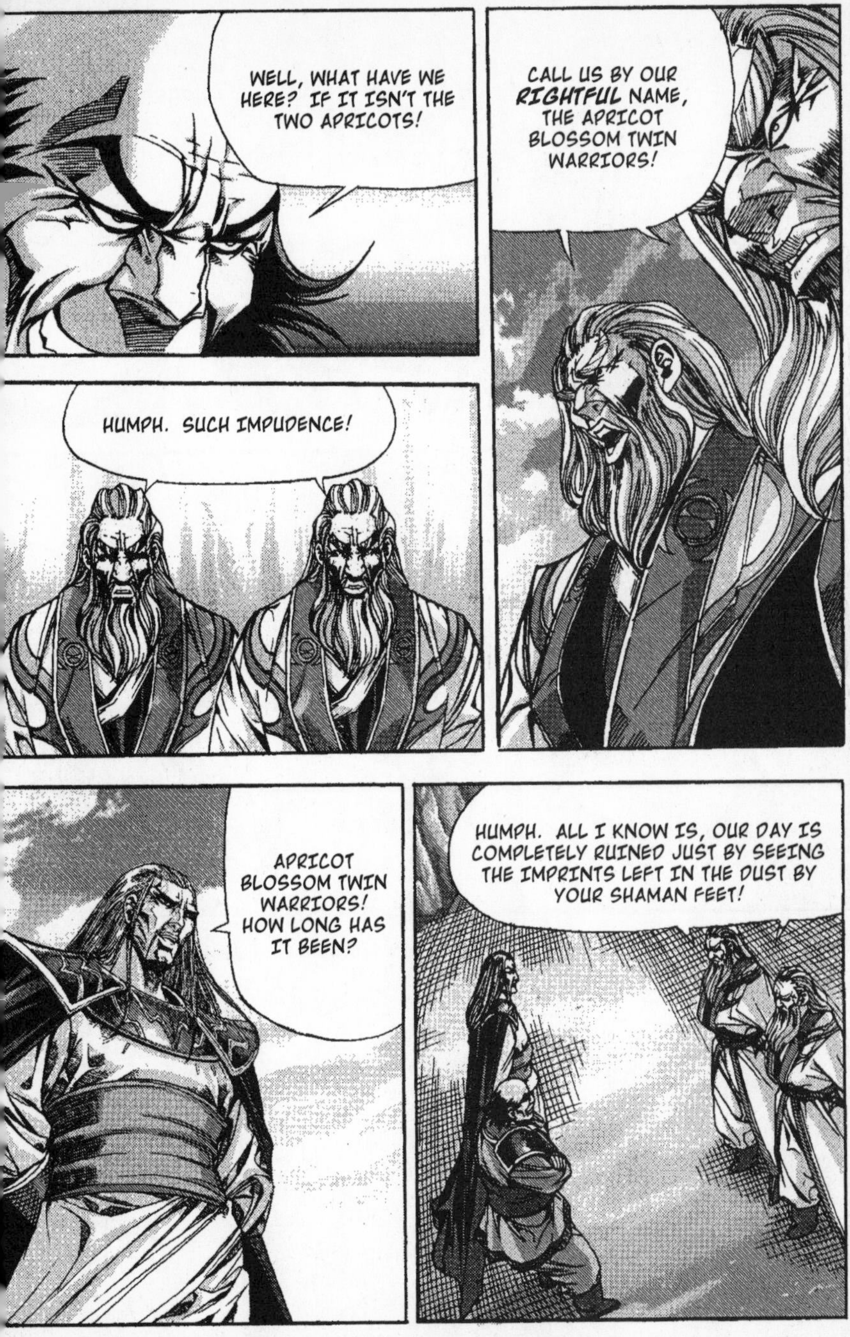
WELL, WHAT HAVE WE HERE? IF IT ISN'T THE TWO APRICOTS!
CALL US BY OUR **RIGHTFUL** NAME, THE APRICOT BLOSSOM TWIN WARRIORS!
HUMPH. SUCH IMPUDENCE!
APRICOT BLOSSOM TWIN WARRIORS! HOW LONG HAS IT BEEN?
HUMPH. ALL I KNOW IS, OUR DAY IS COMPLETELY RUINED JUST BY SEEING THE IMPRINTS LEFT IN THE DUST BY YOUR SHAMAN FEET!

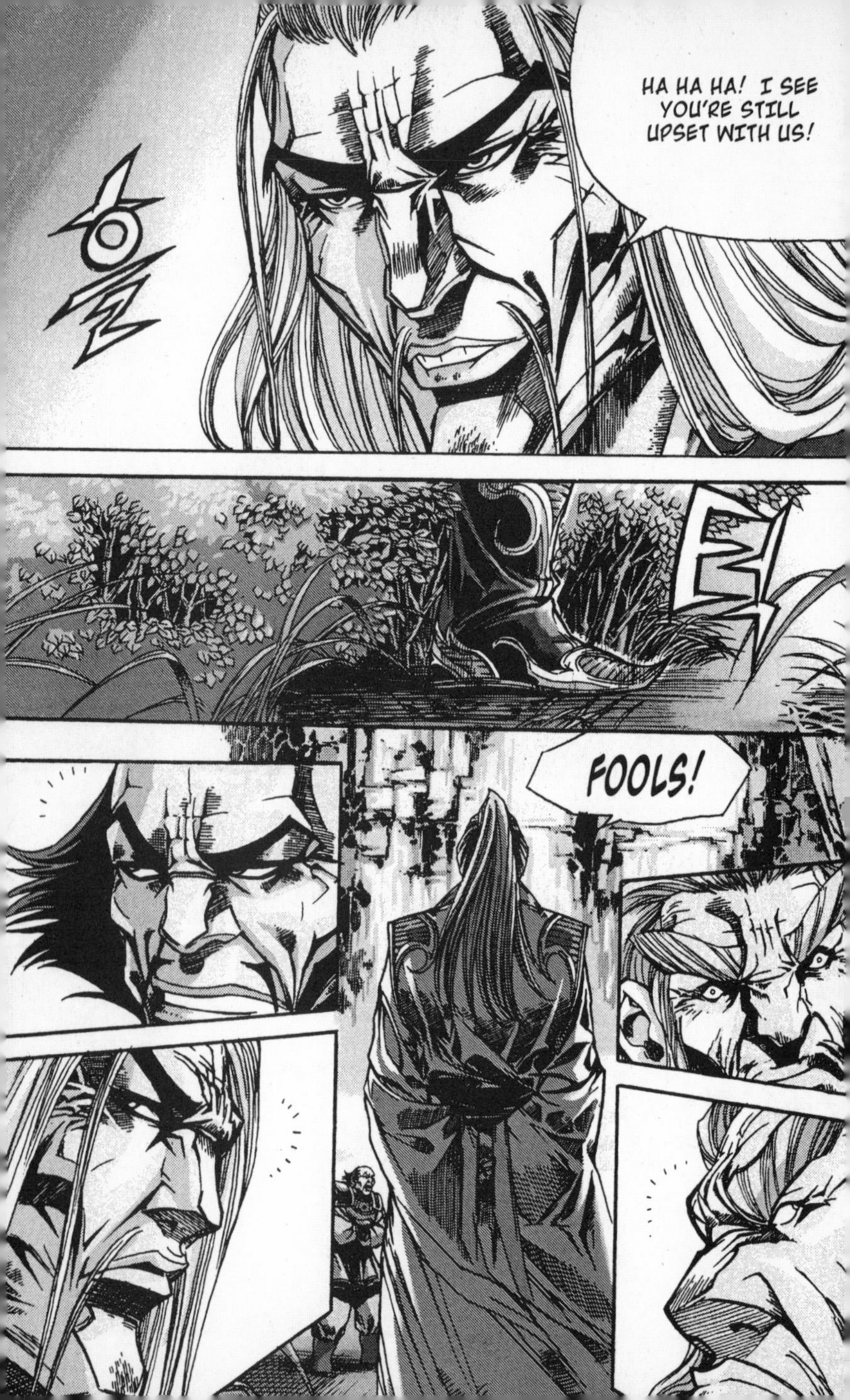
HA HA HA! I SEE YOU'RE STILL UPSET WITH US!
FOOLS!

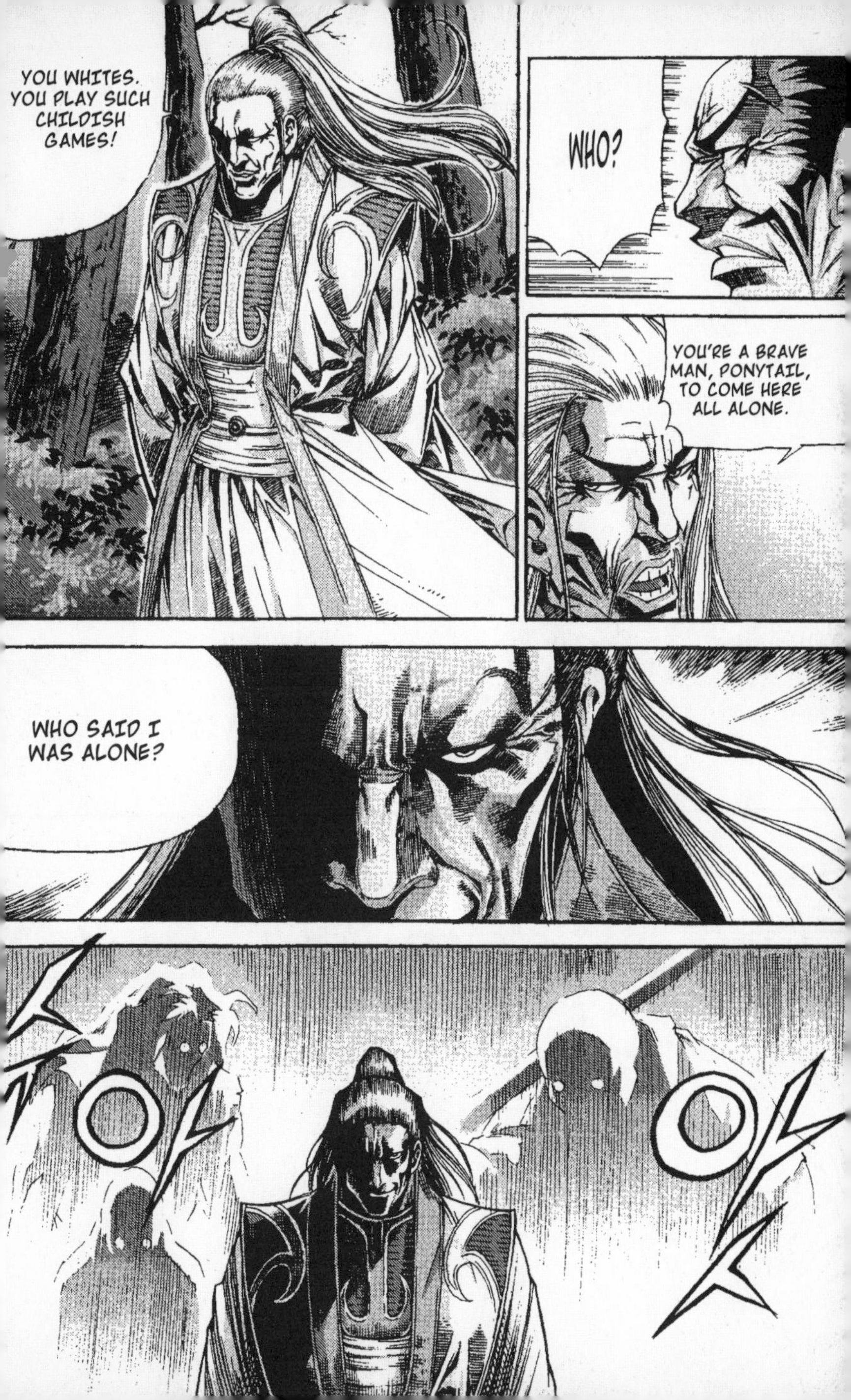
YOU WHITES. YOU PLAY SUCH CHILDISH GAMES!
WHO?
YOU'RE A BRAVE MAN, PONYTAIL, TO COME HERE ALL ALONE.
WHO SAID I WAS ALONE?

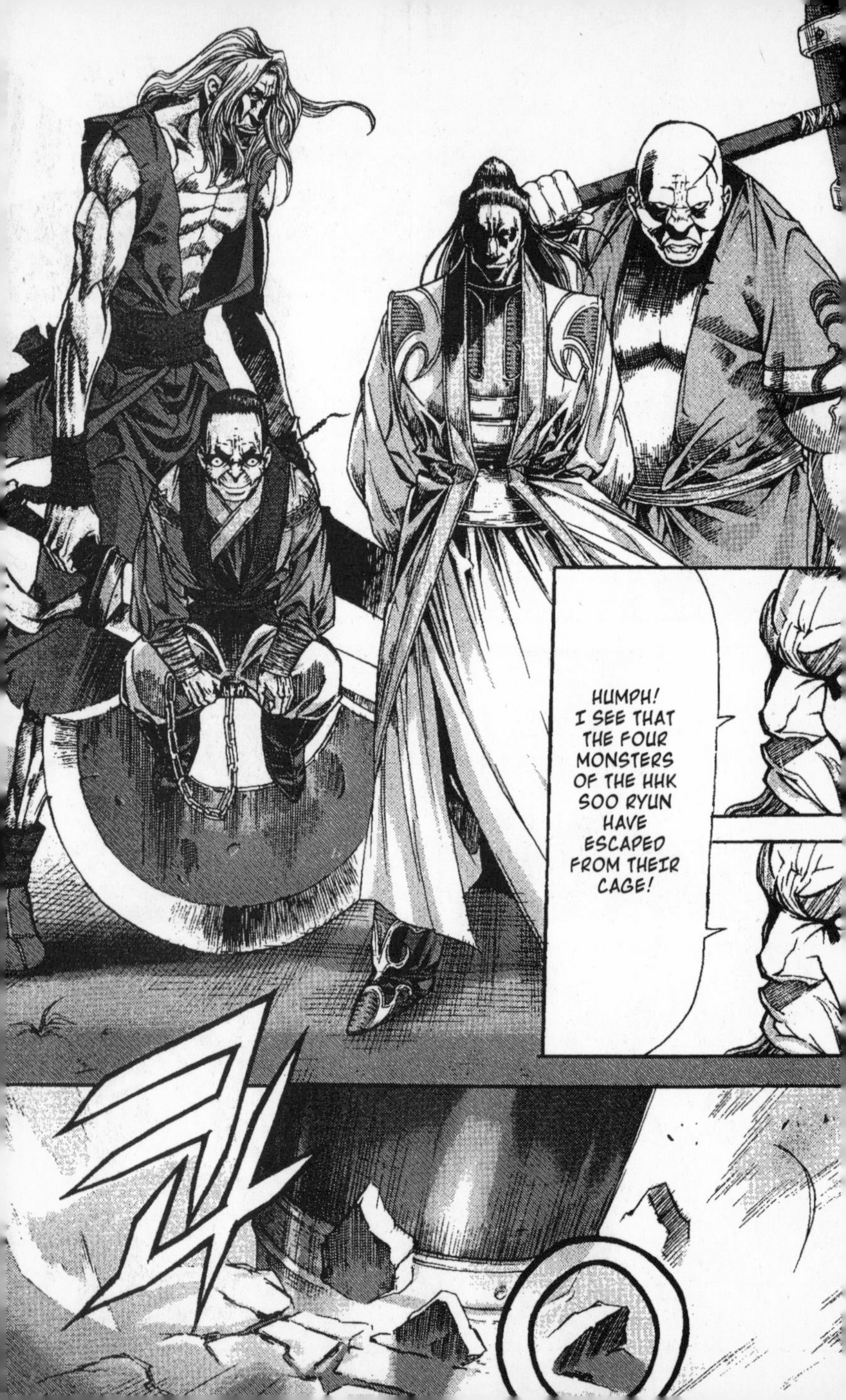
HUMPH! I SEE THAT THE FOUR MONSTERS OF THE HHK SOO RYUN HAVE ESCAPED FROM THEIR CAGE!

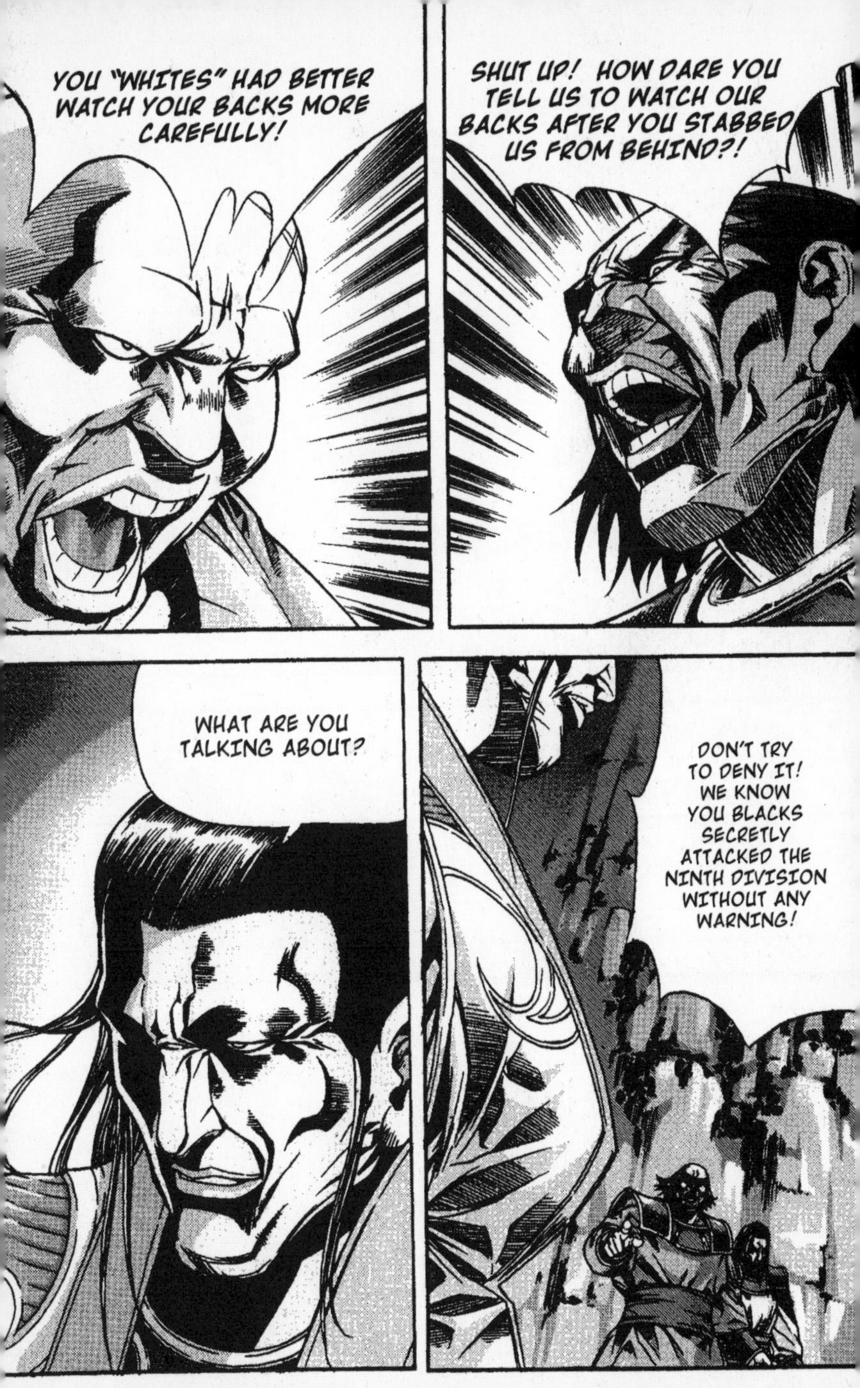
YOU "WHITES" HAD BETTER WATCH YOUR BACKS MORE CAREFULLY!
SHUT UP! HOW DARE YOU TELL US TO WATCH OUR BACKS AFTER YOU STABBED US FROM BEHIND?!
WHAT ARE YOU TALKING ABOUT?
DON'T TRY TO DENY IT! WE KNOW YOU BLACKS SECRETLY ATTACKED THE NINTH DIVISION WITHOUT ANY WARNING!

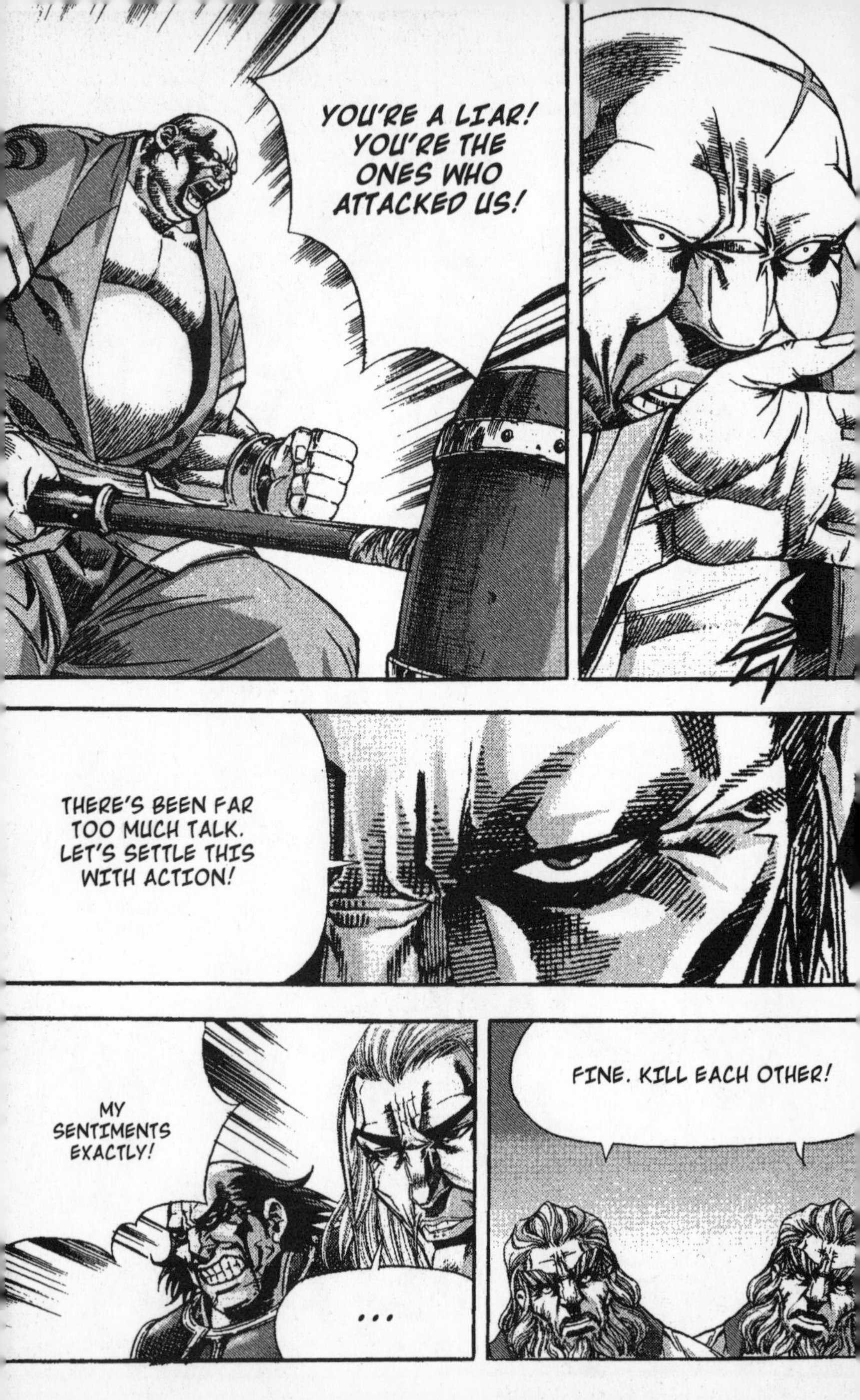
YOU'RE A LIAR! YOU'RE THE ONES WHO ATTACKED US!
THERE'S BEEN FAR TOO MUCH TALK. LET'S SETTLE THIS WITH ACTION!
MY SENTIMENTS EXACTLY!
...
FINE. KILL EACH OTHER!

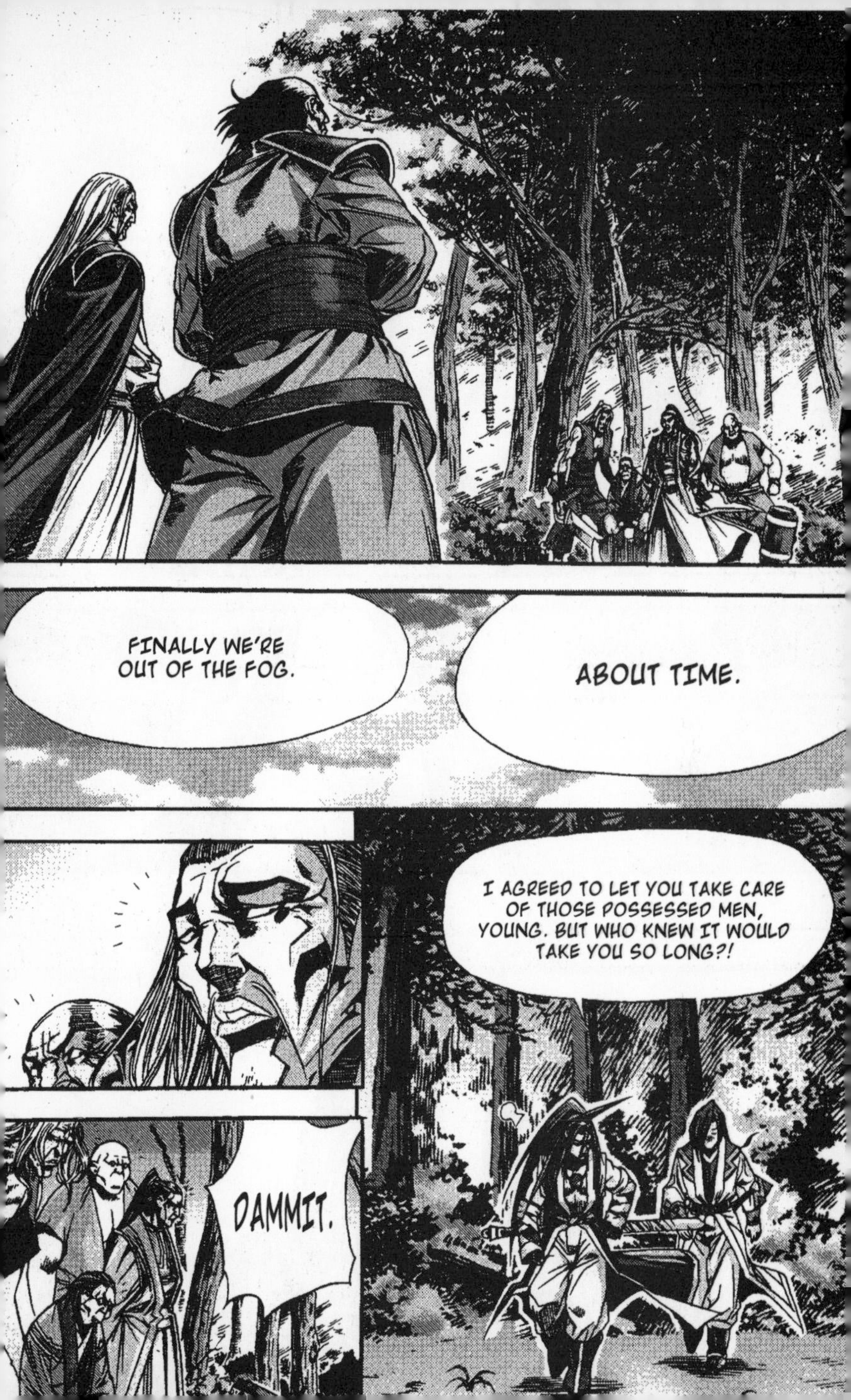
FINALLY WE'RE OUT OF THE FOG.
ABOUT TIME.
I AGREED TO LET YOU TAKE CARE OF THOSE POSSESSED MEN, YOUNG. BUT WHO KNEW IT WOULD TAKE YOU SO LONG?!
DAMMIT.

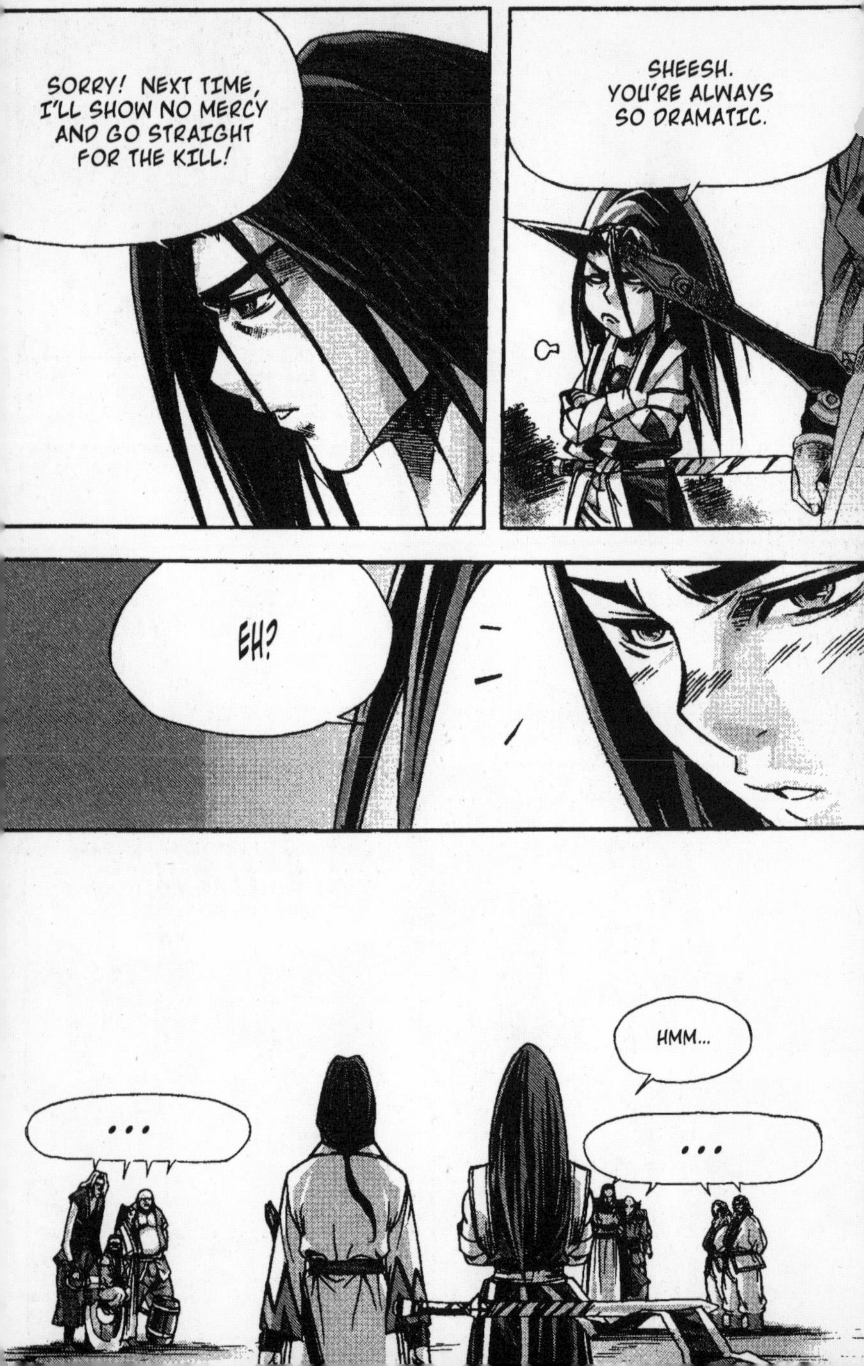
SORRY! NEXT TIME, I'LL SHOW NO MERCY AND GO STRAIGHT FOR THE KILL!
SHEESH. YOU'RE ALWAYS SO DRAMATIC.
EH?
HMM...
...
...

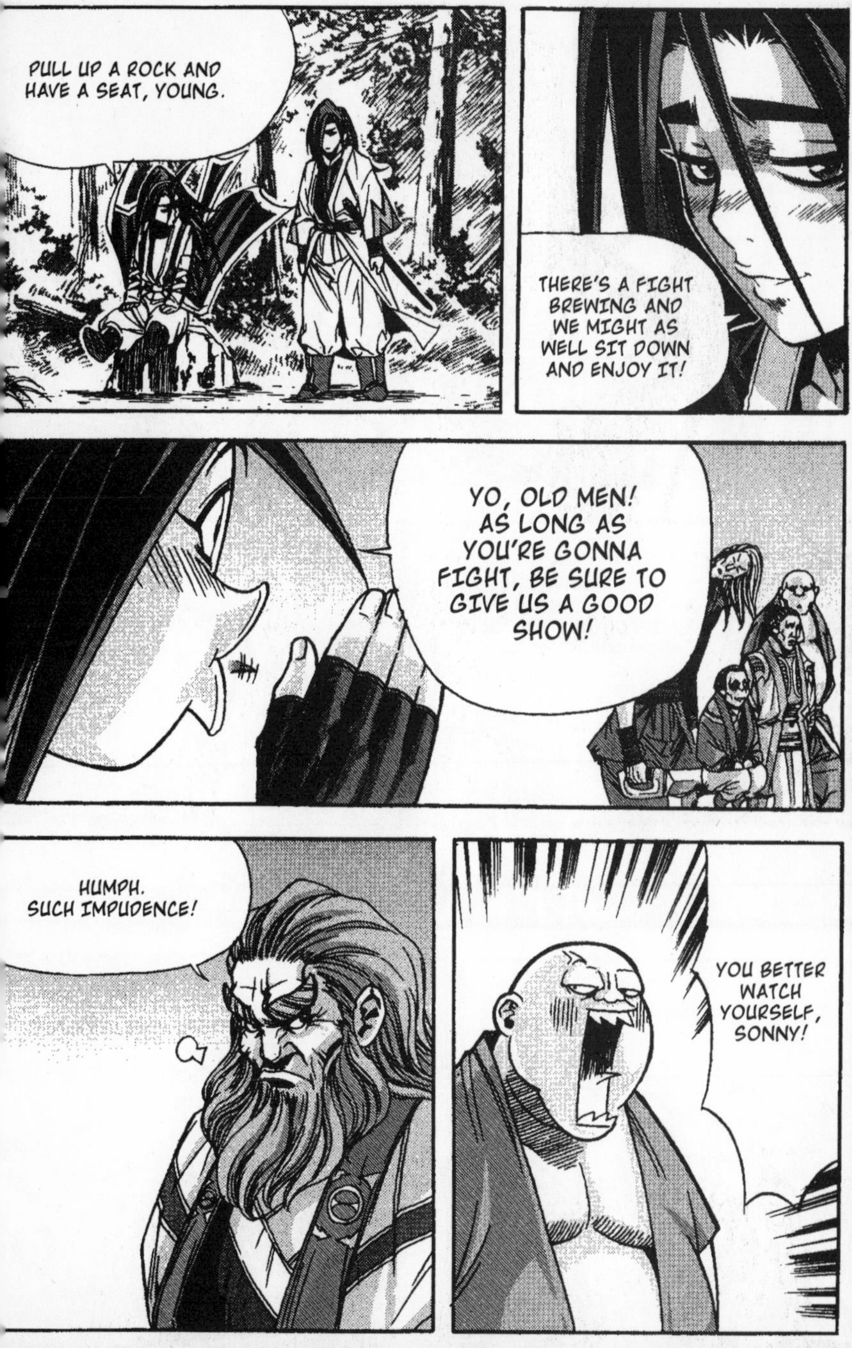
PULL UP A ROCK AND HAVE A SEAT, YOUNG.
THERE'S A FIGHT BREWING AND WE MIGHT AS WELL SIT DOWN AND ENJOY IT!
YO, OLD MEN! AS LONG AS YOU'RE GONNA FIGHT, BE SURE TO GIVE US A GOOD SHOW!
HUMPH. SUCH IMPUDENCE!
YOU BETTER WATCH YOURSELF, SONNY!

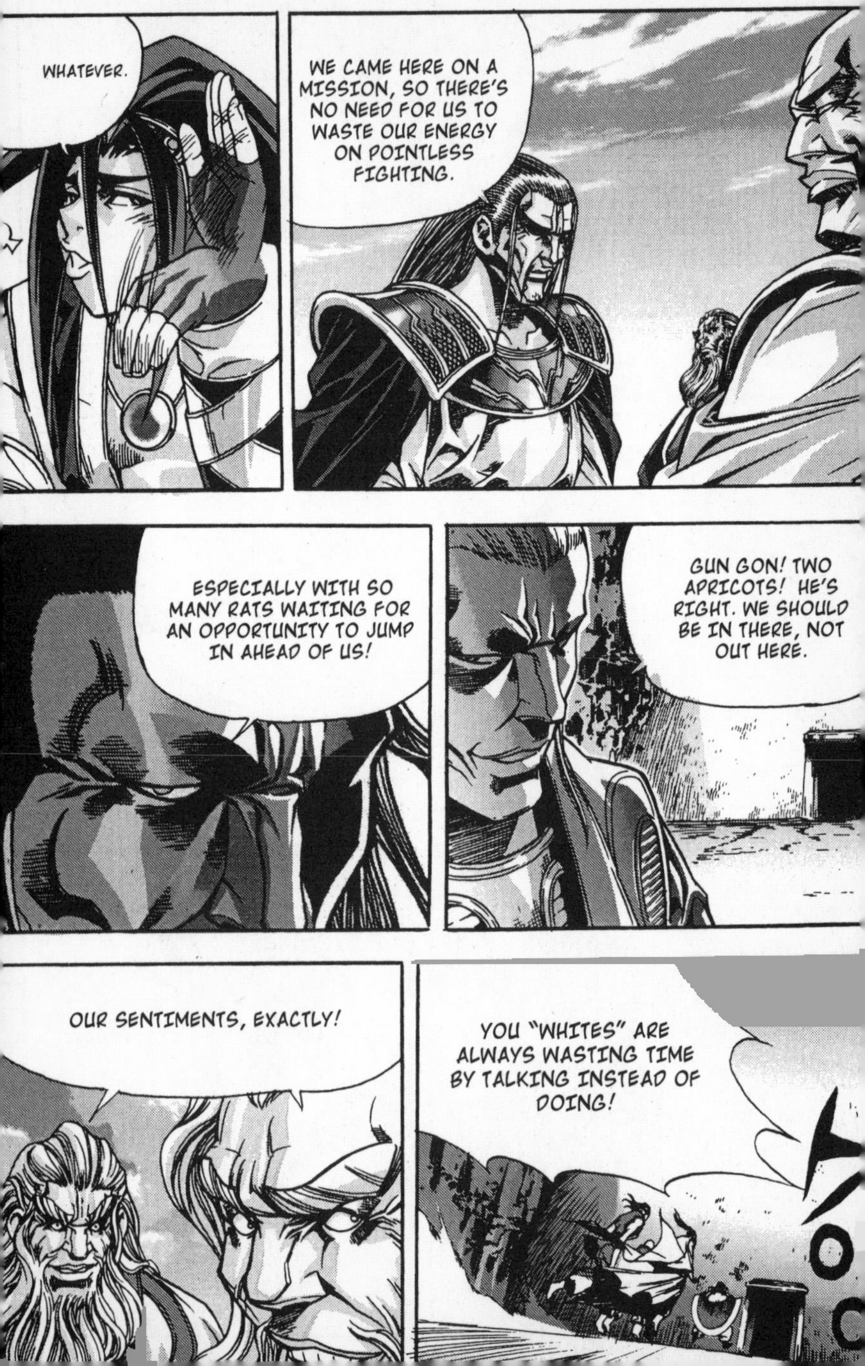
WHATEVER.
WE CAME HERE ON A MISSION, SO THERE'S NO NEED FOR US TO WASTE OUR ENERGY ON POINTLESS FIGHTING.
ESPECIALLY WITH SO MANY RATS WAITING FOR AN OPPORTUNITY TO JUMP IN AHEAD OF US!
GUN GON! TWO APRICOTS! HE'S RIGHT. WE SHOULD BE IN THERE, NOT OUT HERE.
OUR SENTIMENTS, EXACTLY!
YOU "WHITES" ARE ALWAYS WASTING TIME BY TALKING INSTEAD OF DOING!

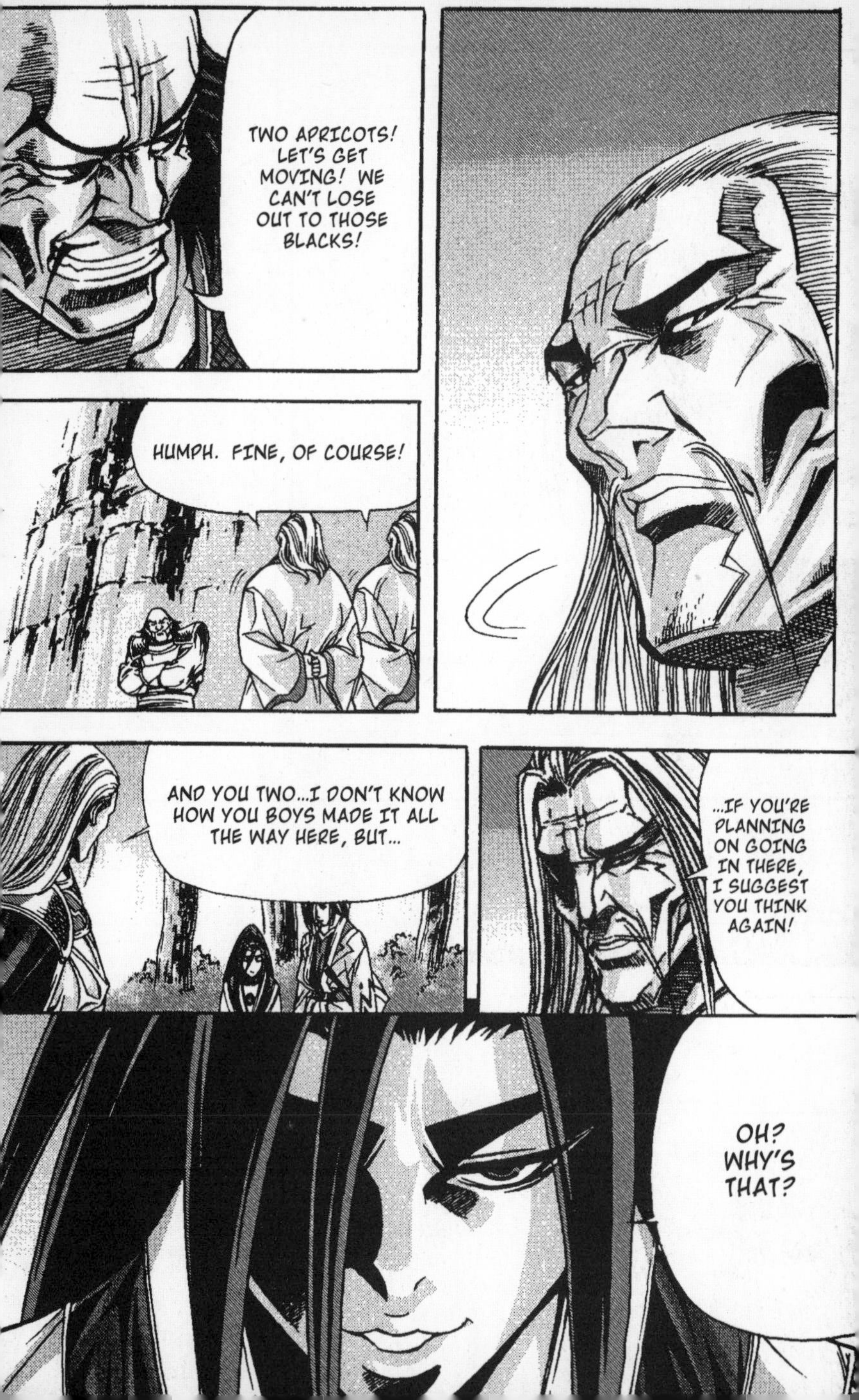
TWO APRICOTS! LET'S GET MOVING! WE CAN'T LOSE OUT TO THOSE BLACKS!
HUMPH. FINE, OF COURSE!
AND YOU TWO...I DON'T KNOW HOW YOU BOYS MADE IT ALL THE WAY HERE, BUT...
...IF YOU'RE PLANNING ON GOING IN THERE, I SUGGEST YOU THINK AGAIN!
OH? WHY'S THAT?

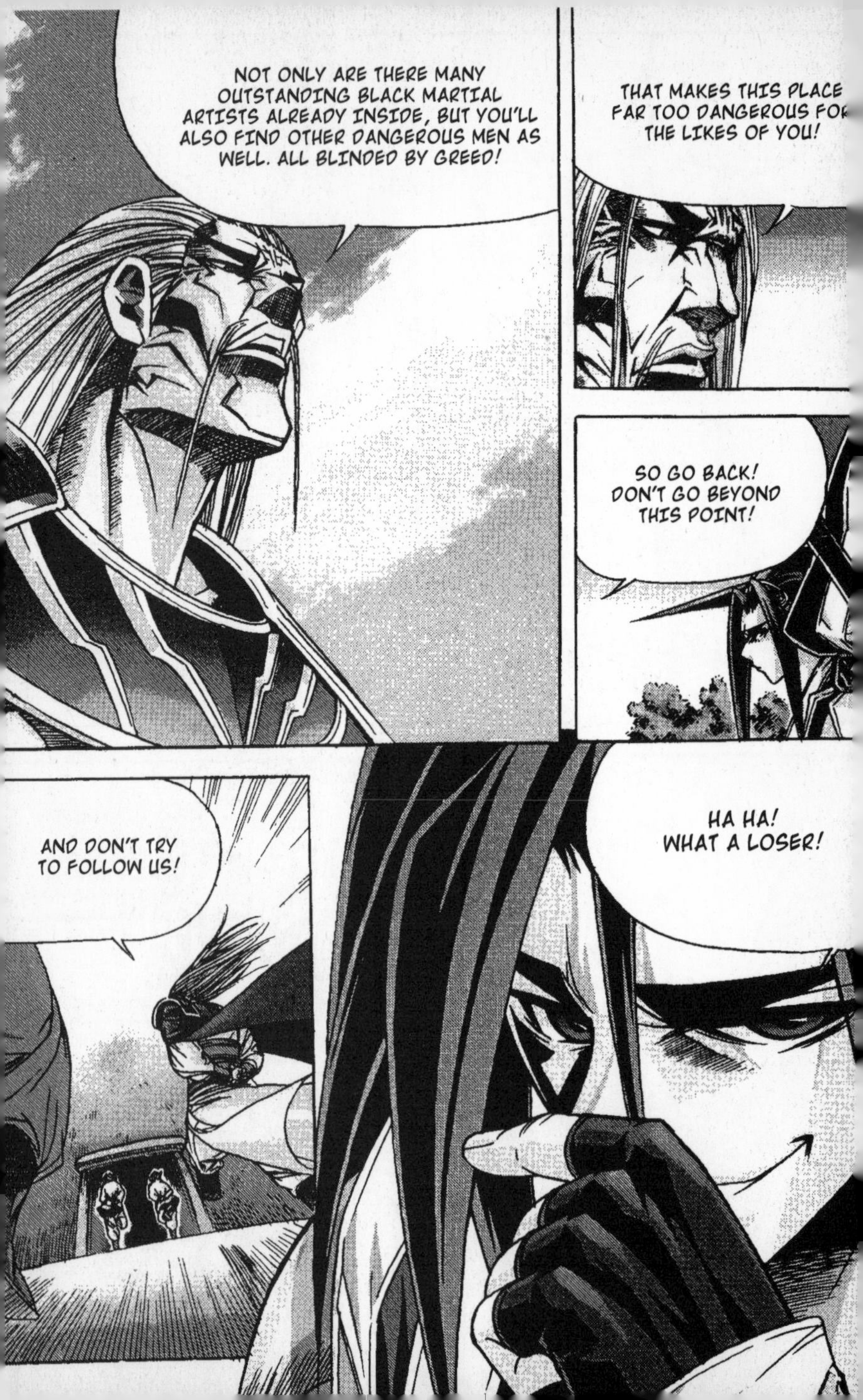
NOT ONLY ARE THERE MANY OUTSTANDING BLACK MARTIAL ARTISTS ALREADY INSIDE, BUT YOU'LL ALSO FIND OTHER DANGEROUS MEN AS WELL. ALL BLINDED BY GREED!
THAT MAKES THIS PLACE FAR TOO DANGEROUS FOR THE LIKES OF YOU!
SO GO BACK! DON'T GO BEYOND THIS POINT!
AND DON'T TRY TO FOLLOW US!
HA HA! WHAT A LOSER!

KING OF HELL

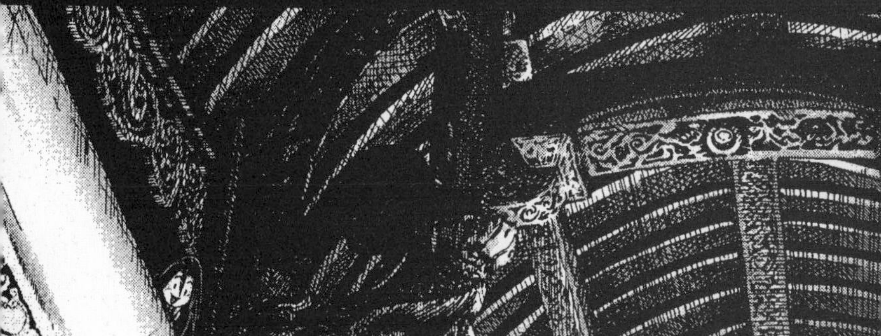

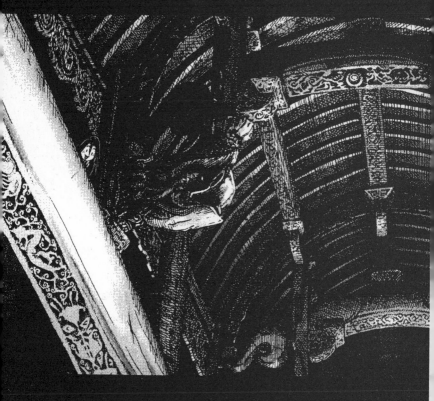

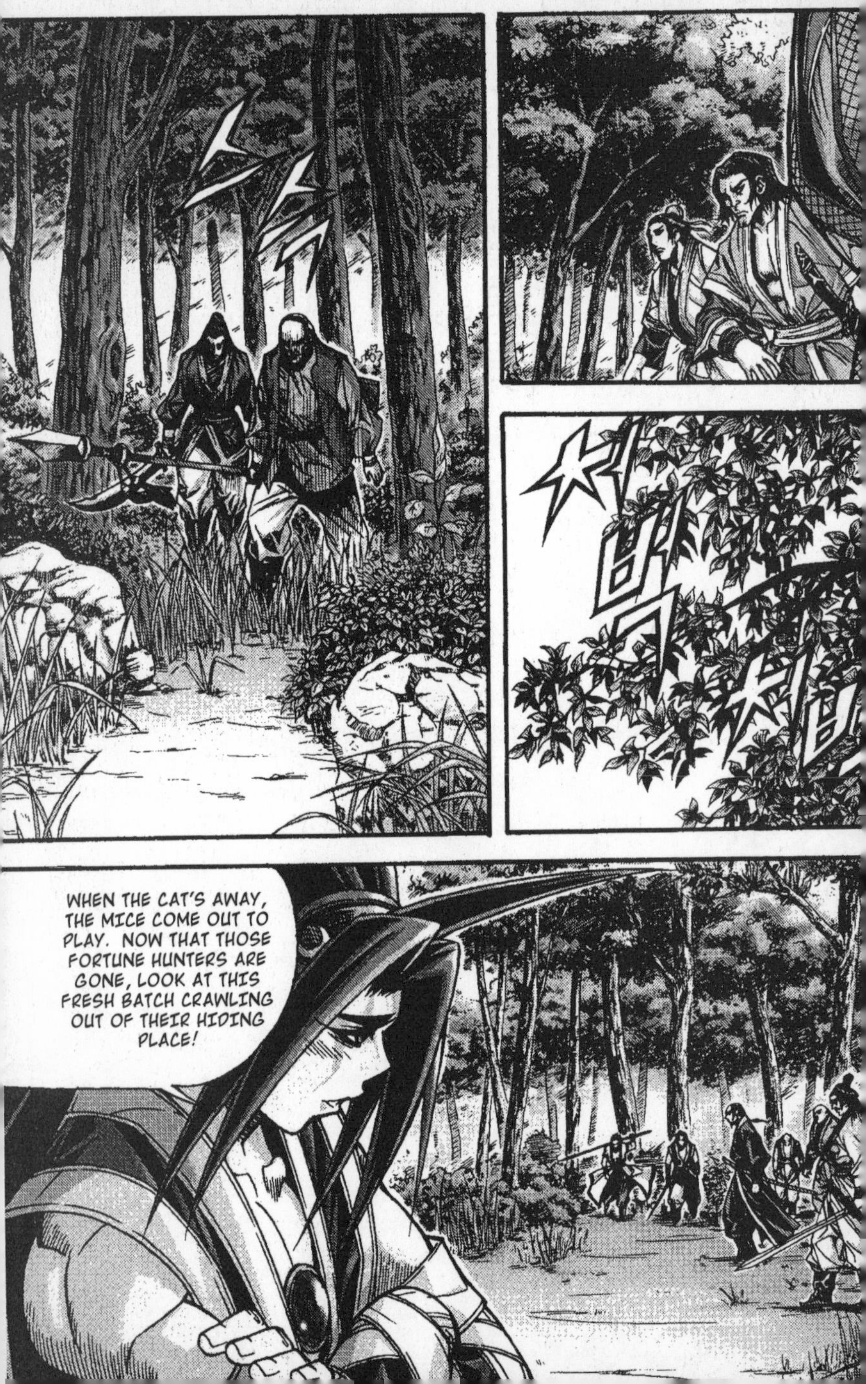
WHEN THE CAT'S AWAY, THE MICE COME OUT TO PLAY. NOW THAT THOSE FORTUNE HUNTERS ARE GONE, LOOK AT THIS FRESH BATCH CRAWLING OUT OF THEIR HIDING PLACE!

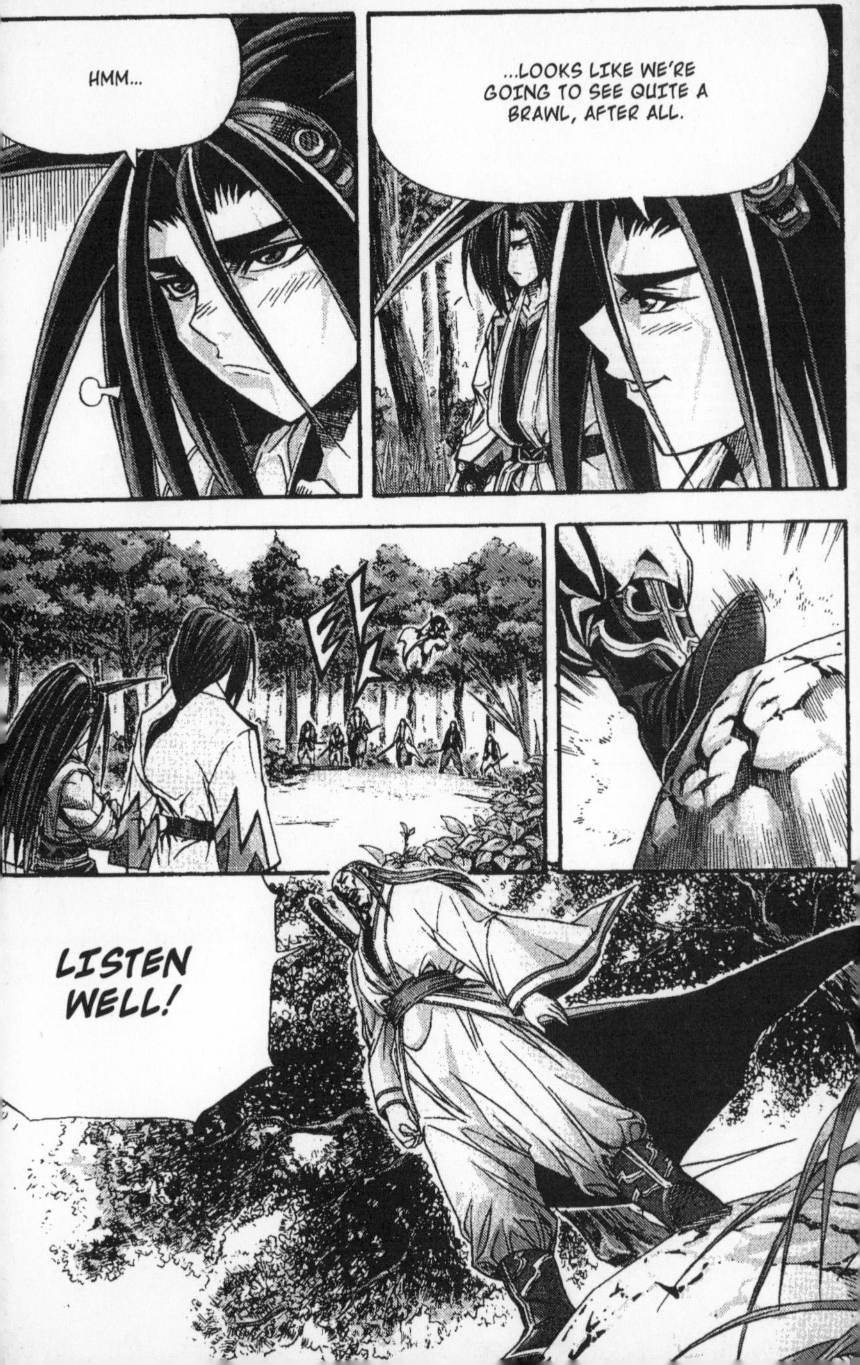
HMM...
...LOOKS LIKE WE'RE GOING TO SEE QUITE A BRAWL, AFTER ALL.
LISTEN WELL!

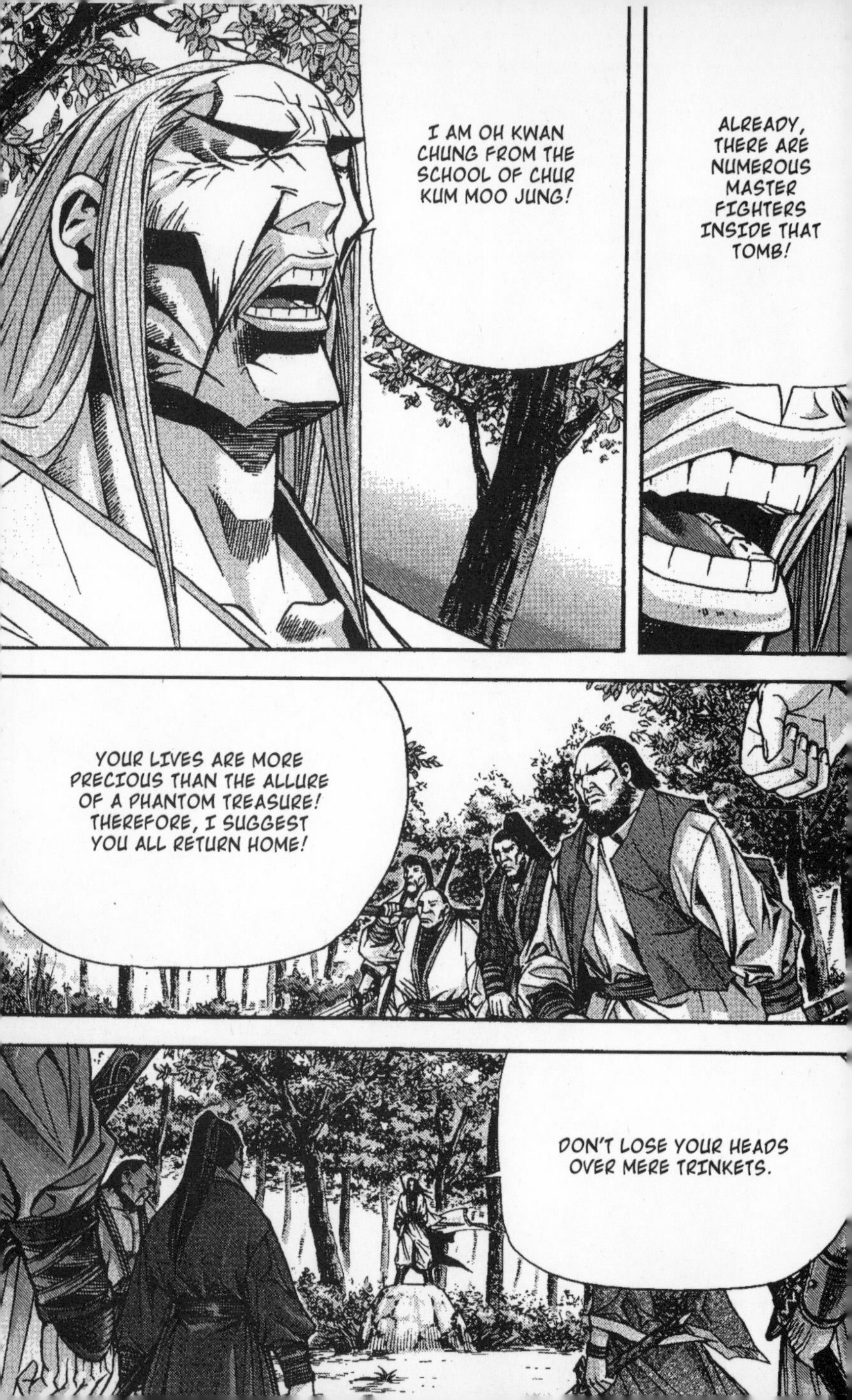
I AM OH KWAN CHUNG FROM THE SCHOOL OF CHUR KUM MOO JUNG!
ALREADY, THERE ARE NUMEROUS MASTER FIGHTERS INSIDE THAT TOMB!
YOUR LIVES ARE MORE PRECIOUS THAN THE ALLURE OF A PHANTOM TREASURE! THEREFORE, I SUGGEST YOU ALL RETURN HOME!
DON'T LOSE YOUR HEADS OVER MERE TRINKETS.

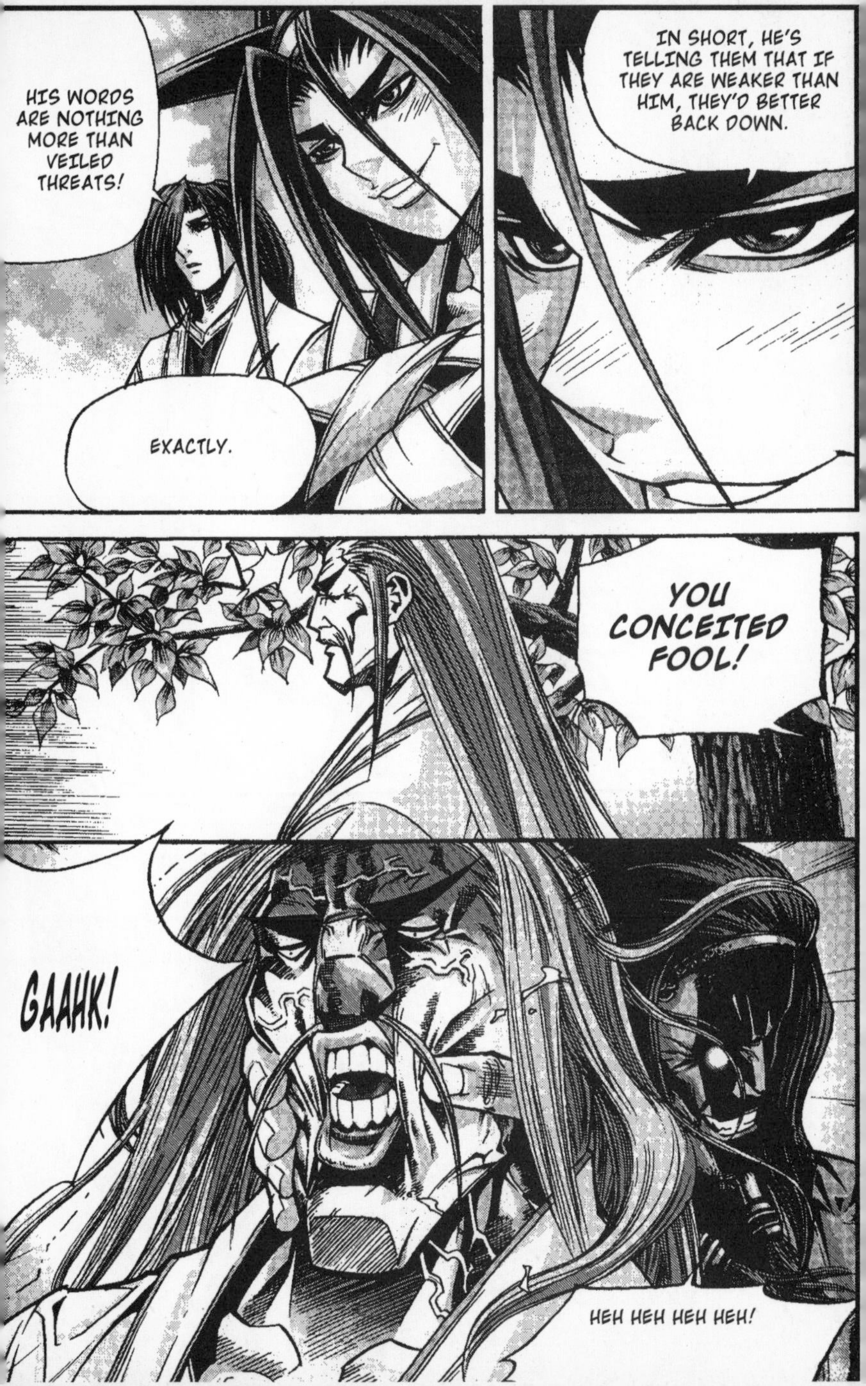
HIS WORDS ARE NOTHING MORE THAN VEILED THREATS!
EXACTLY.
IN SHORT, HE'S TELLING THEM THAT IF THEY ARE WEAKER THAN HIM, THEY'D BETTER BACK DOWN.
YOU CONCEITED FOOL!
GAAHK!
HEH HEH HEH HEH!

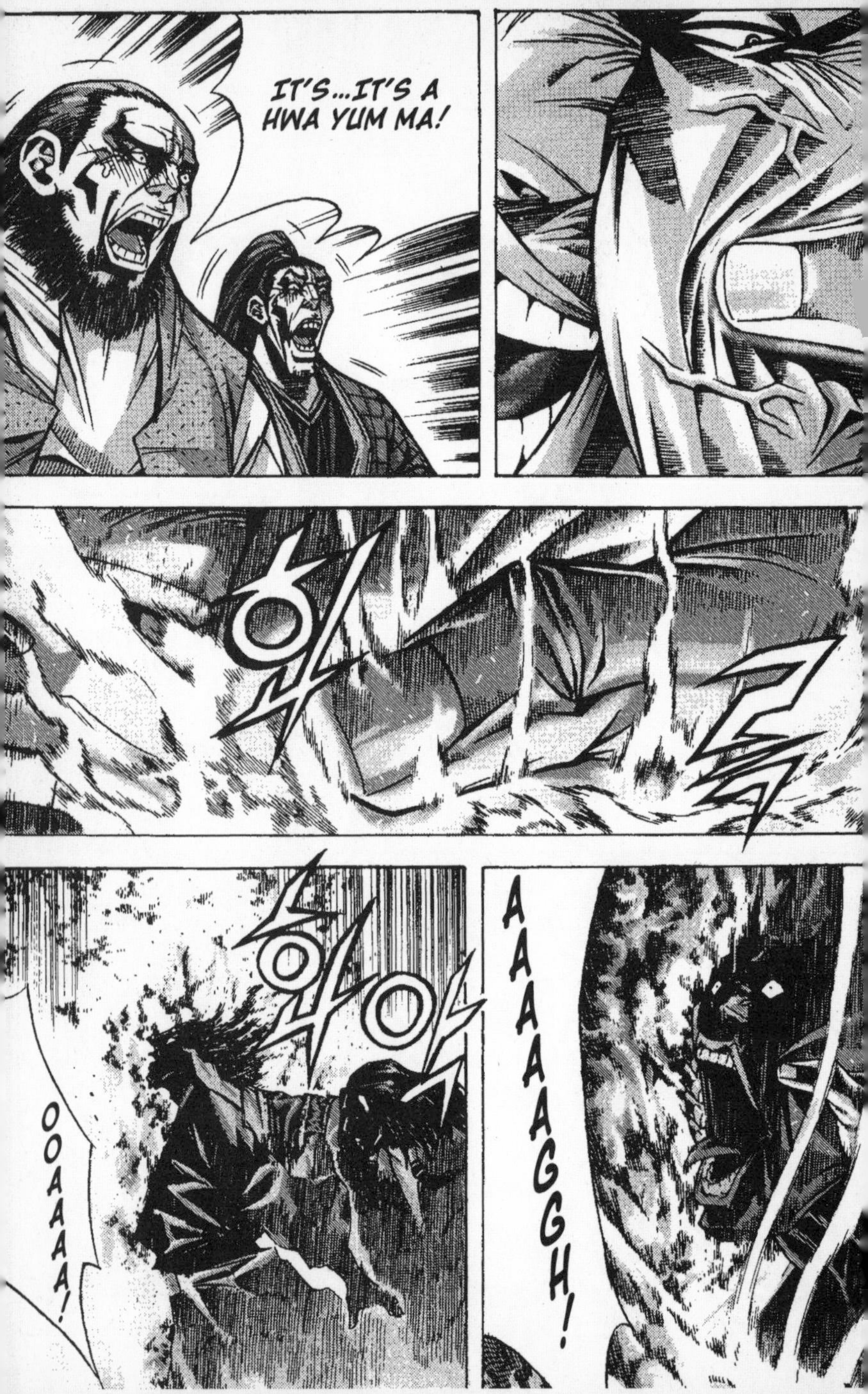
IT'S...IT'S A HWA YUM MA!
OOAAAA!
AAAAAAGGH!

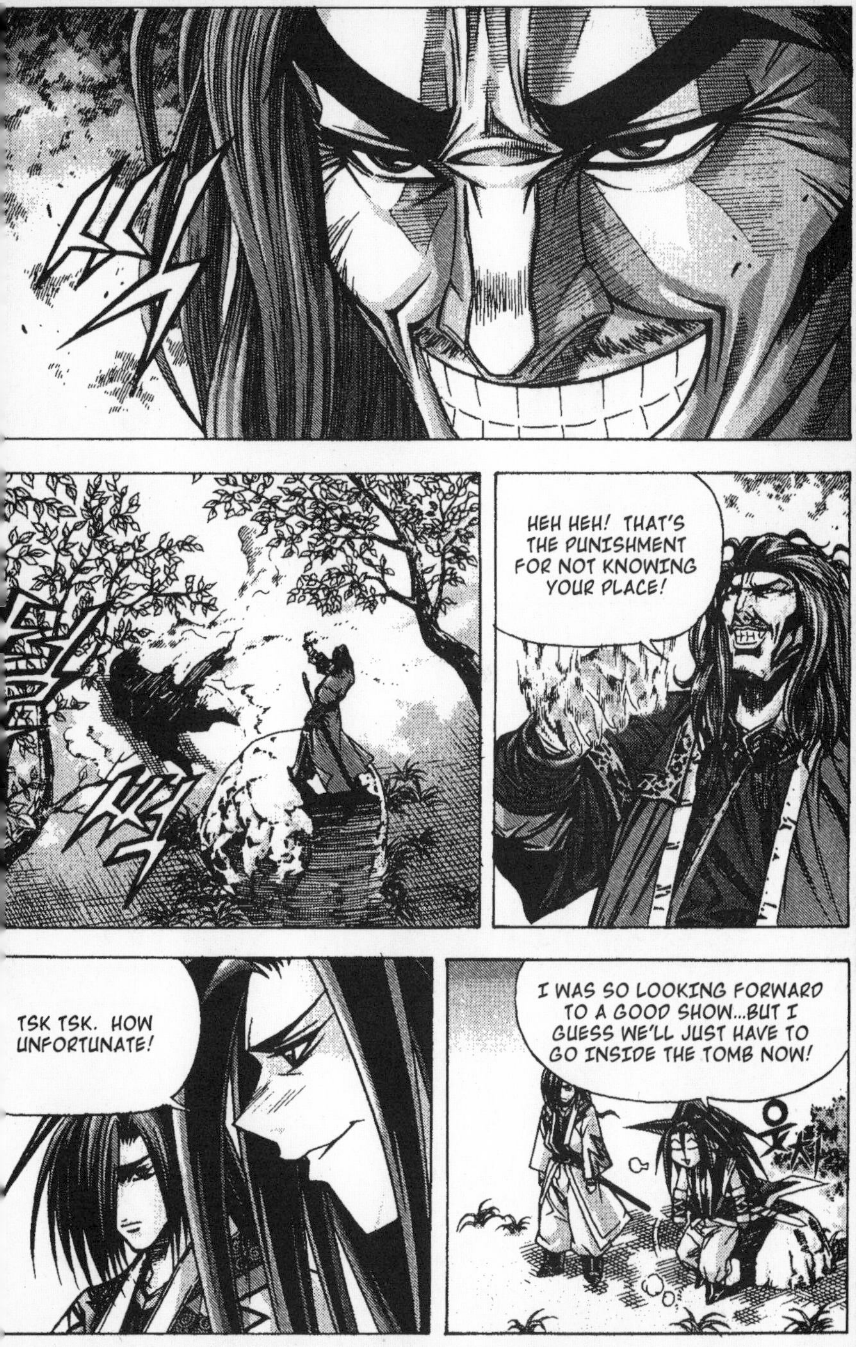
HEH HEH! THAT'S THE PUNISHMENT FOR NOT KNOWING YOUR PLACE!
TSK TSK. HOW UNFORTUNATE!
I WAS SO LOOKING FORWARD TO A GOOD SHOW...BUT I GUESS WE'LL JUST HAVE TO GO INSIDE THE TOMB NOW!

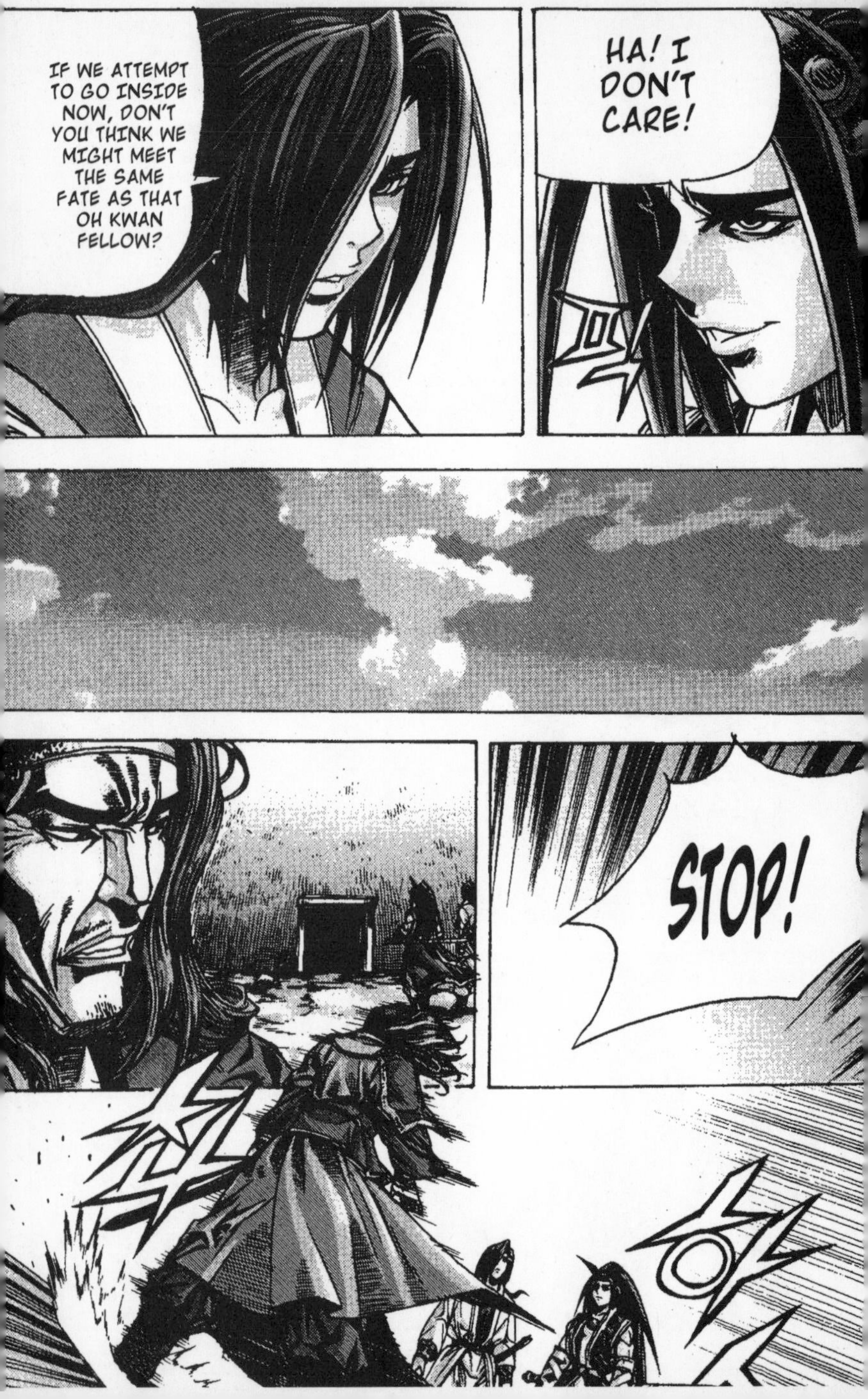
IF WE ATTEMPT TO GO INSIDE NOW, DON'T YOU THINK WE MIGHT MEET THE SAME FATE AS THAT OH KWAN FELLOW?
HA! I DON'T CARE!
STOP!

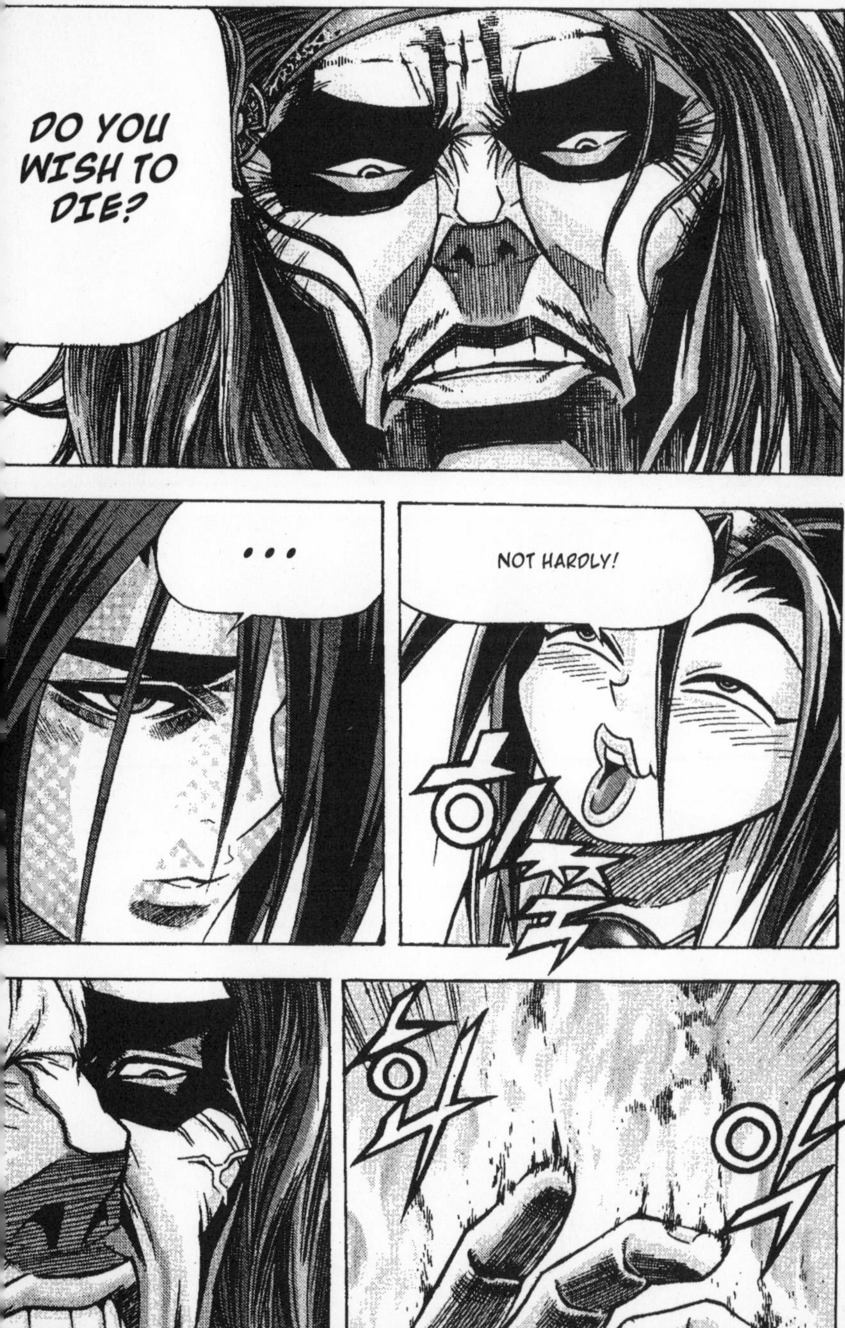
DO YOU WISH TO DIE?
...
NOT HARDLY!

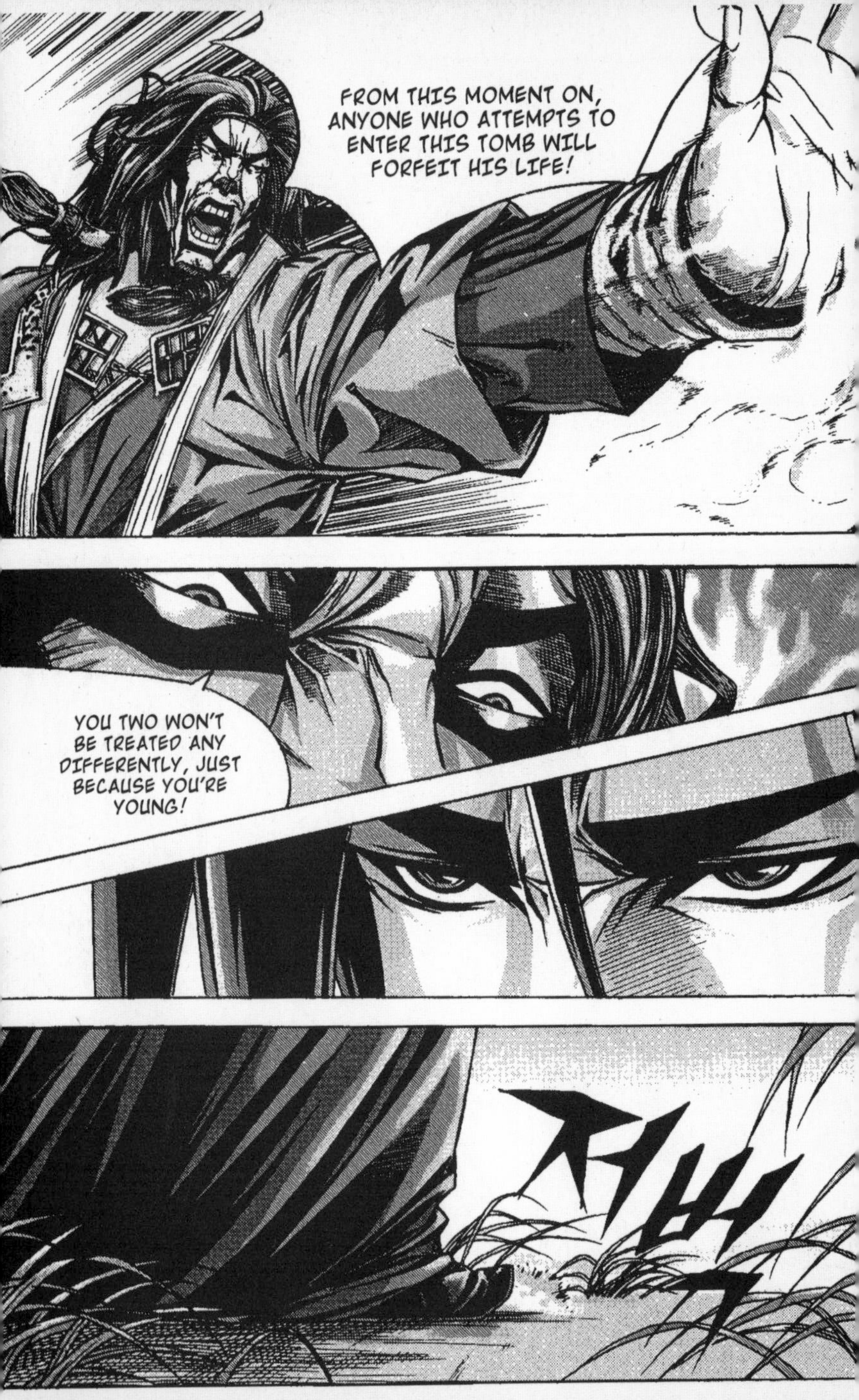
FROM THIS MOMENT ON, ANYONE WHO ATTEMPTS TO ENTER THIS TOMB WILL FORFEIT HIS LIFE!
YOU TWO WON'T BE TREATED ANY DIFFERENTLY, JUST BECAUSE YOU'RE YOUNG!

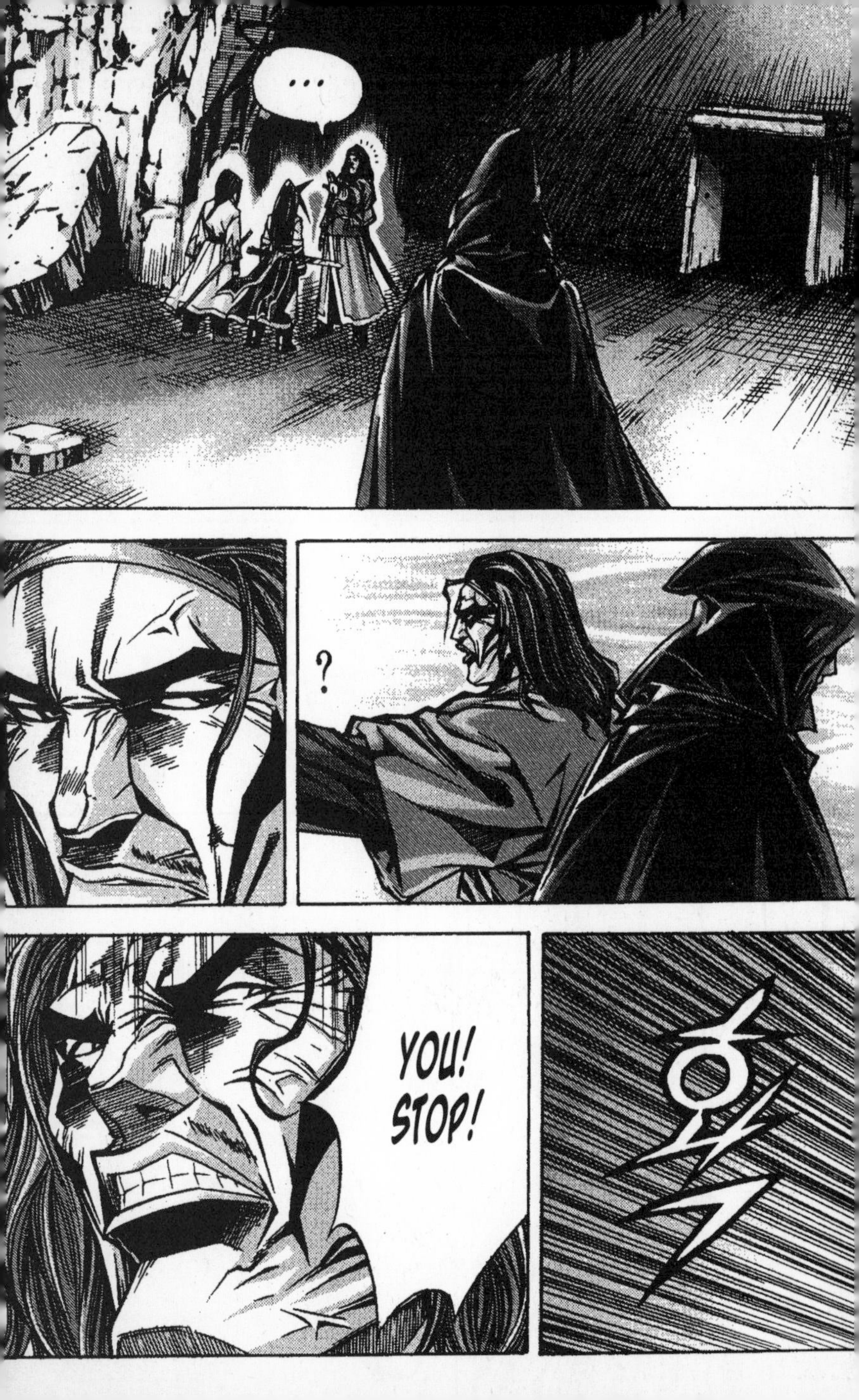
...
?
YOU! STOP!

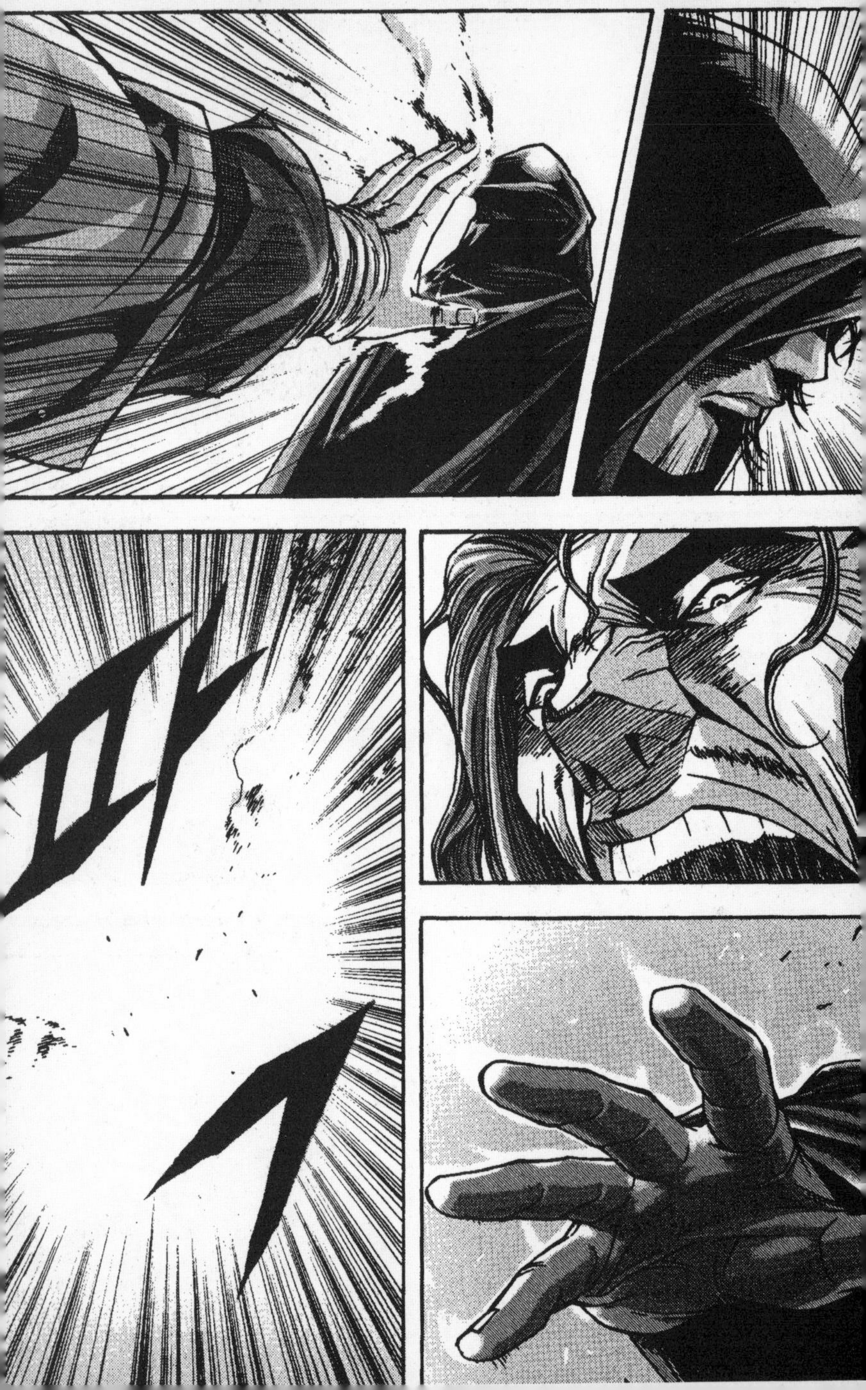

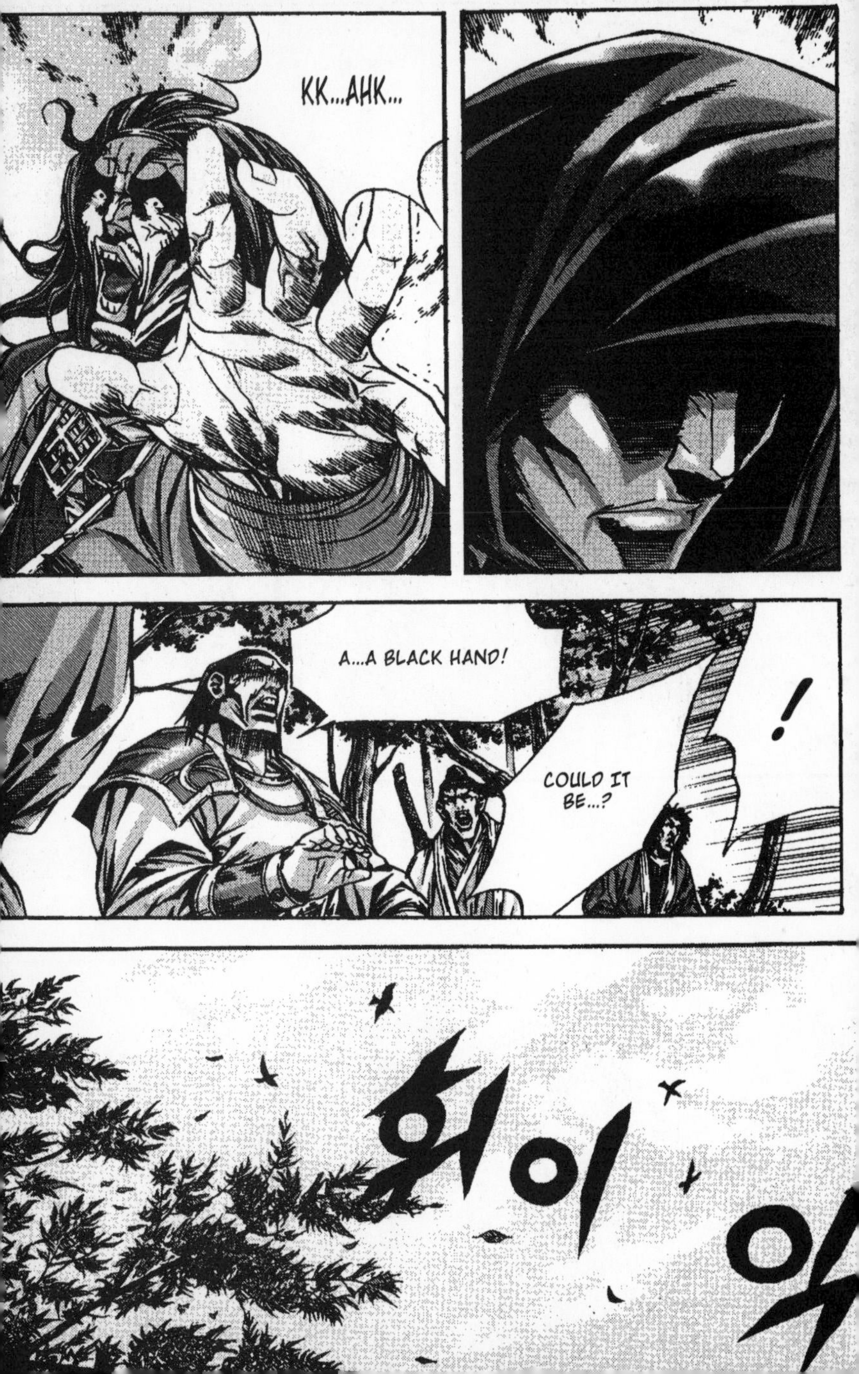
KK...AHK...
A...A BLACK HAND!
!
COULD IT BE...?

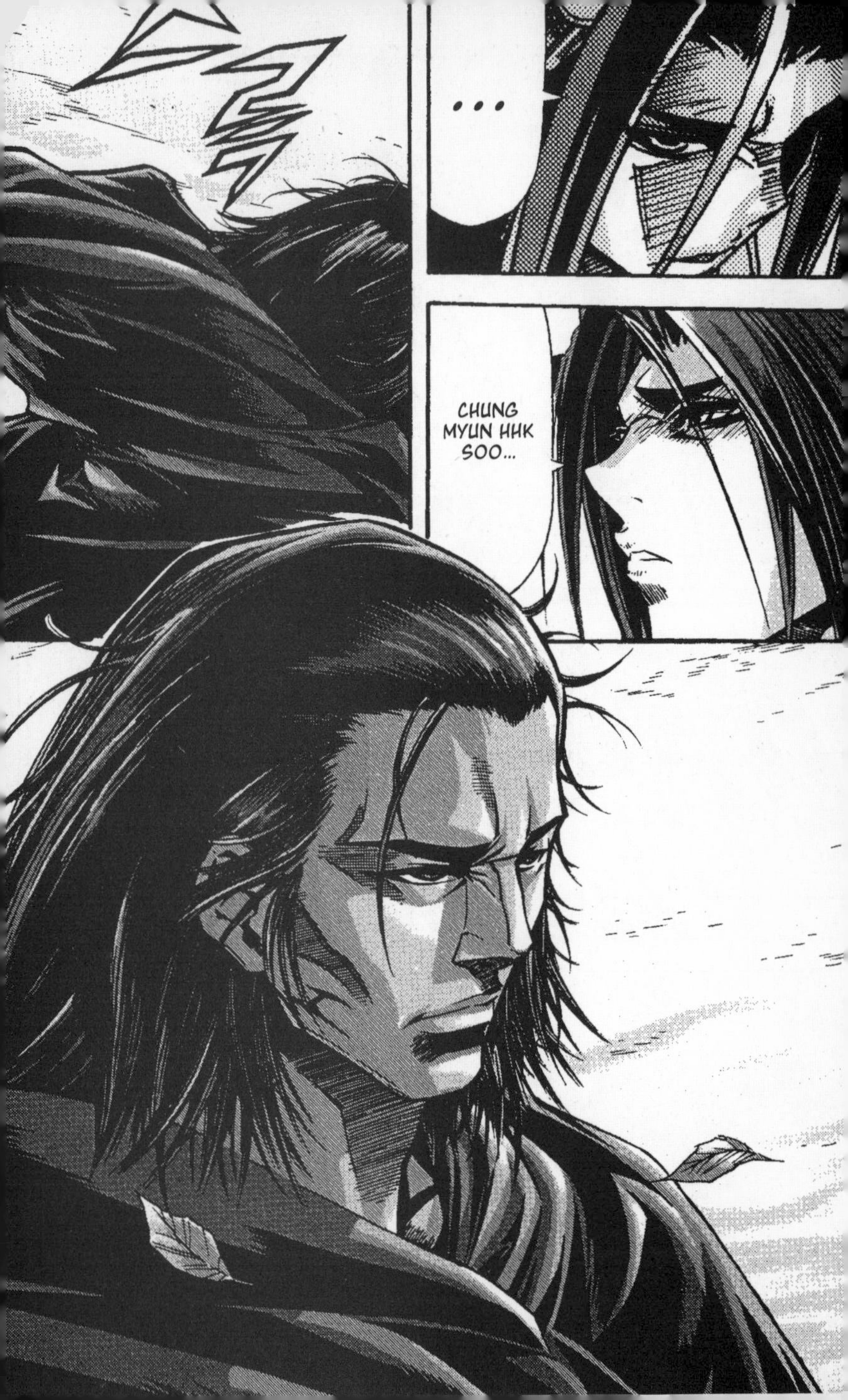
...
CHUNG MYUN HHK SOO...

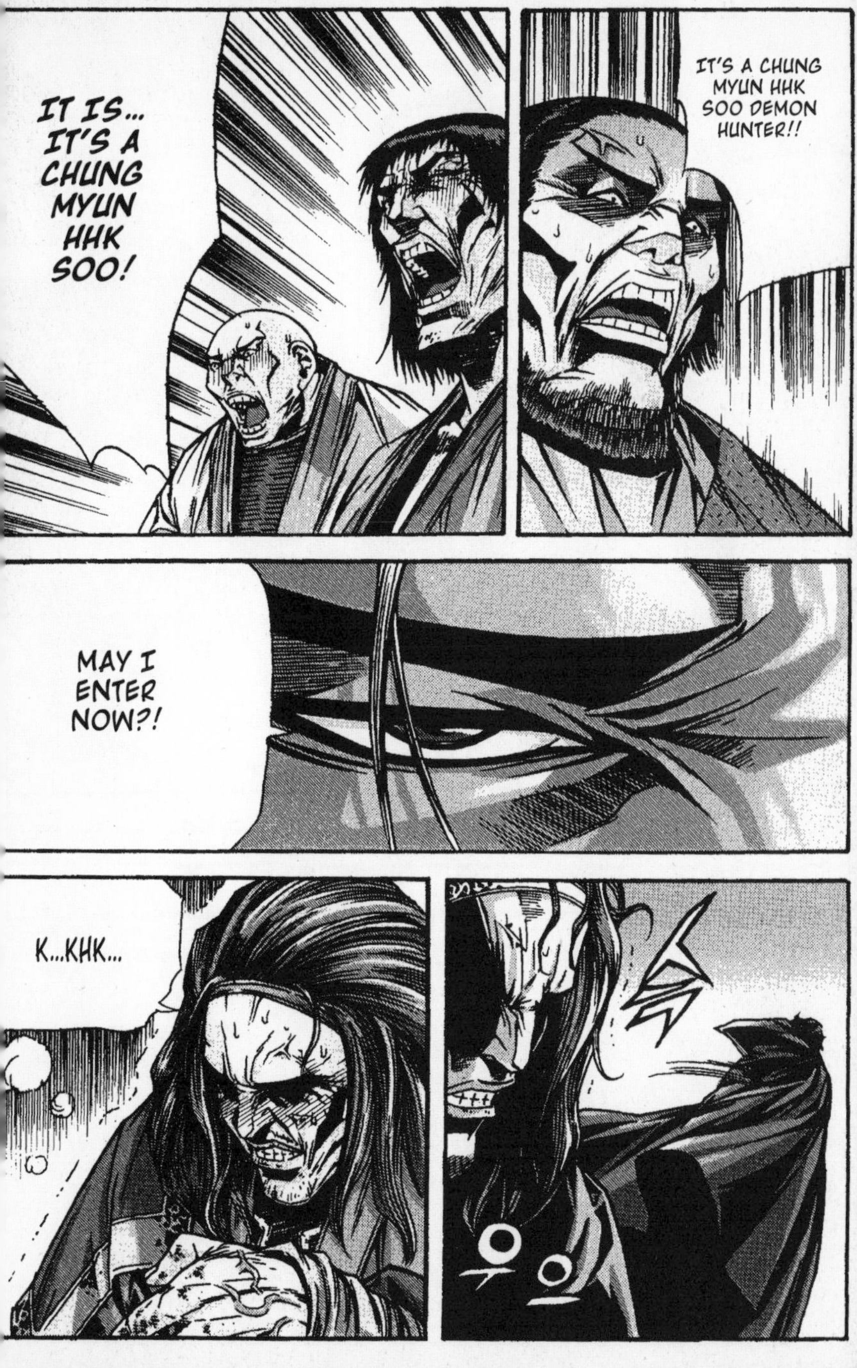
IT IS... IT'S A CHUNG MYUN HHK SOO!
IT'S A CHUNG MYUN HHK SOO DEMON HUNTER!!
MAY I ENTER NOW?!
K...KHK...

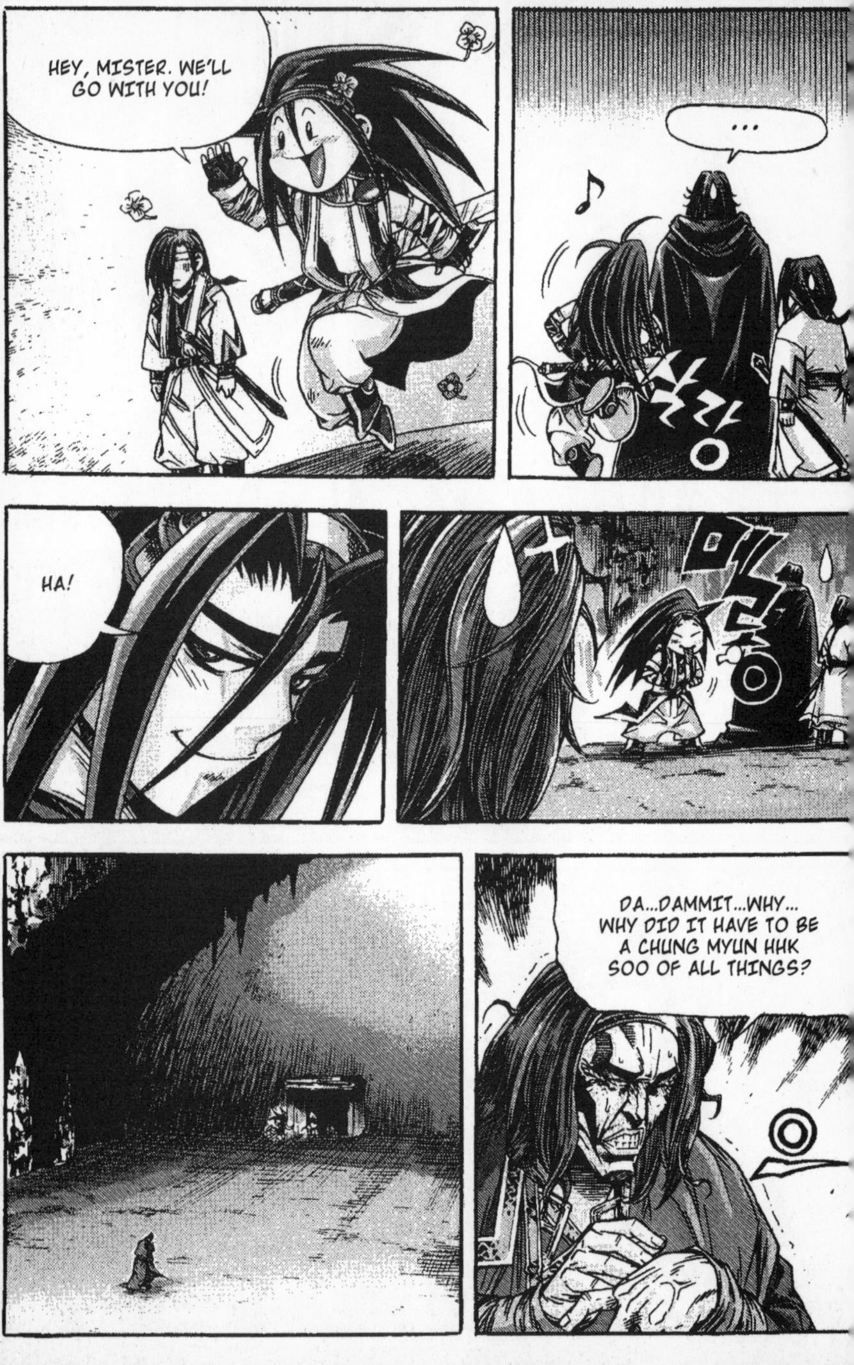
HEY, MISTER. WE'LL GO WITH YOU!
...
HA!
DA...DAMMIT...WHY... WHY DID IT HAVE TO BE A CHUNG MYUN HHK SOO OF ALL THINGS?

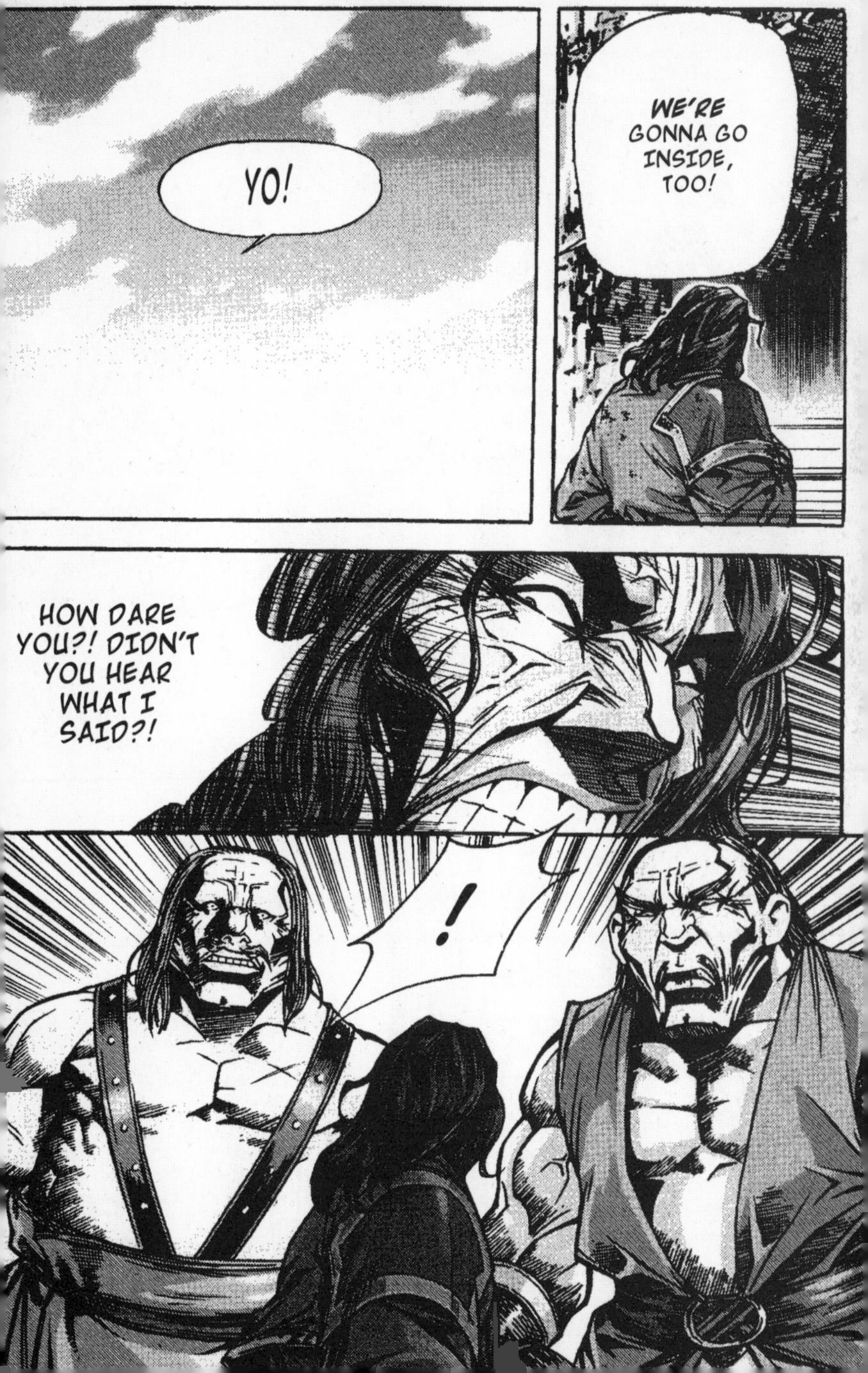
YO!
WE'RE GONNA GO INSIDE, TOO!
HOW DARE YOU?! DIDN'T YOU HEAR WHAT I SAID?!
!

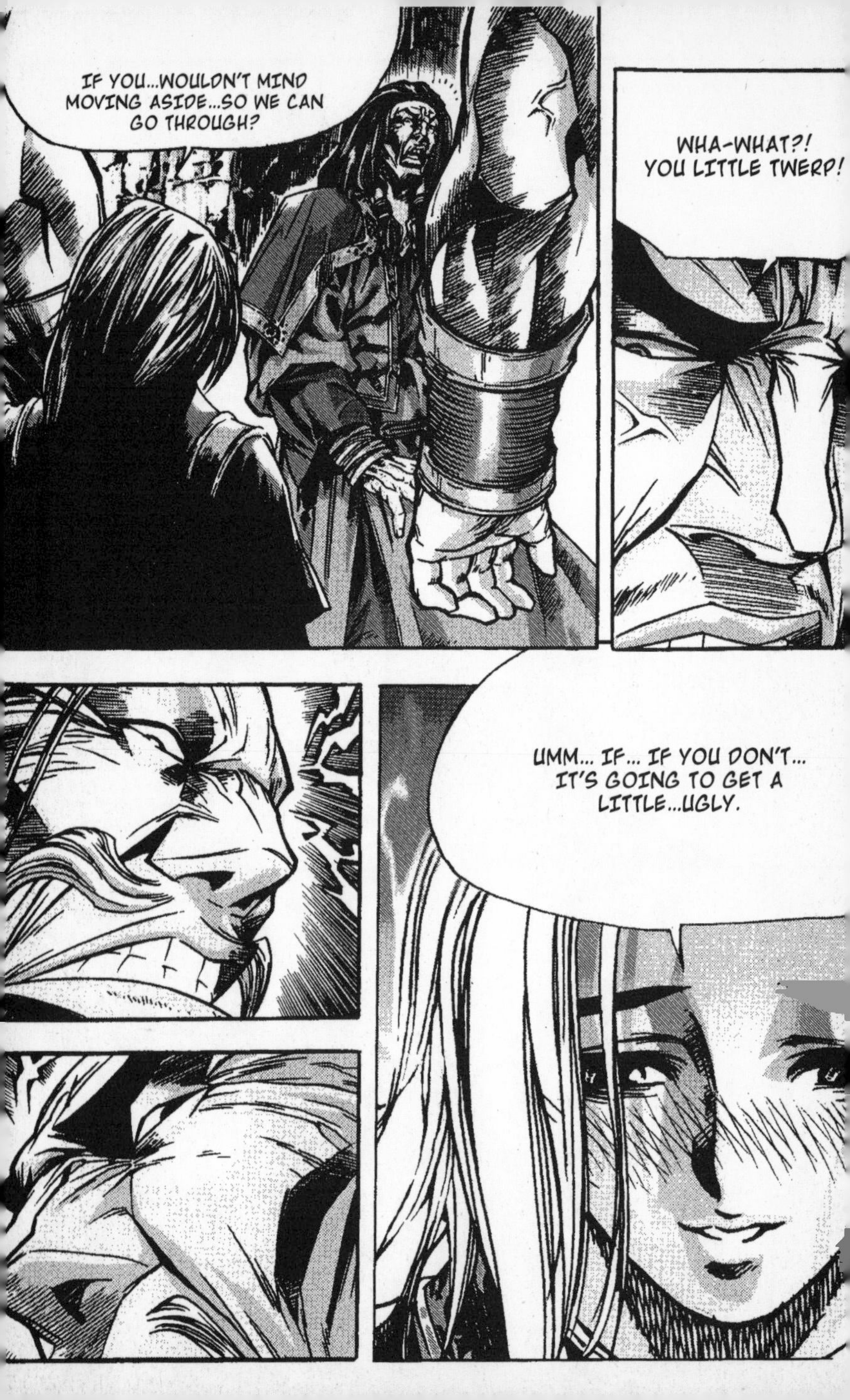
IF YOU...WOULDN'T MIND MOVING ASIDE...SO WE CAN GO THROUGH?
WHA-WHAT?! YOU LITTLE TWERP!
UMM... IF... IF YOU DON'T... IT'S GOING TO GET A LITTLE...UGLY.

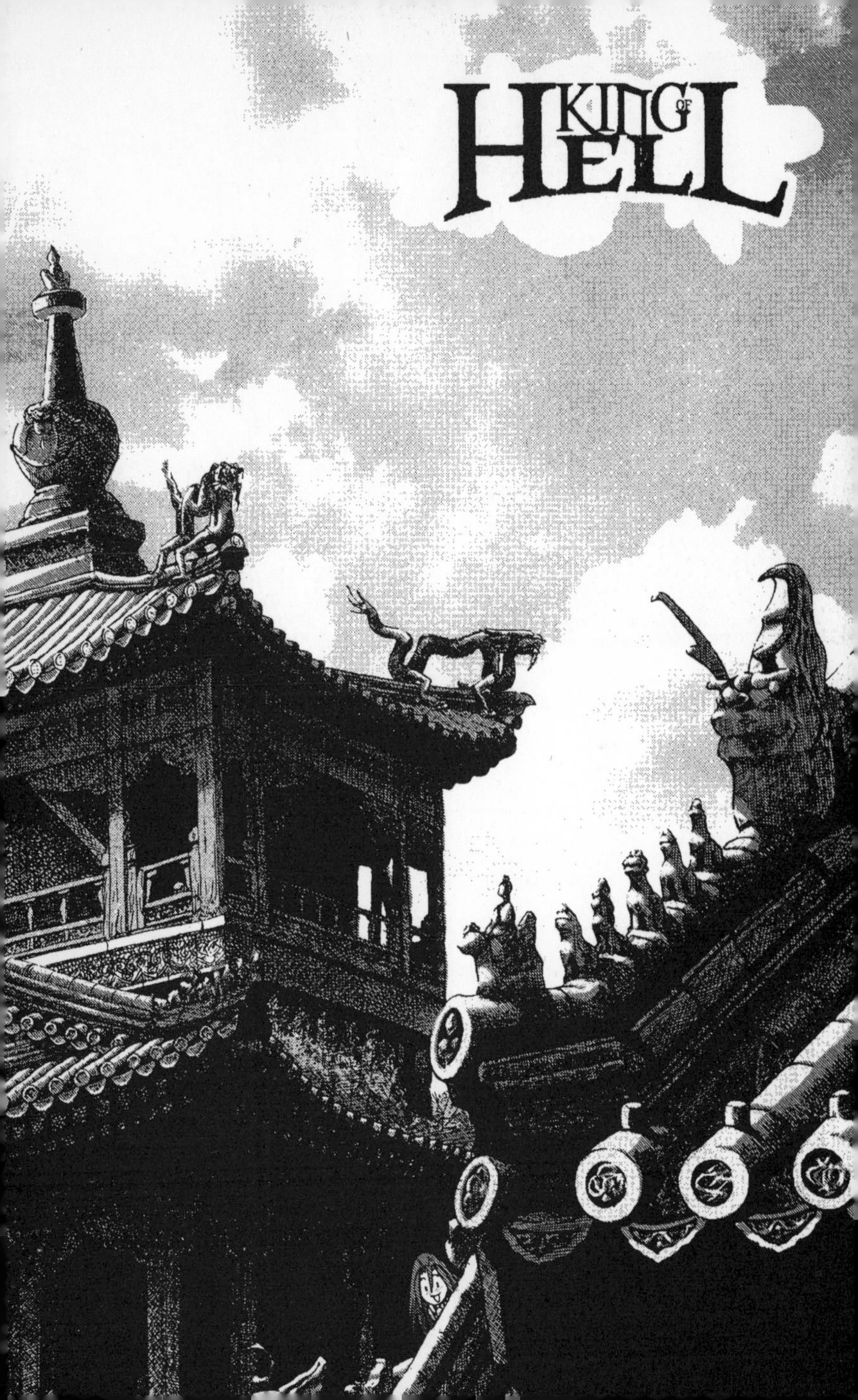
KING OF HELL

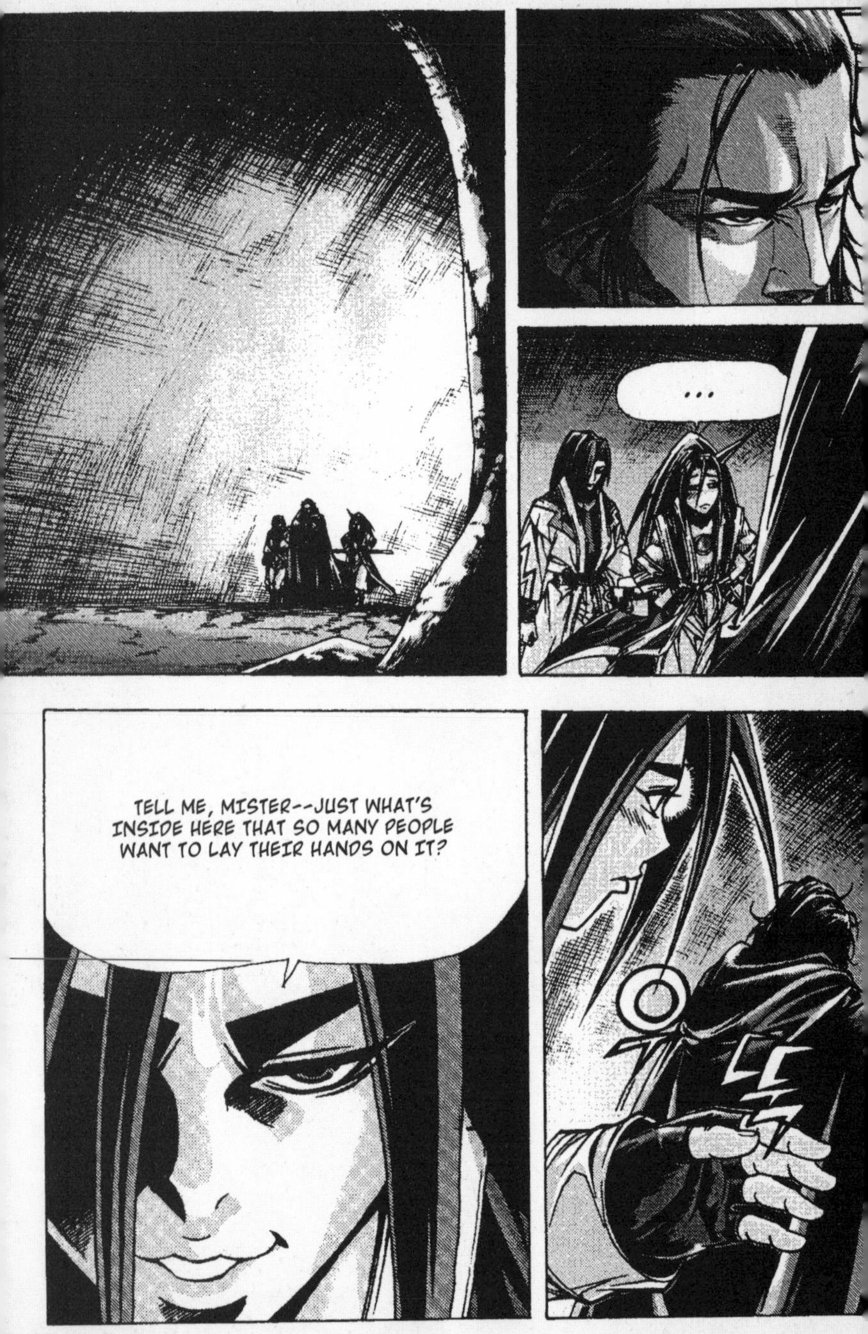
...
TELL ME, MISTER--JUST WHAT'S INSIDE HERE THAT SO MANY PEOPLE WANT TO LAY THEIR HANDS ON IT?

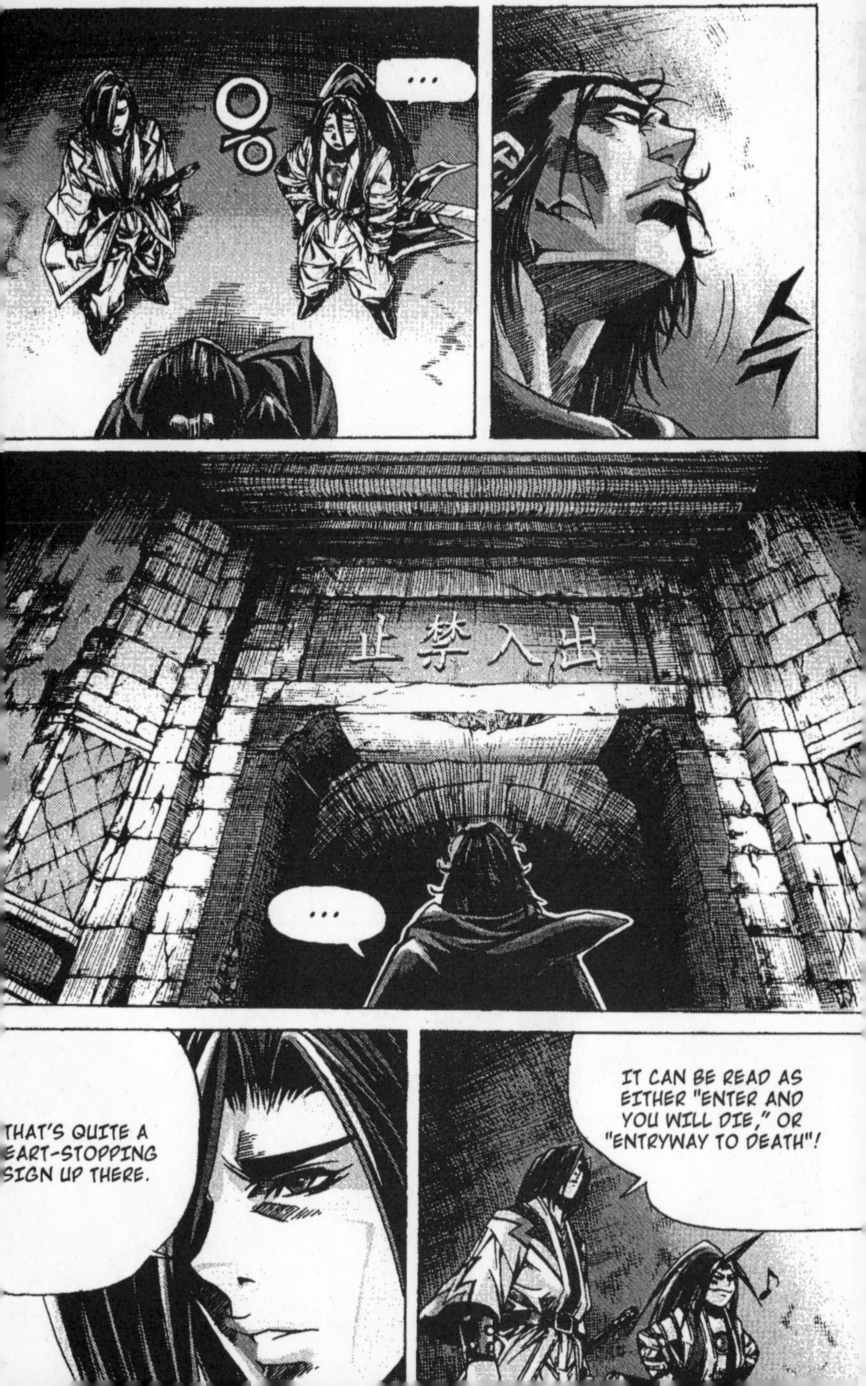
...
出入禁止
...
THAT'S QUITE A EART-STOPPING SIGN UP THERE.
IT CAN BE READ AS EITHER "ENTER AND YOU WILL DIE," OR "ENTRYWAY TO DEATH"!

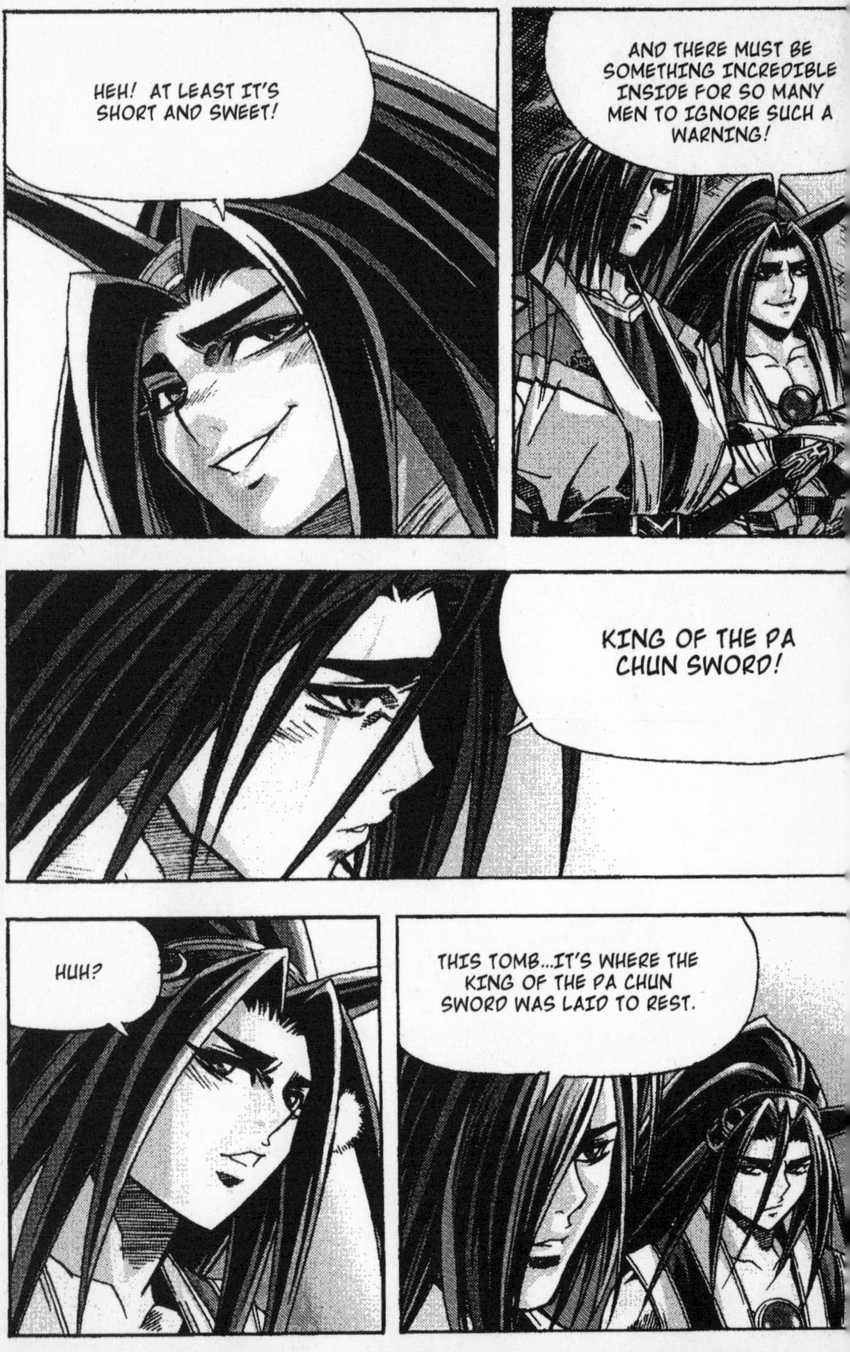
HEH! AT LEAST IT'S SHORT AND SWEET!
AND THERE MUST BE SOMETHING INCREDIBLE INSIDE FOR SO MANY MEN TO IGNORE SUCH A WARNING!
KING OF THE PA CHUN SWORD!
HUH?
THIS TOMB...IT'S WHERE THE KING OF THE PA CHUN SWORD WAS LAID TO REST.

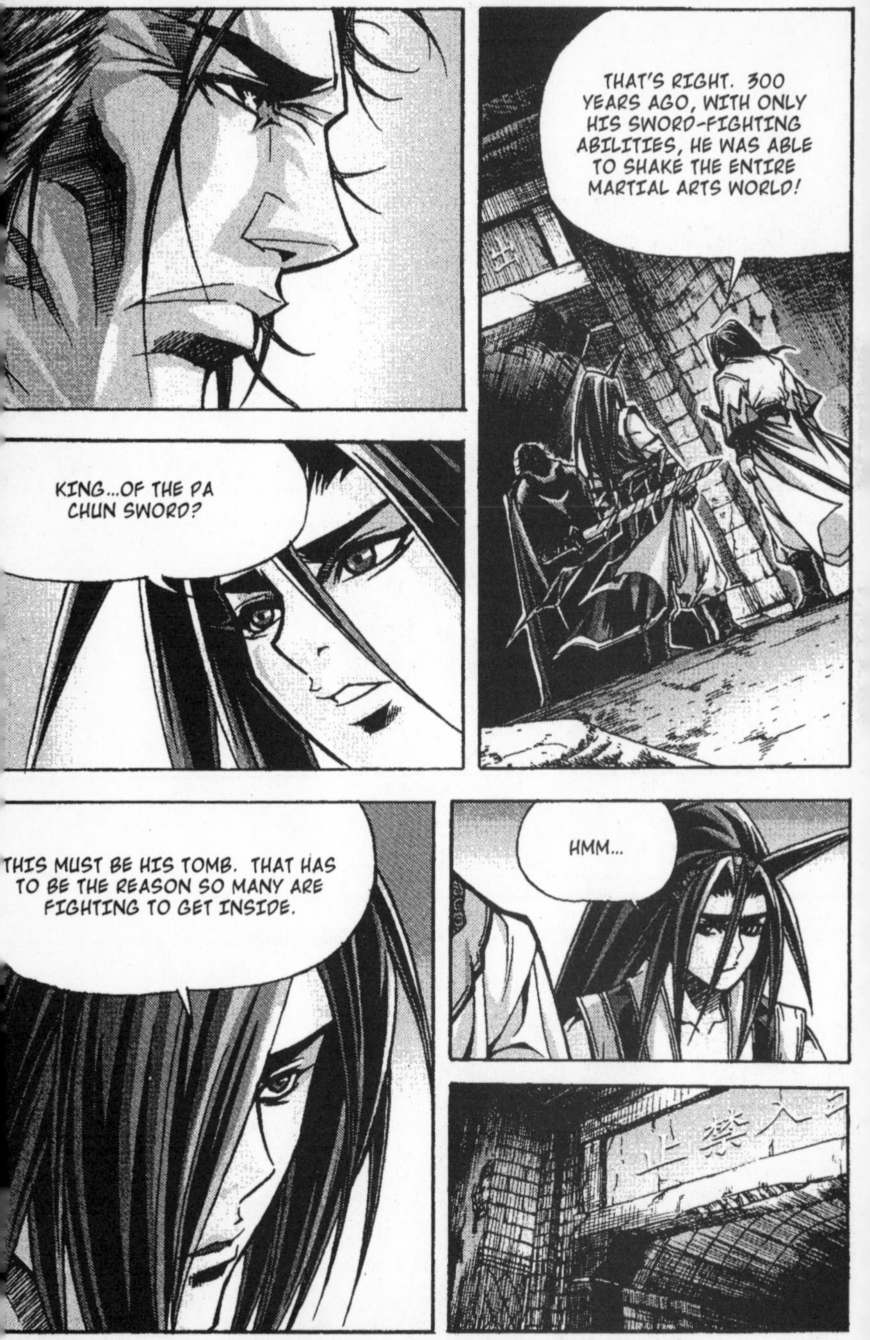
THAT'S RIGHT. 300 YEARS AGO, WITH ONLY HIS SWORD-FIGHTING ABILITIES, HE WAS ABLE TO SHAKE THE ENTIRE MARTIAL ARTS WORLD!
KING...OF THE PA CHUN SWORD?
THIS MUST BE HIS TOMB. THAT HAS TO BE THE REASON SO MANY ARE FIGHTING TO GET INSIDE.
HMM...

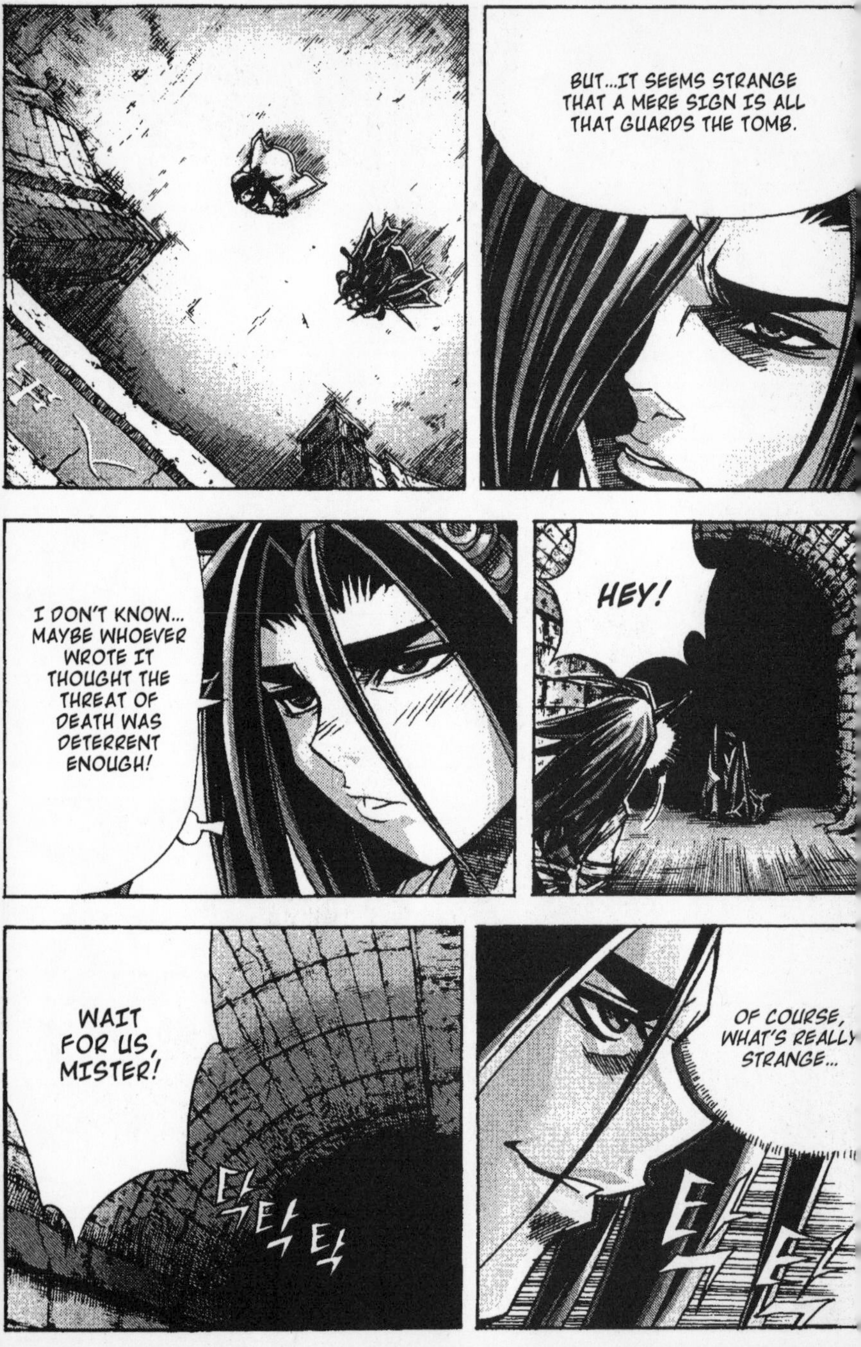
BUT...IT SEEMS STRANGE THAT A MERE SIGN IS ALL THAT GUARDS THE TOMB.
I DON'T KNOW... MAYBE WHOEVER WROTE IT THOUGHT THE THREAT OF DEATH WAS DETERRENT ENOUGH!
HEY!
WAIT FOR US, MISTER!
OF COURSE, WHAT'S REALLY STRANGE...

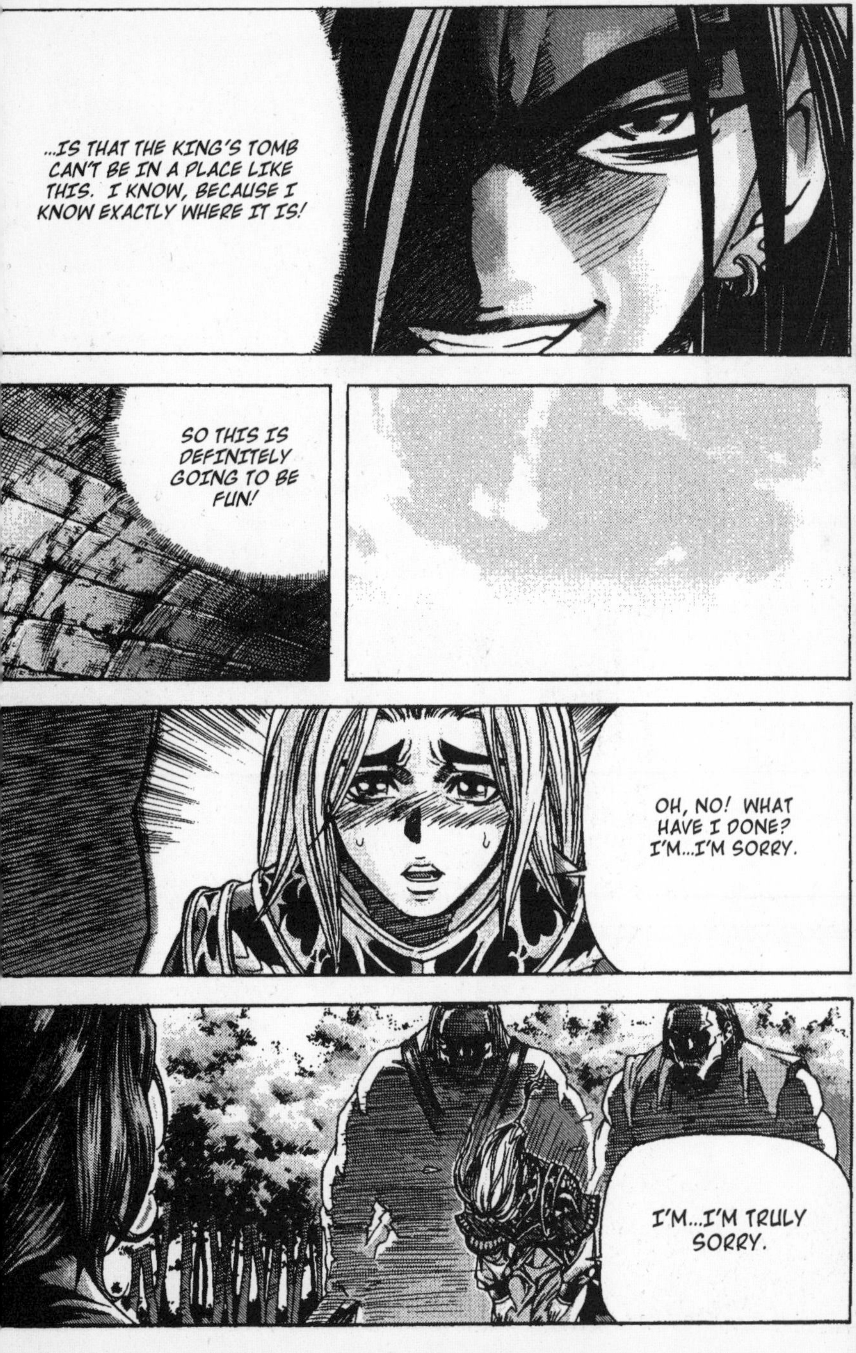
...IS THAT THE KING'S TOMB CAN'T BE IN A PLACE LIKE THIS. I KNOW, BECAUSE I KNOW EXACTLY WHERE IT IS!
SO THIS IS DEFINITELY GOING TO BE FUN!
OH, NO! WHAT HAVE I DONE? I'M...I'M SORRY.
I'M...I'M TRULY SORRY.

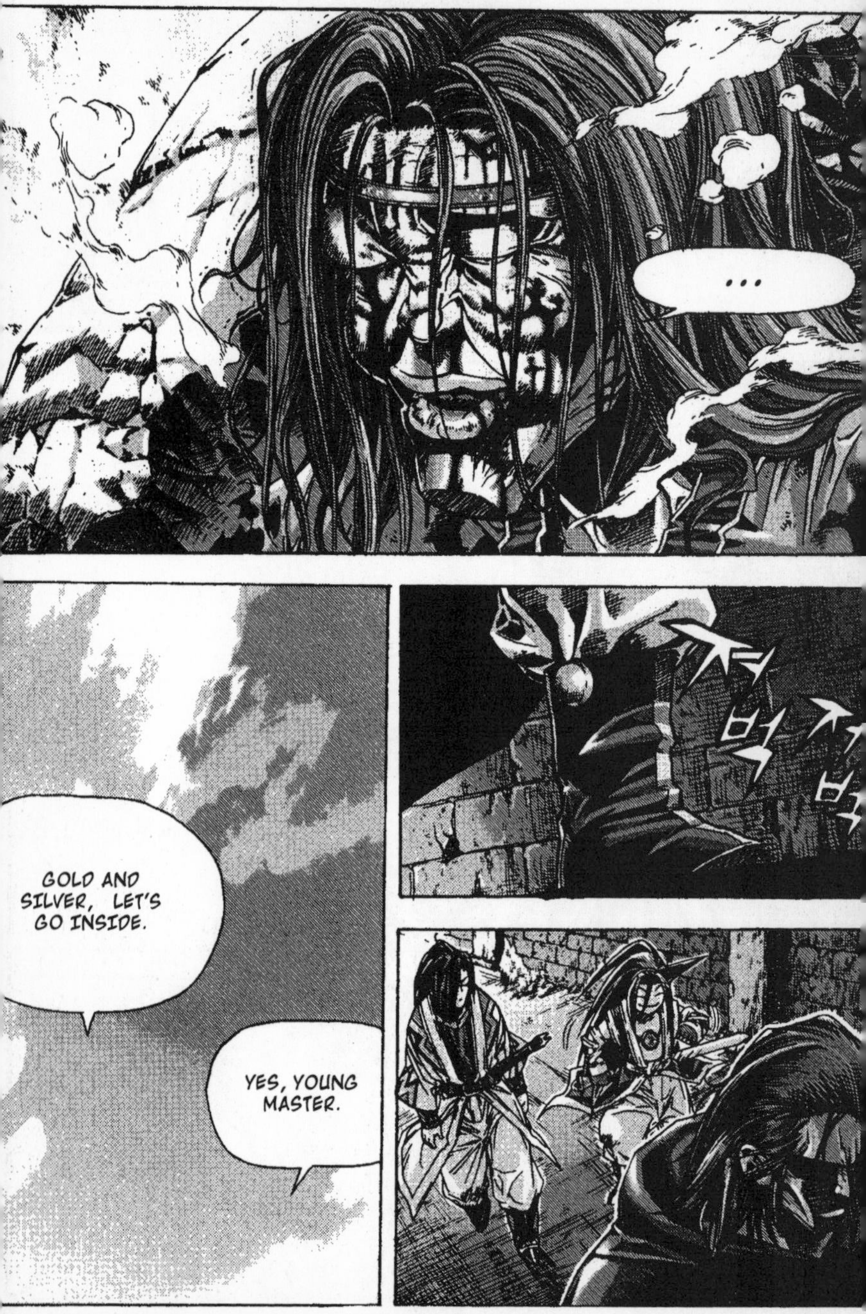
...
GOLD AND SILVER, LET'S GO INSIDE.
YES, YOUNG MASTER.

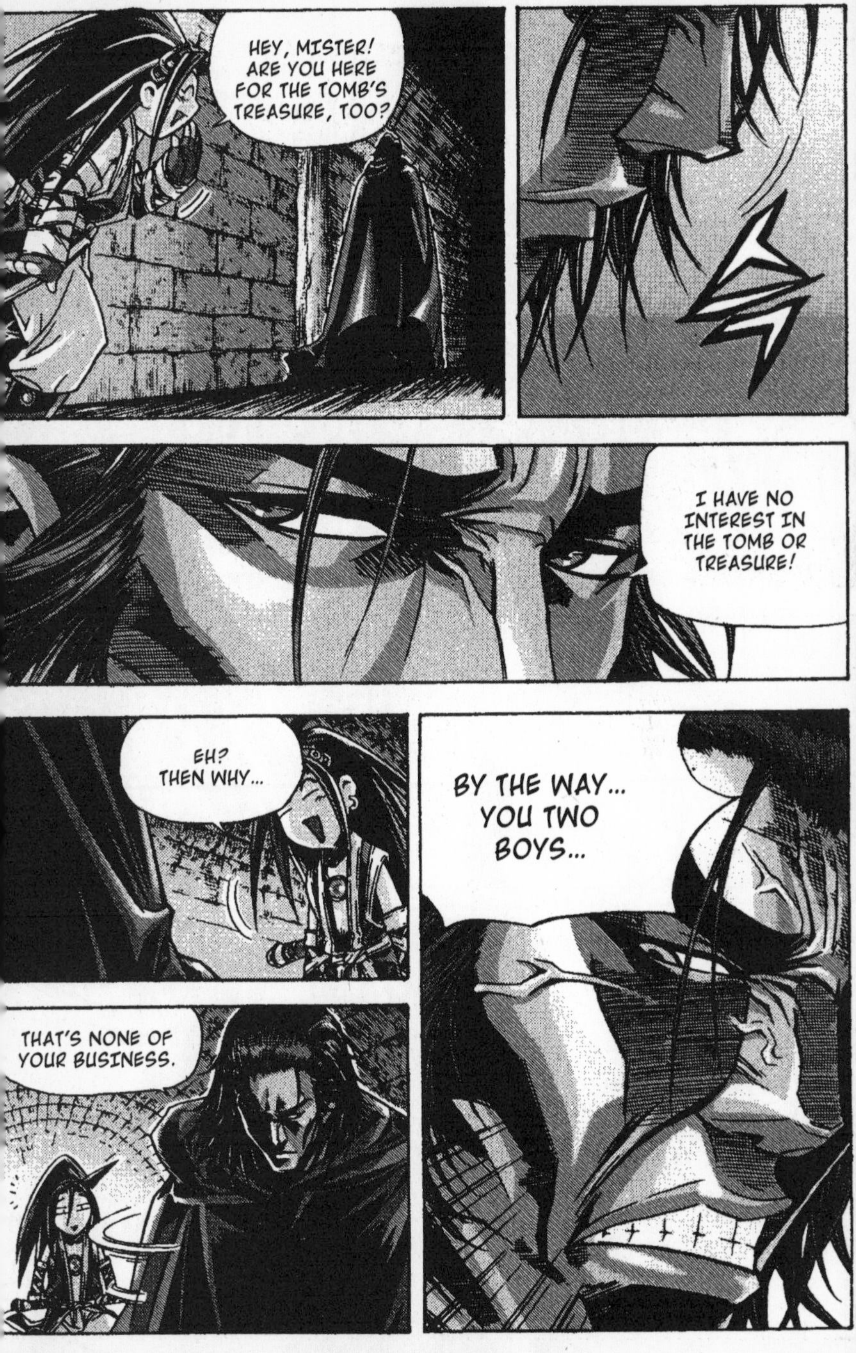
HEY, MISTER! ARE YOU HERE FOR THE TOMB'S TREASURE, TOO?
I HAVE NO INTEREST IN THE TOMB OR TREASURE!
EH? THEN WHY...
THAT'S NONE OF YOUR BUSINESS.
BY THE WAY... YOU TWO BOYS...

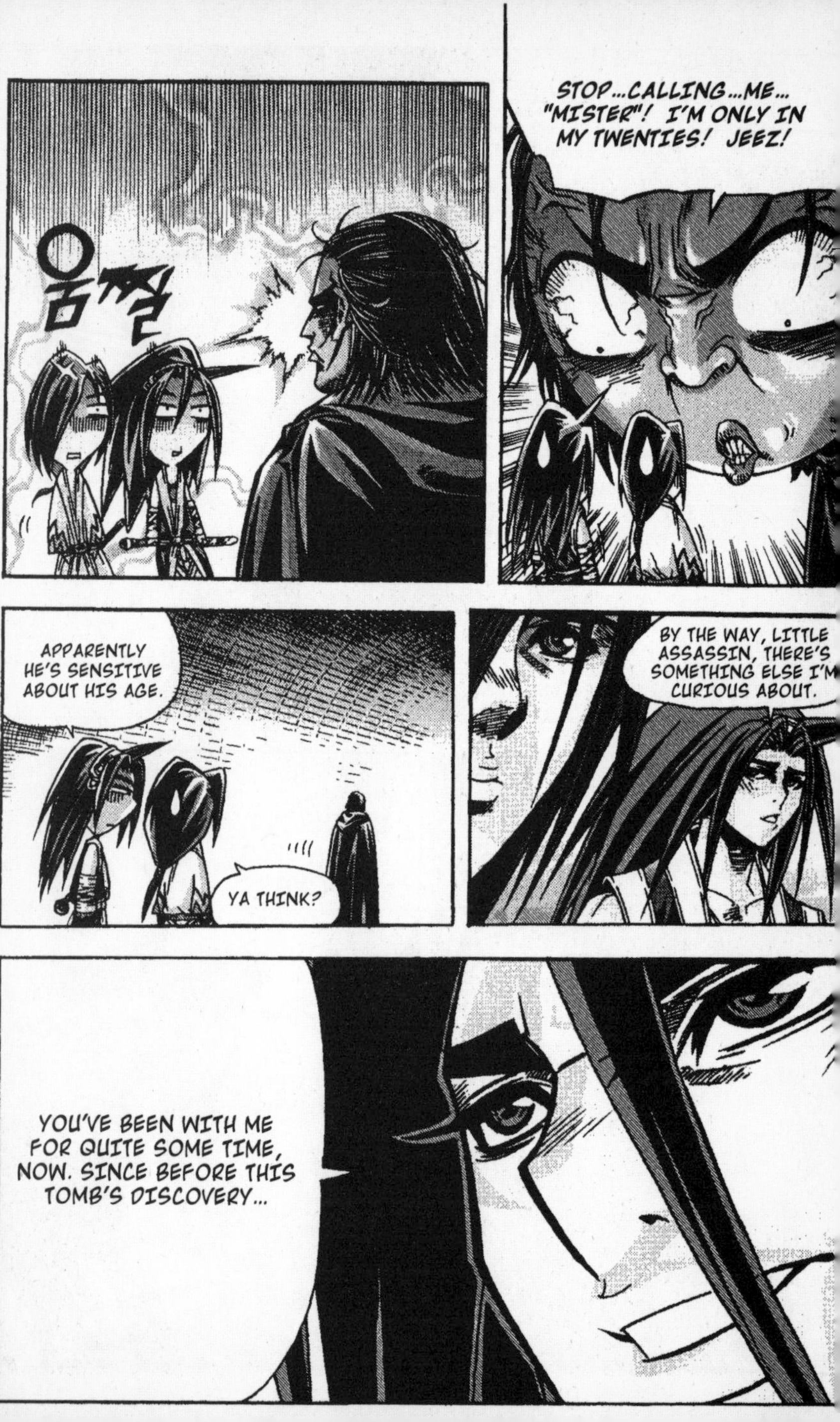
움찔
STOP...CALLING...ME... "MISTER"! I'M ONLY IN MY TWENTIES! JEEZ!
APPARENTLY HE'S SENSITIVE ABOUT HIS AGE.
YA THINK?
BY THE WAY, LITTLE ASSASSIN, THERE'S SOMETHING ELSE I'M CURIOUS ABOUT.
YOU'VE BEEN WITH ME FOR QUITE SOME TIME, NOW. SINCE BEFORE THIS TOMB'S DISCOVERY...

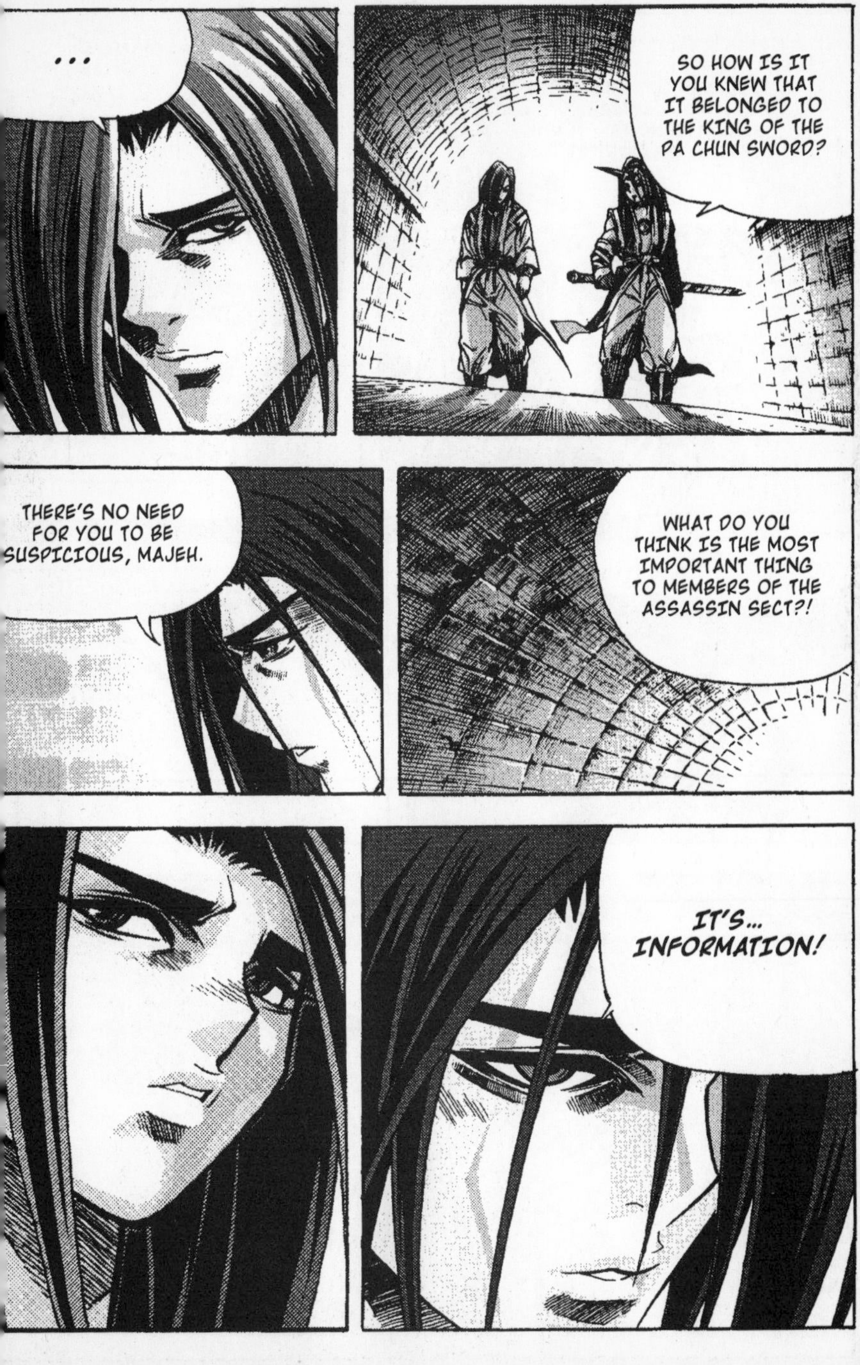
...
SO HOW IS IT YOU KNEW THAT IT BELONGED TO THE KING OF THE PA CHUN SWORD?
THERE'S NO NEED FOR YOU TO BE SUSPICIOUS, MAJEH.
WHAT DO YOU THINK IS THE MOST IMPORTANT THING TO MEMBERS OF THE ASSASSIN SECT?!
IT'S... INFORMATION!

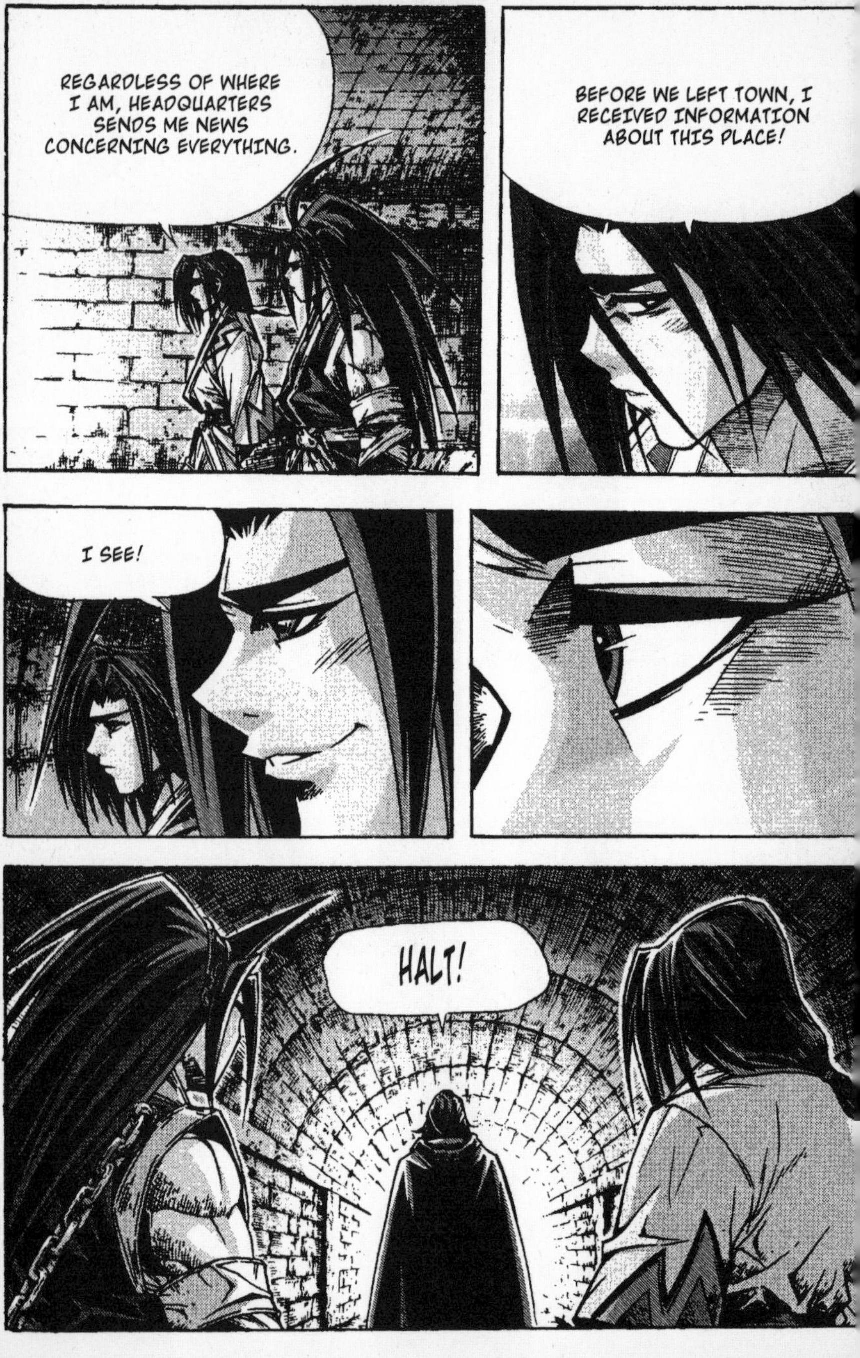
REGARDLESS OF WHERE I AM, HEADQUARTERS SENDS ME NEWS CONCERNING EVERYTHING.
BEFORE WE LEFT TOWN, I RECEIVED INFORMATION ABOUT THIS PLACE!
I SEE!
HALT!

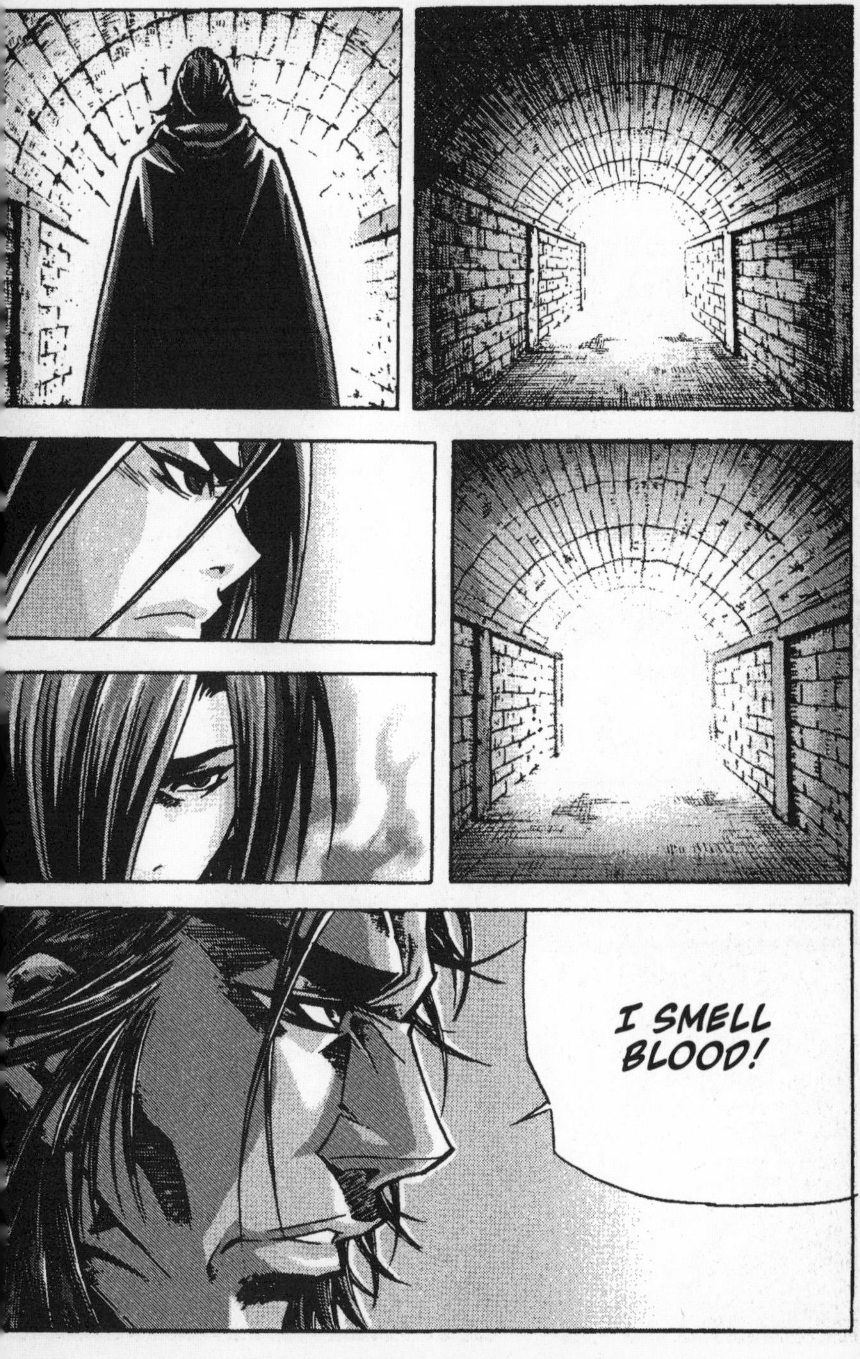
I SMELL BLOOD!

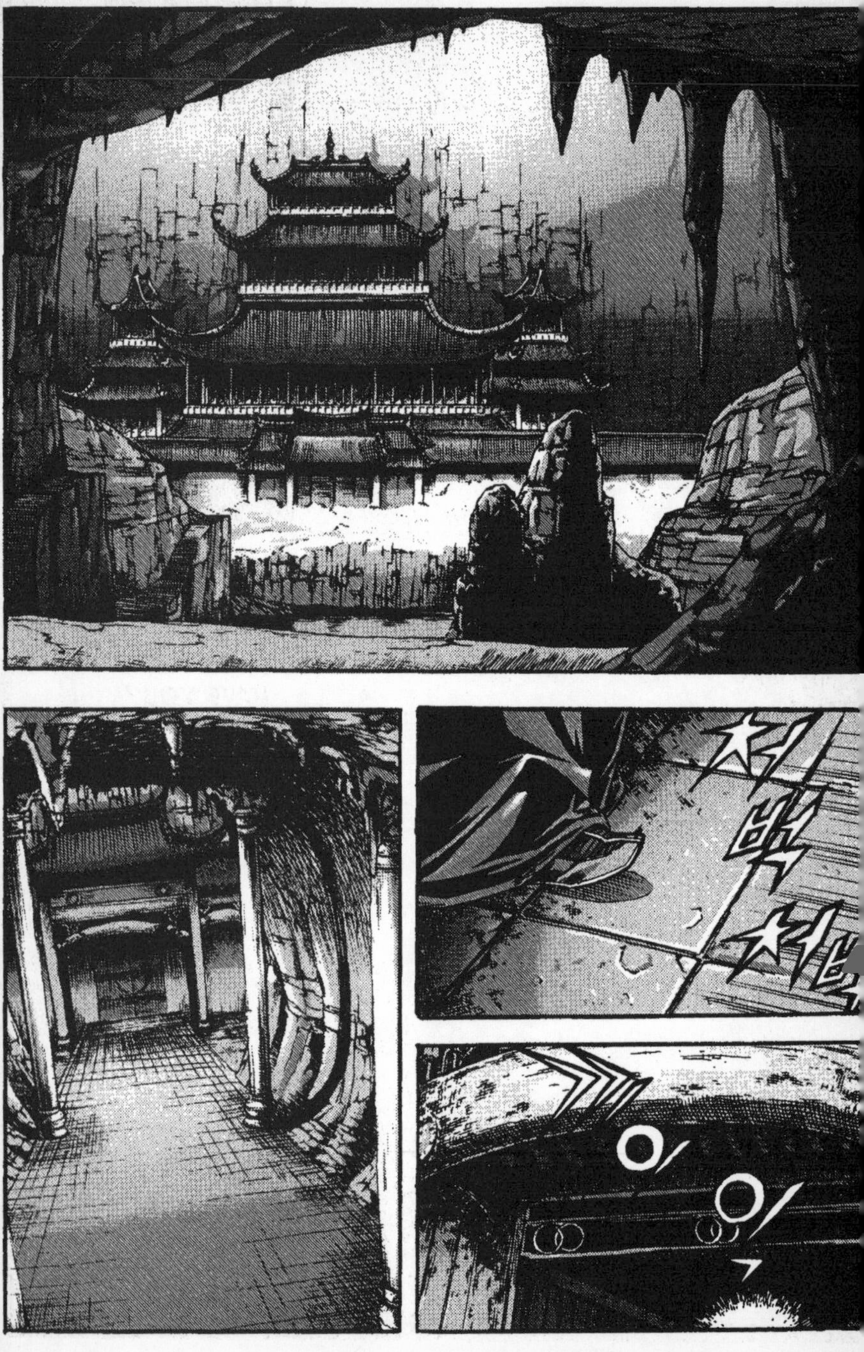
척벅 척
이 이

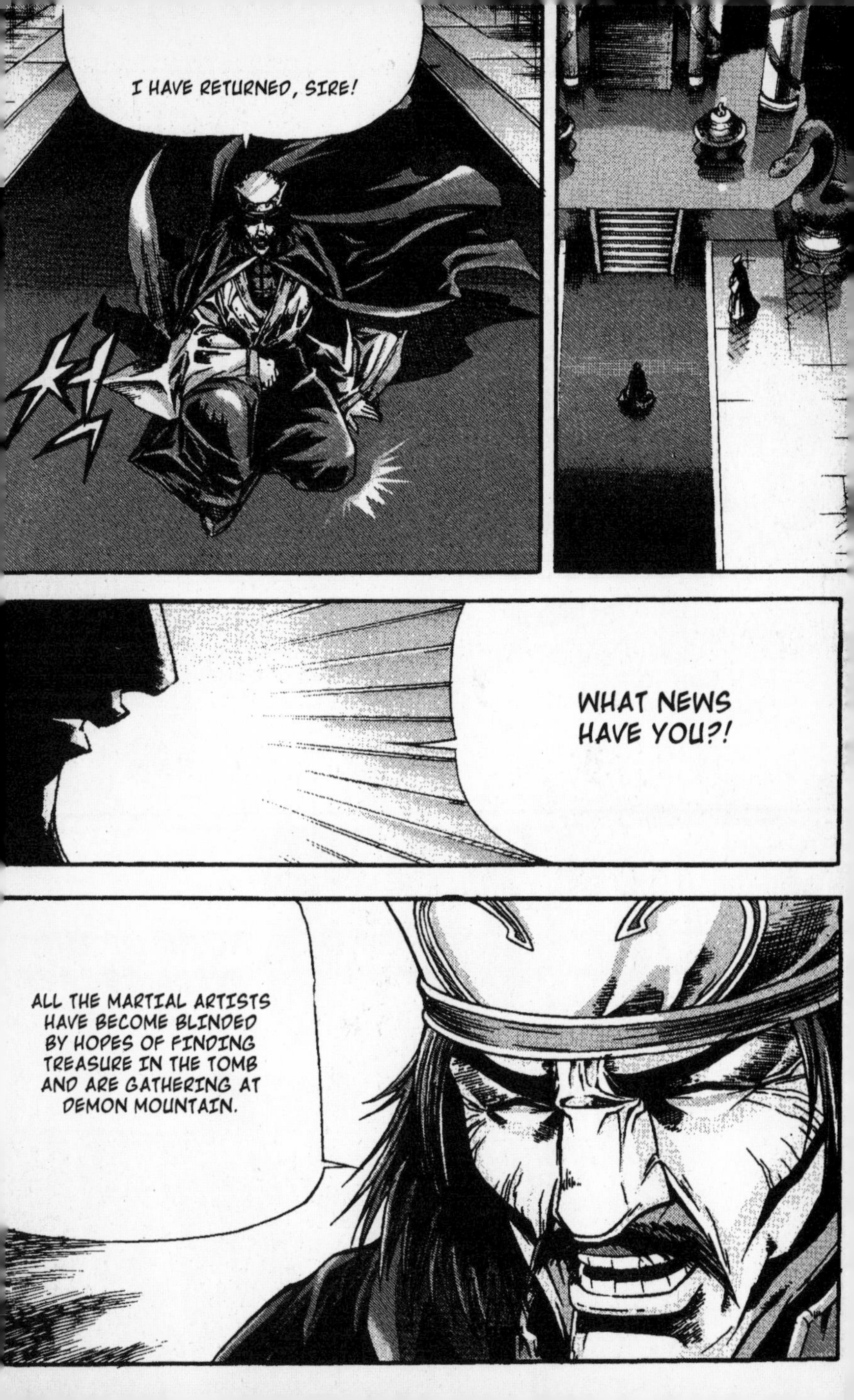
I HAVE RETURNED, SIRE!
WHAT NEWS HAVE YOU?!
ALL THE MARTIAL ARTISTS HAVE BECOME BLINDED BY HOPES OF FINDING TREASURE IN THE TOMB AND ARE GATHERING AT DEMON MOUNTAIN.

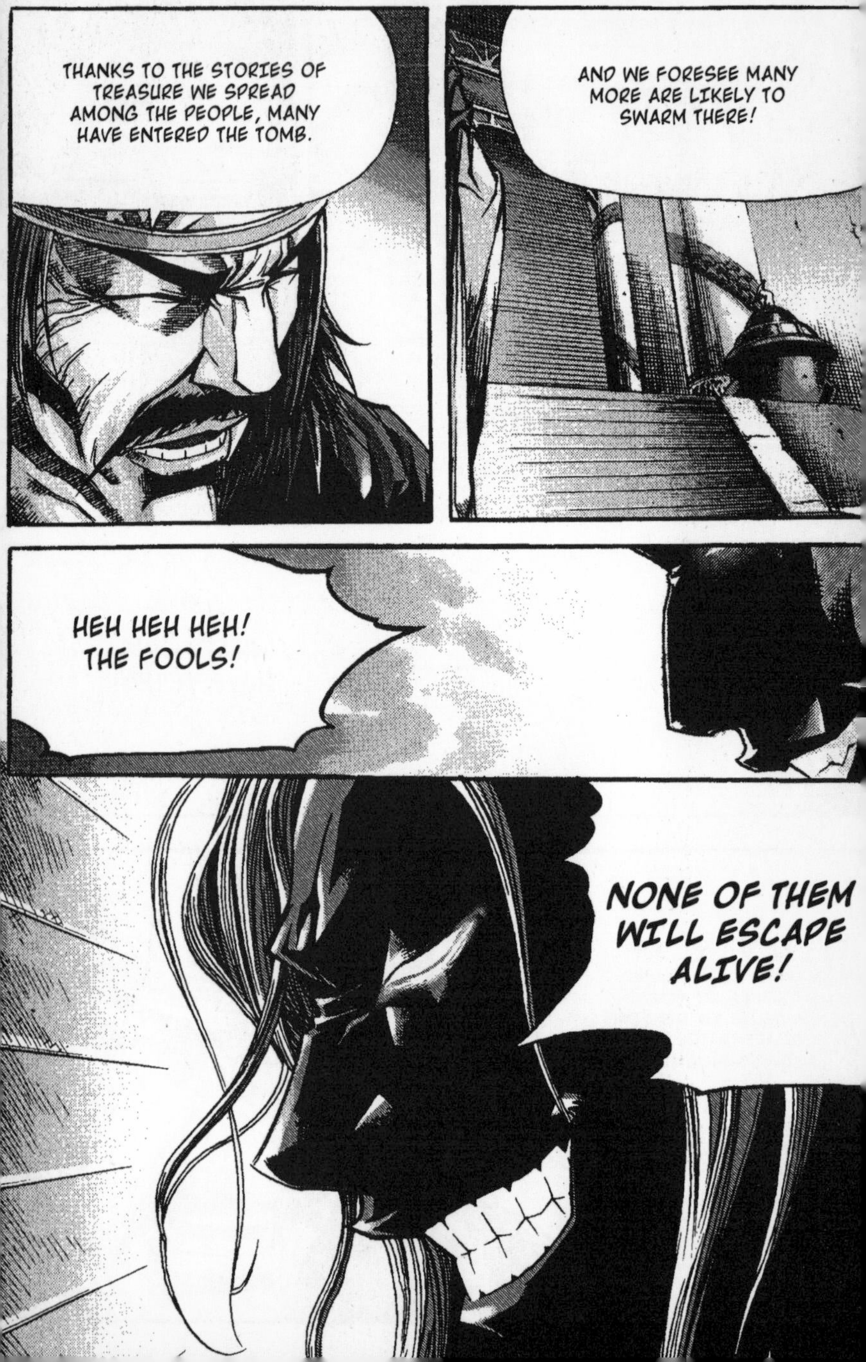
THANKS TO THE STORIES OF TREASURE WE SPREAD AMONG THE PEOPLE, MANY HAVE ENTERED THE TOMB.
AND WE FORESEE MANY MORE ARE LIKELY TO SWARM THERE!
HEH HEH HEH! THE FOOLS!
NONE OF THEM WILL ESCAPE ALIVE!

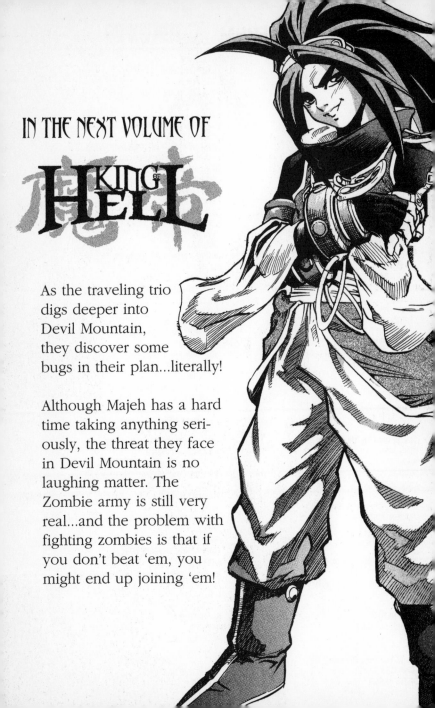

IN THE NEXT VOLUME OF

KING OF HELL

As the traveling trio digs deeper into Devil Mountain, they discover some bugs in their plan...literally!

Although Majeh has a hard time taking anything seriously, the threat they face in Devil Mountain is no laughing matter. The Zombie army is still very real...and the problem with fighting zombies is that if you don't beat 'em, you might end up joining 'em!

ALSO AVAILABLE FROM  TOKYOPOP®

ALSO AVAILABLE FROM  TOKYOPOP®

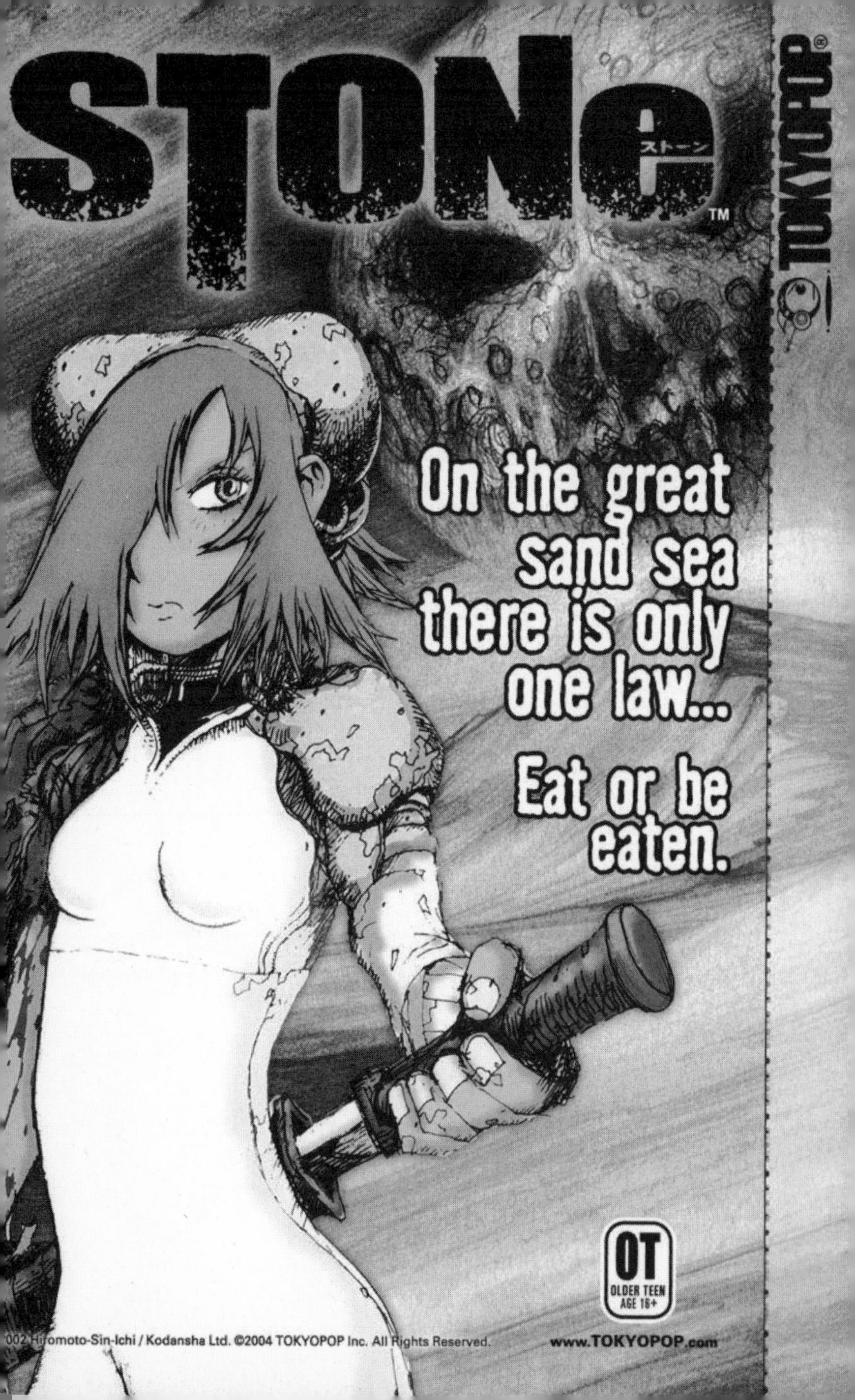
STONe™
ストーン
TOKYOPOP®
On the great sand sea there is only one law...
Eat or be eaten.
OT
OLDER TEEN AGE 16+
002 Hiromoto-Sin-Ichi / Kodansha Ltd. ©2004 TOKYOPOP Inc. All Rights Reserved.
www.TOKYOPOP.com

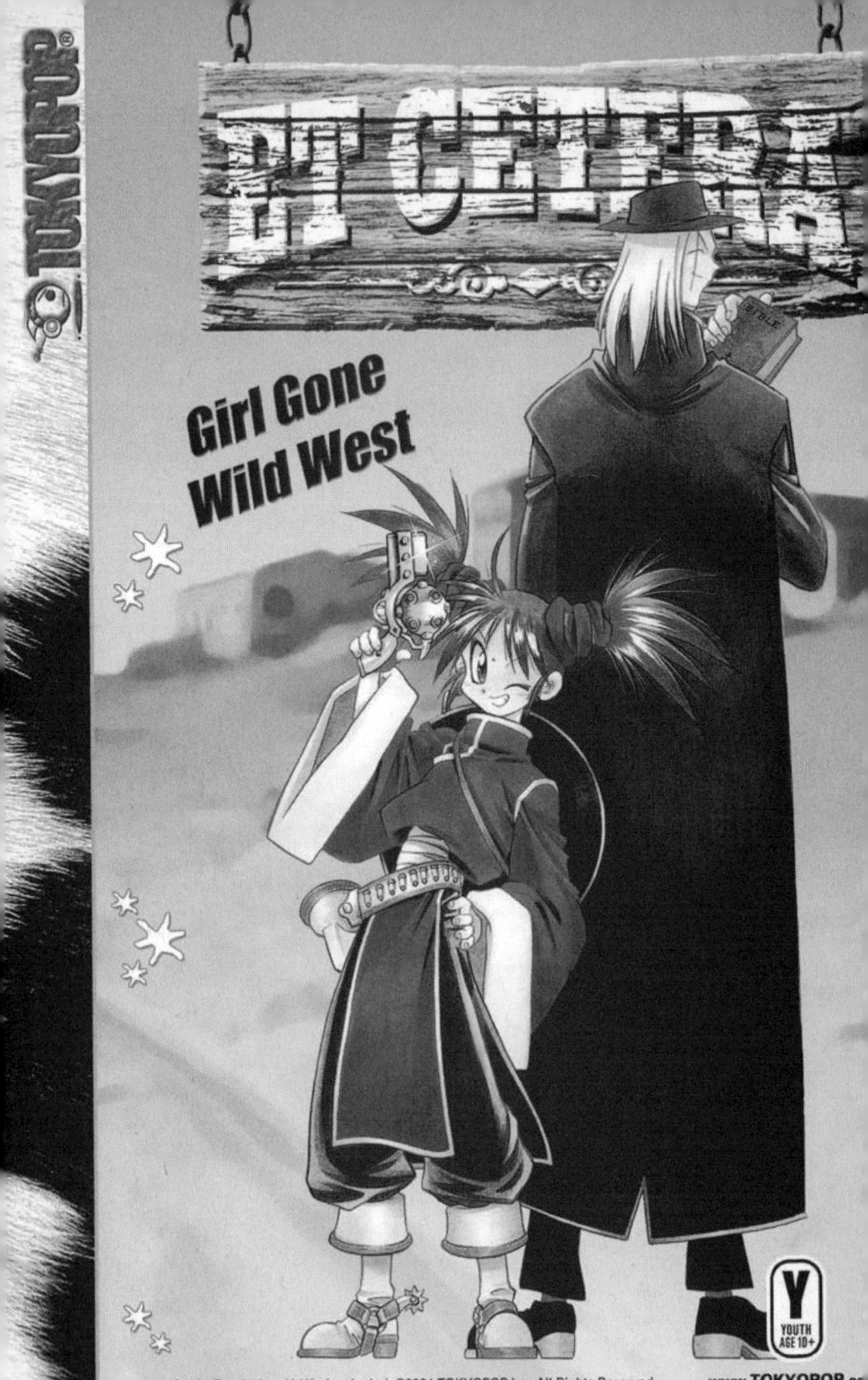
TOKYOPOP
Girl Gone
Wild West
BIBLE
Y
YOUTH
AGE 10+

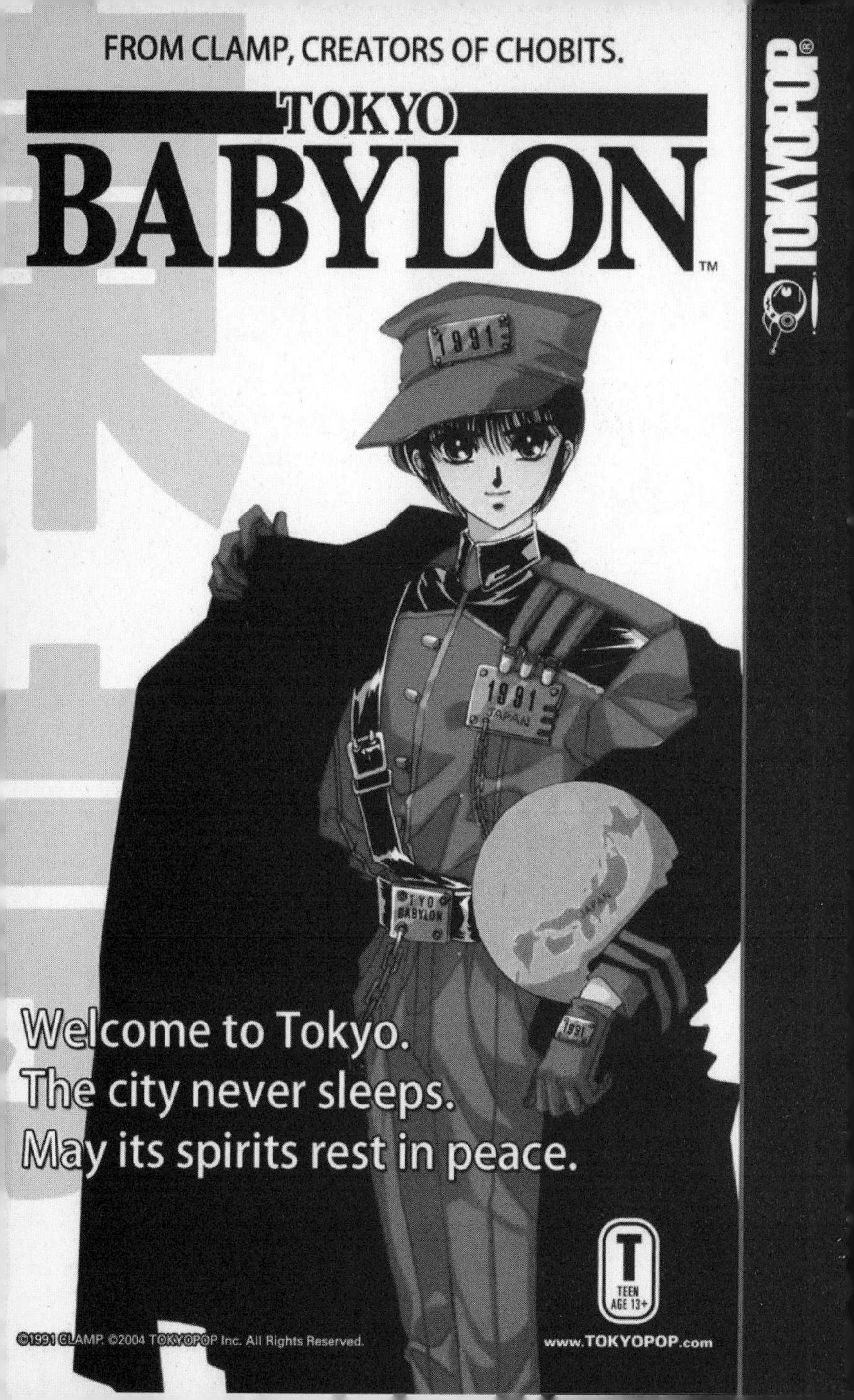
FROM CLAMP, CREATORS OF CHOBITS.
TOKYO BABYLON™
TOKYOPOP
Welcome to Tokyo.
The city never sleeps.
May its spirits rest in peace.
T TEEN AGE 13+
©1991 CLAMP. ©2004 TOKYOPOP Inc. All Rights Reserved.
www.TOKYOPOP.com

CHRONICLES OF THE
CURSED SWORD

BY YEO BEOP-RYONG

A living sword forged in darkness
A hero born outside the light
One can destroy the other
But both can save the world.

**Available Now At Your Favorite
Book And Comic Stores.**

TOKYOPOP

www.TOKYOPOP.com